W9-AKC-713

IMPORTANT

HERE IS YOUR REGISTRATION CODE TO ACCESS MCGRAW-HILL PREMIUM CONTENT AND MCGRAW-HILL ONLINE RESOURCES

For key premium online resources you need THIS CODE to gain access. Once the code is entered, you will be able to use the web resources for the length of your course.

Access is provided only if you have purchased a new book.

If the registration code is missing from this book, the registration screen on our website, and within your WebCT or Blackboard course will tell you how to obtain your new code. Your registration code can be used only once to establish access. It is not transferable.

To gain access to these online resources

1. **USE** your web browser to go to: www.mhhe.com/schaefersm2

2. **CLICK** on "First Time User"

3. **ENTER** the Registration Code printed on the tear-off bookmark on the right

4. After you have entered your registration code, click on "Register"

5. **FOLLOW** the instructions to setup your personal UserID and Password

6. **WRITE** your UserID and Password down for future reference. Keep it in a safe place.

If your course is using WebCT or Blackboard, you'll be able to use this code to access the McGraw-Hill content within your instructor's online course.

To gain access to the McGraw-Hill content in your instructor's WebCT or Blackboard course simply log into the course with the user ID and Password provided by your instructor. Enter the registration code exactly as it appears to the right when prompted by the system. You will only need to use this code the first time you click on McGraw-Hill content.

These instructions are specifically for student access. Instructors are not required to register via the above instructions.

The McGraw-Hill Companies

McGraw Hill Higher Education

Thank you, and welcome to your McGraw-Hill Online Resources.

ISBN 0-07-299779-6 T/A SCHAEFER: SOCIOLOGY MATTERS, 2/E

REGISTRATION CODE

VSVG-Y2SB-O2R9-XIDU-WLZC

REGISTRATION CODE

The McGraw-Hill Companies

McGraw Hill Higher Education

Sociology Matters

Sociology Matters

Second Edition

Richard T. Schaefer
DePaul University

Boston Burr Ridge, IL Dubuque, IA Madison, WI New York
San Francisco St. Louis Bangkok Bogotá Caracas Kuala Lumpur
Lisbon London Madrid Mexico City Milan Montreal New Delhi
Santiago Seoul Singapore Sydney Taipei Toronto

The McGraw·Hill Companies

Higher Education

SOCIOLOGY MATTERS Second edition
Published by McGraw-Hill, a business unit of The McGraw-Hill Companies, Inc., 1221 Avenue of the Americas, New
York, NY 10020. Copyright © 2006, 2004, by The McGraw-Hill Companies, Inc. All rights reserved. No part of this
publication may be reproduced or distributed in any form or by any means, or stored in a database or retrieval system,
without the prior written consent of The McGraw-Hill Companies, Inc., including, but not limited to, in any network or
other electronic storage or transmission, or broadcast for distance learning. Some ancillaries, including electronic and
print components, may not be available to customers outside the United States.

This book is printed on acid-free paper.

1 2 3 4 5 6 7 8 9 0 DOC/DOC 0 9 8 7 6 5

ISBN   0-07-299775-3

Publisher: *Phillip A. Butcher*
Sponsoring editor: *Sherith H. Pankratz*
Senior developmental editor: *Thomas B. Holmes*
Senior marketing manager: *Daniel M. Loch*
Media producer: *Jessica Bodie*
Senior project manager: *Diane M. Folliard*
Production supervisor: *Janean A. Utley*
Design manager: *Laurie Entringer*
Media supplement producer: *Nancy Garcia*
Photo research coordinator: *Nora Agbayani*
Art editor: *Emma Ghiselli*
Cover image: *© Rainer Grosskopf/Getty Images*
Typeface: *10/12 Times Roman*
Compositor: *ProGraphics*
Printer: *R.R. Donnelley and Sons*

Library of Congress Cataloging-in-Publication Data

Schaefer, Richard T.
      Sociology matters / Richard T. Schaefer.—2nd ed.
         p. cm.
      Includes bibliographical references and index.
      ISBN 0-07-299775-3 (alk. paper)
         1. Sociology. 2. Cultural relations. 3. Social stratification. I. Title.
   HM447.S33 2006
   301--dc22
                                                                                                            2005041595

www.mhhe.com

iv

Dedication

To my wife, Sandy

About the Author

RICHARD T. SCHAEFER
Professor, DePaul University
B.A. Northwestern University
M.A., Ph.D. University of Chicago

Growing up in Chicago at a time when neighborhoods were going through transitions in ethnic and racial composition, Richard T. Schaefer found himself increasingly intrigued by what was happening, how people were reacting, and how these changes were affecting neighborhoods and people's jobs. His interest in social issues caused him to gravitate to sociology courses at Northwestern University, where he received a B.A. in sociology.

"Originally as an undergraduate I thought I would go on to law school and become a lawyer. But after taking a few sociology courses, I found myself wanting to learn more about what sociologists studied, and fascinated by the kinds of questions they raised." This fascination led him to obtain his M.A. and Ph.D. in sociology from the University of Chicago. Dr. Schaefer's continuing interest in race relations led him to write his master's thesis on the membership of the Ku Klux Klan and his doctoral thesis on racial prejudice and race relations in Great Britain.

Dr. Schaefer went on to become a professor of sociology, and now teaches at DePaul University in Chicago. In 2004 he was named to the Vincent DePaul professorship in recognition of his undergraduate teaching and scholarship. He has taught introductory sociology for over 30 years to students in colleges, adult education programs, nursing programs, and even a maximum-security prison. Dr. Schaefer's love of teaching is apparent in his interaction with his students. "I find myself constantly learning from the students who are in my classes and from reading what they write. Their insights into the material we read or current events that we discuss often become part of future course material and sometimes even find their way into my writing."

Dr. Schaefer is author of the ninth edition of *Sociology* (McGraw-Hill, 2005) and the sixth edition of *Sociology: A Brief Introduction* (McGraw-Hill, 2006). Dr. Schaefer is also the author of *Racial and Ethnic Groups,* now in its tenth edition, and *Race and Ethnicity in the United States,* third edition. His articles and book reviews have appeared in many journals, including *American Journal of Sociology; Phylon: A Review of Race and Culture; Contemporary Sociology; Sociology and Social Research; Sociological Quarterly;* and *Teaching Sociology.* He served as president of the Midwest Sociological Society from 1994 to 1995.

Dr. Schaefer's advice to students is to "look at the material and make connections to your own life and experiences. Sociology will make you a more attentive observer of how people in groups interact and function. It will also make you more aware of people's different needs and interests—and perhaps more ready to work for the common good, while still recognizing the individuality of each person."

Preface

Sociology has been my life's work for several decades. In the classroom and in the pages of my textbooks, I have tried to spark students' interest in the discipline by showing them its real-life implications. My aim has been to convince students that sociology is more than just another academic pursuit, an exercise in scholarship for the sake of scholarship. Sociology illuminates the world around us—our families, schools, neighborhoods, and other familiar institutions we have lived with all our lives. It puts into larger perspective our culture and our socialization—the way we come to be the way we are. Sociology makes us think deeply about the divide between ourselves and those of different races, classes, and ethnicities. It forces us to recognize the effects of power, technological advances, and the increasingly rapid process of social change on our own lives. Sociology matters—to you, me, and everyone with a stake in the society we live in.

This concise volume stresses the same theme, in fewer pages and with fewer illustrations and study aids. *Sociology Matters* is intended for instructors who desire an especially short, relatively inexpensive introductory text. This text covers the essential content in *Sociology: A Brief Introduction,* Sixth Edition, in much the same depth. Its 11 chapters can be covered easily in a quarter- or semester-long course, together with other materials instructors might wish to add.

Major Emphases

Like the brief sixth edition of *Sociology,* this volume includes comprehensive, balanced coverage of the major theoretical perspectives. Chapter 1 introduces, defines, and contrasts the functionalist, conflict, and interactionist perspectives, as well as the increasingly important feminist approach. Later chapters use these distinctive viewpoints to explore topics such as deviance (Chapter 4); social stratification (Chapter 5); race and ethnicity (Chapter 6); gender (Chapter 7); social institutions (Chapters 8 and 9); communities, health, and the environment (Chapter 10); and social change (Chapter 11).

This volume also includes strong coverage of gender, race, ethnicity, and social class. Three entire chapters are devoted to these topics: Chapter 5, on stratification in the United States and global inequality; Chapter 6, on race and ethnicity; and Chapter 7, on gender. Related discussions appear throughout the book. For instance, Chapter 3 examines race and gender as ascribed statuses; Chapter 4, racial profiling and the perceived seriousness of white-collar crime; Chapter 10, the connection between health and a person's social class, race, ethnicity, and gender; and Chapter 11, the role of gender in social movements.

Finally, this volume includes considerable cross-cultural coverage. Chapter 2, which opens with a vignette on technological and cultural change in Bhutan, covers the development of culture around the world. Chapter 4 covers international crime rates. Chapter 5 treats social stratification from a global perspective, including coverage of world systems analysis, dependency theory, modernization theory, the development of multinational corporations, and the global economy. Chapter 7 covers Margaret Mead's work on cross-cultural differences in gender roles. Chapter 8 takes a global view of the family. Chapter 10, which opens with a vignette on global population growth, treats global environmental issues. And Chapter 11 covers global social change.

Special Features

This volume offers a variety of learning aids designed to help students understand and review basic concepts, including:

- Chapter outline
- Chapter-opening vignette with chapter overview
- *Use Your Sociological Imagination* sections, which prompt students to apply their knowledge of sociology to the world around them
- Tables and figures, some with sticker-style captions and Think About It questions
- Photographs and cartoons
- Online Learning Center icons, which alert students to relevant material on the book's companion website
- Boldfaced key terms
- *Sociology Matters* sections at the end of each chapter, which point out the relevance of a chapter's content to students' lives
- Numbered 10-point chapter summary
- End-of-chapter key terms list with page references
- End-of-book glossary with page references

What's New in the Second Edition?

The most important changes in this edition include the following (refer as well to the chapter-by-chapter list of changes on pages x–xiii).

CONTENT

- The chapter on social institutions has been split in two to allow for expanded coverage of family and religion (Chapter 8) as well as education and the economy (Chapter 9).
- Fifteen new key terms have been added, along with expanded coverage: *globalization* and the *life course approach* (Chapter 2); *collective decision making, minimal hierarchy,* and *work team* (Chapter 3); the *estate system* and the *feminization of poverty* (Chapter 5); *racial profiling* (Chapter 6); *religious belief, religious experience,* and *religious ritual* (Chapter 8); the *hidden curriculum, credentialism,* and *downsizing* (Chapter 9); and the *brain drain* (Chapter 10).
- Coverage of numerous other topics has been augmented or added, including: norms, values, and symbols (Chapter 2); the media as an agent of socialization (Chapter 2); immigration (Chapter 6); institutional discrimination (Chapter 6); urban growth and development (Chapter 10); the interactionist approach to physician training (Chapter 10); HIV/AIDS (Chapter 10); the technology gap between core and periphery nations (Chapter 11); and sex selection and human cloning (Chapter 11).

PEDAGOGY

- Eleven new Summing Up tables pull together coverage of the major theoretical perspectives.
- Five new figures illustrate important sociological trends and developments.
- Two new chapter-opening passages spark student interest.
- Two new cartoons highlight sociological issues.
- A new *Use Your Sociological Imagination* exercise helps students to think like a sociologist.

Supplements and Internet Resources

A wealth of complimentary teaching and learning resources is available to students and instructors who use *Sociology Matters.* Students will benefit from the free study aids and topical activities accessible to them at McGraw-Hill's website, www.mhhe.com/schaefersm2. Among these features are:

- Student self-quizzes
- Internet Connection

- Learning Objectives
- What Concept Am I? game
- Correlation guide to the *Reel Society* interactive movie CD-ROM, a supplementary program that uses actors and stories to bring basic sociological concepts to life

Instructors also have an Online Learning Center devoted to their needs. They may choose from the following resources:

- Instructor's Resource Manual
- Computerized Test Bank
- Instructor's Resource CD-ROM with Computerized Test Bank, including the Instructor's Resource Manual and PowerPoint slides
- Online Learning Center (includes quizzes, activities, and PowerPoint masters)
- Correlation guide to *Reel Society,* an interactive movie available on CD-ROM (can be used to stimulate classroom discussion of basic sociological concepts)
- Two hours of Video Lecture Launcher footage on two VHS tapes, drawn from the NBC News archives

What's New in Each Chapter?

CHAPTER 1: THE SOCIOLOGICAL VIEW

- Discussion of the decline in religious observance among young people in the United States
- Discussion of the different symbolic meanings of the Confederate flag
- Discussion of a study of violence in children's television programming as an example of the use of existing sources
- Summing Up table: "Major Research Designs"

CHAPTER 2: CULTURE AND SOCIALIZATION

- Updated chapter-opening vignette on the effect of television on Bhutan's culture
- Key term coverage of globalization
- Expanded coverage of norms, including changing norms regarding interracial marriage and Muslim norms regarding touching by strangers
- Expanded coverage of values, specifically changing values among college students

- Updated illustration of the argots spoken by subcultures: terms used by New York City sanitation workers
- Updated illustration of ethnocentrism: U.S. versus Iraqi attitudes regarding favoritism toward kin
- Summing Up table: "Major Theoretical Perspectives on Culture"
- Expanded coverage of symbols, specifically the controversy over the acceptability of the Muslim headscarf in French schools
- Key term coverage of the life course approach
- Expanded coverage of the media as an agent of socialization, specifically the role of the Internet in children's socialization, with figure

CHAPTER 3: SOCIAL STRUCTURE, GROUPS, AND ORGANIZATIONS

- Application of the results of Zimbardo's prison experiment to the Abu Ghraib prisoner abuse scandal in Iraq
- Summing Up table: "Stages of Sociocultural Evolution"
- Revised and expanded section, "The Changing Workplace," including key term coverage of collective decision making, minimal hierarchy, and work teams

CHAPTER 4: DEVIANCE AND SOCIAL CONTROL

- Chapter-opening vignette on backyard wrestling
- *Use Your Sociological Imagination* exercise on Merton's theory of deviance
- Summing Up table: "Approaches to Deviance"
- Cartoon on white-collar crime

CHAPTER 5: STRATIFICATION IN THE UNITED STATES AND GLOBAL INEQUALITY

- Key term coverage of the estate system
- Summing Up table: "Two Major Perspectives on Social Stratification"
- Figure: "Distribution of Income in the United States, 2002" (pyramid graph)
- Figure: "U.S. Minimum Wage Adjusted for Inflation, 1950–2002"
- Key term coverage of the feminization of poverty
- Discussion of the desperate economic situation in sub-Saharan Africa

CHAPTER 6: INEQUALITY BY RACE AND ETHNICITY

- Discussion of the Immigration Control Act of 1986
- Cartoon on illegal immigration
- Key term coverage of racial profiling
- Summing Up table: "Sociological Perspectives on Race"
- Discussion of Devah Pager's experiment on racial discrimination in employment
- Updated figure: "U.S. Median Income by Race, Ethnicity, and Gender, 2003"
- Updated table: "Median Income by Race and Sex, Holding Education Constant, 2003"

CHAPTER 7: INEQUALITY BY GENDER

- Chapter opening on the pervasive gender gap in median earnings in the United States
- Summing Up table: "Sociological Perspectives on Gender"
- Updated figure: "Trends in U.S. Women's Participation in the Paid Labor Force"
- Updated table: "U.S. Women in Selected Occupations"
- Updated discussion of the double jeopardy of minority women, based on new income statistics

CHAPTER 8: SOCIAL INSTITUTIONS: FAMILY AND RELIGION

- First of two separate chapters on social institutions
- Figure: "U.S. Households by Family Type, 1940–2003"
- Section on sociological views of the family (functionalist, conflict, interactionist, feminist)
- Summing Up table: "Sociological Perspectives on the Family"
- Section on religious behavior (belief, ritual, experience)
- Summing Up table: "Sociological Perspectives on Religion"

CHAPTER 9: SOCIAL INSTITUTIONS: EDUCATION, GOVERNMENT, AND THE ECONOMY

- Second of two separate chapters on social institutions
- Section on sociological perspectives on education (functionalist, conflict, interactionist)

- Summing Up table: "Sociological Perspectives on Education"
- Figure: "Power Elite Models" (Mills, Domhoff)
- Figure: "Racial and Ethnic Composition of the U.S. Labor Force, 1980 and 2020 (projection)"
- Expanded section on deindustrialization, including "offshoring," or the outsourcing of office and professional jobs to foreign countries

CHAPTER 10: POPULATION, COMMUNITY, HEALTH, AND THE ENVIRONMENT

- Expanded discussion of the social consequences of rampant urban growth and development, illustrated by Las Vegas
- Key term coverage of the brain drain
- Discussion of how physicians learn their roles (interactionist approach)
- Expanded coverage of HIV/AIDS
- Updated figure: "Percentage of People without Health Insurance, 2003"

CHAPTER 11: SOCIAL MOVEMENTS, SOCIAL CHANGE, AND TECHNOLOGY

- Updated chapter-opening vignette on downloading of music from the Internet
- Summing Up table: "Contributions to Social Movement Theory"
- Expanded discussion of the gap in computer technology between core and periphery nations
- Discussion of the trend toward outsourcing of service and professional jobs to semiperiphery nations
- Discussion of sex selection of embryos prior to in vitro fertilization
- Discussion of legislation regarding human cloning

Acknowledgments

Elizabeth Morgan, who collaborated with me on the first edition, as well as on several editions of my longer introductory textbooks for undergraduates, brought her experience and knowledge to the second edition of *Sociology Matters*.

I deeply appreciate the contributions my editors made to this book. Thom Holmes, a senior developmental editor at McGraw-Hill, continued to help to shape this fresh approach to sociology for undergraduates.

Rhona Robbin, director of development and media technology, oversaw the project, lending her expertise and experience to its development. I received strong support and encouragement from Phillip Butcher, publisher; Sherith Pankratz, sponsoring editor; Dan Loch, marketing manager; and Jessica Bodie and Nancy Garcia, media technology producers. Additional guidance and support came from Trish Starner, editorial assistant; Diane Folliard, senior project manager; Laurie Entringer, design manager; Janean Utley, production supervisor; Nora Agbayani, photo editor; and Judy Brody, permissions editor.

I would especially like to acknowledge Rebecca Matthews of the University of Iowa, for her work on the instructor's resource manual and test bank; Lynn Newhart of Rockford College, for developing the materials in the Online Learning Center; and Gerry Williams, for his work on the PowerPoint slides for this book.

As is evident from these acknowledgments, the preparation of a textbook is truly a team effort. The most valuable member of this effort continues to be my wife, Sandy, who provides the support so necessary to my creative and scholarly activities.

I have had the good fortune to be able to introduce students to sociology for many years. Those students have been enormously helpful in spurring my own sociological imagination. In ways I can fully appreciate but cannot fully acknowledge, their questions in class and queries in the hallway have found their way into this textbook.

Richard T. Schaefer

www.schaefersociology.net/schaeferrt@aol.com

As a full-service publisher of quality educational products, McGraw-Hill does much more than just sell textbooks to your students. We create and publish an extensive array of print, video, and digital supplements to support instruction on your campus. Orders of new (versus used) textbooks help us to defray the cost of developing such supplements, which is substantial. Please consult your local McGraw-Hill representative to learn about the availability of the supplements that accompany Sociology Matters. *If you are not sure who your representative is, you can find him or her by using the Rep Locator at www.mhhe.com.*

Academic Reviewers

Many sociologists reviewed this book and offered constructive and thorough evaluations of its content. I would like to thank the following reviewers for their thoughtful comments on the manuscript and its features:

Henry Borne
Holy Cross College

Todd E. Bernhardt
Broward Community College

Barbara Feldman
Seton Hall University

Cynthia Ganote
Vanderbilt University

William Gronfein
*Indiana University–Purdue
University Indianapolis*

Bram Hamovitch
Lakeland Community College

Kathleen S. Lowney
Valdosta State University

Scott Lukas
Lake Tahoe College

Stephanie M. McClure
University of Georgia

Dennis McGrath
*Community College of
Philadelphia*

Melanie Moore
University of Northern Colorado

Nelson Pichardo
Central Washington University

James R. Robinson
Oklahoma State University

Leonard A. Steverson
South Georgia College

Laurel Tripp
University of Maine

Meifang Zhang
Midlands Technical College

Brief Contents

Chapter 1   *The Sociological View*   *1*

Chapter 2   *Culture and Socialization*   *33*

Chapter 3   *Social Structure, Groups, and Organizations*   *64*

Chapter 4   *Deviance and Social Control*   *87*

Chapter 5   *Stratification in the United States and Global Inequality*   *111*

Chapter 6   *Inequality by Race and Ethnicity*   *142*

Chapter 7   *Inequality by Gender*   *165*

Chapter 8   *Social Institutions: Family and Religion*   *184*

Chapter 9   *Social Institutions: Education, Government, and the Economy*   *205*

Chapter 10 *Population, Community, Health, and the Environment*   *232*

Chapter 11 *Social Movements, Social Change, and Technology*   *264*

Contents

Preface   *vii*

Chapter 1   *The Sociological View*   *1*

What Is Sociology?   *2*

The Sociological Imagination   *3*
Sociology and the Social Sciences   *4*
Sociology and Common Sense   *5*

What Is Sociological Theory?   *6*

The Development of Sociology   *8*

Early Thinkers: Comte, Martineau, and Spencer   *8*
Émile Durkheim   *9*
Max Weber   *10*
Karl Marx   *10*
Modern Developments   *11*

Major Theoretical Perspectives   *13*

Functionalist Perspective   *13*
Conflict Perspective   *14*
Interactionist Perspective   *16*
The Sociological Approach   *17*

What Is the Scientific Method?   *18*

Defining the Problem   *19*
Reviewing the Literature   *20*
Formulating the Hypothesis   *20*
Collecting and Analyzing Data   *21*
Developing the Conclusion   *22*
In Summary: The Scientific Method   *23*

Major Research Designs   *24*

Surveys   *24*
Observation   *25*
Experiments   *26*
Use of Existing Sources   *27*

Ethics of Research   *27*

Applied and Clinical Sociology   *28*

Summary   *30*

xvii

Chapter 2   *Culture and Socialization*   *33*

Culture and Society   *34*

Development of Culture around the World   *35*

Cultural Universals   *36*
Innovation   *36*
Globalization, Diffusion, and Technology   *36*

Elements of Culture   *38*

Language   *38*
Norms   *39*
Sanctions   *41*
Values   *42*

Culture and the Dominant Ideology   *43*

Cultural Variation   *44*

Subcultures   *44*
Countercultures   *45*
Culture Shock   *46*
Ethnocentrism   *47*
Cultural Relativism   *48*

The Role of Socialization   *48*

Environment: The Impact of Isolation   *49*
Heredity: The Impact of Biology   *50*

The Self and Socialization   *50*

Cooley: Looking-Glass Self   *51*
Mead: Stages of the Self   *51*
Mead: Theory of the Self   *53*
Goffman: Presentation of the Self   *54*

Socialization and the Life Course   *54*

The Life Course   *54*
Anticipatory Socialization and Resocialization   *55*

Agents of Socialization   *56*

Family   *56*
School   *57*
Peer Group   *58*
Mass Media and Technology   *59*
Workplace   *60*
The State   *61*

Summary   *62*

Chapter 3   *Social Structure, Groups, and Organizations*   *64*

Defining and Reconstructing Reality   *65*

Elements of Social Structure   *66*

Statuses   *66*
Social Roles   *68*
Groups   *70*
Social Networks and Technology   *72*
Social Institutions   *72*

Social Structure in Global Perspective   *73*

Tönnies's Gemeinschaft *and* Gesellschaft   *74*
Lenski's Sociocultural Evolution Approach   *74*

Understanding Organizations   *78*

Formal Organizations and Bureaucracies   *78*
Characteristics of a Bureaucracy   *78*
Bureaucracy and Organizational Culture   *82*

The Changing Workplace   *83*

Summary   *84*

Chapter 4   *Deviance and Social Control*   *87*

Social Control   *88*

Conformity and Obedience   *89*
Informal and Formal Social Control   *90*
Law and Society   *91*

What Is Deviance?   *92*

Explaining Deviance   *93*

Functionalist Perspective   *94*
Interactionist Perspective   *96*
Labeling Theory   *99*
Conflict Theory   *100*
Feminist Perspective   *101*

Crime   *101*

Types of Crime   *102*
Crime Statistics   *105*

Summary   *108*

Chapter 5   *Stratification in the United States and Global Inequality*   *111*

Understanding Stratification   *112*

  Systems of Stratification   112
  Perspectives on Stratification   115
  Is Stratification Universal?   117

Stratification by Social Class   *120*

  Measuring Social Class   120
  Wealth and Income   122
  Poverty   124
  Life Chances   128

Social Mobility   *129*

  Open versus Closed Stratification Systems   130
  Types of Social Mobility   130
  Social Mobility in the United States   130

Global Inequality   *132*

  Legacy of Colonialism   133
  Globalization   135
  Multinational Corporations   136
  Modernization   138

Summary   *139*

Chapter 6   *Inequality by Race and Ethnicity*   *142*

The Privileges of the Dominant   *143*

The Social Construction of Race and Ethnicity   *144*

Race, Ethnicity, and Minority Groups   *145*

  Minority Groups   146
  Race   148
  Ethnicity   148

Immigration and New Ethnic Groups   *149*

  History of Immigration   150
  Functions of Immigration   152
  The Conflict Approach to Immigration   152

Explaining Inequality by Race and Ethnicity   *153*

  The Functionalist View   153
  The Conflict Response   154
  The Interactionist Approach   155

Patterns of Prejudice and Discrimination   *155*

    Discriminatory Behavior   156

    Institutional Discrimination   157

    Measuring Discrimination   159

Summary   *162*

Chapter 7   *Inequality by Gender   165*

The Social Construction of Gender   *166*

    Gender-Role Socialization   167

    Women's and Men's Gender Roles   167

    A Cross-Cultural Perspective   169

Explaining Inequality by Gender   *169*

    The Functionalist View   169

    The Conflict Response   170

    The Feminist Perspective   171

    The Interactionist Perspective   172

Women: The Oppressed Majority   *173*

    Sexism and Sex Discrimination   174

    Sexual Harassment   174

    The Status of Women Worldwide   175

    Women in the Workforce of the United States   176

    The Social Consequences of Women's Employment   179

The Double Jeopardy of Minority Women   *180*

Summary   *182*

Chapter 8   *Social Institutions: Family and Religion   184*

Studying Social Institutions   *185*

    Functionalist View   185

    Conflict View   187

    Interactionist View   188

The Family: A Global View   *189*

    Composition: What Is the Family?   189

    Kinship Patterns: To Whom Are We Related?   191

    Authority Patterns: Who Rules?   192

Studying the Family   *193*

    Functionalist View   193

    Conflict View   194

    Interactionist View   194

    Feminist View   195

Religion as a Social Institution   *196*

The Integrative Function of Religion   196
Religion and Social Support   198
Religion and Social Change   198
Religion and Social Control: A Conflict View   199

Religious Behavior   *200*

Belief   201
Ritual   201
Experience   202

Summary   *203*

Chapter 9   *Social Institutions: Education, Government, and the Economy   205*

Sociological Perspectives on Education   *206*

Functionalist View   206
Conflict View   208
Interactionist View   211

Education: Schools as Formal Organizations   *211*

Bureaucratization of Schools   212
Teachers: Employees and Instructors   214
Student Subcultures   214

Government: Authority and Power   *216*

Types of Authority   217
Who Rules in the United States?   218

Economic Systems   *222*

Capitalism   222
Socialism   224

Economic Transformation   *225*

The Changing Face of the Workforce   225
Deindustrialization   227

Summary   *230*

Chapter 10   *Population, Community, Health, and the Environment   232*

Demography: The Study of Population   *233*

Malthus's Thesis and Marx's Response   233
Studying Population Today   235
Elements of Demography   235

How Did Communities Originate?   *236*

   Early Communities   236
   Preindustrial Cities   237
   Industrial and Postindustrial Cities   238

Urbanization and Its Consequences   *240*

   Functionalist View: Urban Ecology   241
   Conflict View: New Urban Sociology   243

Health and Illness: Sociological Perspectives   *244*

   Functionalist Approach   245
   Conflict Approach   246
   Interactionist Approach   248
   Labeling Approach   248

Social Epidemiology   *250*

   Social Class   251
   Race and Ethnicity   252
   Gender   253
   Age   254

The Environment: The World and Our Place in It   *255*

   Environmental Problems: An Overview   256
   Human Ecology   257
   A Conflict View of Environmental Issues   258
   Environmental Justice   259

Summary   *261*

Chapter 11 *Social Movements, Social Change, and Technology*   *264*

Social Movements   *265*

   The Relative Deprivation Approach   266
   The Resource Mobilization Approach   266
   Gender and Social Movements   268
   New Social Movements   269

Theories of Social Change   *270*

   Evolutionary Theory   270
   Functionalist Theory   271
   Conflict Theory   272
   Global Social Change   273

Resistance to Social Change   *274*

   Economic and Cultural Factors   275
   Resistance to Technology   276

Technology and the Future   277
   Computer Technology   277
   Biotechnology   278

Technology and Society   281
   Culture and Social Interaction   281
   Social Control   283
   Stratification and Inequality   284

Summary   286

Glossary   289
References   299
Acknowledgments   329
Photo Credits   331
Index   333

The Sociological View

What Is Sociology?

What Is Sociological Theory?

The Development of Sociology

Major Theoretical Perspectives

What Is the Scientific Method?

Major Research Designs

Ethics of Research

Applied and Clinical Sociology

On your way to work one morning, you glance around the neighborhood. You are one of only a few walkers, despite the fine fall weather. In the early morning mist, the cars on the street—mostly SUVs—are sending plumes of exhaust into the chill autumn air. Each of the small luxury trucks carries only one person. Why, you wonder, does everyone need an SUV? Why can't people carpool?

Up ahead, motorists dash to and from their cars to the convenience store across the street. You crave a cup of coffee, the gourmet kind the convenience store sells. You pick up your pace. On reaching the store you order a pricey cup of Premium Mountain Roast, whose aroma fills the warm, cozy shop. As you wait, you watch an attendant sell a lottery ticket to a woman in an old, frayed overcoat. Why, you wonder, is she spending her money on lottery tickets? She could use a new coat.

These are questions anyone with curiosity might ask. Yet there are other questions we could ask, more searching questions about the society in which these scenes take place. If air pollution is a problem, why doesn't the government invest more in public transportation? If gambling on the street is illegal, why is the state running a lottery—essentially a gambling business—in a convenience store? And what about that cup of premium coffee you bought? Chances are the beans were grown in Mexico, Colombia, or Guatemala, where the workers who harvested them may not have received a living wage. Why do so many of the products we buy in the United States—coffee, chocolate, sneakers—come from other nations, and why can't the workers who produce them afford to buy them?

These are a few of the questions a sociologist might ask about the scene you just witnessed. Sociologists study social patterns that many people share. As the sociologist C. Wright Mills wrote over 40 years ago, if one person is unemployed, his difficulty is a personal problem, but if thousands of people are unemployed, their difficulty is a social problem. Sociologists look for root causes of such social patterns in the way society is organized and governed (Mills [1959] 2000a).

As a field of study, sociology is extremely broad in scope. You'll see throughout this book the tremendous range of topics sociologists investigate—from tattooing to TV viewing, from neighborhood groups to global economic patterns, from peer pressure to class consciousness. Sociologists look at how other people influence your behavior; how the government, religion, and the economy affect you; and how you yourself affect others. These aren't just academic questions. Sociology matters because it illuminates your life and your world, whether you are going to school, working for pay, or raising a family.

This first chapter introduces sociology as a social science, one that is characterized by a special skill called the *sociological imagination*. We'll meet three pioneering thinkers—Émile Durkheim, Max Weber, and Karl Marx—and discuss the theoretical perspectives that grew out of their work. We'll see how sociologists use the scientific method to investigate the many questions they pose. Sociologists use surveys, observation, experiments, and existing sources in their research; they often wrestle with ethical issues that arise during their studies. We'll examine some practical uses for their research at the end of the chapter.

What Is Sociology?

Sociology is the systematic study of social behavior and human groups. It focuses primarily on the influence of social relationships on people's attitudes and behavior and on how societies are established and change. This textbook deals with such varied topics as families, the workplace, street gangs, business firms, political parties, genetic engineering, schools, religions, and labor unions. It is concerned with love, poverty, conformity, discrimination, illness, technology, and community.

THE SOCIOLOGICAL IMAGINATION

In attempting to understand social behavior, sociologists rely on an unusual type of creative thinking. C. Wright Mills described such thinking as the *sociological imagination*—an awareness of the relationship between an individual and the wider society. This awareness allows all of us (not just sociologists) to comprehend the links between our immediate, personal social settings and the remote, impersonal social world that surrounds us and helps to shape us (Mills [1959] 2000a).

A key element in the sociological imagination is the ability to view one's own society as an outsider would, rather than only from the perspective of personal experiences and cultural biases. Consider something as simple as the practice of eating while walking. In the United States people think nothing of consuming coffee or chocolate as they walk along the street. Sociologists would see this as a pattern of acceptable behavior because others regard it as acceptable. Yet sociologists need to go beyond one culture to place the practice in perspective. This "normal" behavior is quite unacceptable in some other parts of the world. For example, in Japan people do not eat while walking. Streetside sellers and vending machines dispense food everywhere, but the Japanese will stop to eat or drink whatever they buy before they continue on their way. In their eyes, to engage in another activity while eating shows disrespect for the food preparers, even if the food comes out of a vending machine.

The sociological imagination allows us to go beyond personal experiences and observations to understand broader public issues. Divorce, for example, is unquestionably a personal hardship for a husband and wife who split apart. However, C. Wright Mills advocated using the sociological imagination to view divorce not simply as the personal problem of a particular man or woman, but rather as a societal concern. From this perspective, an increase in the divorce rate serves to redefine a major social institution, the family. Today, households frequently include stepparents and half-sisters or -brothers whose parents have divorced and remarried.

Sociological imagination can bring new understanding to daily life around us. Since 1992, sociologists David Miller and Richard Schaefer (this textbook's author) have studied the food bank system of the United States, which distributes food to hungry individuals and families. On the face of it, food banks seem above reproach. After all, as Miller and Schaefer learned in their research, more than one out of four children in the United States is hungry. One-third of the nation's homeless people report eating one meal per day or less. What could be wrong with charities redistributing to pantries and shelters food that used to be destined for landfills? In 2003, for example, Second Harvest, a food distribution organization, redistributed 1.8 billion pounds of food from hundreds of individual and corporate donors to more than 50,000 food pantries, soup kitchens, and social service agencies.

Many observers would uncritically applaud the distribution of tons of food to 26 million needy Americans. But let's look deeper. While supportive of and personally involved in such efforts, Miller and Schaefer (1993) have drawn on the sociological imagination to offer a more probing view of these activities. They note that powerful forces in our society—such as the federal government, major food retailers, and other large corporations—have joined in charitable food distribution arrangements. Perhaps as a result, the focus of such relief programs is too restricted. The homeless are to be fed, not housed; the unemployed are to be given meals, not jobs. Relief efforts assist hungry individuals and families without challenging the existing social order (for example, by demanding a redistribution of wealth). Of course, without these limited successes in distributing food, starving people might assault patrons of restaurants, loot grocery stores, or literally die of starvation on the steps of city halls and across from the White House. Such critical thinking is typical of sociologists, as they draw on the sociological imagination to study a social issue—in this case, hunger in the United States (Second Harvest 2003).

The sociological imagination is an empowering tool. It allows us to look beyond a limited understanding of things to see the world and its people in a new way and through a broader lens than we might otherwise use. It may be as simple as understanding why a roommate prefers country music to hip hop, or it may open up a whole different way of understanding whole populations in the world. For example, in the aftermath of the terrorist attacks on the United States on September 11, 2001, many citizens wanted to understand how Muslims throughout the world perceived their country, and why. From time to time this textbook will offer you the chance to exercise your own sociological imagination in a variety of situations. We'll begin with one that may be close to home for you.

Use Your Sociological Imagination

You attend a rock concert one night and a religious service the next morning. What differences do you see in how the two audiences behave and in how they respond to the leader? What might account for these differences?

SOCIOLOGY AND THE SOCIAL SCIENCES

Is sociology a science? The term *science* refers to the body of knowledge obtained by methods based on systematic observation. Like researchers in other scientific disciplines, sociologists engage in organized, systematic study of phenomena (in this case, human behavior) in order to enhance understanding. All scientists, whether studying mushrooms or murderers, attempt to collect precise information through methods of study that are as objective as possible. They rely on careful recording of observations and accumulation of data.

Of course, there is a great difference between sociology and physics, between psychology and astronomy. For this reason, the sciences are commonly divided into natural and social sciences. *Natural science* is the study of the physical features of nature and the ways in which they interact and change. Astronomy, biology, chemistry, geology, and physics are all natural sciences. *Social science* is the study of various aspects of human society. The social sciences include sociology, anthropology, economics, history, psychology, and political science.

These social science disciplines have a common focus on the social behavior of people, yet each has a particular orientation. Anthropologists usually study past cultures and preindustrial societies that continue today, as well as the origins of men and women. Economists explore the ways in which people produce and exchange goods and services, along with money and other resources. Historians are concerned with the peoples and events of the past and their significance for us today. Political scientists study international relations, the workings of government, and the exercise of power and authority. Psychologists investigate personality and individual behavior. So what does *sociology* focus on? It emphasizes the influence that society has on people's attitudes and behavior and the ways in which people shape society. Humans are social animals; therefore, sociologists scientifically examine our social relationships with others.

Let's consider how the different social sciences might approach the hotly debated issue of handgun control. Many people today, concerned about the misuse of firearms in the United States, are calling for restrictions on the purchase and use of handguns. Political scientists studying this issue would look at the impact of political action groups, such as the National Rifle Association (NRA), on lawmakers. Historians would examine how guns were used over time in our country and elsewhere. Anthropologists would focus on the use of weapons in a variety of cultures as means of protection as well as symbols of power. Psychologists would look at individual cases and assess the impact handguns have on their owners as well as on individual victims of gunfire. Economists would be interested in how the manufacture and sale of firearms affect communities.

And what approach would sociologists take? They might look at who owns handguns in the United States. They would ask: What explains the significant gender, racial, age, and geographic differences in gun ownership? How would these differences affect the formulation of social policy by city, state, and federal governments? They would examine data from different states to evaluate the effect of gun restrictions on the incidence of firearm accidents or violent crimes involving firearms. They would consider how cultural values and media portrayals influence people's desire to own firearms. Sociologists might also look at data that show how the United States compares to other nations in handgun ownership and use.

SOCIOLOGY AND COMMON SENSE

Sociology focuses on the study of human behavior. Yet we all have experience with human behavior and at least some knowledge of it. All of us might well have theories about why people buy lottery tickets, for example, or why people become homeless. Our theories and opinions typically come from "common sense"—that is, from our experiences and conversations, from what we read, from what we see on television, and so forth.

In our daily lives, we rely on common sense to get us through many unfamiliar situations. However, this commonsense knowledge, while sometimes accurate, is not always reliable, because it rests on commonly held beliefs rather than on systematic analysis of facts. It was once considered "common sense" to accept the idea that the earth was flat—a view rightly questioned by Pythagoras and Aristotle. Incorrect commonsense notions are not just a part of the distant past; they remain with us today.

In the United States, "common sense" tells us that religious fervor has been rising among young adults. "Common sense" tells us that people panic when faced with natural disasters, such as floods and earthquakes, or in the wake of tragedies such as the attacks on New York City and Washington, D.C., on September 11, 2001. However, these particular "commonsense" notions—like the notion that the earth is flat—are untrue; neither of them is supported by sociological research.

What *does* research have to tell us about these questions? Through 2003, annual surveys of first-year college students show a decline in the percentage who attend religious services even occasionally. Increasing numbers of college students claim to have no religious preference. The trend encompasses not just organized religion but other forms of spirituality as well. Fewer students pray or meditate today than in the past, and fewer consider their level of spirituality to be very high (Sax et al. 2003).

Similarly, disasters do not generally produce panic. In the aftermath of natural disasters and even explosions, greater social organization and structure emerge to deal with a community's problems. In the United States, an emergency operations group often coordinates public services, as well as certain services normally performed by the private sector, such as food distribution. Decision making becomes more centralized.

Like other social scientists, sociologists do not accept something as a fact because "everyone knows it." Instead, each piece of information must be tested and recorded, then analyzed in relationship to other data. Sociologists rely on scientific studies in order to describe and understand a social environment. At times, the findings of sociologists may seem like common sense because they deal with aspects of everyday life. The difference is that such findings have been *tested* by researchers. Common sense now tells us that the earth is round. But this particular commonsense notion is based on centuries of scientific work that upholds the breakthroughs made by Pythagoras and Aristotle.

What Is Sociological Theory?

Why do people commit suicide? One traditional commonsense answer is that people inherit the desire to kill themselves. Another view is that sunspots drive people to take their own lives. These explanations may not seem especially convincing to contemporary researchers, but they represent beliefs widely held as recently as 1900.

Sociologists are not particularly interested in why any one individual commits suicide; they are more concerned with identifying the social forces that systematically cause some people to take their own lives. In order to undertake this research, sociologists develop a theory that offers a general explanation of suicidal behavior.

We can think of theories as attempts to explain events, forces, materials, ideas, or behavior in a comprehensive manner. Within sociology, a *theory* is a set of statements that seeks to explain problems, actions, or behavior. An effective theory may have both explanatory and predictive power. That is, it can help us to see the relationships among seemingly isolated phenomena, as well as to understand how one type of change in an environment leads to others.

Émile Durkheim ([1897] 1951) looked into suicide data in great detail and developed a highly original theory about the relationship between suicide and social factors. He was primarily concerned not with the personalities of individual suicide victims, but rather with suicide *rates* and how they varied from country to country. As a result, when he looked at the number of reported suicides in France, England, and Denmark in 1869, he noted the total population of each country so that he could determine the rate of suicide in each. He found that whereas England had only 67 reported suicides per million inhabitants, France had 135 per million and Denmark had 277 per million. The question then became: "Why did Denmark have a comparatively high rate of reported suicides?"

Durkheim went much deeper into his investigation of suicide rates; the result was his landmark work *Suicide,* published in 1897. Durkheim refused to automatically accept unproven explanations regarding suicide, including the beliefs that cosmic forces or inherited tendencies caused such deaths. Instead, he focused on such problems as the cohesiveness or lack of cohesiveness of religious, social, and occupational groups.

Durkheim's research suggested that suicide, while a solitary act, is related to group life. Protestants had much higher suicide rates than Catholics; the unmarried had much higher rates than married people; soldiers were more likely to take their lives than civilians. In addition, there seemed to be higher rates of suicide in times of peace than in times of war and revolution, and in times of economic instability and recession rather than in times of prosperity. Durkheim concluded that the suicide rate of a society reflected the extent to which people were or were not integrated into the group life of the society.

Émile Durkheim, like many other social scientists, developed a theory to explain how individual behavior can be understood within a social context. He pointed out the influence of groups and societal forces on what had always been viewed as a highly personal act. Clearly,

Durkheim offered a more *scientific* explanation for the causes of suicide than that of sunspots or inherited tendencies. His theory has predictive power, since it suggests that suicide rates will rise or fall in conjunction with certain social and economic changes.

The Development of Sociology

People have always been curious about sociological matters—such as how we get along with others, what we do for a living, and whom we select as our leaders. Philosophers and religious authorities of ancient and medieval societies made countless observations about human behavior. They did not test or verify their observations scientifically; nevertheless, those observations often became the foundation for moral codes. Several of the early social philosophers predicted that a systematic study of human behavior would one day emerge. Beginning in the 19th century, European theorists made pioneering contributions to the development of a science of human behavior.

EARLY THINKERS: COMTE, MARTINEAU, AND SPENCER

The 19th century was an unsettled time in France. The French monarchy had been deposed in the revolution of 1789, and Napoleon had subsequently suffered defeat in his effort to conquer Europe. Amid this chaos, philosophers considered how society might be improved. Auguste Comte (1798–1857), credited with being the most influential of the philosophers of the early 1800s, believed that a theoretical science of society and a systematic investigation of behavior were needed to improve French society. He coined the term *sociology* to apply to the science of human behavior.

Writing in the 1800s, Comte feared that the excesses of the French Revolution had permanently impaired France's stability. Yet he hoped that the systematic study of social behavior would eventually lead to more rational human interactions. In Comte's hierarchy of sciences, sociology was at the top. He called it the "queen," and its practitioners "scientist-priests." This French theorist did not simply give sociology its name; he also presented a rather ambitious challenge to the fledgling discipline.

Scholars learned of Comte's works largely through translations by the English sociologist Harriet Martineau (1802–1876). As a sociologist, Martineau was a pathbreaker in her own right. She offered insightful observations of the customs and social practices of both her native Britain and the United States. Martineau's book *Society in America* ([1837] 1962) examines religion, politics, child rearing, and immigration in the young nation. Martineau gives special attention to social class distinctions and to such factors as gender and race.

Martineau's writings emphasized the impact that the economy, law, trade, and population could have on the social problems of contemporary society. She spoke out in favor of the rights of women, the emancipation of slaves, and religious tolerance. In Martineau's (1896) view, intellectuals and scholars should not simply offer observations of social conditions; they should act on their convictions in a manner that will benefit society. That is why Martineau conducted research on the nature of female employment and pointed to the need for further investigation of the issue (Lengermann and Niebrugge-Brantley 1998).

Another important contributor to the discipline of sociology was Herbert Spencer (1820–1903). A relatively prosperous Victorian Englishman, Spencer (unlike Martineau) did not feel compelled to correct or improve society; instead, he merely hoped to understand it better. Drawing on Charles Darwin's study *On the Origin of Species,* Spencer applied the concept of evolution of the species to societies in order to explain how they change, or evolve, over time. Similarly, he adapted Darwin's evolutionary view of the "survival of the fittest" by arguing that it is "natural" that some people are rich while others are poor.

Spencer's approach to societal change was extremely popular in his own lifetime. Unlike Comte, Spencer suggested that since societies are bound to change eventually, one need not be highly critical of present social arrangements or work actively for social change. This viewpoint appealed to many influential people in England and the United States who had a vested interest in the status quo and were suspicious of social thinkers who endorsed change.

ÉMILE DURKHEIM

Émile Durkheim made many pioneering contributions to sociology, including his important theoretical work on suicide. The son of a rabbi, Durkheim (1858–1917) was educated in both France and Germany. He established an impressive academic reputation and was appointed one of the first professors of sociology in France. Above all, Durkheim will be remembered for his insistence that behavior must be understood within a larger social context, not just in individualistic terms.

As one example of this emphasis, Durkheim ([1912] 2001) developed a fundamental thesis to help understand all forms of society. Through intensive study of the Arunta, an Australian tribe, he focused on the functions that religion performs and underscored the role that group life plays in defining what we consider to be religious. Durkheim concluded that like other forms of group behavior, religion reinforces a group's solidarity.

Like many other sociologists, Durkheim did not limit his interests to one aspect of social behavior. Later in this book, we will consider his thinking on crime and punishment, religion, and the workplace. Few sociologists have had such a dramatic impact on so many different areas within the discipline.

MAX WEBER

Another important early theorist was Max Weber (pronounced "VAY-ber"). Born in Germany in 1864, Weber studied legal and economic history, but he gradually developed an interest in sociology. Eventually, he became a professor at various German universities. Weber taught his students that they should employ **Verstehen,** the German word for "understanding" or "insight," in their intellectual work. He pointed out that we cannot analyze much of our social behavior by the same criteria we use to measure weight or temperature. To fully comprehend behavior, we must learn the subjective meanings people attach to their actions—how they themselves view and explain their behavior.

We also owe credit to Weber for a key conceptual tool: the ideal type. An **ideal type** is a construct, a made-up model that serves as a measuring rod against which actual cases can be evaluated. In his own works, Weber identified various characteristics of bureaucracy as an ideal type (discussed in detail in Chapter 3). In presenting this model of bureaucracy, Weber was not describing any particular organization, nor was he using the term *ideal* in a way that suggested a positive evaluation. Instead, his purpose was to provide a useful standard for measuring how bureaucratic an actual organization is (Gerth and Mills 1958). Later in this textbook, we will use the concept of an ideal type to study the family, religion, authority, and economic systems and to analyze bureaucracy.

KARL MARX

Karl Marx (1818–1883) shared with Durkheim and Weber a dual interest in abstract philosophical issues and the concrete reality of everyday life. Unlike them, Marx was so critical of existing institutions that a conventional academic career was impossible for him. He spent most of his life in exile from his native Germany.

Marx's personal life was a difficult struggle. When a paper that he had written was suppressed, he fled to France. In Paris, he met Friedrich Engels (1820–1895), with whom he formed a lifelong friendship. The two lived at a time when European and North American economic life was increasingly dominated by the factory rather than the farm.

In 1847, Marx and Engels attended secret meetings in London of an illegal coalition of labor unions known as the Communist League. The following year, they prepared a platform called *The Communist Manifesto,* in which they argued that the masses of people who have no resources other than their labor (whom they referred to as the *proletariat*) should unite to fight for the overthrow of capitalist societies.

In Marx's analysis, society was fundamentally divided between classes that clash in pursuit of their own class interests. When he examined the industrial societies of his time, such as Germany, England, and the United States, he saw the factory as the center of conflict between the exploiters (the owners of the means of production) and the exploited (the workers). Marx viewed these relationships in systematic terms; that is, he believed that an entire system of economic, social, and political relationships maintained the power and dominance of the owners over the workers. Consequently, Marx and Engels argued, the working class needed to *overthrow* the existing class system. Marx's influence on contemporary thinking has been dramatic. His writings inspired those who were later to lead communist revolutions in Russia, China, Cuba, Vietnam, and elsewhere.

Even apart from the political revolutions that his work fostered, Marx's significance is profound. Marx emphasized the *group* identifications and associations that influence an individual's place in society. This area of study is the major focus of contemporary sociology. Throughout this textbook, we will consider how membership in a particular gender classification, age group, racial group, or economic class affects a person's attitudes and behavior. In an important sense, we can trace this way of understanding society back to the pioneering work of Karl Marx.

MODERN DEVELOPMENTS

Sociology today builds on the firm foundation developed by Émile Durkheim, Max Weber, and Karl Marx. However, the discipline has certainly not remained stagnant over the last 100 years. While Europeans have continued to make contributions, sociologists from throughout the world, and especially the United States, have advanced sociological theory and research. Their new insights have helped us to better understand the workings of society.

Charles Horton Cooley.   Charles Horton Cooley (1864–1929) was typical of the sociologists who came to prominence in the early 1900s. Born in Ann Arbor, Michigan, Cooley received his graduate training in economics, but later became a sociology professor at the University of Michigan. Like other early sociologists, he had become interested in this "new" discipline while pursuing a related area of study.

Cooley shared the desire of Durkheim, Weber, and Marx to learn more about society. But to do so effectively, he preferred to use the sociological perspective to look first at smaller units—intimate, face-to-face groups such as families, gangs, and friendship networks. He saw these groups as the seedbeds of society, in the sense that they shape people's ideals, beliefs, values, and social nature. Cooley's work increased our understanding of groups of relatively small size.

Jane Addams.   In the early 1900s, many leading sociologists in the United States saw themselves as social reformers dedicated to systematically studying and then improving a corrupt society. They were genuinely concerned about the lives of immigrants in the nation's growing cities, whether those immigrants came from Europe or from the rural American south. Early female sociologists, in particular, often took active roles in poor urban areas as leaders of community centers known as settlement houses. For example, Jane Addams (1860–1935), a member of the American Sociological Society, cofounded the famous Chicago settlement, Hull House.

Addams and other pioneering female sociologists commonly combined intellectual inquiry, social service work, and political activism—all with the goal of assisting the underprivileged and creating a more egalitarian society. For example, working with the Black journalist and educator Ida Wells-Barnett, Addams successfully prevented racial segregation in the Chicago public schools. Addams's efforts to establish a juvenile court system and a women's trade union also reveal the practical focus of her work (Addams 1910, 1930; Deegan 1991; Lengermann and Niebrugge-Brantley 1998).

By the middle of the 20th century, however, the focus of the discipline had shifted. Sociologists for the most part restricted themselves to theorizing and gathering information; the aim of transforming society was left to social workers and others. This shift away from social reform was accompanied by a growing commitment to scientific methods of research and to value-free interpretation of data. Not all sociologists were happy with this emphasis. A new organization, the Society for the Study of Social Problems, was created in 1950 to deal more directly with social inequality and other social ills.

Robert Merton.   Sociologist Robert Merton (1910–2003) made an important contribution to the field by successfully combining theory and research. Born in 1910 to Slavic immigrant parents in Philadelphia, Merton subsequently won a scholarship to Temple University. He continued his studies at Harvard, where he acquired his lifelong interest in sociology. Merton's teaching career was based at Columbia University.

Merton produced a theory that is one of the most frequently cited explanations of deviant behavior. He noted different ways in which people attempt to achieve success in life. In his view, some may deviate from the socially agreed-upon goal of accumulating material goods or the socially accepted means of achieving that goal. For example, in Merton's classification scheme, "innovators" are people who accept the goal of pursuing material wealth but use illegal means to do so, including robbery, burglary, and extortion. Merton based his explanation of crime on individual behavior—influenced by society's approved goals and means—yet it has wider applications. It helps to account for the high crime rates among the nation's poor, who may see no hope of advancing themselves through traditional roads to success. Chapter 4 discusses Merton's theory in greater detail.

Today sociology reflects the diverse contributions of earlier theorists. As sociologists approach such topics as divorce, drug addiction, and religious cults, they can draw on the theoretical insights of the discipline's pioneers. A careful reader can hear Comte, Durkheim, Weber, Marx, Cooley, Addams, and many others speaking through the pages of current research. Sociology has also broadened beyond the intellectual confines of North America and Europe. Contributions to the discipline now come from sociologists studying and researching human behavior in other parts of the world. In describing the work of today's sociologists, it is helpful to examine a number of influential theoretical approaches (also known as *perspectives*).

Major Theoretical Perspectives

Sociologists view society in different ways. Some see the world basically as a stable and ongoing entity. They are impressed with the endurance of the family, organized religion, and other social institutions. Some sociologists see society in terms of many groups in conflict, competing for scarce resources. To other sociologists, the most fascinating aspects of the social world are the everyday, routine interactions among individuals that we often take for granted. These three views, the ones most widely used by sociologists, are the functionalist, conflict, and interactionist perspectives. Together, they will provide an introductory look at the discipline.

FUNCTIONALIST PERSPECTIVE

Think of society as a living organism in which each part of the organism contributes to its survival. This view is the *functionalist perspective* (also referred to as the *structural functionalist approach*). The functionalist perspective emphasizes the way that the parts of a society are structured to maintain its stability.

Talcott Parsons (1902–1979), a Harvard University sociologist, was a key figure in the development of functionalist theory. Parsons had been greatly influenced by the work of Émile Durkheim, Max Weber, and other European sociologists. For over four decades, Parsons dominated sociology in the United States with his advocacy of functionalism. He saw any society as a vast network of connected parts, each of which helps to maintain the system as a whole. According to the functionalist approach, if an aspect of social life does not contribute to a society's stability or survival—if it does not serve some identifiably useful function or promote value consensus among members of a society—it will not be passed on from one generation to the next.

Let's examine prostitution as an example of the functionalist perspective. Why is it that a practice so widely condemned continues to display such persistence and vitality? Functionalists suggest that prostitution satisfies needs that may not be readily met through more socially acceptable forms of behavior, such as courtship or marriage. The "buyer" receives sex without any responsibility for procreation or sentimental attachment; at the same time, the "seller" makes a living through the exchange.

Such an examination leads us to conclude that prostitution does perform certain functions that society seems to need. However, that is not to suggest that prostitution is a desirable or legitimate form of social behavior. Functionalists do not make such judgments. Rather, advocates of the functionalist perspective hope to explain how an aspect of society that is so frequently attacked can nevertheless manage to survive (K. Davis 1937).

Manifest and Latent Functions.   A college catalog typically states various functions of the institution. It may inform you, for example, that the university intends to "offer each student a broad education in classical and contemporary thought, in the humanities, in the sciences, and in the arts." However, it would be quite a surprise to find a catalog that declared, "This university was founded in 1895 to keep people between the ages of 18 and 22 out of the job market, thus reducing unemployment." No college catalog will declare that as the purpose of the university. Yet societal institutions serve many functions, some of them quite subtle. The university, in fact, *does* delay people's entry into the job market.

Robert Merton (1968) made an important distinction between manifest and latent functions. *Manifest functions* of institutions are open, stated, conscious functions. They involve the intended, recognized consequences of an aspect of society, such as the university's role in certifying academic competence and excellence. By contrast, *latent functions* are unconscious or unintended functions that may reflect hidden purposes of an institution. One latent function of universities is to hold down unemployment. Another is to serve as a meeting ground for people seeking marital partners.

CONFLICT PERSPECTIVE

In contrast to the functionalists' emphasis on stability and consensus, conflict sociologists see the social world in continual struggle. Proponents of the *conflict perspective* assume that social behavior is best understood in terms of conflict or tension between competing groups. Such conflict need not be violent; it can take the form of labor negotiations, party politics, competition between religious groups for members, or disputes over the federal budget.

Throughout most of the 1900s, advocates of the functionalist perspective had the upper hand among sociologists in the United States. However, proponents of the conflict approach have become increasingly persuasive since the late 1960s. The widespread social unrest resulting from battles over civil rights, bitter divisions over the war in Vietnam, the rise of the feminist and gay liberation movements, the Watergate scandal, urban riots, and confrontations at abortion clinics offered support for the conflict approach—the view that our social world is characterized by continual struggle between competing groups. Currently, sociologists accept conflict theory as one valid way to gain insight into a society.

The Marxist View. As we saw earlier, Karl Marx viewed the struggle between social classes as inevitable, given the exploitation of workers under capitalism. Expanding on Marx's work, sociologists and other social scientists have come to see conflict not merely as a class phenomenon but as a part of everyday life in all societies. In studying any culture, organization, or social group, sociologists want to know who benefits, who suffers, and who dominates at the expense of others. They are concerned with the conflicts between women and men, parents and children, cities and suburbs, and Whites and Blacks, to name only a few. Conflict theorists are interested in how society's institutions—including the family, government, religion, education, and the media—may help to maintain the privileges of some groups and keep others in a subservient position. Their emphasis on social change and the redistribution of resources makes conflict theorists more "radical" and "activist" than functionalists (Dahrendorf 1959).

A Different Voice: W. E. B. Du Bois. One important contribution of conflict theory is that it has encouraged sociologists to view society through the eyes of those segments of the population that rarely influence decision making. Some Black sociologists, including W. E. B. Du Bois (1868–1963), conducted research that they hoped would assist in the struggle for a racially egalitarian society. Du Bois believed that knowledge was essential to combating prejudice and achieving tolerance and justice. Sociologists, he contended, must draw on scientific principles to study social problems such as those experienced by Blacks in the United States, in order to separate accepted opinion from fact. He himself documented Blacks' relatively low status in Philadelphia and Atlanta. Through his in-depth studies of urban life, both White and Black, Du Bois made a major contribution to sociology.

Du Bois had little patience for theorists such as Herbert Spencer, who seemed content with the status quo. He believed that the granting of full political rights to Blacks in the United States was essential to their social and economic progress. Because many of his ideas challenged the status quo, he did not find a receptive audience within either the government or the academic world. As a result, Du Bois became increasingly involved with organizations whose members questioned the established social order, and he helped to found the National Association for the Advancement of Colored People, better known as the NAACP (Lewis 1994, 2000).

The increasingly diverse views within sociology in recent years have led to some valuable research, especially for African Americans. For many years, African Americans were understandably wary of participating in medical research studies, because those studies had been used for such purposes as justifying slavery or determining the impact of untreated syphilis. Now, however, African American sociologists and other social scientists are working to involve Blacks in useful ethnic medical research on such diseases as diabetes and sickle cell anemia, two disorders that strike Black populations especially hard (Young and Deakins 2001).

Feminist Perspective.   Sociologists began embracing the feminist perspective in the 1970s, although it has a long tradition in many other disciplines. Proponents of the *feminist perspective* view inequity based on gender as central to all behavior and organization. Because this perspective clearly focuses on one aspect of inequality, it is often allied with the conflict perspective. But unlike conflict theorists, those who hold to the feminist perspective tend to focus on the relationships of everyday life, just as interactionists would. Drawing on the work of Marx and Engels, many contemporary feminist theorists view women's subordination as inherent in capitalist societies. Some radical feminist theorists, however, view the oppression of women as inevitable in *all* male-dominated societies, including those labeled as *capitalist, socialist,* and *communist.*

Feminist scholarship has broadened our understanding of social behavior by taking it beyond the White male point of view. For example, a family's social standing is no longer defined solely by the husband's position and income. Feminist scholars have not only challenged stereotyping of women; they have argued for a gender-balanced study of society in which women's experiences and contributions are as visible as those of men (England 1999; Komarovsky 1991; Tuchman 1992).

INTERACTIONIST PERSPECTIVE

Workers interacting on the job, encounters in public places like bus stops and parks, behavior in small groups—these are all aspects of microsociology that catch the attention of interactionists. Whereas functionalist and conflict theorists both analyze large-scale, societywide patterns of behavior, proponents of the *interactionist perspective* generalize about everyday forms of social interaction in order to understand society as a whole. In the 1990s, for example, the workings of juries became a subject of public scrutiny. High-profile trials ended in verdicts that left some people shaking their heads. Long before jury members were being interviewed on their front lawns following trials, interactionists tried to better understand behavior in the small-group setting of a jury deliberation room.

While the functionalist and conflict approaches were initiated in Europe, interactionism developed first in the United States. George Herbert Mead (1863–1931) is widely regarded as the founder of the interactionist perspective. Mead taught at the University of Chicago from 1893 until his death. His sociological analysis, like that of Charles Horton Cooley, often focused on human interactions within one-to-one situations and small groups. Mead was interested in observing the most minute forms of communication—smiles, frowns, the nodding of one's head—and in understanding how such individual behavior was influenced by the larger context of a group or society. Despite his innovative views, Mead only occasionally wrote articles, and never a book. He was an extremely popular teacher; in fact, most of his insights have come to us through edited volumes of lectures that his students published after his death.

Interactionism is a sociological framework in which human beings are seen to be living in a world of meaningful objects. These "objects" may include material things, actions, other people, relationships, and even symbols. The interactionist perspective is sometimes referred to as the *symbolic interactionist perspective,* because interactionists see symbols as an especially important part of human communication. Symbols carry shared social meanings that are generally recognized by all members of a society. However, some symbols carry different meanings for different groups of people. To some people in the United States, for example, the Confederate flag symbolizes respect for their rich cultural heritage; to others, it represents the subjugation of their civil rights.

Different cultures may use different symbols to convey the same idea. For example, consider the different ways various societies portray suicide without the use of words. People in the United States point a finger at the head (shooting); urban Japanese bring a fist against the stomach (stabbing); and the South Fore of Papua, New Guinea, clench a hand at the throat (hanging). These symbolic interactions are classified as a form of **nonverbal communication,** which can include many other gestures, facial expressions, and postures.

What symbols at your college or university have special meaning for students?

THE SOCIOLOGICAL APPROACH

Which perspective should a sociologist use in studying human behavior? Functionalist? Conflict? Interactionist? Feminist? In fact, sociologists make use of all the perspectives summarized in Table 1–1 (see page 18), since each offers unique insights into the same issue. We can gain the broadest understanding of our society, then, by drawing on all the major perspectives, noting where they overlap and where they diverge.

Although no one approach is "correct," and sociologists draw on all of them for various purposes, many sociologists tend to favor one particular perspective over others. A sociologist's theoretical orientation influences his or her approach to a research problem in important ways. The choice of what to study, how to study it, and what questions to pose (or not to pose) can all be influenced by a researcher's theoretical orientation. In the next part of this chapter, we will see how sociologists have

Table 1–1 Comparing Major Theoretical Perspectives

	Functionalist	**Conflict**	**Interactionist**
View of society	Stable, well integrated	Characterized by tension and struggle between groups	Active in influencing and affecting everyday social interaction
View of the individual	People are socialized to perform societal functions	People are shaped by power, coercion, and authority	People manipulate symbols and create their social worlds through interaction
View of the social order	Maintained through cooperation and consensus	Maintained through force and coercion	Maintained by shared understanding of everyday behavior
View of social change	Predictable, reinforcing	Change takes place all the time and may have positive consequences	Reflected in people's social positions and their communications with others
Example	Public punishments reinforce the social order	Laws reinforce the positions of those in power	People respect laws or disobey them based on their own past experience

adapted the scientific method to their discipline and how they apply that method in surveys, case observations, and experiments. Bear in mind, though, that even with meticulous attention to all the steps in the scientific method, a researcher's work will always be guided by his or her theoretical viewpoint. Research results, like theories, shine a spotlight on one part of the stage, leaving other parts in relative darkness.

What Is the Scientific Method?

Like all of us, sociologists are interested in the central questions of our time. Is the family falling apart? Why is there so much crime in the United States? Is the world lagging behind in its ability to feed the population? Such issues concern most people, whether or not they have academic training. However, unlike the typical citizen, the sociologist is committed to using the scientific method in studying society. The ***scientific method*** is a systematic, organized series of steps that ensures maximum objectivity and consistency in researching a problem.

Many of us will never actually conduct scientific research. Why, then, is it important that we understand the scientific method? Because it plays a major role in the workings of our society. Residents of the United States are constantly being bombarded with "facts" or "data." A television reporter informs us that "one in every two marriages in this country now ends in divorce." An advertiser cites supposedly scientific studies to prove that a

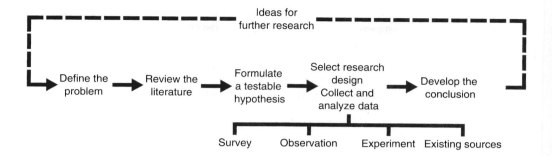

Figure 1–1
The Scientific Method

particular product is superior. Such claims may be accurate or exaggerated. We can better evaluate such information—and will not be fooled so easily—if we are familiar with the standards of scientific research. These standards are quite stringent and demand as strict adherence as possible.

The scientific method requires precise preparation in developing useful research. Otherwise, the research data collected may not prove accurate. Sociologists and other researchers follow five basic steps in the scientific method: (1) defining the problem, (2) reviewing the literature, (3) formulating the hypothesis, (4) selecting the research design and then collecting and analyzing data, and (5) developing the conclusion (see Figure 1–1). We'll use an actual example to illustrate the workings of the scientific method.

DEFINING THE PROBLEM

Does it "pay" to go to college? Some people make great sacrifices and work hard to get a college education. Parents borrow money for their children's tuition. Students work part-time jobs or even take full-time positions while attending evening or weekend classes. Does it pay off? Are there monetary returns for getting that degree?

The first step in any research project is to state as clearly as possible what you hope to investigate—that is, *define the problem.* In this instance, we are interested in knowing how schooling relates to income. We want to find out the earnings of people with different levels of formal schooling. Early on, any social science researcher must develop an operational definition of each concept being studied. An ***operational definition*** is an explanation of an abstract concept that is specific enough to allow a researcher to assess the concept. For example, a sociologist interested in status might use membership in exclusive social clubs as an operational definition of status. Someone studying prejudice might consider a person's unwillingness to hire or work with members of minority groups as an operational definition of prejudice. In our example, we need to develop two operational definitions—one for education and the other for earnings—in order to study whether it pays to get advanced educational degrees.

Initially, we will take a functionalist perspective (although we may end up incorporating other approaches). We will argue that opportunities for more earning power are related to level of schooling and that schools prepare students for employment.

REVIEWING THE LITERATURE

By conducting a *review of the literature*—the relevant scholarly studies and information—researchers refine the problem under study, clarify possible techniques to be used in collecting data, and eliminate or reduce avoidable mistakes. In our example, we would examine information about the salaries for different occupations. We would see if jobs that require more academic training are better rewarded. It would also be appropriate to review other studies on the relationship between education and income.

The review of the literature would soon tell us that many other factors besides years of schooling influence earning potential. For example, we would learn that the children of richer parents are more likely to go to college than those from modest backgrounds. As a result, we might consider the possibility that those parents may also help their children to secure better-paying jobs after graduation.

FORMULATING THE HYPOTHESIS

After reviewing earlier research and drawing on the contributions of sociological theorists, the researchers may then *formulate the hypothesis*. A **hypothesis** is a speculative statement about the relationship between two or more factors known as *variables*. Income, religion, occupation, and gender can all serve as variables in a study. We can define a **variable** as a measurable trait or characteristic that is subject to change under different conditions.

Researchers who formulate a hypothesis generally must suggest how one aspect of human behavior influences or affects another. The variable hypothesized to cause or influence another is called the **independent variable.** The second variable is termed the **dependent variable** because its action "depends" on the influence of the independent variable.

Our hypothesis is that the higher one's educational degree, the more money a person will earn. The independent variable that is to be measured is the level of educational degree. The variable that is thought to "depend" on it—income—must also be measured.

Identifying independent and dependent variables is a critical step in clarifying cause-and-effect relationships. **Causal logic** involves the relationship between a condition or variable and a particular consequence, with one event leading to the other. Under causal logic, being less integrated into society (the independent variable) may be directly related to or produce a greater likelihood of suicide (the dependent variable).

Similarly, parents' income levels (an independent variable) may affect the likelihood that their children will enroll in college (a dependent variable). Later in life, the level of education their children achieve (independent variable) may be directly related to their children's income levels (dependent variable). Note that income level can be either an independent or a dependent variable, depending on the causal relationship.

A *correlation* exists when a change in one variable coincides with a change in the other. Correlations are an indication that causality *may* be present; they do not necessarily indicate causation. For example, data indicate that working mothers are more likely to have delinquent children than are mothers who do not work outside the home. But this correlation is actually *caused* by a third variable: family income. Lower-class households are more likely to have a full-time working mother; at the same time, reported rates of delinquency are higher in that class than in other economic levels. Consequently, while having a mother who works outside the home is correlated with delinquency, it does not *cause* delinquency. Sociologists seek to identify the *causal* link between variables; they generally describe the causal link in their hypotheses.

COLLECTING AND ANALYZING DATA

How do you test a hypothesis to determine if it is supported or refuted? You need to collect information, using one of the research designs described later in the chapter. The research design guides the researcher in collecting and analyzing data.

Selecting the Sample. In most studies, social scientists must carefully select what is known as a *sample*. A *sample* is a selection from a larger population that is statistically representative of that population. There are many kinds of samples, but the one social scientists use most frequently is the random sample. In a *random sample,* every member of an entire population being studied has the same chance of being selected. Thus, if researchers want to examine the opinions of people listed in a city directory (a book that, unlike the telephone directory, lists all households), they might use a computer to randomly select names from the directory. This selection would constitute a random sample. The advantage of using specialized sampling techniques is that sociologists do not need to question everyone in a population.

It is all too easy to confuse the careful scientific techniques used in representative sampling with the many *nonscientific* polls that receive much more media attention. For example, television viewers and radio listeners are encouraged to e-mail their views on today's headlines or on political contests. Such polls reflect nothing more than the views of those who happened to see the television program (or hear the radio broadcast) and took the time, perhaps at some cost, to register their opinions. These data do not necessarily reflect (and indeed may distort) the views of the broader population. Not everyone has access to a television or radio or has the time to watch or listen to a program or the means and/or inclination to send e-mail. Similar problems are raised by the "mail-back" questionnaires found in many magazines and by "mall intercepts," in which shoppers are asked about some issue. Even when these techniques include answers from tens of thousands of people, they will be far less accurate than a carefully selected representative sample of 1,500 respondents.

For the purposes of our example, we will use information collected in the General Social Survey (GSS). Since 1972, the National Opinion Research Center (NORC) has conducted this national survey 24 times, most recently in 2002. Each time, a representative sample of the adult population is interviewed on a variety of topics for about one and a half hours. The author of this book examined the responses of the 2,765 people interviewed in 2002, especially concerning their level of education and income.

Ensuring Validity and Reliability.   The scientific method requires that research results be both valid and reliable. *Validity* refers to the degree to which a scale or measure truly reflects the phenomenon under study. *Reliability* refers to the extent to which a measure produces consistent results. A valid measure of income depends on gathering accurate data. Various studies show that people are reasonably accurate in knowing how much money they earned in the most recent year. One problem of reliability is that some people may not *disclose* accurate information, but most do. In the General Social Survey, only 9 percent of the respondents refused to give their income, and another 5 percent said they did not know what their income was. That means 86 percent of the respondents gave their incomes, which we can assume were reasonably accurate (given their other responses about occupation and years in the labor force).

DEVELOPING THE CONCLUSION

Scientific studies, including those conducted by sociologists, do not aim to answer all the questions that can be raised about a particular subject. Therefore, the conclusion of a research study represents both an end and a beginning. It terminates a specific phase of the investigation, but it should also generate ideas for future study.

Supporting Hypotheses.   In our example, we find that the data support our hypothesis: People with more formal schooling *do* earn more money. As Table 1–2 shows, as a group, those with a high school diploma earn more than those who failed to complete high school, but those with an associate's degree earn more than high school graduates. The relationship continues through more advanced levels of schooling; those with graduate degrees earn the most.

Table 1–2 Income by Education

Income Group	Educational Level (Percentage of Graduates in Each Income Group)				
	Less Than High School Education	High School Diploma	Associate's Degree	BA/BS	Graduate Degree
Under $15,000	50%	31%	11%	17%	11%
$15,000–$24,999	25	22	18	12	8
$25,000–$34,999	14	26	32	22	17
$35,000–$59,999	7	15	18	23	25
$60,000 and over	4	6	21	26	39
Total	100%	100%	100%	100%	100%

SOURCE: Author's analysis of General Social Survey 2002 in J. A. Davis et al. 2003.

Sociological studies do not always generate data that support the original hypothesis. In many instances, a hypothesis is refuted, and researchers must reformulate their conclusions. Unexpected results may also lead sociologists to reexamine their methodology and make changes in the research design.

Controlling for Other Factors.   A *control variable* is a factor held constant to test the relative impact of the independent variable. For example, if researchers wanted to know how adults in the United States feel about restrictions on smoking in public places, they would probably attempt to use a respondent's smoking behavior as a control variable. That is, how do smokers versus nonsmokers feel about smoking in public places? The researchers would compile separate statistics on how smokers and nonsmokers feel about antismoking regulations.

Our study of the influence of education on income suggests that not everyone enjoys equal educational opportunities, a disparity that is one of the causes of social inequality. Since education affects a person's income, we may wish to call on the conflict perspective to explore this topic further. What impact does a person's race or gender have? Is a woman with a college degree likely to earn as much as a man with similar schooling? Later in this textbook we will consider these other factors and variables. We will examine the impact that education has on income, while controlling for variables such as gender and race.

IN SUMMARY: THE SCIENTIFIC METHOD

Let's summarize the process of the scientific method through a review of our example. We *defined a problem* (the question of whether it pays to get higher educational degrees). We *reviewed the literature* (other studies of the relationship between education and income) and *formulated a hypothesis* (the higher one's educational degree, the more money a person will earn). We *collected and analyzed the data,* making sure the sample was representative and the data were valid and reliable. Finally, we *developed the conclusion:* The data do support our hypothesis about the influence of education on income.

Major Research Designs

An important aspect of sociological research is deciding how to collect the data. A ***research design*** is a detailed plan or method for obtaining data scientifically. Selection of a research design requires creativity and ingenuity. This choice will directly influence both the cost of the project and the amount of time needed to collect the results of the research. Research designs that sociologists use regularly to generate data include surveys, observation, experiments, and existing sources.

SURVEYS

Almost all of us have responded to surveys of one kind or another. We may have been asked what kind of detergent we use, which presidential candidate we intend to vote for, or what our favorite television program is. A ***survey*** is a study, generally in the form of an interview or questionnaire, that provides researchers with information about how people think and act. Among the United States' best-known surveys of opinion are the Gallup poll and the Harris poll. As anyone who watches the news knows, these polls have become a staple of political life.

In preparing to conduct a survey, sociologists must not only develop representative samples; they must exercise great care in the wording of questions. An effective survey question must be simple and clear enough for people to understand it. It must also be specific enough so that there are no problems in interpreting the results. Open-ended questions ("What do you think of the programming on educational television?") must be carefully phrased to solicit the type of information desired. Surveys can be indispensable sources of information, but only if the sampling is done properly and the questions are worded accurately and without bias.

There are two main forms of surveys: the ***interview,*** in which a researcher obtains information through face-to-face or telephone questioning, and the ***questionnaire,*** a printed or written form used to obtain information from a respondent. Each of these has its own advantages. An interviewer can obtain a high response rate, because people find it more difficult to turn down a personal request for an interview than to throw away a written questionnaire. In addition, a skillful interviewer can go beyond written questions and probe for a subject's underlying feelings and reasons. On the other hand, questionnaires have the advantage of being cheaper, especially in large samples.

Surveys are an example of *quantitative research,* in which scientists collect and report data primarily in numerical form. Most of the survey research discussed so far in this book has been quantitative. While this type of research is appropriate for large samples, it doesn't offer great depth and detail on a topic. That is why researchers also make use of *qualitative research,* which relies on what scientists see in field and naturalistic settings. Qualitative research often focuses on small groups and communities rather than on large groups or whole nations. The most common form of qualitative research is *observation.*

OBSERVATION

Investigators who collect information through direct participation in and/or closely watching a group or community under study are engaged in *observation.* This method allows sociologists to examine certain behaviors and communities that could not be investigated through other research techniques.

An increasingly popular form of qualitative research in sociology today is *ethnography.* **Ethnography** refers to the study of an entire social setting through extended, systematic observation. Typically, an ethnographic description emphasizes how the subjects themselves view their social reality. Anthropologists rely heavily on ethnography. Much as an anthropologist seeks to understand the people of some Polynesian island, the sociologist as ethnographer seeks to understand and present to us an entire way of life in some setting.

In some cases, the sociologist actually joins a group for a period to get an accurate sense of how it operates. This approach is called *participant observation.* During the late 1930s, in a classic example of participant-observation research, William F. Whyte moved into a low-income Italian neighborhood in Boston. For nearly four years he was a member of the social circle of "corner boys" that he describes in *Street Corner Society.* Whyte revealed his identity to these men and joined in their conversations, bowling, and other leisure-time activities. His goal was to gain greater insight into the community that these men had established. As Whyte (1981:303) listened to Doc, the leader of the group, he "learned the answers to questions I would not even have had the sense to ask if I had been getting my information solely on an interviewing basis." Whyte's work was especially valuable, since at the time, the academic world had little direct knowledge of the poor and tended to rely on the records of social service agencies, hospitals, and courts for information (Adler and Johnson 1992).

The initial challenge that Whyte faced—and that every participant observer encounters—was to gain acceptance into an unfamiliar group. It is no simple matter for a college-trained sociologist to win the trust of a religious cult, a youth gang, a poor Appalachian community, or a circle of skid row residents. Doing so requires a great deal of patience and an accepting, nonthreatening personality on the part of the observer.

Observation research poses other complex challenges for the investigator. Sociologists must be able to fully understand what they are observing. In a sense, then, researchers must learn to see the world as the group sees it in order to fully comprehend the events taking place around them.

EXPERIMENTS

When sociologists want to study a possible cause-and-effect relationship, they may conduct experiments. An *experiment* is an artificially created situation that allows the researcher to manipulate variables.

In the classic method of conducting an experiment, two groups of people are selected and matched for similar characteristics, such as age or education. The researchers then assign one of the groups to be the experimental group and the other to be the control group. The *experimental group* is exposed to an independent variable; the *control group* is not. Thus, if scientists were testing a new type of antibiotic drug, they would administer that drug to an experimental group but not to a control group.

Sociologists don't often rely on this classic form of experiment, because it generally involves manipulating human behavior in an inappropriate manner, especially in a laboratory setting. However, sociologists do try to re-create experimental conditions in the field. For example, they may compare children's performance in two schools that follow different curricula.

In some experiments, just as in observation research, the presence of a social scientist or other observer may affect the behavior of the people being studied. The recognition of this phenomenon grew out of an experiment conducted during the 1920s and 1930s at the Hawthorne plant of the Western Electric Company. A group of researchers set out to determine how to improve the productivity of workers at the plant. The investigators manipulated such variables as the lighting and working hours to see what impact the changes would have on productivity. To their surprise, they found that *every* step they took seemed to increase productivity. Even measures that seemed likely to have the opposite effect, such as reducing the amount of lighting in the plant, led to higher productivity.

Why did the plant's employees work harder even under less favorable conditions? Their behavior apparently was influenced by the greater attention being paid to them in the course of the research and by the novelty of being subjects in an experiment. Since that time, sociologists have used the term *Hawthorne effect* to refer to the unintended influence of observers or experiments on subjects of research, who deviate from their typical behavior because they realize that they are under observation (Lang 1992).

Use Your Sociological Imagination

You are a researcher interested in the effect of TV-watching on schoolchildren's grades. How would you go about setting up an experiment to measure the effect?

USE OF EXISTING SOURCES

Sociologists do not necessarily need to collect new data in order to conduct research and test hypotheses. The term **secondary analysis** refers to a variety of research techniques that make use of previously collected and publicly accessible information and data. Generally, in conducting secondary analysis, researchers utilize data in ways unintended by the initial collectors of information. For example, census data that were compiled for specific uses by the federal government are also valuable to marketing specialists in locating everything from bicycle stores to nursing homes.

Sociologists consider secondary analysis to be *nonreactive,* since it does not influence people's behavior. For example, Émile Durkheim's statistical analysis of suicide neither increased nor decreased human self-destruction. Researchers, then, can avoid the Hawthorne effect by using secondary analysis.

Many social scientists find it useful to study cultural, economic, and political documents, including newspapers, periodicals, radio and television tapes, the Internet, scripts, diaries, songs, folklore, and legal papers, to name some examples. In examining these sources, researchers employ a technique known as **content analysis,** which is the systematic coding and objective recording of data, guided by some rationale.

Researchers today are analyzing the nature and extent of violence contained in children's television programming. In a recent study, they found that 69 percent of the shows specifically intended for children ages 12 and under contained violence. Though a comparison with non-children's programming showed little difference in the total amount of time devoted to violence, it did show that children's programs contain more scenes of violence than other programs (B. Wilson et al. 2002).

Table 1–3 on page 28 summarizes the advantages and disadvantages of the four major research designs.

Ethics of Research

A biochemist cannot inject a drug into a human being unless the drug has been thoroughly tested and the subject agrees to the shot. To do otherwise would be both unethical and illegal. Sociologists must also abide by certain specific standards in conducting research, called a **code of ethics.** The professional society of the discipline, the American Sociological Association (ASA), first published its *Code of Ethics* in 1971 (revised most recently in 1997), which put forth the following basic principles:

1. Maintain objectivity and integrity in research.
2. Respect the subject's right to privacy and dignity.
3. Protect subjects from personal harm.

summingUP

Table 1–3 Major Research Designs

Method	Examples	Advantages	Limitations
Survey	Questionnaires Interviews	Yields information about specific issues	Can be expensive and time-consuming
Observation	Ethnography	Yields detailed information about specific groups or organizations	Involves months if not years of labor-intensive data gathering
Experiment	Deliberate manipulation of people's social behavior	Yields direct measures of people's behavior	Ethical limitations on the degree to which subjects' behavior can be manipulated
Existing sources/ secondary analysis	Analysis of census or health data Analysis of films or TV commercials	Cost-efficiency	Limited to data collected for some other purpose

4. Preserve confidentiality.

5. Seek informed consent when data are collected from research participants or when behavior occurs in a private context.

6. Acknowledge research collaboration and assistance.

7. Disclose all sources of financial support. (American Sociological Association 1997)

Most sociological research uses *people* as sources of information—as respondents to survey questions, subjects of observation, or participants in experiments. In all cases, sociologists need to be certain that they are not invading the privacy of their subjects. Generally, they handle this responsibility by assuring them anonymity and by guaranteeing the confidentiality of personal information.

We have examined the process of sociological research, including related ethical considerations, in detail. But not all sociologists are researchers. Some practice what has come to be known as applied sociology, or the application of sociological knowledge to real-world social problems.

Applied and Clinical Sociology

Sociology matters because it addresses real issues that affect people's lives. Many early sociologists—notably, Jane Addams and George Herbert Mead—were strong advocates for social reform. They wanted their theories and findings to be relevant to policymakers and to people's lives in general. For instance, Mead was the treasurer of Hull House, where for many years he used his theory to improve the lives of those who were powerless (especially immigrants). He also served on committees dealing with Chicago's labor problems and with public education. Today, *applied sociology* is defined as the use of the discipline of sociology with the specific intent of yielding practical applications for human behavior and organizations.

Often, the goal of such work is to assist in resolving a social problem. For example, in the last 35 years, eight presidents of the United States have established commissions to delve into major societal concerns facing our nation. Sociologists are often asked to apply their expertise to such issues as violence, pornography, crime, immigration, and population. In Europe, both academic and governmental research departments are offering increasing financial support for applied studies.

Growing interest in applied sociology has led to such specializations as medical sociology and environmental sociology. The former includes research on how health care professionals and patients deal with disease. For example, medical sociologists have studied the social impact of the AIDS crisis on families, friends, and communities. Environmental sociologists examine the relationship between human societies and the physical environment. One focus of their work is the issue of "environmental justice" (see Chapter 10), which has been raised because researchers and community activists have found that hazardous waste dumps are especially likely to be found in poor and minority neighborhoods (M. Martin 1996).

The growing popularity of applied sociology has led to the rise of the specialty of clinical sociology. Louis Wirth (1931) wrote about clinical sociology more than 70 years ago, but the term itself has become popular only in recent years. While applied sociologists may simply evaluate social issues, *clinical sociology* is dedicated to altering social relationships (as in family therapy) or to restructuring social institutions (as in the reorganization of a medical center).

Applied sociologists generally leave it to others to act on their evaluations. By contrast, clinical sociologists take direct responsibility for implementation and view those with whom they work as their clients. This specialty has become increasingly attractive to graduate students in sociology because it offers an opportunity to apply intellectual learning in a practical way. Up to now, a shrinking job market in the academic world has made such alternative career routes appealing.

Applied and clinical sociology can be contrasted with *basic* (or *pure*) *sociology,* which seeks a more profound knowledge of the fundamental aspects of social phenomena. This type of research is not necessarily meant to generate specific applications, although such ideas may result once findings are analyzed. When Durkheim studied suicide rates, he was not primarily interested in discovering a way to eliminate suicide. In this sense, his research was an example of basic rather than applied sociology.

What issues facing your local community would you like to address with applied sociological research?

Sociology Matters

Sociology matters because it offers new insights into what is going on around you, in your own life as well as in the larger society. Consider the purpose of a college education:

- What are your own reasons for going to college? Are you interested only in academics, or did you enroll for the social life as well? Does your college encourage you to pursue both, and if so, why?

- How does your pursuit of a college education impact society as a whole? What are the social effects of your decision to become a student, both now and later in life, after you receive your degree?

Sociology also matters because sociologists follow a systematic research design to reach their conclusions. Consider the importance of careful research:

- Have you ever acted on incomplete information, or even misinformation? What were the results?

- What might be the result if legislators or government policy makers were to base their actions on faulty research?

CHAPTER RESOURCES

Summary

Sociology is the systematic study of social behavior and human groups. This chapter presented a brief history of the discipline and introduced the concept of the **sociological imagination.** It surveyed sociological **theory,** including contemporary perspectives, and suggested some practical uses for theory. This chapter also presented the principles of the **scientific method** and showed how sociologists use them in their research.

1. The **sociological imagination** is an awareness of the relationship between an individual and the wider society. It is based on an ability to view society as an outsider might, rather than from the perspective of an insider.

2. Sociologists employ **theory** to explain problems, actions, or behavior. Nineteenth-century thinkers who contributed to the development of sociological theory include Émile Durkheim, who pioneered work on suicide; Max Weber, a German thinker who taught the need for *Verstehen,* or "insight," in intellectual work; and Karl Marx, a German intellectual who emphasized the importance of class conflict.

3. Today, several theoretical perspectives guide sociological research. The **functionalist perspective** holds that society is structured in ways that maintain social stability, so that social change tends to be slow and evolutionary.

4. The **conflict perspective,** on the other hand, emphasizes the importance of conflict between competing social groups, so that social change tends to be swift and revolutionary. A related perspective, the *feminist perspective,* stresses conflict based on gender inequality.

5. The **feminist perspective** stresses gender as the key to understanding social interactions. Feminist sociologists charge that too often, scholars concentrate on male social roles, ignoring male–female differences in behavior.

6. The **interactionist perspective** is concerned primarily with the everyday ways in which individuals shape their society and are shaped by it. Interactionists see social change as an ongoing and very personal process.

7. The **scientific method** includes five steps: defining the problem; reviewing the literature; formulating the *hypothesis;* selecting the **research design** and collecting and analyzing data; and developing the conclusion. The **hypothesis** states a possible relationship between two or more variables, usually one **independent variable** and a **dependent variable** that is thought to be related to it.

8. To avoid having to test everyone in a population, sociologists use a **sample** that is representative of the general population. Using a representative sample lends **validity** and **reliability** to the results of scientific research.

9. Sociologists use four major **research designs** in their work: **surveys** of the population; personal **observation** of behaviors and communities; **experiments** that test hypothetical cause-and-effect relationships; and analysis of existing sources.

10. **Applied sociology**—the practical application of the discipline to problems in human behavior and organizations—is a growing field that includes community research, environmental sociology, and **clinical sociology.**

www.mhhe.com/schaefersm2
Visit the Online Learning Center
for *Sociology Matters* to access
quizzes, review activities, and
other learning tools.

Key Terms

applied sociology, 29

basic sociology, 29

causal logic, 20

clinical sociology, 29

code of ethics, 27

conflict perspective, 14

content analysis, 27

control group, 26

control variable, 23

correlation, 21

dependent variable, 20

ethnography, 25

experiment, 26

experimental group, 26

feminist perspective, 16

functionalist perspective, 13

Hawthorne effect, 26

hypothesis, 20

ideal type, 10

independent variable, 20

interactionist perspective, 16

interview, 24

latent function, 14

manifest function, 14

natural science, 4

nonverbal communication, 17

observation, 25

operational definition, 19

qualitative research, 25

quantitative research, 25

questionnaire, 24

random sample, 21

reliability, 22

research design, 24

sample, 21

science, 4

scientific method, 18

secondary analysis, 27

social science, 4

sociological imagination, 3

sociology, 2

survey, 24

theory, 7

validity, 22

variable, 20

Verstehen, 10

Culture and Socialization

Culture and Society

Development of Culture around the World

Elements of Culture

Culture and the Dominant Ideology

Cultural Variation

The Role of Socialization

The Self and Socialization

Socialization and the Life Course

Agents of Socialization

In Bhutan, a country of about 2 million people in the heart of the Himalayas, a quiet revolution is taking place. Until recently, residents of the geographically isolated country had almost no contact with Western media. The king of Bhutan, fearing that foreign influences would undermine the country's traditional Buddhist values, had long blocked broadcast television. But by 1998, a new king had ascended the throne, one who defined his goal as maximizing his subjects' Gross National Happiness. Determined to transform the small monarchy into a constitutional democracy, he saw television not as a corrupter of his people's values, but as a vehicle for their civic education.

In 1999 the king told his subjects they could subscribe to cable television—a luxury few of them could afford. "Not everything you see will be good," he warned (*The Guardian* 2003:5). Soon images and ideas most Bhutanese had never seen or heard of were flashing across their new television screens. HBO, *Larry King Live,* pornography, professional wrestling—all poured uncensored into people's homes. Schoolchildren were particularly ill-prepared for what they saw. Some were deeply disturbed by the violence of professional wrestling; others took to copying it, even at school.

Three years later, the country that was founded on the Buddhist principle of nonviolence suffered its first-ever crime wave. Stories of murder, theft, drug addiction, and even embezzlement by public servants shocked residents of the once sheltered Shangri-la. Though government officials have refrained from judgment, a group of Bhutanese researchers that has studied the rise in crime puts the blame squarely on the effects of cable television (BBC 2004; *The Guardian* 2003).

Throughout the world, the transforming effects of Western media are troubling those who value their traditional cultures. Even without a background in sociology, these people know that their culture is fundamental to their society. In this chapter we will learn that all societies share certain basic cultural elements, even though they may express those elements differently. We will see how cultures change, whether from within or in response to outside influences, such as the media. And we will learn how culture reinforces the power of the dominant classes in society.

Culture also affects the basic attitudes, values, and behaviors that children learn through a process called **socialization.** It can even affect a child's **personality**—the individual characteristics, attitudes, needs, and behaviors that set one person apart from another. Throughout the life course, culture prescribes the roles people take and the ceremonies they participate in as they pass from one life stage to another. It molds the most fundamental institutions of society, from the family, schools, and peer groups to the mass media, the workplace, and the state. Culture, in other words, is all-encompassing.

Culture and Society

Culture is the totality of learned, socially transmitted customs, knowledge, material objects, and behavior. It includes the ideas, values, customs, and artifacts (for example, DVDs, comic books, and birth control devices) of groups of people. Patriotic attachment to the flag of the United States is an aspect of culture, as is a national passion for the tango in Argentina.

Sometimes people refer to a particular person as "very cultured" or to a city as having "lots of culture." That use of the term *culture* is different from our use in this textbook. In sociological terms, *culture* does not refer solely to the fine arts and refined intellectual taste. It consists of *all* objects and ideas within a society, including ice cream cones, rock music, and slang words. Sociologists consider both a portrait by Rembrandt and a portrait by a billboard painter to be aspects of a culture. A tribe that cultivates soil by hand has just as much culture as a people that relies on computer-operated machinery. Each people has a distinctive culture with its own characteristic ways of gathering and preparing food, constructing homes, structuring the family, and promoting standards of right and wrong.

The fact that you share a similar culture with others helps to define the group or society to which you belong. A fairly large number of people are said to constitute a *society* when they live in the same territory, are relatively independent of people outside it, and participate in a common culture. The city of Los Angeles is more populous than many nations of the world, yet sociologists do not consider it a society in its own right. Rather, it is part of—and dependent on—the larger society of the United States.

A society is the largest form of human group. It consists of people who share a common heritage and culture. Members of the society learn this culture and transmit it from one generation to the next. They even preserve their distinctive culture through literature, art, video recordings, and other means of expression. If it were not for the social transmission of culture, each generation would have to reinvent television, not to mention the wheel.

Having a common culture also simplifies many day-to-day interactions. For example, when you buy an airline ticket, you know you don't need to bring along hundreds of dollars in cash. You can pay with a credit card. When you are part of a society, you can take many small (as well as more important) cultural patterns for granted. You assume that theaters will provide seats for the audience, that physicians will not disclose confidential information, and that parents will be careful when crossing the street with young children. All these assumptions reflect basic values, beliefs, and customs of the culture of the United States.

Language is a critical element of culture that sets humans apart from other species. Members of a society generally share a common language, which facilitates day-to-day exchanges with others. When you ask a hardware store clerk for a flashlight, you don't need to draw a picture of the instrument. You share the same cultural term for a small, portable, battery-operated light. However, in England you would need to ask for an "electric torch." Of course, even within the same society, a term can have a number of different meanings. In the United States, the words *grass* and *weed* signify both forage for grazing animals and an intoxicating drug.

Development of Culture around the World

Though cultures differ in their customs, artifacts, and languages, they all share certain basic characteristics. In this section we will see how those characteristics change as cultures develop, and how cultures influence one another through their technological, commercial, and artistic achievements.

CULTURAL UNIVERSALS

All societies, despite their differences, have developed certain general practices known as *cultural universals.* Many cultural universals are, in fact, adaptations to meet essential human needs, such as people's need for food, shelter, and clothing. Anthropologist George Murdock (1945:124) compiled a list of cultural universals that included athletic sports, cooking, funeral ceremonies, medicine, and sexual restrictions.

The cultural practices listed by Murdock may be universal, but the manner in which they are expressed varies from culture to culture. For example, one society may let its members choose their own marriage partners. Another may encourage marriages arranged by the parents.

Not only does the expression of cultural universals vary from one society to another; it may also change dramatically over time within a society. Each generation, and each year for that matter, most human cultures change and expand through the processes of innovation and diffusion.

INNOVATION

The process of introducing a new idea or object to a culture is known as *innovation.* Innovation interests sociologists because of the potential social consequences of introducing something new. There are two forms of innovation: discovery and invention. A *discovery* involves making known or sharing the existence of some aspect of reality. The finding of the DNA molecule and the identification of a new moon of Saturn are both acts of discovery. A significant factor in the process of discovery is the sharing of newfound knowledge with others. By contrast, an *invention* results when existing cultural items are combined into a form that did not exist before. The bow and arrow, the automobile, and the Internet are all examples of inventions, as are Protestantism and democracy.

GLOBALIZATION, DIFFUSION, AND TECHNOLOGY

The familiar green Starbucks logo beckons you into a comfortable coffee shop where you can order decaf latte and a cinnamon ring. What's unusual about that? This Starbucks happens to be located in the heart of Beijing's Forbidden City, just outside the Palace of Heavenly Purity, former residence of Chinese emperors. In 2002 it was one of 25 Starbucks stores in China; four years later there were more than 90. The success of Starbucks in a country in which coffee drinking is still a novelty (most Chinese are tea drinkers) has been striking (*China Daily* 2004).

The emergence of Starbucks in China illustrates a rapidly escalating trend called *globalization.* **Globalization** may be defined as the worldwide integration of government policies, cultures, social movements, and financial markets through trade and the exchange of ideas. While public discussion of globalization is relatively recent, intellectuals have been pondering its social consequences for a long time. Karl Marx and Friedrich Engels warned in *The Communist Manifesto* (written in 1848) of a world market that would lead to production in distant lands, sweeping away existing working relationships. Today, more and more cultural expressions and practices are crossing national borders, transforming the traditions and customs of the societies exposed to them. Sociologists use the term *diffusion* to refer to the process by which a cultural item spreads from group to group or society to society. Diffusion can occur through a variety of means, among them exploration, military conquest, missionary work, the influence of the mass media, tourism, and the Internet.

Sociologist George Ritzer (2000) coined the term *McDonaldization* to describe the process through which the principles of the fast-food restaurant have come to dominate certain sectors of society, both in the United States and throughout the world. For example, hair salons and medical clinics now take walk-in appointments. In Hong Kong, sex selection clinics offer a menu of items, from fertility enhancement to methods of increasing the likelihood of producing a child of the desired sex. Religious groups—from evangelical preachers on local stations or websites to priests at the Vatican Television Center—use marketing techniques similar to those that are used to sell Happy Meals.

McDonaldization is associated with the melding of cultures, so that we see more and more similarities in cultural expression. In Japan, for example, African entrepreneurs have found a thriving market for hip-hop fashions popularized by teens in the United States. In Austria, the McDonald's organization itself has drawn on Austrians' love of coffee, cake, and conversation to create the McCafe fast-food chain. Many critical observers believe that McDonaldization and globalization serve to dilute the distinctive aspects of a society's culture (Alfino et al. 1998; Ritzer 2004).

Some societies try to protect themselves from the invasion of too much culture from other countries, especially the economically dominant United States. The Canadian government, for example, requires that 35 percent of a station's daytime radio programming be devoted to Canadian songs or artists. In Brazil, a toy manufacturer has eclipsed Barbie's popularity by designing Susi, a doll that looks more like Brazilian girls. Susi has a slightly smaller chest, much wider thighs, and darker skin than Barbie. Her wardrobe includes the skimpy bikinis favored on Brazilian beaches as well as a soccer shirt honoring the Brazilian team. According to the toy company's marketing director, "We wanted Susi to be more Latin, more voluptuous. We Latins appreciate those attributes." Brazilians seem to agree: Five Susi dolls are sold for every two Barbies (DePalma 1999; Downie 2000).

Technology in its many forms has increased the speed of cultural diffusion and broadened the distribution of cultural elements. Sociologist Gerhard Lenski has defined *technology* as "cultural information about how to use the material resources of the environment to satisfy human

Use Your Sociological Imagination

If you grew up in your parents' generation—without computers, e-mail, the Internet, pagers, and cell phones—how would your daily life differ from the one you lead today?

needs and desires" (Nolan and Lenski 2004:37). Today's technological developments no longer need await publication in journals with limited circulation. Press conferences, often carried simultaneously on the Internet, now trumpet new developments.

Sociologist William F. Ogburn (1922) made a useful distinction between the elements of material and nonmaterial culture. *Material culture* refers to the physical or technological aspects of our daily lives, including food items, houses, factories, and raw materials. *Nonmaterial culture* refers to ways of using material objects and to customs, beliefs, philosophies, governments, and patterns of communication. Generally, the nonmaterial culture is more resistant to change than the material culture. Ogburn introduced the term *culture lag* to refer to the period of maladjustment when the nonmaterial culture is still struggling to adapt to new material conditions. For example, the ethics of using the Internet, particularly issues concerning privacy and censorship, have not yet caught up with the explosion in Internet use and technology.

Elements of Culture

Each culture considers its own distinctive ways of handling basic societal tasks to be "natural." But in fact, methods of education, marital ceremonies, religious doctrines, and other aspects of culture are learned and transmitted through human interactions within specific societies. Parents in India are accustomed to arranging marriages for their children; parents in the United States leave marital decisions up to their offspring. Lifelong residents of Naples consider it natural to speak Italian; lifelong residents of Buenos Aires feel the same way about Spanish. Let's take a look at the major aspects of culture that shape the way the members of a society live: language, norms, sanctions, and values.

LANGUAGE

The English language makes extensive use of words dealing with war. We speak of "conquering" space, "fighting the battle" of the budget, "waging war" on drugs, making a "killing" on the stock market, and "bombing" an examination; something monumental or great is "the bomb." An observer from an entirely different and warless culture could gauge the importance that war and the military have had in our lives simply by recognizing the prominence that militaristic terms have in our language. Similarly, cattle are so important to the Nuer of southern Sudan that they have more than 400 words to describe them (Haviland et al. 2005).

Language is, in fact, the foundation of every culture. *Language* is an abstract system of word meanings and symbols for all aspects of culture. It includes speech, written characters, numerals, symbols, and gestures and expressions of nonverbal communication.

Though language is a cultural universal, striking differences in the use of language are evident around the world. Such is the case even when two countries use the same spoken language. For example, an English-speaking person from the United States who is visiting London may be puzzled the first time an English friend says "I'll ring you up." The friend means "I'll call you on the telephone." Similarly, the meanings of nonverbal gestures tend to vary from one culture to another. The positive "thumbs up" gesture used in the United States has only vulgar connotations in Greece (Ekman et al. 1984).

The thumbs-up gesture is an example of *nonverbal communication,* or the use of gestures, facial expressions, and other visual images to communicate. If you are in the midst of a friendly meeting and one member suddenly sits back, folds his arms, and turns down the corners of his mouth, you know at once that trouble has arrived. When you see a friend in tears, you may give her a quick hug. After winning a big game you probably high-five your teammates. These are all examples of nonverbal communication.

We are not born with these expressions. We learn them, just as we learn other forms of language, from people who share our culture. That is as true for the basic expressions of happiness and sadness as it is for more complex emotions, such as shame or distress (Fridlund et al. 1987).

Like other forms of language, nonverbal communication is not the same in all cultures. For example, sociological research shows that people from various cultures differ in the degree to which they touch others during the course of normal social interaction.

NORMS

"Wash your hands before dinner." "Thou shalt not kill." "Respect your elders." All societies have ways of encouraging and enforcing what they view as appropriate behavior while discouraging and punishing what they consider to be improper behavior. *Norms* are the established standards of behavior maintained by a society.

For a norm to become significant, it must be widely shared and understood. For example, in movie theaters in the United States, we typically expect that people will be quiet while the film is shown. Of course, the application of this norm can vary, depending on the particular film and type of audience. People who are viewing a serious artistic film will be more likely to insist on the norm of silence than those watching a slapstick comedy or horror movie.

Types of Norms.   Sociologists distinguish between norms in two ways. First, norms are classified as either formal or informal. *Formal norms* generally have been written down and specify strict punishment of violators. In the United States, we often formalize norms into laws, which must be very precise in defining proper and improper behavior.

Sociologist Donald Black (1995) has termed *law* "governmental social control," meaning formal norms that are enforced by the state. Laws are just one example of formal norms. The requirements for a college major and the rules of a card game are also considered formal norms.

By contrast, *informal norms* are generally understood but are not precisely recorded. Standards of proper dress are a common example of informal norms. Our society has no specific punishment or sanction for a person who comes to school, say, wearing a monkey suit. Making fun of the nonconforming student is usually the most likely response.

Norms are also classified by their relative importance to society. When classified in this way, they are known as *mores* and *folkways.*

Mores (pronounced "MOR-ays") are norms deemed highly necessary to the welfare of a society, often because they embody the most cherished principles of a people. Each society demands obedience to its mores; violations can lead to severe penalties. Thus, the United States has strong mores against murder, treason, and child abuse, which have been institutionalized into formal norms.

Folkways are norms governing everyday behavior. Folkways play an important role in shaping the daily behavior of members of a culture. Still, society is less likely to formalize folkways than mores, and their violation raises comparatively little concern. For example, walking up a "down" escalator in a department store challenges our standards of appropriate behavior, but it will not result in a fine or a jail sentence.

In many societies around the world, folkways exist to reinforce patterns of male dominance. In traditional Buddhist areas of southeast Asia, various folkways reveal men's hierarchical position above women. On trains, women do not sleep in upper berths above men. Hospitals that house men on the first floor do not place women patients on the second floor. Even on clotheslines, folkways dictate male dominance: women's attire is hung lower than that of men (Bulle 1987).

Use Your Sociological Imagination

You are a high school principal. What norms would you want to govern students' behavior? How might those norms differ from those typical of college students?

Acceptance of Norms.   People do not follow norms, whether mores or folkways, in all situations. In some cases, they can evade a norm because they know it is weakly enforced. It is illegal for U.S. teenagers to drink alcoholic beverages, yet drinking by minors is common throughout the nation. In fact, teenage alcoholism is a serious social problem.

Norms are violated in some instances because one norm conflicts with another. For example, suppose one night you hear the screams of the woman next door, who is being beaten by her husband. If you decide to intervene by ringing their doorbell or calling the police, you are violating the norm of "minding your own business," while at the same time following the norm of assisting a victim of violence.

Even when norms do not conflict, there are always exceptions. Under different circumstances, the same action can cause one to be viewed as either a hero or a villain. Secretly taping telephone conversations is normally considered illegal and abhorrent. However, it can be done with a court order to obtain valid evidence for a criminal trial. We would heap praise on a government agent who uses such methods to convict an organized crime boss or detect a planned terrorist attack. Similarly, we tolerate killing another human being in self-defense, and we actually reward killing in warfare.

Acceptance of norms is subject to change as the political, economic, and social conditions of a culture are transformed. Until the 1960s, for example, formal norms throughout much of the United States prohibited the marriage of people from different racial groups. Over the last half century, however, such legal prohibitions were cast aside. The process of change can be seen today in the increasing acceptance of single parents and growing support for the legalization of marriage between same-sex couples (see Chapter 8).

When circumstances require the sudden violation of long-standing cultural norms, the change can upset an entire population. In Iraq, where Muslim custom strictly forbids touching by strangers, for men but especially for women, the war that began in 2003 has brought numerous daily violations of the norm. Outside important mosques, government offices, and other facilities likely to be targeted by terrorists, visitors must now be patted down and have their bags searched by Iraqi security guards. To reduce the discomfort caused by the procedure, women are searched by female guards and men by male guards. Despite that concession, and the fact that many Iraqis admit or even insist on the need for such measures, people still wince at the invasion of their personal privacy. In reaction to the searches, Iraqi women have begun to limit the contents of the bags they carry or simply to leave their bags at home (Rubin 2003).

SANCTIONS

Suppose a football coach sends a 12th player onto the field. Or imagine a college graduate showing up in shorts for a job interview at an accounting firm. Consider a driver who neglects to put any money into a parking meter. These people have violated widely shared and understood norms. So what happens? In each of these situations, the person will receive sanctions if his or her behavior is detected.

Sanctions are penalties and rewards for conduct concerning a social norm. Note that the concept of *reward* is included in this definition. Conformity to a norm can lead to positive sanctions such as a pay raise, a medal, a word of gratitude, or a pat on the back. Negative sanctions include fines, threats, imprisonment, and stares of contempt.

Table 2–1 (page 42) summarizes the relationship between norms and sanctions. As you can see, the sanctions associated with formal norms (those that are written down and codified) tend to be formal as well. If a coach sends too many players onto the field, the team will be penalized 15 yards. The driver who fails to put money in the parking meter will be ticketed and expected to pay a fine. But sanctions for violations of

Table 2–1 Norms and Sanctions

Norms	Sanctions	
	Positive	Negative
Formal	Salary bonus	Demotion
	Testimonial dinner	Firing from a job
	Medal	Jail sentence
	Diploma	Expulsion
Informal	Smile	Frown
	Compliment	Humiliation
	Cheers	Belittling

informal norms can vary. The college graduate who comes to the job interview in shorts will probably lose any chance of getting the job; on the other hand, he or she might be so brilliant the interviewer will overlook the unconventional attire.

The entire fabric of norms and sanctions in a culture reflects that culture's values and priorities. The most cherished values will be most heavily sanctioned; matters regarded as less critical will carry light and informal sanctions.

VALUES

Though we all have our own personal sets of standards—which may include caring, fitness, or success in business—we also share a general set of objectives as members of a society. Cultural *values* are collective conceptions of what is considered good, desirable, and proper—or bad, undesirable, and improper. They indicate what people in a given culture prefer, as well as what they find important and morally right or wrong. Values may be specific, such as honoring one's parents and owning a home, or they may be more general, such as health, love, and democracy. Of course, the members of a society do not uniformly share its values. Angry political debates and billboards promoting conflicting causes tell us that much.

Values influence people's behavior and serve as criteria for evaluating the actions of others. There is often a direct relationship among a culture's values, norms, and sanctions. For example, if a culture highly values the institution of marriage, it may have norms (and strict sanctions) that prohibit the act of adultery. If a culture views private property as a basic value, it will probably have stiff laws against theft and vandalism.

Socially shared, intensely felt values are a fundamental part of life in the United States. Even so, our values can and do change. Each year more than 276,000 entering college students at 413 of the nation's four-year colleges fill out a questionnaire about their attitudes. Because this survey focuses on an array of issues, beliefs, and life goals, it is commonly cited as a barometer of the nation's values. The respondents are asked what values are personally important to them. Over the last 36 years, the value of "being very well-off financially" has shown the strongest gain in popularity; the proportion of first-year college students who endorse this value as "essential" or "very important" rose from 44 percent in 1967 to 74 percent in 2003. In contrast, the value that has shown the most striking decline in endorsement by students is "developing a meaningful philosophy of life." While this value was the most popular in the 1967 survey, endorsed by more than 80 percent of the respondents, it had fallen to ninth place on the list by 2003, when it was endorsed by less than 40 percent of students entering college.

During the 1980s and 1990s, support for values having to do with money, power, and status grew. At the same time, support for certain values having to do with social awareness and altruism, such as "helping others," declined. According to the 2003 nationwide survey, only 39 percent of first-year college students stated that "influencing social values" was an "essential" or "very important" goal. The proportion of students for whom "helping to promote racial understanding" was an essential or very important goal reached a record high of 42 percent in 1992, but fell to 31 percent in 2003. Like other aspects of culture, such as language and norms, a nation's values are not necessarily fixed (Astin et al. 1994; Sax et al. 2003:27).

Culture and the Dominant Ideology

Functionalist and conflict theorists agree that culture and society are mutually supportive, but for different reasons. Functionalists maintain that social stability requires a consensus and the support of society's members; strong central values and common norms provide that support. This view of culture became popular in sociology beginning in the 1950s. It was borrowed from British anthropologists who saw cultural traits as a stabilizing element in a culture. From a functionalist perspective, a cultural trait or practice will persist if it performs functions that society seems to need or contributes to overall social stability and consensus.

Conflict theorists agree that a common culture may exist, but they argue that it serves to maintain the privileges of certain groups. Moreover, in protecting their own self-interest, powerful groups may keep others in a subservient position. The term ***dominant ideology*** describes the set of cultural beliefs and practices that help to maintain powerful social, economic, and political interests. This concept was first used by Hungarian Marxist Georg Lukacs (1923) and Italian Marxist Antonio Gramsci (1929); it did not gain an audience in the United States until the early 1970s. In Karl Marx's view, a capitalist society has a dominant ideology that serves the interests of the ruling class.

From a conflict perspective, the dominant ideology has major social significance. Not only do a society's most powerful groups and institutions control wealth and property; even more important, they control the means of producing beliefs about reality through religion, education, and the media. From a feminist perspective, if all a society's most important institutions tell women they should be subservient to men, that dominant ideology will help to control women and keep them in a subordinate position (Abercrombie et al. 1980, 1990; Robertson 1988).

A growing number of social scientists believe it is not easy to identify a "core culture" in the United States. For support, they point to the lack of consensus on national values, the diffusion of cultural traits, the diversity within our culture, and the changing views of young people. Yet there is no way of denying that certain expressions of values have greater influence than others, even in so complex a society as the United States.

Cultural Variation

Each culture has a unique character. Inuit tribes in northern Canada—wrapped in furs and dieting on whale blubber—have little in common with farmers in Southeast Asia, who dress for the heat and subsist mainly on the rice they grow in their paddies. Cultures adapt to meet specific sets of circumstances, such as climate, level of technology, population, and geography. This adaptation to different conditions shows up in differences in all elements of culture, including norms, sanctions, values, and language. Thus, despite the presence of cultural universals such as courtship and religion, there is still great diversity among the world's many cultures. Moreover, even *within* a single nation, certain segments of the populace develop cultural patterns that differ from the patterns of the dominant society.

SUBCULTURES

Rodeo riders, residents of a retirement community, workers on an offshore oil rig—all are examples of what sociologists refer to as *subcultures*. A **subculture** is a segment of society that shares a distinctive pattern of mores, folkways, and values that differs from the pattern of the larger society. In a sense, a subculture can be thought of as a culture existing within a larger, dominant culture. The existence of many subcultures is characteristic of complex societies such as the United States.

Members of a subculture participate in the dominant culture while at the same time engaging in unique and distinctive forms of behavior. Frequently, a subculture will develop an ***argot,*** or specialized language, that distinguishes it from the wider society. For example, New York

City's sanitation workers have developed a humorous argot for use on a job that is so dirty and smelly, most people wouldn't consider doing it. Terms such as *g-man, honey boat* (a garbage scow or barge) and *airmail* (trash thrown from an upper-story window) date back to the 1940s and 1950s. More recent coinages include *disco rice* (maggots) and *urban whitefish* (used condoms). Administrators at the sanitation department practice a more reserved humor than those who work on the trucks. When they send a *honey boat* to New Jersey, they're not dumping the city's garbage; they're *exporting* it.

Argot allows "insiders," the members of the subculture, to understand words with special meanings. It also establishes patterns of communication that "outsiders" can't understand. Sociologists associated with the interactionist perspective emphasize that language and symbols offer a powerful way for a subculture to feel cohesive and maintain its identity. Nevertheless, insiders' argot sometimes creeps into mainstream usage, as policymakers at New York's sanitation department have discovered. They invented the term *nimby* ("not in my backyard") to describe New Yorkers' attitude toward the construction of new sanitation facilities. Recently they have been using the terms *banana* ("Build absolutely nothing anywhere near anyone") and *nope* ("not on planet earth") (Urbina 2004).

Subcultures develop in a number of ways. Often a subculture emerges because a segment of society faces problems or even privileges unique to its position. Subcultures may be based on common age (teenagers or old people), region (Appalachians), ethnic heritage (Cuban Americans), occupation (firefighters), or beliefs (deaf activists working to preserve deaf culture). Certain subcultures, such as computer hackers, develop because of a shared interest or hobby. In still other subcultures, such as that of prison inmates, members have been excluded from conventional society and are forced to develop alternative ways of living.

Functionalist and conflict theorists agree that variation exists within a culture. Functionalists view subcultures as variations of particular social environments and as evidence that differences can exist within a common culture. However, conflict theorists suggest that variation often reflects the inequality of social arrangements within a society. From a conflict perspective, the challenge to dominant social norms mounted by African American activists, the feminist movement, and the disability rights movement reflects inequity based on race, gender, and disability status. Conflict theorists also argue that subcultures sometimes emerge when the dominant society unsuccessfully tries to suppress a practice, such as the use of illegal drugs.

COUNTERCULTURES

By the end of the 1960s, an extensive subculture had emerged in the United States, composed of young people turned off by a society they believed was too materialistic and technological. This group included

"IT'S ENDLESS. WE JOIN A COUNTER-CULTURE; IT BECOMES THE CULTURE. WE JOIN ANOTHER COUNTER-CULTURE; IT BECOMES THE CULTURE..."

primarily political radicals and "hippies" who had "dropped out" of mainstream social institutions. These young men and women rejected the pressure to accumulate more and more cars, larger and larger homes, and an endless array of material goods. Instead, they expressed a desire to live in a culture based on more humanistic values, such as sharing, love, and coexistence with the environment. As a political force, this subculture opposed the United States' involvement in the war in Vietnam and encouraged draft resistance (Flacks 1971; Roszak 1969).

When a subculture conspicuously and deliberately *opposes* certain aspects of the larger culture, it is known as a ***counterculture.*** Countercultures typically thrive among the young, who have the least investment in the existing culture. In most cases, a 20-year-old can adjust to new cultural standards more easily than someone who has spent 60 years following the patterns of the dominant culture (Zellner 1995).

In the wake of the World Trade Center attack of September 11, 2001, people around the United States learned of the existence of terrorist groups operating as a counterculture within their country. This was a situation that generations have lived with in Northern Ireland, Israel, the Palestinian territory, and many other parts of the world. Worldwide, terrorist cells are not necessarily fueled only by outsiders. Frequently people become disenchanted with the policies of their own country, and a few take very violent steps.

CULTURE SHOCK

Anyone who feels disoriented, uncertain, out of place, even fearful when immersed in an unfamiliar culture may be experiencing ***culture shock.*** For example, a resident of the United States who visits certain areas in China

Use Your Sociological Imagination

You arrive in a developing African country as a Peace Corps volunteer. What aspects of this very different culture do you think would be the hardest to adjust to? What might the citizens of that country find shocking about your culture?

and wants local meat for dinner may be stunned to learn that the specialty is dog meat. Similarly, someone from a strict Islamic culture may be shocked upon first seeing the comparatively provocative dress styles and open displays of affection common in the United States and Europe.

All of us, to some extent, take for granted the cultural practices of our society. As a result, it can be surprising and even disturbing to realize that other cultures do not follow our "way of life." The fact is, customs that seem strange to us are considered normal and proper in other cultures, which may see *our* mores and folkways as odd.

ETHNOCENTRISM

Many everyday statements reflect our attitude that our culture is best. We use terms such as *underdeveloped, backward,* and *primitive* to refer to other societies. What "we" believe is a religion; what "they" believe is superstition and mythology.

It is tempting to evaluate the practices of other cultures from our own perspective. Sociologist William Graham Sumner (1906) coined the term **ethnocentrism** to refer to the tendency to assume that one's own culture and way of life represent the norm or are superior to all others. The ethnocentric person sees his or her own group as the center or defining point of culture and views all other cultures as deviations from what is "normal."

Recently, ethnocentric value judgments have complicated U.S. efforts at democratic reform of the Iraqi government. Before the 2003 war in Iraq, U.S. planners had assumed that Iraqis would adapt to a new form of government in the same way the Germans and Japanese did following World War II. But in the Iraqi culture, unlike the German and Japanese cultures, loyalty to the family and the extended clan comes before patriotism and the common good. In a country in which almost half of all people, even those in the cities, marry a first or second cousin, citizens are predisposed to favor their own kin in government and business dealings. Why trust a stranger from outside the family? What Westerners would criticize as nepotism, then, is actually an acceptable, even admirable, practice to Iraqis (J. Tierney 2003).

Functionalists point out that ethnocentrism serves to maintain a sense of solidarity by promoting group pride. Denigrating other nations and cultures can enhance our patriotic feelings and belief that our own way of life is superior. Yet this type of social stability is established at the expense of other peoples. Of course, ethnocentrism is hardly limited to citizens of the United States. Visitors from many African cultures are surprised at the disrespect that children in the United States show their parents. People from India may be repelled by our practice of living in the same household with dogs and cats. All these people may feel comforted by their membership in cultures that in their view are superior to ours.

CULTURAL RELATIVISM

While ethnocentrism is the evaluation of foreign cultures using the familiar culture of the observer as a standard of correct behavior, ***cultural relativism*** is the evaluation of a people's behavior from the perspective of their own culture. Cultural relativism places a priority on understanding other cultures rather than dismissing them as "strange" or "exotic." Unlike ethnocentrism, cultural relativism employs a kind of *value neutrality* in scientific study, which Max Weber saw as being extremely important.

Cultural relativism stresses that different social contexts give rise to different norms and values. Thus, we must examine practices such as polygamy, bullfighting, and monarchy within the particular contexts of the cultures in which they are found. While cultural relativism does not suggest that we must unquestionably *accept* every cultural variation, it does require a serious and unbiased effort to evaluate norms, values, and customs in light of their distinctive culture.

How one views a culture—whether from an ethnocentric point of view or through the lens of cultural relativism—has important consequences for social policy. A hot issue today is the extent to which a nation should accommodate nonnative language speakers by sponsoring bilingual programs. Educational programs, whether for native or nonnative speakers, are part of the process of socialization, the subject of the next section.

Table 2–2 summarizes the major theoretical perspectives on culture.

The Role of Socialization

What makes us who we are? Is it the genes we are born with, or the environment we grow up in? Researchers have traditionally clashed over the

summingUP

Table 2–2 Major Theoretical Perspectives on Culture

	Functionalist Perspective	**Conflict Perspective**	**Interactionist Perspective**
Norms	Reinforce societal standards	Reinforce patterns of dominance	Are maintained through face-to-face interaction
Values	Are collective conceptions of what is good	May perpetuate social inequality	Are defined and redefined through social interaction
Culture and Society	Culture reflects a society's strong central values	Culture reflects a society's dominant ideology	A society's core culture is perpetuated through daily social interactions
Cultural Variation	Subcultures serve the interests of subgroups Ethnocentrism reinforces group solidarity	Countercultures question the dominant social order Ethnocentrism devalues groups	Customs and traditions are transmitted through intergroup contact and through the media

relative importance of biological and environmental factors in human development, a conflict called the *nature versus nurture* (or *heredity versus environment*) debate. Today, most social scientists have moved beyond this debate, acknowledging instead the *interaction* of the two variables in shaping human development. However, we can better appreciate how heredity and environment interact to influence the socialization process if we first examine situations in which one factor operates almost entirely without the other (Homans 1979).

ENVIRONMENT: THE IMPACT OF ISOLATION

In the 1994 movie *Nell,* Jodie Foster played a young woman hidden from birth by her mother in a backwoods cabin. Raised without normal human contact, Nell crouches like an animal, screams wildly, and speaks or sings in a language all her own. The movie was drawn from the actual account of an emaciated 16-year-old boy who appeared mysteriously in 1828 in the town square of Nuremberg, Germany (Lipson 1994).

Some viewers may have found the story of Nell difficult to believe, but the painful childhood of a girl called Isabelle was all too real. For the first six years of her life, Isabelle lived in almost total seclusion in a darkened room. She had little contact with other people, with the exception of her mother, who could neither speak nor hear. Isabelle's grandparents had been so deeply ashamed of her illegitimate birth that they kept her hidden away from the world. Ohio authorities finally discovered the child in 1938, when Isabelle's mother escaped from her parents' home, taking her daughter with her.

When Isabelle was discovered at age six, she could not speak; she could merely make various croaking sounds. Her only communications with her mother were simple gestures. Isabelle had been largely deprived of the typical interactions and socialization experiences of childhood. Since she had seen few people, she initially showed a strong fear of strangers and reacted almost like a wild animal when confronted with an unfamiliar person. As she became accustomed to seeing certain individuals, her reaction changed to one of extreme apathy. At first, observers believed that Isabelle was deaf, but she soon began to react to nearby sounds. On tests of maturity, she scored at the level of an infant rather than a six-year-old.

Specialists developed a systematic training program to help Isabelle adapt to human relationships and socialization. After a few days of training, she made her first attempt to verbalize. Although she started slowly, Isabelle passed quickly through six years of development. In a little over two months she was speaking in complete sentences. Nine months later she could identify both words and sentences. Before Isabelle reached the age of nine she was ready to attend school with other children. By her 14th year she was in sixth grade, doing well in school, and emotionally well-adjusted.

What events in your life have had a strong influence on who you are?

Yet without an opportunity to experience socialization in her first six years, Isabelle had been hardly human in the social sense when she was first discovered. Her inability to communicate at the time of her discovery—despite her physical and cognitive potential to learn—and her remarkable progress over the next few years underscore the impact of socialization on human development (K. Davis 1940, 1947).

Increasingly, researchers are emphasizing the importance of early socialization experiences for children who grow up in more normal environments. We know now that it is not enough to care for an infant's physical needs; parents must also concern themselves with children's social development. If, for example, children are discouraged from having friends, they will miss out on social interactions that are critical for emotional growth.

HEREDITY: THE IMPACT OF BIOLOGY

Do the *social* traits that human groups display have biological origins? Given the continuing debate over the relative influences of heredity and the environment, there has been renewed interest in sociobiology in recent years. *Sociobiology* is the systematic study of the biological bases of human social behavior. Sociobiologists assert that many of the cultural traits humans display, such as the almost universal expectation that women will be nurturers and men will be providers, are not learned but are rooted in our genetic makeup (E. O. Wilson 1975, 1978).

Some researchers insist that intellectual interest in sociobiology will only deflect serious study of the more significant influence on human behavior, socialization. Yet Lois Wladis Hoffman (1985), in her presidential address to the Society for the Psychological Study of Social Issues, argued that sociobiology poses a valuable challenge to social scientists to better document their own research. Interactionists, for example, could show that social behavior is not programmed by human biology, but instead adjusts continually to the attitudes and responses of others.

Certainly most social scientists would agree that there is a biological basis for social behavior. But there is less support for the more extreme positions taken by certain advocates of sociobiology. Like interactionists, conflict theorists and functionalists believe that people's behavior rather than their genetic structure defines social reality. Conflict theorists fear that the sociobiological approach could be used as an argument against efforts to assist disadvantaged people, such as schoolchildren who are not competing successfully (E. O. Wilson 2000; see also Guterman 2000; Segerstråle 2000).

The Self and Socialization

We all have various perceptions, feelings, and beliefs about who we are and what we are like. How do we come to develop these? Do they change as we age?

We were not born with these understandings. Building on the work of George Herbert Mead (1964b), sociologists recognize that we create our own designation: the self. The *self* is a distinct identity that sets us apart from others. It is not a static phenomenon, but continues to develop and change throughout our lives.

Sociologists and psychologists alike have expressed interest in how the individual develops and modifies the sense of self as a result of social interaction. The work of sociologists Charles Horton Cooley and George Herbert Mead, pioneers of the interactionist approach, has been especially useful in furthering our understanding of these important issues (Gecas 1982).

COOLEY: LOOKING-GLASS SELF

In the early 1900s, Charles Horton Cooley advanced the belief that we learn who we are by interacting with others. Our view of ourselves, then, comes not only from direct contemplation of our personal qualities but also from our impressions of how others perceive us. Cooley used the phrase *looking-glass self* to emphasize that the self is the product of our social interactions with other people.

The process of developing a self-identity or self-concept has three phases. First, we imagine how we present ourselves to others—to relatives, friends, even strangers on the street. Then we imagine how others evaluate us (attractive, intelligent, shy, or strange). Finally, we develop some sort of feeling about ourselves, such as respect or shame, as a result of these impressions (Cooley 1902).

A subtle but critical aspect of Cooley's looking-glass self is that it results from an individual's "imagination" of how others view him or her. As a result, we can develop self-identities based on *incorrect* perceptions of how others see us. A student may react strongly to a teacher's criticism and decide (wrongly) that the instructor views him or her as stupid. This misperception can easily be converted into a negative self-identity through the following process: (1) the teacher criticized me, (2) the teacher must think that I'm stupid, (3) I *am* stupid. Yet self-identities are also subject to change. If the student receives an "A" at the end of the course, he or she will probably no longer feel stupid.

MEAD: STAGES OF THE SELF

George Herbert Mead continued Cooley's exploration of interactionist theory. Mead (1934, 1964a) developed a useful model of the process by which the self emerges, defined by three distinct stages: the preparatory stage, the play stage, and the game stage.

The Preparatory Stage.   During the *preparatory stage,* children imitate the people around them, especially family members with whom they continually interact. Thus, a small child will bang on a piece of wood while a parent is engaged in carpentry work, or will try to throw a ball if an older sibling is doing so nearby.

As they grow older, children become more adept at using symbols to communicate with others. *Symbols* are the gestures, objects, and language that form the basis of human communication. By interacting with relatives and friends, as well as by watching cartoons on television and looking at picture books, children in the preparatory stage begin to understand the use of symbols.

In multicultural societies, cultural differences in the meaning of symbols create the potential for conflict. For example, the symbolic headscarf that Muslim women wear recently became a major social issue in France. For years French public schools have banned overt signs of religion, such as large crosses, skullcaps, and headscarves. Muslim students who violated the informal dress code were expelled. In 2003, amid growing controversy, a government advisory panel recommended that the French Parliament strengthen the ban by writing it into law. The issue is a particularly thorny one because of the conflicting cultural meanings these symbols carry. To many of the French, the headscarf symbolizes the submission of women—an unwelcome connotation in a society that places a high value on egalitarianism. To others it represents a challenge to the French way of life. Thus, 69 percent of the French surveyed on the issue supported the ban. But to Muslims, the headscarf symbolizes modesty and respectability. Muslim schoolchildren take this symbol very seriously (*The Economist* 2004a).

The Play Stage.   Mead was among the first to analyze the relationship of symbols to socialization. As children develop skill in communicating through symbols, they gradually become more aware of social relationships. As a result, during the *play stage,* the child begins to pretend to be other people. Just as an actor "becomes" a character, a child becomes a doctor, parent, superhero, or ship captain.

In fact, Mead noted that an important aspect of the play stage is role playing. *Role taking* is the process of mentally assuming the perspective of another in order to respond from that imagined viewpoint. Through this process, a young child will gradually learn when it is best to ask a parent for favors. If the parent usually comes home from work in a bad mood, the child will wait until after dinner, when the parent is more relaxed and approachable.

The Game Stage.   In Mead's third stage, the *game stage,* the child of about eight or nine years old no longer just plays roles, but begins to consider several tasks and relationships simultaneously. At this point in development, children grasp not only their own social positions, but also those of others around them—just as in a football game the players must understand their own and everyone else's positions. Consider a girl or boy who is part of a scout troop out on a weekend hike in the mountains. The child must understand what he or she is expected to do, but must also recognize the responsibilities of other scouts and of the leaders. This is the final stage of development in Mead's model; the child can now respond to numerous members of the social environment.

Mead uses the term **generalized other** to refer to the attitudes, viewpoints, and expectations of society as a whole that a child takes into account in his or her behavior. Simply put, this concept suggests that when an individual acts, he or she takes into account an entire group of people. For example, a child will not act courteously merely to please a particular parent. Rather, the child comes to understand that courtesy is a widespread social value endorsed by parents, teachers, and religious leaders.

In the game stage, children can take a more sophisticated view of people and their social environment. They now understand what specific occupations and social positions are, and no longer equate Mr. Williams only with the role of "librarian" or Ms. Franks only with "principal." It has become clear to the child that Mr. Williams can be a librarian, a parent, and a marathon runner at the same time, and that Ms. Franks is one of many principals in our society. Thus, the child has reached a new level of sophistication in his or her observations of individuals and institutions.

MEAD: THEORY OF THE SELF

Mead is best known for his theory of the self. According to Mead (1964b), the self begins as the privileged center of a person's world. Young children picture themselves as the focus of everything around them and find it difficult to consider the perspectives of others. When shown a mountain scene and asked to describe what an observer on the opposite side of the mountain sees (such as a lake or hikers), they describe only objects visible from their own vantage point. This childhood tendency to place ourselves at the center of events never entirely disappears. Many people with a fear of flying automatically assume that if any plane goes down, it will be the one they are on. And who reads the horoscope section in the paper without looking at their own horoscope first? Why else do we buy lottery tickets, if we don't imagine ourselves winning?

Nonetheless, as people mature, the self changes and begins to reflect greater concern for the reactions of others. Mead used the term **significant others** to refer to those individuals who are most important in the development of the self. Parents, friends, co-workers, coaches, and teachers are often among those who play a major role in shaping a person's self. Many young people, for example, find themselves drawn to the same kind of work their parents engage in.

In some instances, studies of significant others have generated controversy among researchers. For example, some researchers contend that African American adolescents are more "peer-oriented" than their White counterparts because of presumed weaknesses in Black families. However, investigations indicate that this hasty conclusion was based on limited studies focused on less affluent Blacks. In fact, there appears to be little difference in the people African Americans and Whites

Who have been your significant others? Are you someone else's significant other?

from similar economic backgrounds regard as their significant others (Giordano et al. 1993; Juhasz 1989).

GOFFMAN: PRESENTATION OF THE SELF

How do we manage our "self"? How do we display to others who we are? Erving Goffman, a sociologist associated with the interactionist perspective, suggested that many of our daily activities involve attempts to convey impressions of who we are.

Early in life, the individual learns to slant his or her presentation of the self in order to create distinctive appearances and satisfy particular audiences. Goffman (1959) refers to this altering of the presentation of the self as ***impression management.*** In analyzing such everyday social interactions, Goffman makes so many explicit parallels to the theater that his view has been termed the ***dramaturgical approach.*** According to this perspective, people resemble performers in action. For example, a clerk may try to appear busier than he or she actually is if a supervisor happens to be watching. A customer in a singles' bar may try to look as if he or she is waiting for a particular person to arrive.

Goffman's work on the self represents a logical progression of the sociological work begun by Cooley and Mead on how personality is acquired through socialization and how we manage the presentation of the self to others. Cooley stressed the process by which we come to create a self; Mead focused on how the self develops as we learn to interact with others; Goffman emphasized the ways in which we consciously create images of ourselves for others.

Socialization and the Life Course

THE LIFE COURSE

What was the last rite of passage you participated in? Was it formal or informal?

Among the Kota people of the Congo, adolescents paint themselves blue. Mexican American girls go on a daylong religious retreat before dancing the night away. Egyptian mothers step over their newborn infants seven times, and students at the U.S. Naval Academy throw their hats in the air. These are all ways of celebrating ***rites of passage,*** a means of dramatizing and validating changes in a person's status. The Kota rite marks the passage to adulthood. The color blue, viewed as the color of death, symbolizes the death of childhood. Hispanic girls celebrate reaching womanhood at age 15 with a *quinceañera* ceremony. In many Latino communities in the United States, the popularity of the *quinceañera* supports a network of party planners, caterers, dress designers, and the Miss Quinceañera Latina pageant.

These specific ceremonies mark stages of development in the life course. They indicate that the process of socialization continues through all stages of the life cycle. In fact, some researchers have chosen to concentrate on socialization as a lifelong process. Sociologists and other social scientists who take such a *life-course approach* look closely at the social factors that influence people throughout their lives, from birth to death. They recognize that biological changes mold but do not dictate human behavior.

ANTICIPATORY SOCIALIZATION AND RESOCIALIZATION

The development of a social self is literally a lifelong transformation that begins in the crib and continues even as one prepares for death. Two types of socialization occur at many points throughout the life course: anticipatory socialization and resocialization.

Anticipatory socialization refers to the processes of socialization in which a person "rehearses" for future positions, occupations, and social relationships. A culture can function more efficiently and smoothly if members become acquainted with the norms, values, and behavior associated with a social position before actually assuming that status. Preparation for many aspects of adult life begins with anticipatory socialization during childhood and adolescence and continues throughout our lives as we prepare for new responsibilities.

Occasionally, assuming new social and occupational positions requires us to *unlearn* an established orientation. **Resocialization** refers to the process of discarding former behavior patterns and accepting new ones as part of a transition in one's life. Often resocialization occurs when there is an explicit effort to transform an individual, as happens in reform schools, therapy groups, prisons, religious conversion settings, and political indoctrination camps. The process of resocialization typically involves considerable stress for the individual, much more so than socialization in general or even anticipatory socialization (Gecas 1982).

Resocialization is particularly effective when it occurs within a total institution. Erving Goffman (1961) coined the term *total institution* to refer to institutions such as prisons, the military, mental hospitals, and convents, which regulate all aspects of a person's life under a single authority. Because the total institution is generally cut off from the rest of society, it provides for all the needs of its members. Quite literally, the crew of a merchant vessel at sea becomes part of a total institution. So elaborate are its requirements, so all-encompassing its activities, a total institution often represents a miniature society.

Goffman (1961) identified four common traits of total institutions, as follows:

1. All aspects of life are conducted in the same place under the control of a single authority.

2. Any activities within the institution are conducted in the company of others in the same circumstances—for example, army recruits or novices in a convent.

3. The authorities devise rules and schedule activities without consulting the participants.

4. All aspects of life within a total institution are designed to fulfill the purpose of the organization. Thus, all activities in a monastery might be centered on prayer and communion with God.

People often lose their individuality within total institutions. For example, a person entering prison may experience the humiliation of a **degradation ceremony** as he or she is stripped of clothing, jewelry, and other personal possessions. From this point on, scheduled daily routines allow for little or no personal initiative. The individual becomes secondary and rather invisible in the overbearing social environment (Garfinkel 1956).

Agents of Socialization

As we have seen, in the United States the life course is defined by rather gradual movement from one stage of socialization to the next. The continuing and lifelong socialization process involves many different social forces that influence our lives and alter our self-images.

The family is the most important agent of socialization in the United States, especially for children. We'll also give particular attention in this chapter to five other agents of socialization: the school, the peer group, the mass media, the workplace, and the state.

FAMILY

Children in Amish communities are raised in a highly structured and disciplined manner. But they are not immune to the temptations posed by their peers in the non-Amish world—"rebellious" acts such as dancing, drinking, and riding in cars. Still, Amish families don't get too concerned; they know the strong influence they ultimately exert over their offspring. The same is true for the family in general. It is tempting to say that the "peer group" or even the "media" really raise children these days, especially when the spotlight falls on young people involved in shooting sprees and hate crimes. Almost all available research, however, shows that the role of the family in socializing a child cannot be overestimated (Williams 1998; for a different view see J. R. Harris 1998).

The lifelong process of learning begins shortly after birth. Since newborns can hear, see, smell, taste, and feel heat, cold, and pain, they are constantly orienting themselves to the surrounding world. Human beings, especially family members, constitute an important part of their social environment. People minister to the baby's needs by feeding, cleansing, carrying, and comforting the baby.

The term *gender role* refers to expectations regarding the proper behavior, attitudes, and activities of males and females. For example, we traditionally think of "toughness" as masculine—and desirable in men but not women—while we view "tenderness" as feminine. Yet other cultures do not necessarily assign these qualities to each gender in the way that our culture does.

As the primary agents of childhood socialization, parents play a critical role in guiding children into those gender roles deemed appropriate in a society. Other adults, older siblings, the mass media, and religious and educational institutions also have a noticeable impact on a child's socialization into feminine and masculine norms. A culture or subculture may require that one sex or the other take primary responsibility for the socialization of children, economic support of the family, or religious or intellectual leadership.

Interactionists remind us that socialization concerning not only masculinity and femininity, but also marriage and parenthood, begins in childhood as a part of family life. Children observe their parents as they express affection, deal with finances, quarrel, complain about in-laws, and so forth. These experiences represent an informal process of anticipatory socialization. The child develops a tentative model of what being married and being a parent are like.

Typically, parents are thought to have a positive effect on their children's socialization. But that is not always the case. A survey of nearly 600 teens in New York, Texas, Florida, and California indicated that 20 percent had shared drugs other than alcohol with their parents, and about 5 percent were actually introduced to drugs by their mothers or fathers. Approximately 1.5 million children under the age of 18, or 2 percent of all U.S. youths, have a parent in a state or federal prison at some time during the year. Socialization within the family, whether positive or negative, is a powerful process (Leinwand 2000; Mumola 2000).

SCHOOL

Where did you learn the national anthem? Who taught you about the heroes of the American Revolution? Where were you first tested on your knowledge of your culture? Like the family, schools have an explicit mandate to socialize people in the United States—and especially children—into the norms and values of our culture.

As conflict theorists Samuel Bowles and Herbert Gintis (1976) have observed, schools in this country foster competition through built-in systems of reward and punishment, such as grades and evaluations by teachers. Consequently, a child who is working intently to learn a new skill can sometimes come to feel stupid and unsuccessful. However, as the self matures, children become capable of increasingly realistic assessments of their intellectual, physical, and social abilities.

Functionalists point out that as agents of socialization, schools fulfill the function of teaching children the values and customs of the larger society. Conflict theorists agree but add that schools can reinforce the divisive aspects of society, especially those of social class. For example, higher education in the United States is costly despite the existence of financial aid programs. Students from affluent backgrounds have an advantage in gaining access to universities and professional training. At the same time, less affluent young people may never receive the preparation that would qualify them for the best-paying and most prestigious jobs.

In other cultures as well, schools serve socialization functions. During the 1980s, for example, Japanese parents and educators were distressed to realize that children were gradually losing the knack of eating with chopsticks. The trend became a national issue in 1997, when school lunch programs introduced plastic "sporks" (combined fork and spoon, used frequently in the United States). National leaders, responding to the public outcry, banished sporks in favor of *hashi* (chopsticks). On a more serious note, Japanese schools have come under increasing pressure in recent years as working parents have abdicated more and more responsibility to educational institutions. To rectify the imbalance, the Japanese government in 1998 promoted a guide to better parenting, calling on parents to read more with their children, allow for more playtime, limit TV watching, and plan family activities (Gauette 1998).

PEER GROUP

Ask 13-year-olds who matters most in their lives and they are likely to answer "friends." As a child grows older, the family becomes somewhat less important in a person's social development, and peer groups increasingly assume the role of Mead's significant others. Within the peer group, young people associate with others who are approximately their own age and who often enjoy a similar social status.

Peer groups can ease the transition to adult responsibilities. At home, parents tend to dominate; at school, the teenager must contend with teachers and administrators. But within the peer group, each member can assert himself or herself in a way that may not be possible elsewhere. Nevertheless, almost all adolescents in our culture remain economically dependent on their parents, and most are emotionally dependent as well.

Peers can be the source of harassment as well as support. This problem has received considerable attention in Japan, where bullying in school is a constant fact of life. Groups of students act together to humiliate, disgrace, or torment a specific student, a practice known in Japan as *ijime*. Most students go along with the bullying out of fear that they themselves might become the target. In some cases the *ijime* has led to a child's suicide. In 1998, the situation became so desperate that a volunteer association set up a 24-hour telephone hotline in Tokyo just for children. The success of the effort convinced the government to sponsor a nationwide hotline system (Matsushita 1999; Sugimoto 1997).

MASS MEDIA AND TECHNOLOGY

In the last 80 years, media innovations—radio, motion pictures, recorded music, television, and the Internet—have become important agents of socialization. The Internet, in particular, is becoming an important influence in the socialization of children in the United States. According to one study of youths in Silicon Valley, California, about 33 percent of children in the area went online every day in 2002. As Figure 2–1 shows, in a typical week the children spent between 2 hours or less and 10 hours or more instant-messaging, chatting online, and surfing the Net.

Even more than the Internet, television is a critical force in children's socialization. Remarkably, 32 percent of children under the age of 7 and 53 percent of all children ages 12 to 18 have their own television set. In all, young people in the United States spend 5.5 hours per day with some form of media, mostly television. Little wonder that the American Academy of Pediatrics has urged parents not to allow

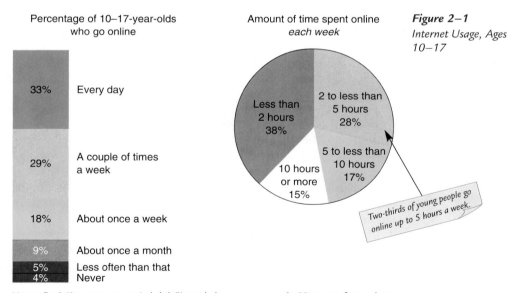

Figure 2–1
Internet Usage, Ages 10–17

NOTES: *Don't Know responses not included. Pie graph shows usage among the 80 percent of respondents who said they went online once a week or more. Based on a survey of 804 randomly selected youths, Silicon Valley, late 2002.* SOURCE: Kaiser Family Foundation/*San Jose Mercury News* 2003.

Think About It
How did your use of the Internet when you were younger compare to these survey results?

children under 2 years old to watch television. Parents should also avoid using any kind of media as an electronic baby-sitter and should try to create an "electronic media–free" environment in their children's rooms (Rideout et al. 1999).

Television, however, is not always a negative socializing influence. Television programs and even commercials can introduce young people to unfamiliar lifestyles and cultures. Not only do children in the United States learn about life in "faraway lands," but inner-city children learn about the lives of farm children and vice versa. The same goes for children living in other countries.

Sociologists and other social scientists have also begun to consider the impact of technology on socialization, especially as it applies to family life. The Silicon Valley Cultures Project studied families in California's Silicon Valley (a technological corridor) for 10 years, beginning in 1991. Although these families may not be typical, they probably represent a lifestyle that more and more households will approximate. The researchers have found that technology in the form of e-mail, webpages, cellular phones, voice mail, digital organizers, and pagers is allowing householders to let outsiders do everything from grocery shopping to soccer pools. They are also finding that families are socialized into multitasking (doing more than one task at a time) as the social norm; devoting one's full attention to one task—even eating or driving—is less and less common on a typical day (Silicon Valley Cultures Project 2002).

WORKPLACE

Learning to behave appropriately in the workplace is a fundamental aspect of human socialization. In the United States, working full-time confirms one's adult status; it indicates to all that one has passed out of adolescence. In a sense, socialization into an occupation can represent both a harsh reality ("I have to work in order to buy food and pay the rent") and the realization of an ambition ("I've always wanted to be an airline pilot") (Moore 1968:862).

Once, "going to work" began with the end of one's formal schooling, but that is no longer the case, at least not in the United States. More and more young people work today, and not just for a parent or relative. Adolescents generally seek jobs in order to make spending money; 80 percent of high school seniors say that little or none of what they earn goes to family expenses. They rarely look on their employment as a means of exploring vocational interests or getting on-the-job training (Cooper 1998).

College students today recognize that occupational socialization is not socialization into one lifetime occupation. They anticipate going through a number of jobs. A survey of college students and recent graduates found that 78 percent plan to stay with their employer for no longer than three years. One out of every four anticipate staying with a first employer only one year (Jobtrak.com 2000).

THE STATE

Social scientists have increasingly recognized the importance of the state as an agent of socialization because of its growing impact on the life course. Traditionally, family members have served as the primary caregivers in our culture, but in the 20th century, the family's protective function has steadily been transferred to outside agencies such as hospitals, mental health clinics, and insurance companies. The state runs many of these agencies, or licenses and regulates them (Ogburn and Tibbits 1934).

In the past, heads of households and local groups such as religious organizations influenced the life course most significantly. Today, however, national interests are increasingly influencing the individual as a citizen and an economic actor. For example, labor unions and political parties serve as intermediaries between the individual and the state.

The state has had a noteworthy impact on the life course by reinstituting rites of passage that had disappeared in agricultural societies and in periods of early industrialization. For example, government regulations stipulate the ages at which a person may drive a car, drink alcohol, vote in elections, marry without parental permission, work overtime, and retire. These regulations do not constitute strict rites of passage: most 18-year-olds choose not to vote, and most people choose their age of retirement without reference to government dictates. Still, the state shapes the socialization process by regulating the life course to some degree and by influencing our views of appropriate behavior at particular ages (Mayer and Schoepflin 1989).

Sociology Matters

Sociology matters because it raises your awareness of cultural patterns you would otherwise take for granted.

- What culture and/or subcultures do you belong to? Have you ever questioned your culture's norms and values?
- How does your culture relate to cultures in other societies? Do you feel comfortable in mainstream society?

Sociology matters, too, because it shows you how you became who you are.

- How do you view yourself as you interact with others around you? How do you think you formed this view of yourself?
- What people, groups, or social institutions have been particularly important in helping you to define who you are?

CHAPTER RESOURCES

Summary

Culture is the totality of learned, socially transmitted customs, knowledge, material objects, and behavior that defines the group or **society** to which we belong. People learn these elements of culture through the lifelong process of **socialization.** This chapter presented the basic elements that are common to all cultures, as well as variations that distinguish one culture from another. It examined the role of socialization in human development, including the way in which people develop their concept of the **self.** It closed with a description of the major agents of socialization.

1. **Cultural universals** are general practices that are found in every culture, including courtship, family, games, language, medicine, religion, and sexual restrictions. The manner in which these universal practices are expressed varies from one culture to the next, however.

2. In recent decades, international trade and the exchange of ideas have accelerated cultural change. Sociologists use the term **globalization** to refer to the resulting worldwide integration of government policies, cultures, social movements, and financial markets.

3. **Language,** an important element of culture, includes speech, writing, and symbols, as well as gestures and other forms of nonverbal communication. Language both describes and shapes culture.

4. **Norms** are the standards of behavior members of a society are expected to uphold. Norms may be **formal**—written down—or **informal**—generally understood. **Sanctions** are the rewards and punishments meted out to those who comply with or violate social norms.

5. Every culture has a **dominant ideology**—a set of beliefs and practices that reinforce powerful social, economic, and political interests. Large cultures may include **subcultures**—groups of people who share norms and values that differ from those of the larger society, and may contradict the dominant ideology.

6. Most people use their own culture as the standard for evaluating other cultures, a perspective that is called **ethnocentrism.** Some sociologists attempt to see other cultures as members of those cultures see them, a perspective called **cultural relativism.**

7. The process of **socialization** to a society's cultural values is influenced both by the environment and by heredity. The study of the biological bases of social behavior is called **sociobiology.**

8. Charles Horton Cooley asserted that we learn who we are by interacting with others, a phenomenon he called the **looking-glass self.** Another interactionist, George Herbert Mead, proposed a three-stage theory of the development of the **self.**

9. Erving Goffman showed that many of our daily activities involve attempts to convey distinct impressions of who we are, a process he called **impression management.**

10. Sociologists who take a **life-course approach** to the study of socialization are interested in the social factors that influence people throughout their lives, from birth to death. The primary agents in this process are the family, schools, peer groups, the mass media and technology, the workplace, and the state.

www.mhhe.com/schaefersm2
Visit the Online Learning Center for *Sociology Matters* to access quizzes, review activities, and other learning tools.

Key Terms

anticipatory socialization, 55

argot, 44

counterculture, 46

cultural relativism, 48

cultural universal, 36

culture, 34

culture lag, 38

culture shock, 46

degradation ceremony, 56

diffusion, 37

discovery, 36

dominant ideology, 43

dramaturgical approach, 54

ethnocentrism, 47

folkway, 40

formal norm, 39

gender role, 57

generalized other, 53

globalization, 36

impression management, 54

informal norm, 40

innovation, 36

invention, 36

language, 38

law, 40

life-course approach, 55

looking-glass self, 51

material culture, 38

McDonaldization, 37

mores, 40

nonmaterial culture, 38

norm, 39

personality, 34

resocialization, 55

rite of passage, 54

role taking, 52

sanction, 41

self, 51

significant other, 53

socialization, 34

society, 35

sociobiology, 50

subculture, 44

symbol, 52

technology, 37

total institution, 55

value, 42

3

Social Structure, Groups, and Organizations

Defining and
Reconstructing Reality

Elements of Social Structure

Social Structure in
Global Perspective

Understanding Organizations

The Changing Workplace

In the early 1970s, social psychologist Philip Zimbardo asked seventy male students at Stanford University to participate in an unorthodox experiment: a mock prison he had set up in the basement of a campus building. Using a coin toss, Zimbardo assigned half the subjects to play the role of prisoner and half to act as prison guards. He told the "guards" to make up their own rules for running the prison, then waited to see what would happen (Haney et al. 1973; Zimbardo et al. 2003).

The results both astonished and frightened Zimbardo. Virtually overnight, the guards became tough enforcers of the rules, shouting curt commands at the prisoners. Some became cruel and abusive; one even forced a prisoner into "solitary confinement" in a closet. The prisoners reacted just as swiftly: some became depressed, apathetic, and helpless; others, rebellious and angry. In just six days, the situation became so intolerable that Zimbardo was forced to abandon the study. Given the anxiety and distress he had observed in the student prisoners, continuing the experiment would have been unethical.

In this study, college students adopted predictable patterns of behavior (those expected of guards and prisoners) when they were placed together in a mock prison. Sociologists use the term *social interaction* to refer to the ways in which people respond to one another. Social interactions need not be face to face; talking over the telephone and communicating via e-mail are also forms of social interaction. In Zimbardo's mock prison experiment, the social interactions between guards and prisoners were highly impersonal. Guards wore reflective sunglasses that made eye contact impossible and addressed prisoners by number rather than by name.

As in many real-life prisons, the simulated prison at Stanford had a social structure in which guards held virtually total control over prisoners. Formally defined, *social structure* is the way in which a society is organized into predictable relationships. Clearly, the prison's social structure influenced how the guards and prisoners interacted. As Zimbardo (et al. 2003:546) noted, it was a real prison "in the minds of the jailers and their captives." The experiment, conducted more than 30 years ago, has since been repeated—with similar findings— both in the United States and in other countries.

Zimbardo's experiment took on new relevance in 2004, in the wake of shocking revelations of prisoner abuse at the U.S.-run Abu Ghraib military facility in Iraq. Graphic photos showed U.S. soldiers humiliating naked Iraqi prisoners and threatening to attack them with police dogs. The structure of the wartime prison, coupled with intense pressure on military intelligence officers to secure information regarding terrorist plots, contributed to the breakdown in the guards' behavior. But Zimbardo himself noted that the guards' depraved conduct could have been predicted simply on the basis of his research (Zarembo 2004; Zimbardo 2004).

The concepts of social interaction and social structure are closely linked to groups and organizations. Often, social interactions take place in groups of friends, relatives, or coworkers, or in formal organizations such as universities and prisons. Whatever the setting, an underlying social structure dictates the relationships among members of the group or organization, and the ways in which they respond to one another. In this chapter we will study the basic elements of social structure, from individual social status and social roles to groups, social networks, and social institutions. We will examine two theories of social structure that apply not just to our own society, but to societies around the world. And we will look at the special characteristics of formal organizations, including bureaucracies. The chapter closes with a quick glimpse at the way new technologies are changing our social interactions.

Defining and Reconstructing Reality

How do we define our social reality? As an example, let's consider something as simple as how we regard tattoos. Even as recently as a few years ago, most of us in the United States considered tattoos to be "weird" or "kooky." We associated them with fringe countercultural groups, such as punk rockers, biker gangs, and skinheads. Among many people, a tattoo elicited an automatic negative response. Now, however, there are so many tattooed people, including society's trendsetters and major sports figures, and the ritual of getting a tattoo has become so legitimized, that we regard tattoos differently. At this point, as a result of increased social interactions with tattooed people, tattoos look perfectly at home to us in a number of settings.

The ability to define social reality reflects a group's power within a society. In fact, one of the most crucial aspects of the relationship between dominant and subordinate groups is the ability of the dominant or majority group to define a society's values. Sociologist William I. Thomas (1923), an early critic of theories of racial and gender differences, recognized that the "definition of the situation" could mold the thinking and personality of the individual. Writing from an interactionist perspective, Thomas observed that people respond not only to the objective features of a person or situation but also to the *meaning* the person or situation has for them. For example, in Philip Zimbardo's mock prison experiment, student "guards" and "prisoners" accepted the definition of the situation (including the traditional roles and behavior associated with being a guard or prisoner) and acted accordingly.

Let's take a closer look at the elements of social structure that help to define social reality.

Elements of Social Structure

We can examine predictable social relationships in terms of five elements: statuses, social roles, groups, social networks, and social institutions. These elements make up a social structure just as a foundation, walls, and ceilings make up a building's structure. The elements of social structure are developed through the lifelong process of socialization, described in Chapter 2.

STATUSES

We normally think of a person's "status" as having to do with influence, wealth, and fame. However, sociologists use the term **status** to refer to any of the full range of socially defined positions within a large group or society, from the lowest to the highest position. Within our society, a person can occupy the status of president of the United States, fruit picker, son or daughter, violinist, teenager, resident of Minneapolis, dental technician, or neighbor. A person can hold a number of statuses at the same time.

Ascribed and Achieved Status. Sociologists view some statuses as *ascribed* and others as *achieved* (see Figure 3–1). An **ascribed status** is "assigned" to a person by society without regard for the person's unique

Figure 3–1
Social Statuses

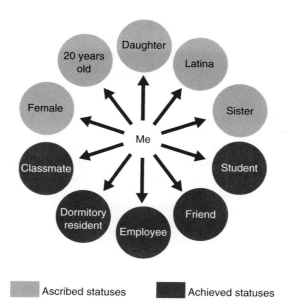

Ascribed statuses   Achieved statuses

Think About It
The person in this figure—"me"—occupies many positions in society, each of which involves distinct statuses. How would you define *your* statuses? Which have the most influence in your life?

talents or characteristics. Generally, this assignment takes place at birth; thus, a person's racial background, gender, and age are all considered ascribed statuses. Though these characteristics are biological in origin, they are significant mainly because of the *social* meanings they have in our culture. Conflict theorists are especially interested in ascribed statuses, since they often confer privileges or reflect a person's membership in a subordinate group. The social meanings of race, ethnicity, and gender will be analyzed more fully in Chapters 6 and 7.

In most cases, we can do little to change an ascribed status. But we can attempt to change the traditional constraints associated with such statuses. For example, the Gray Panthers—an activist political group founded in 1971 to work for the rights of older people—have tried to modify society's negative and confining stereotypes of the elderly. As a result of their work and that of other groups supporting older citizens, the ascribed status of "senior citizen" is no longer as difficult for millions of older people.

Unlike ascribed statuses, an ***achieved status*** comes to us largely through our own efforts. Both "bank president" and "prison guard" are achieved statuses, as are "lawyer," "pianist," "sorority member," "convict," and "social worker." You must do something to acquire an achieved status—go to school, learn a skill, establish a friendship, or invent a new product. As we will see in the next section, our ascribed status heavily influences our achieved status. Being male, for example, decreases the likelihood that a person will consider becoming a child care worker.

Master Status. Each person holds many different and sometimes conflicting statuses; some may connote higher social positions and some, lower positions. How, then, do others view one's overall social position? According to sociologist Everett Hughes (1945), societies deal with such inconsistencies by agreeing that certain statuses are more important than others. A *master status* is a status that dominates others and thereby determines a person's general position within society. For example, Arthur Ashe, who died of AIDS in 1993, had a remarkable career as a tennis star, but at the end of his life, his status as a well-known personality with AIDS may have outweighed his statuses as a retired athlete, an author, and a political activist. Throughout the world many people with disabilities find that their status as "disabled" receives undue weight, and overshadows their actual ability to perform successfully in meaningful employment.

Our society gives so much importance to race and gender that they often dominate our lives. These ascribed statuses frequently influence achieved status. The African American activist Malcolm X (1925–1965), an eloquent and controversial advocate of Black power and Black pride in the early 1960s, recalled that his feelings and perspectives changed dramatically when he was in eighth grade. His English teacher, a White man, advised him that his goal of becoming a lawyer was "no realistic goal for a nigger" and encouraged him instead to become a carpenter. Malcolm X (1964:37) found that his position as a Black man (ascribed status) was an obstacle to his dream of becoming a lawyer (achieved status). In the United States, the ascribed statuses of race and gender can function as master statuses that impact one's potential to achieve a desired professional and social status.

SOCIAL ROLES

What Are Social Roles? Throughout our lives, we acquire what sociologists call *social roles*. A *social role* is a set of expectations for people who occupy a given social position or status. Thus, in the United States, we expect that cab drivers will know how to get around a city, that receptionists will be reliable in handling phone messages, and that police officers will take action if they see a citizen being threatened. With each distinctive social status—whether ascribed or achieved— come particular role expectations. However, actual performance varies from individual to individual. One secretary may assume extensive administrative responsibilities, while another may focus on clerical duties. Similarly, in Philip Zimbardo's mock prison experiment, some students were brutal and sadistic guards, but others were not.

Roles are a significant component of social structure. Viewed from a functionalist perspective, roles contribute to a society's stability by enabling members to anticipate the behavior of others and to pattern their own actions accordingly. Yet social roles can also be dysfunctional, by restricting people's interactions and relationships. If we view a person only as a "police officer" or a "supervisor," it will be difficult to relate to the person as a friend or neighbor.

Role Conflict.   Imagine the delicate situation of a woman who has worked for a decade on an assembly line in an electrical plant and has recently been named supervisor of the unit she worked in. How is this woman expected to relate to her longtime friends and coworkers? Should she still go out to lunch with them, as she has done almost daily for years? Is it her responsibility to recommend the firing of an old friend who cannot keep up with the demands of the assembly line?

Role conflict occurs when incompatible expectations arise from two or more social positions held by the same person. Fulfillment of the roles associated with one status may directly violate the roles linked to a second status. In the example above, the newly promoted supervisor will most likely experience a sharp conflict between her social and occupational roles. Role conflicts call for important ethical choices. So, the new supervisor will have to make a difficult decision about how much allegiance she owes her friend and how much she owes her employer.

Another type of role conflict occurs when individuals move into occupations that are not common among people with their ascribed status. Male preschool teachers and female police officers experience this type of role conflict. In the latter case, female officers must strive to reconcile their workplace role in law enforcement with the societal view of a woman's role, which does not embrace many skills needed in police work. And while female police officers encounter sexual harassment, as women do throughout the labor force, they must also deal with the "code of silence," an informal norm that precludes their implicating fellow officers in wrongdoing (S. Martin 1994).

Use Your Sociological Imagination

If you were a male nurse, what aspects of role conflict would you need to consider? Now imagine you are a professional boxer and a woman. What conflicting role expectations might that involve? In both cases, how well do you think you would handle role conflict?

Role Strain.   Role conflict describes the situation of a person dealing with the challenge of occupying two social positions simultaneously. However, even a single position can cause problems. Sociologists use the term *role strain* to describe the situation that occurs when the same social position imposes conflicting demands and expectations.

In the prison experiment described in the chapter opening, social psychologist Philip Zimbardo unexpectedly experienced role strain. He initially saw himself merely as a college professor directing an imaginative experiment in which students played the roles of either guard or inmate. However, he soon found that as a professor, he is also expected to look after the welfare of the students, or at least not to endanger them. Eventually he resolved the role strain by making the difficult decision to terminate the experiment. Twenty-five years later, in a television interview, he was still reflecting on the challenge of the role strain he confronted (CBS News 1998).

GROUPS

In sociological terms, a **group** is any number of people with similar norms, values, and expectations who interact with one another on a regular basis. The members of a women's basketball team, of a hospital's business office, or of a symphony orchestra constitute a group. However, the residents of a suburb would not be considered a group, since they rarely interact with one another at one time.

Every society is composed of many groups in which daily social interaction takes place. People seek out groups to establish friendships, to accomplish certain goals, and to fulfill the social roles they have acquired. Groups, then, play a vital part in a society's social structure. Much of our social interaction takes place within groups and is influenced by their norms and sanctions. Being a teenager or a retired person takes on special meaning when you interact within a group designed for people with that particular status. The expectations associated with many social roles, including those accompanying the statuses of brother, sister, and student, become more clearly defined in the context of a group.

Primary and Secondary Groups.   Charles Horton Cooley (1902) coined the term **primary group** to refer to a small group characterized by intimate, face-to-face association and cooperation. The members of a street gang constitute a primary group; so do members of a family living in the same household, as well as a group of "sisters" in a college sorority.

Primary groups play a pivotal role both in the socialization process (see Chapter 2) and in the development of roles and statuses. Indeed, primary groups can be instrumental in a person's day-to-day existence. When we find ourselves identifying closely with a group, it is probably a primary group.

Table 3–1 Comparison of Primary and Secondary Groups

Primary Group	Secondary Group
Generally small	Usually large
Relatively long period of interaction	Relatively short duration, often temporary
Intimate, face-to-face association	Little social intimacy or mutual understanding
Some emotional depth in relationships	Relationships generally superficial
Cooperative, friendly	Formal and impersonal

summing**UP**

We also participate in many groups that are not characterized by close bonds of friendship, such as large college classes and business associations. The term *secondary group* refers to a formal, impersonal group in which there is little social intimacy or mutual understanding (see Table 3–1). The distinction between primary and secondary groups is not always clear-cut. Some social clubs may become so large and impersonal that they no longer function as primary groups.

In-Groups and Out-Groups.   A group can hold special meaning for members because of its relationship to other groups. People in one group sometimes feel antagonistic to or threatened by another group, especially if that group is perceived as being different culturally or racially. Sociologists explain these "we" and "they" feelings using two terms first employed by William Graham Sumner (1906): *in-group* and *out-group.*

An *in-group* can be defined as any group or category to which people feel they belong. Simply put, it comprises everyone who is regarded as "we" or "us." The in-group may be as narrow as a teenage clique or as broad as an entire society. The very existence of an in-group implies that there is an out-group viewed as "they" or "them." An *out-group* is a group or category to which people feel they do *not* belong.

Conflict between in-groups and out-groups can turn violent. In 1999 two disaffected students at Columbine High School in Littleton, Colorado, launched an attack on the school that left 15 students and teachers dead, including themselves. The gunmen, members of an out-group that other students referred to as the Trenchcoat Mafia, apparently resented the taunting of an in-group referred to as the Jocks. Similar episodes have occurred in schools across the nation, where rejected adolescents, overwhelmed by personal and family problems, peer group pressure, academic responsibilities, or media images of violence, have struck out against more popular classmates.

Try putting yourself in the shoes of an out-group member. What does your in-group look like from that perspective?

Reference Groups.   Both in-groups and primary groups can dramatically influence the way an individual thinks and behaves. Sociologists call any group that individuals use as a standard in evaluating themselves and their own behavior a *reference group.* For example, a high school student who aspires to join a social circle of hip-hop music devotees will pattern his or her behavior after that of the group. The student will begin dressing like these peers, downloading the same music, and hanging out at the same stores and clubs.

Reference groups have two basic purposes. First, they serve a normative function by setting and enforcing standards of conduct and belief. The high school student who wants the approval of the hip-hop crowd will have to follow the group's dictates, at least to some extent. Second, reference groups perform a comparison function by serving as a standard against which people can measure themselves and others. An actor will evaluate himself or herself against a reference group composed of others in the acting profession (Merton and Kitt 1950).

SOCIAL NETWORKS AND TECHNOLOGY

Groups do not merely serve to define other elements of the social structure, such as roles and statuses; they also serve as an intermediate link between the individual and the larger society. We are all members of a number of different groups, and through our acquaintances make connections with people in different social circles. These connections are known as a *social network*—that is, a series of social relationships that links a person directly to others, and through them indirectly to still more people. Social networks may constrain people by limiting the range of their interactions, yet may also empower them by making available vast resources (Lin 1999).

Involvement in social networks—commonly known as *networking*—is especially valuable in finding employment. Albert Einstein was successful in finding a job only when a classmate's father put him in touch with his future employer. These kinds of contacts, even those that are weak and distant, can be crucial in establishing social networks and facilitating transmission of information.

Recently, the word *network* has taken on new meaning thanks to the development of personal computers and the Internet. E-mail, chat rooms, and electronic bulletin boards have greatly extended the reach of our social networks, which were once based primarily on word of mouth. Today, potential mates can meet online, no matter where they live. Job seekers can check job openings around the world, and special interest groups can disseminate their messages internationally.

In 2001, the anthrax scare and the mobilization of troops for the Afghanistan conflict combined to increase our reliance on e-mail in unintended ways. Concerns about the delivery of anthrax spores in posted mail led many people and organizations to accept only electronic mail. At the same time, military personnel sent overseas turned increasingly to e-mail to stay in touch with friends and family members at home. Aboard one aircraft carrier, for example, the 5,000 crew members had to sign up a day in advance for a half hour of computer time. All told, they wrote and read about 60,000 e-mails a day. Contrast this with the situation a few years ago, when sailors had to wait as long as a month for a letter from home. As one crew member said, "Without e-mail, I'd be going even crazier than I already am" (Stack 2001:A3).

If you were deaf, what impact might Instant Messaging over the Internet have on you?

SOCIAL INSTITUTIONS

The mass media, the government, the economy, the family, and the health care system are all examples of social institutions found in our society. *Social institutions* are organized patterns of beliefs and

Even though you may not be totally sure whom you are "talking to" online, the Internet has added a massive new dimension to social interaction.

behavior centered on basic social needs, such as replacing personnel (the family) and preserving order (the government).

A close look at social institutions gives sociologists insight into the structure of a society. Consider religion, for example. The institution of religion adapts to the segment of society that it serves. Church work has very different meanings for ministers who serve a skid row area or a suburban middle-class community. Religious leaders assigned to a skid row mission will focus on tending to the ill and providing food and shelter. Clergy in the suburbs will focus on counseling those considering marriage and divorce, arranging youth activities, and overseeing cultural events. (We will examine social institutions in detail in Chapters 8 and 9.)

Social Structure in Global Perspective

Modern societies are complex, especially when compared with earlier social arrangements. Sociologists Ferdinand Tönnies and Gerhard Lenski have offered two ways to contrast modern societies with simpler forms of social structure.

TÖNNIES'S *GEMEINSCHAFT* AND *GESELLSCHAFT*

Ferdinand Tönnies (1855–1936) was appalled by the rise of an industrial city in his native Germany during the late 1800s. In his view, the city marked a dramatic change from the ideal type of a close-knit community, which Tönnies termed *Gemeinschaft,* to that of an impersonal mass society, or *Gesellschaft* (Tönnies [1887] 1988).

The *Gemeinschaft* (pronounced guh-MINE-shoft) community is typical of rural life. It is a small community in which people have similar backgrounds and life experiences. Virtually everyone knows one another, so that social interactions are intimate and familiar, almost as one might find among kinfolk. A commitment to the larger social group and a sense of togetherness characterize the community. People relate to others in a personal way, not just as "clerk" or "manager." With this personal interaction, however, comes little privacy.

Social control in the *Gemeinschaft* community is maintained through informal means, such as moral persuasion, gossip, and even gestures. These techniques work effectively because people genuinely care about how others feel toward them. Social change is relatively limited in the *Gemeinschaft;* the lives of members of one generation may be quite similar to those of their grandparents.

By contrast, the *Gesellschaft* (pronounced guh-ZELL-shoft) is an ideal type characteristic of modern urban life. Most people are strangers and feel little in common with other community residents. Relationships are governed by social roles that grow out of immediate tasks, such as purchasing a product or arranging a business meeting. Self-interest dominates, and little consensus exists concerning values or commitment to the group. As a result, social control must rely on more formal techniques, such as laws and legally defined punishments. Social change is an important aspect of life in the *Gesellschaft;* it can be strikingly evident, even within a single generation.

Sociologists have used these two terms to compare social structures stressing close relationships with those that emphasize impersonal ties. It is easy to view the *Gemeinschaft* with nostalgia, as a far better way of life than the "rat race" of contemporary existence. However, the more intimate relationships of the *Gemeinschaft* come at a price. The prejudice and discrimination found there can be quite confining; ascribed statuses such as family background often outweigh a person's unique talents and achievements. In addition, the *Gemeinschaft* tends to be distrustful of the individual who seeks to be creative or just to be different.

LENSKI'S SOCIOCULTURAL EVOLUTION APPROACH

Sociologist Gerhard Lenski takes a very different view of society and social structure. Rather than distinguishing between two opposite types of society, as Tönnies did, Lenski sees human societies as undergoing a process of change characterized by a dominant pattern known as *socio-cultural evolution.* This term refers to the "process of change and development in human societies that results from cumulative growth in their stores of cultural information" (Nolan and Lenski 2004:366).

In Lenski's view, a society's level of technology is critical to the way it is organized. Lenski defines *technology* as "cultural information about how to use the material resources of the environment to satisfy human needs and desires" (Nolan and Lenski 2004:37). The available technology does not completely define the form that a particular society and its social structure take. Nevertheless, a low level of technology may limit the degree to which a society can depend on such things as irrigation or complex machinery. As technology advances, society evolves from a preindustrial to an industrial and then a postindustrial stage.

Preindustrial Societies.   How does a preindustrial society organize its economy? If we know that, it is possible to categorize the society. The first type of preindustrial society to emerge in human history was the *hunting-and-gathering society*, in which people simply relied on whatever foods and fibers were readily available. Technology in such societies is minimal. Organized in groups, people move constantly in search of food. There is little division of labor into specialized tasks.

Hunting-and-gathering societies are composed of small, widely dispersed groups. Each group consists almost entirely of people related to one another. As a result, kinship ties are the source of authority and influence, and the social institution of the family takes on a particularly important role. Tönnies would certainly view such societies as examples of *Gemeinschaft.*

Since resources are scarce, there is relatively little inequality in hunting-and-gathering societies in terms of material goods. Social differentiation is based on ascribed statuses such as gender, age, and family background. By the close of the 20th century, the last hunting-and-gathering societies had virtually disappeared.

Horticultural societies, in which people plant seeds and crops rather than merely subsist on available foods, emerged about 10,000 to 12,000 years ago. Members of horticultural societies are much less nomadic than hunters and gatherers. They place greater emphasis on the production of tools and household objects. Yet their technology remains rather limited: They cultivate crops with the aid of digging sticks or hoes (Wilford 1997).

The last stage of preindustrial development is the *agrarian society,* which emerged about 5,000 years ago. As in horticultural societies, members of agrarian societies are engaged primarily in the production of food. However, the introduction of new technological innovations such as the plow allows farmers to dramatically increase their crop yield. Farmers can cultivate the same fields over generations, allowing the emergence of still larger settlements.

Industrial Societies.   Although the industrial revolution did not topple monarchs, it produced changes every bit as significant as those resulting from political revolutions. The industrial revolution, which took place largely in England during the period 1760 to 1830, was a scientific revolution focused on the application of nonanimal (mechanical) sources of power to labor tasks. An *industrial society* is a society that depends on mechanization to produce its goods and services. Industrial societies rely on new inventions that facilitate agricultural and industrial production, and on new sources of energy, such as steam.

As the industrial revolution proceeded, a new form of social structure emerged. Many societies underwent an irrevocable shift from an agrarian-oriented economy to an industrial base. No longer did a typical individual or a family make an entire product. Instead, specialization of tasks and manufacturing of goods became increasingly common. Workers, generally men but also women and even children, left their family homesteads to work in central locations such as factories.

The process of industrialization had distinctive social consequences. Families and communities could not continue to function as self-sufficient units. Individuals, villages, and regions began to exchange goods and services and to become interdependent. As people came to rely on the labor of members of other communities, the family lost its unique position as the source of power and authority. The need for specialized knowledge led to more formalized education, and education emerged as a social institution distinct from the family.

Postindustrial and Postmodern Societies.   When the sociocultural evolutionary approach first appeared in the 1960s, sociologists paid relatively little attention to how maturing industrialized societies may change with the emergence of even more advanced forms of technology. Since then, Lenski and other sociologists have studied the significant changes in the occupational structure of industrial societies as they shift from manufacturing to service economies. Social scientists call these technologically advanced nations *postindustrial societies,* defined by sociologist Daniel Bell (1999) as societies whose economic systems are engaged primarily in the processing and control of information. The main output of a postindustrial society is services rather than manufactured goods. Large numbers of people become involved in occupations devoted to the teaching, generation, or dissemination of ideas.

Bell views this transition from industrial to postindustrial society as a positive development. He sees a general decline in organized working-class groups and a rise in interest groups concerned with such national issues as health, education, and the environment. Bell's outlook is functionalist because he portrays postindustrial society as basically consensual. Organizations and interest groups, he predicts, will engage in an open and competitive process of decision making. The level of conflict between diverse groups will diminish, strengthening social stability.

Table 3–2 Stages of Sociocultural Evolution

Societal Type	First Appearance	Characteristics
Hunting-and-gathering	Beginning of human life	Nomadic; reliance on readily available food and fibers
Horticultural	About 10,000 to 12,000 years ago	More settled; development of agriculture and limited technology
Agrarian	About 5,000 years ago	Larger, more stable settlements; improved technology and increased crop yields
Industrial	1760–1850	Reliance on mechanical power and new sources of energy; centralized workplaces; economic interdependence; formal education
Postindustrial	1960s	Reliance on services, especially the processing and control of information; expanded middle class
Postmodern	Latter 1970s	High technology; mass consumption of consumer goods and media images; cross-cultural integration

More recently, sociologists have gone beyond discussion of postindustrial societies to the postmodern society. A ***postmodern society*** is a technologically sophisticated society that is preoccupied with consumer goods and media images. Such societies consume goods and information on a mass scale. Postmodern theorists take a global perspective, noting the ways that aspects of culture cross national boundaries. For example, residents of the United States may listen to reggae music from Jamaica, eat sushi and other types of Japanese food, and wear clogs from Sweden. Table 3–2 summarizes the six stages of sociocultural evolution (Brannigan 1992; Lyotard 1993).

Ferdinand Tönnies and Gerhard Lenski present two visions of society's social structure. While different, both approaches are useful; this textbook will draw on both. Lenski's sociocultural evolutionary approach emphasizes a historical perspective. It does not picture different types of social structure coexisting within the same society. Consequently, one would not expect a single society to include hunters and gatherers along with a postmodern culture. Yet sociologists frequently observe that a *Gemeinschaft* and a *Gesellschaft* can be found in the same society. For example, a rural New Hampshire community located less than 100 miles from Boston is linked to the metropolitan area by modern information technology— television and radio, the telephone, and the Internet.

The work of Tönnies and Lenski reminds us that a major focus of sociology has been to identify changes in social structure, and the consequences for human behavior as society shifts to more advanced forms of technology. The social structure becomes increasingly complex, and new social institutions emerge to assume some functions previously performed by the family. These changes, in turn, affect the nature of social interactions. Each individual takes on multiple social roles, and people come to rely partly on social networks rather than solely on kinship ties. As the social structure becomes more complicated, people's relationships tend to become more impersonal, transient, and fragmented. The development of formal organizations and bureaucracies, the subject of the next section, is another outcome of this process.

Understanding Organizations

FORMAL ORGANIZATIONS AND BUREAUCRACIES

As industrial and postmodern societies have shifted to more advanced forms of technology and their social structures have become more complex, our lives have become increasingly dominated by large secondary groups referred to as *formal organizations*. A ***formal organization*** is a group designed for a special purpose and structured for maximum efficiency. The United States Postal Service, the McDonald's fast-food chain, the Boston Pops orchestra, and the college you attend are all examples of formal organizations. Organizations vary in their size, specificity of goals, and degree of efficiency, but all are structured to facilitate the management of large-scale operations. All have a bureaucratic form of organization.

In our society, formal organizations fulfill an enormous variety of personal and societal needs, shaping the lives of every one of us. In fact, formal organizations have become such a dominant force that we must create organizations to supervise other organizations, such as the Securities and Exchange Commission (SEC), which regulates the stock market. Though it sounds much more exciting to say that we live in a "computer age" than in an "age of formal organization," the latter is probably a more accurate description of our times (Azumi and Hage 1972; Etzioni 1964).

CHARACTERISTICS OF A BUREAUCRACY

A ***bureaucracy*** is a component of formal organization in which rules and hierarchical ranking are used to achieve efficiency. Rows of desks staffed by seemingly faceless people, endless lines and forms, impossibly complex language, and frustrating encounters with red tape—all these unpleasant images have combined to make *bureaucracy* a dirty word and an easy target in political campaigns. As a result, few people want to identify their occupation as "bureaucrat," despite the fact that all of us perform various bureaucratic tasks. Elements of bureaucracy enter into almost every occupation in an industrial society.

Max Weber ([1922] 1947) first directed researchers to the significance of bureaucratic structure. In an important sociological advance, Weber emphasized the basic similarity of structure and process found in the otherwise dissimilar enterprises of religion, government, education, and business. Weber saw bureaucracy as a form of organization quite different from the family-run business. For analytical purposes, he developed an ideal type of bureaucracy that would reflect the most characteristic aspects of all human organizations. By *ideal type* Weber meant a construct or model that serves as a measuring rod against which actual cases can be evaluated. In actuality, perfect bureaucracies do not exist; no real-world organization corresponds exactly to Weber's ideal type.

Weber proposed that whether the purpose is to run a church, a corporation, or an army, the ideal bureaucracy displays five basic characteristics. A discussion of those characteristics, as well as the dysfunctions (or potential negative consequences) of a bureaucracy, follows. (Table 3–3 summarizes the discussion.)

1. **Division of Labor.** Specialized experts perform specific tasks. In your college bureaucracy, the admissions officer does not do the job of registrar; the guidance counselor doesn't see to the maintenance of buildings. By working at a specific task, people are more likely to become highly skilled and carry out a job with maximum efficiency. This emphasis on specialization is so basic a part of our lives that we may not realize it is a fairly recent development in Western culture.

   Although the division of labor has certainly enhanced the performance of many complex bureaucracies, in some cases it can lead

summingUP

Table 3–3 Characteristics of a Bureaucracy

Characteristic	Positive Consequence	Negative Consequence	
		For the Individual	For the Organization
Division of labor	Produces efficiency in large-scale organization	Produces trained incapacity	Produces a narrow perspective
Hierarchy of authority	Clarifies who is in command	Deprives employees of a voice in decision making	Permits concealment of mistakes
Written rules and regulations	Let workers know what is expected of them	Stifle initiative and imagination	Lead to goal displacement
Impersonality	Reduces bias	Contributes to cold and uncaring atmosphere	Discourages loyalty to company
Employment based on technical qualifications	Discourages favoritism and reduces petty rivalries	Discourages ambition to improve oneself elsewhere	Promotes Peter principle

to *trained incapacity.* That is, workers become so specialized that they develop blind spots and fail to notice obvious problems. Even worse, they may not care about what is happening in the next department. Some observers believe that such developments have caused workers in the United States to become less productive on the job.

In some cases, the bureaucratic division of labor can have tragic results. In the wake of the coordinated attacks on the World Trade Center and the Pentagon on September 11, 2001, Americans wondered aloud how the FBI and CIA could have failed to detect the terrorists' elaborately planned operation. The problem, in part, turned out to be the division of labor between the FBI, which focuses on domestic matters, and the CIA, which operates overseas. Officials at these intelligence-gathering organizations, both of which are huge bureaucracies, are well-known for jealously guarding information from one another. Subsequent investigations revealed that they knew about Osama bin Laden and his al-Qaeda terrorist network in the early 1990s. Unfortunately, five federal agencies—the CIA, FBI, National Security Agency, Defense Intelligence Agency, and National Reconnaissance Office—failed to share their leads on the network. Although the hijacking of the four commercial airliners used in the massive attacks may not have been preventable, the bureaucratic division of labor definitely hindered efforts to defend against terrorism, and actually undermined U.S. national security.

2. **Hierarchy of Authority.**   Bureaucracies follow the principle of hierarchy; that is, each position is under the supervision of a higher authority. A president heads a college bureaucracy; he or she selects members of the administration, who in turn hire their own staff. In the Roman Catholic church, the pope is the supreme authority; under him sit cardinals, bishops, and so forth.

3. **Written Rules and Regulations.**   What if your sociology professor gave your classmate an A for having such a friendly smile? You might think that wasn't fair—that it was "against the rules."

Rules and regulations, as we all know, are an important characteristic of bureaucracies. Ideally, through such procedures, a bureaucracy ensures uniform performance of every task. This characteristic of a bureaucracy prohibits your classmate from receiving an A for a nice smile, because the rules guarantee that all students will receive essentially the same treatment.

Through written rules and regulations, bureaucracies generally offer employees clear standards for an adequate (or exceptional) performance. In addition, procedures provide a valuable sense of continuity in a bureaucracy. Individual workers will come and go, but the organization's structure and past records give it a life of its own that outlives the services of any one bureaucrat.

Of course, rules and regulations can overshadow the larger goals of an organization to the point that they become dysfunctional. What if a hospital emergency room physician failed to treat a seriously injured person because he or she had no valid proof of U.S. citizenship? If blindly applied, rules no longer serve as a means to achieving an objective, but instead become important (and perhaps too important) in their own right. Robert Merton (1968) has used the term ***goal displacement*** to refer to overzealous conformity to official regulations.

4. **Impersonality.**   Max Weber wrote that in a bureaucracy, work is carried out *sine ira et studio,* "without hatred or passion." Bureaucratic norms dictate that officials perform their duties without the personal consideration of people as individuals. Although this approach is intended to guarantee equal treatment for each person, it also contributes to the often cold and uncaring feeling associated with modern organizations. We typically think of big government and big business when we think of impersonal bureaucracies. But today even small firms have telephone systems that greet callers with an electronic menu.

5. **Employment Based on Technical Qualifications.**   Within the ideal bureaucracy, hiring is based on technical qualifications rather than on favoritism, and performance is measured against specific standards. Written personnel policies dictate who gets promoted; people often have a right to appeal if they believe that particular rules have been violated. Such procedures protect bureaucrats against arbitrary dismissal, provide a measure of security, and encourage loyalty to the organization.

In this sense, the "impersonal" bureaucracy can be considered an improvement over nonbureaucratic organizations. College faculty members, for example, are ideally hired and promoted according to their professional qualifications, including degrees earned and research published, rather than because of whom they know. Once they are granted tenure, their jobs are protected against the whims of a president or dean.

Although ideally, any bureaucracy will value technical and professional competence, personnel decisions do not always follow this ideal pattern. Bureaucratic dysfunctions have become well publicized, particularly because of the work of Laurence J. Peter. According to the ***Peter principle,*** every employee within a hierarchy tends to rise to his or her level of incompetence (Peter and Hull 1969).

These five characteristics of bureaucracy, developed by Max Weber more than 80 years ago, describe an ideal type rather than offering a precise definition of an actual bureaucracy. Not every formal organization will possess all five of Weber's characteristics. In fact, actual bureaucratic organizations can vary widely.

BUREAUCRACY AND ORGANIZATIONAL CULTURE

How does bureaucratization affect the average individual who works in an organization? Early theorists of formal organizations tended to neglect this question. Max Weber, for example, focused on managerial personnel within bureaucracies, but had little to say about workers in industry or clerks in government agencies.

According to the *classical theory* of formal organizations, also known as the *scientific management approach,* workers are motivated almost entirely by economic rewards. This theory stresses that only the physical constraints on workers limit their productivity. Therefore, workers are treated as a resource, much like the machines that began to replace them in the 20th century. Management attempts to achieve maximum work efficiency through scientific planning, established performance standards, and careful supervision of workers and production. Under the scientific management approach, planning includes efficiency studies but not studies of workers' attitudes or job satisfaction.

Not until workers organized unions—and forced management to recognize that they were not objects—did theorists of formal organizations begin to revise the classical approach. Along with management and administrators, social scientists became aware that informal groups of workers have an important impact on organizations. An alternative way of considering bureaucratic dynamics, the *human relations approach,* emphasizes the role of people, communication, and participation within a bureaucracy. This type of analysis reflects the interest of interactionist theorists in small-group behavior. Unlike planning under the scientific management approach, planning based on the human relations perspective focuses on workers' feelings, frustrations, and emotional need for job satisfaction (Perrow 1986).

A series of classic studies illustrates the value of the human relations approach. As we saw in Chapter 1, the Hawthorne studies alerted sociologists to the fact that research subjects may alter their behavior to match the experimenter's expectations. The major focus of the Hawthorne studies, however, was the role of social factors in workers' productivity. One aspect of the research concerned the switchboard-bank wiring room, where 14 men were making parts of switches for telephone equipment. The researchers discovered that these men were producing far below their physical capabilities, which was especially surprising because they could earn more money if they produced more parts.

Why did these men restrict their output? They feared that if they produced switch parts at a faster rate, their pay rate might be reduced, or some of them might lose their jobs. As a result, this group of workers had established their own (unofficial) norm for a proper day's work, with informal rules and sanctions to enforce it. Yet managers were unaware of such practices, and actually believed the men were working as hard as they could (Roethlisberger and Dickson 1939).

The Changing Workplace

Individual businesses, community organizations, and government agencies are always changing, if only because of personnel turnover. But today's factories and corporate offices are undergoing rapid, profound changes unanticipated a century or more ago. Besides the far-reaching impact of technological advances such as computerization, workers must cope with organizational restructuring. For the last several decades, formal organizations have been experimenting with new ways of getting the job done, some of which have significantly altered the workplace.

Collective decision making, or the active involvement of employee problem-solving groups in corporate management, first became popular in the United States in the 1980s. Management gurus had noted the dazzling success of Japanese automobile and consumer products manufacturers. In studying these companies, they found that problem-solving groups were one key to success. At first, such groups concentrated on small problems at specific points in the production line. But today, these groups often cross departmental and divisional boundaries to attack problems rooted in the bureaucratic division of labor. Thus, they require significant adjustment by employees long used to working in a bureaucracy (Ouchi 1981).

Another innovation in the workplace, called *minimal hierarchy,* replaces the traditional bureaucratic hierarchy of authority with a flatter organizational structure. Minimal hierarchy offers workers greater access to those in authority, giving them an opportunity to voice concerns that might not be heard in a traditional bureaucracy. This new organizational structure is thought to minimize the potential for costly and dangerous bureaucratic oversights.

Finally, organizational *work teams* have become increasingly common, even in smaller organizations. There are two types of work team. *Project teams* address ongoing issues, such as safety or compliance with the Americans with Disabilities Act. *Task forces* pursue nonrecurring issues, such as a major building renovation. In both cases, team members are released to some degree from their regular duties in order to contribute to the organizationwide effort (W. Scott 2003).

The common purpose of work teams, minimal hierarchy, and collective decision making is to empower workers. For that reason, these new organizational structures can be exciting for the employees who participate in them. But these innovations rarely touch the vast numbers of workers who perform routine jobs in factories and office buildings. The 22 million part-time workers and 1 million full-time workers who earn the minimum wage or less know little about organizational restructuring (Bureau of Labor Statistics 2004b).

Increasingly, in many industrial countries, workers are turning into telecommuters. *Telecommuters* are employees who work full-time or part-time at home rather than in an outside office, and who are linked to

If your first full-time job after college involved telecommuting, what do you think would be the advantages and disadvantages of working out of a home office? Do you think you would be satisfied as a telecommuter? Why or why not?

supervisors and colleagues through computer terminals, phones, and fax machines. What are the social implications of this shift toward the virtual office? From an interactionist perspective, the workplace is a major source of friendships; restricting face-to-face social opportunities could destroy the trust that is created by "handshake agreements." Thus, telecommuting may move society further along the continuum from *Gemeinschaft* to *Gesellschaft*. On a more positive note, telecommuting may be the first social change that pulls fathers and mothers back into the home rather than pushing them out. The trend, if it continues, should also increase autonomy and job satisfaction for many employees (Castells 2001; DiMaggio et al. 2001).

Sociology Matters

Sociology matters because it defines your social status in terms of a variety of social characteristics and groups.

- What is your ascribed status? What do you hope your achieved status will be some day? Do you have a master status, and if so, how might it impact your achievements?
- What primary and secondary groups do you belong to, and why? How do those groups affect your behavior?
- What social networks and institutions are you involved in? What are their functions, and how can they help you?

CHAPTER RESOURCES

Summary

Through **social structure,** society is organized into predictable relationships that facilitate **social interaction.** The transmission of culture and even the survival of society depend on social interaction. This chapter has presented the basic elements of social structure, from individual **statuses** and the **social roles** that go with them to **groups, social networks,** and **social institutions.** It has examined several theories of social structure and **formal organizations,** including **bureaucracies.**

1. An **ascribed status** is generally assigned to a person at birth, whereas an **achieved status** is attained largely through one's own

effort. In the United States, ascribed statuses such as race and gender can function as **master statuses** that affect one's potential for achievement.

2. The statuses people carry determine the **social roles** they play. People who play more than one social role often suffer from **role conflict,** but even a single role can create **role strain.**

3. Much of our social behavior takes place within **groups.** When we find ourselves identifying closely with a group, it is probably a **primary group.** A **secondary group** is more formal and impersonal.

4. People tend to see the world in terms of **in-groups** (groups to which they belong) and **out-groups** (groups they do not belong to or identify with). **Reference groups** set and enforce standards of social conduct, allowing members to compare themselves to others.

5. Groups serve as links to **social networks** and their vast resources. **Social institutions,** such as government and the family, fulfill essential social functions that other groups cannot, such as preserving order and perpetuating society.

6. The sociologist Ferdinand Tönnies contrasted the close-knit type of community that characterizes rural life, which he called *Gemeinschaft,* with the impersonal type of mass society that characterizes urban life, which he called *Gesellschaft.*

7. In his theory of **sociocultural evolution,** Gerhard Lenski linked the historical development of societies to the technological advances they achieved. Lenski traced their evolution from primitive **hunting-and-gathering societies** to modern-day **postindustrial** and **postmodern societies.**

8. As societies have become more complex, large **formal organizations** and **bureaucracies** have become more powerful and pervasive.

9. Max Weber theorized that in its **ideal type,** every bureaucracy has five basic characteristics: division of labor, hierarchical authority, written rules and regulations, impersonality, and employment based on technical qualifications.

10. While bureaucracy may have stifled individual initiative among workers, recent organizational innovations such as **collective decision making, minimal hierarchy, work teams,** and **telecommuting** may help to reduce bureaucratic dysfunctions.

www.mhhe.com/schaefersm2
Visit the Online Learning Center for *Sociology Matters* to access quizzes, review activities, and other learning tools.

Key Terms

achieved status, 67

agrarian society, 75

ascribed status, 66

bureaucracy, 78

classical theory, 82

collective decision making, 83

formal organization, 78

Gemeinschaft, 74

Gesellschaft, 74

goal displacement, 81

group, 70

horticultural society, 75

human relations approach, 82

hunting-and-gathering society, 75

ideal type, 79

industrial society, 76

in-group, 71

master status, 68

minimal hierarchy, 83

out-group, 71

Peter principle, 81

postindustrial society, 76

postmodern society, 77

primary group, 70

reference group, 71

role conflict, 69

role strain, 69

scientific management approach, 82

secondary group, 71

social institution, 72

social interaction, 64–65

social network, 72

social role, 68

social structure, 65

sociocultural evolution, 75

status, 66

technology, 75

telecommuter, 83

trained incapacity, 80

work team, 83

Deviance and Social Control

Social Control

What Is Deviance?

Explaining Deviance

Crime

Veronika Vester likes to watch her boyfriend, Kidd Krayz, compete in backyard wrestling matches. The boys sometimes use weapons—fire, thumbtacks, barbed wire—as they body-slam and pile-drive each other. At first, Veronika was put off: "I turned around. I couldn't watch it—and then as time goes on, it's just like the normal thing. . . . Now I'm out there yelling, 'Yeah! Hit him!' " (Carpenter 2000:E3).

How did wrestling, a well-respected Olympic sport, degenerate to this point? How does swinging a barbed-wire bat at someone's head become "the normal thing"? Such backyard free-for-alls are crude imitations of the no-holds-barred professional wrestling matches currently shown on television. Through the influence of the media, which glamorize gratuitous violence, teenagers have come to accept a form of entertainment that their parents would brand as deviant.

Who decides what is and is not normal behavior, and how does society attempt to control what people say and do? In this chapter we will study various mechanisms of *social control,* both formal and informal. We will examine several theoretical explanations for *deviance* from social norms. And we will discuss one form of deviance that is subject to strict formal controls: *crime.*

Social Control

As we saw in Chapter 2, each culture, subculture, and group has distinctive norms governing what is deemed appropriate behavior. Laws, dress codes, bylaws of organizations, course requirements, and rules of sports and games all express social norms.

How does a society bring about acceptance of basic norms? The term *social control* refers to the techniques and strategies for preventing deviant behavior in any society. Social control occurs on all levels of society. In the family, we are socialized to obey our parents simply because they are our parents. Peer groups introduce us to informal norms, such as dress codes, that govern the behavior of members. Colleges establish standards they expect of their students. In bureaucratic organizations, workers encounter a formal system of rules and regulations. Finally, the government of every society legislates and enforces social norms.

Most of us respect and accept basic social norms and assume that others will do the same. Even without thinking, we obey the instructions of police officers, follow the day-to-day rules at our jobs, and move to the rear of elevators when people enter. Such behavior reflects an effective process of socialization to the dominant standards of a culture. At the same time, we are well aware that individuals, groups, and institutions *expect* us to act "properly." This expectation carries with it *sanctions,* penalties and rewards for conduct concerning a social norm. If we fail to live up to the norm, we may face punishment through informal sanctions such as fear and ridicule, or formal sanctions such as jail sentences or fines.

The challenge to effective social control is that people often receive competing messages about how to behave. While the state or government may clearly define acceptable behavior, friends or fellow employees may encourage quite different behavior patterns. Binge drinking in college is the perfect example. The larger society frowns on underage drinking and has laws on the books against it. But within the college peer group, binge drinking is generally accepted, with no sanctions attached. Half the men, 41 percent of the women, and close to 80 percent of fraternity and sorority members engage in binge drinking (Wechsler et al. 2002:208).

Functionalists contend that people must respect social norms if any group or society is to survive. In their view, societies literally could not function if massive numbers of people defied standards of appropriate conduct. By contrast, conflict theorists maintain that "successful functioning" of a society will consistently benefit the powerful and work to the disadvantage of other groups. They point out, for example, that widespread resistance to social norms was necessary to overturn the institution of slavery in the United States, to win independence from England, to secure civil rights, to allow women to vote, and to force an end to the war in Vietnam.

CONFORMITY AND OBEDIENCE

Techniques for social control operate on both the group level and the societal level. People we think of as peers or equals influence us to act in particular ways; the same is true of people who hold authority over us or occupy awe-inspiring positions. Stanley Milgram (1975) made a useful distinction between these two important levels of social control.

Milgram defined ***conformity*** as going along with peers—individuals of our own status, who have no special right to direct our behavior. By contrast, ***obedience*** is defined as compliance with higher authorities in a hierarchical structure. Thus, a recruit entering military service will typically *conform* to the habits and language of other recruits and will *obey* the orders of superior officers. Students will *conform* to the drinking behavior of their peers and will *obey* the requests of campus security officers.

If ordered to do so, would you comply with an experimenter's instruction to give people increasingly painful electric shocks? Most people would say no; yet, the research of social psychologist Stanley Milgram (1963, 1975) suggests that most of us *will* obey such orders. In Milgram's words (1975:xi), "Behavior that is unthinkable in an individual . . . acting on his own may be executed without hesitation when carried out under orders."

Milgram placed advertisements in New Haven, Connecticut, newspapers to recruit subjects for what was described as a learning experiment at Yale University. Participants included postal clerks, engineers, high school teachers, and laborers. They were told that the purpose of the research was to investigate the effects of punishment on learning. The experimenter, dressed in a gray technician's coat, explained that in each testing, one subject would be randomly selected as the "learner" and another would function as the "teacher." However, the lottery was rigged so that the "real" subject would always be the teacher, while an associate of Milgram's served as the learner.

At this point, the learner's hand was strapped to an electric apparatus. The teacher was taken to an electronic "shock generator" with 30 graduated lever switches labeled from 15 to 450 volts. Before beginning the experiment, all subjects were given sample shocks of 45 volts, to convince them of the authenticity of the experiment. The experimenter then instructed the teacher to apply shocks of increasing voltage each time the learner gave an incorrect answer on a memory test. Teachers were told that "although the shocks can be extremely painful, they cause no permanent tissue damage." In reality, the learner did not receive any shocks.

The learner acted out a prearranged script, deliberately giving incorrect answers and pretending to be in pain. For example, at 150 volts, the learner would cry out, "Get me out of here!" At 270 volts, the learner would scream in agony. When the shock reached 350 volts, the learner would fall silent. If the teacher wanted to stop the experiment, the experimenter would insist that the teacher continue, using such statements as

"The experiment requires that you continue" and "You have no other choice; you *must* go on" (Milgram 1975:19–23).

The results of this unusual experiment stunned and dismayed Milgram and other social scientists. Almost *two-thirds* of participants fell into the category of "obedient subjects." Why did these subjects obey? Why were they willing to inflict seemingly painful shocks on innocent victims who had never done them any harm? There is no evidence that these subjects were unusually sadistic; few seemed to enjoy administering the shocks. Instead, in Milgram's view, the key to obedience was the experimenter's social role as a "scientist" and "seeker of knowledge."

Milgram pointed out that in the modern industrial world, we are accustomed to submitting to impersonal authority figures whose status is indicated by a title (professor, lieutenant, doctor) or a uniform (the technician's coat). Because we view the authority as larger and more important than the individual, we shift responsibility for our behavior to the authority figure. Milgram's subjects frequently stated, "If it were up to me, I would not have administered shocks." They saw themselves as merely doing their duty (Milgram 1975).

If you were a participant in Milgram's research on obedience, how far do you think you would go in carrying out "orders"? Do you see any ethical problem with the experimenter's manipulation of the subjects?

From an interactionist perspective, one important aspect of Milgram's findings is the fact that in follow-up studies, subjects were less likely to inflict the supposed shocks as they were moved physically closer to their victims. Moreover, interactionists emphasize the effect of *incrementally* administering additional dosages of 15 volts. In effect, the experimenter gradually persuaded the teacher to continue inflicting higher levels of punishment. It is doubtful that anywhere near the two-thirds rate of obedience would have been reached had the experimenter told the teachers to immediately administer 450 volts to the learners (Allen 1978; Katovich 1987).

INFORMAL AND FORMAL SOCIAL CONTROL

The sanctions used to encourage conformity and obedience—and to discourage violation of social norms—are carried out through both informal and formal social control. As the term implies, people use *informal social control* casually to enforce norms. Examples include smiles, laughter, a raised eyebrow, and ridicule.

In the United States and many other cultures, adults often view spanking, slapping, or kicking children as a proper and necessary means of informal social control. Child development specialists counter that such corporal punishment is inappropriate because it teaches children to solve problems through violence. They warn that slapping and spanking can escalate into more serious forms of abuse. Yet, despite a 1998 policy statement by the American Academy of Pediatrics that corporal punishment is not effective and can indeed be harmful, 59 percent of pediatricians support the use of corporal punishment, at least in certain situations. Our culture widely accepts this form of informal social control (Wolraich et al. 1998).

Formal social control is carried out by authorized agents, such as police officers, physicians, school administrators, employers, military officers, and managers of movie theaters. It can serve as a last resort when socialization and informal sanctions do not bring about desired behavior. An increasingly significant means of formal social control in the United States is to imprison people. During the course of a year, 5.7 million adults undergo some form of correctional supervision—jail, prison, probation, or parole. Put another way, almost one out of every 30 adult Americans is subject to this very formal type of social control every year (Beck et al. 2000).

LAW AND SOCIETY

Some norms are so important to a society that they are formalized into laws controlling people's behavior. *Law* may be defined as governmental social control (Black 1995). Some laws, such as the prohibition against murder, are directed at all members of society. Others, such as fishing and hunting regulations, affect particular categories of people. Still others govern the behavior of social institutions (corporate law and laws regarding the taxation of nonprofit enterprises).

Sociologists see the creation of laws as a social process. Laws are created in response to a perceived need for formal social control. Sociologists have sought to explain how and why such perceptions arise. In their view, law is not merely a static body of rules handed down from generation to generation. Rather, it reflects continually changing standards of what is right and wrong, how violations are to be determined, and what sanctions are to be applied (Schur 1968).

Sociologists representing varying theoretical perspectives agree that the legal order reflects the values of those in a position to exercise authority. Therefore, the creation of criminal law can be a most controversial matter. Should it be against the law to employ illegal immigrants in a factory or to have an abortion? Such issues have been bitterly debated because they require a choice among competing values. Not surprisingly, laws that are unpopular—such as the prohibition of alcohol under the Eighteenth Amendment in 1919 and the widespread establishment of a 55-mile-per-hour speed limit on the highway—become difficult to enforce when there is no consensus supporting the underlying norms.

Socialization is actually the primary source of conforming and obedient behavior, including obedience to law. Generally, it is not external pressure from a peer group or authority figure that makes us go along with social norms. Rather, we have internalized such norms as valid and desirable and are committed to observing them. In a profound sense, we want to see ourselves (and to be seen) as loyal, cooperative, responsible, and respectful of others. In the United States and other societies around the world, people are socialized both to want to belong and to fear being viewed as different or deviant.

What Is Deviance?

For sociologists, the term *deviance* does not mean perversion or depravity. Rather, **deviance** is behavior that violates the standards of conduct or expectations of a group or society (Wickman 1991:85). In the United States, alcoholics, compulsive gamblers, and the mentally ill would all be classified as deviants. Being late for class is a deviant act; the same is true of wearing jeans to a formal wedding. On the basis of the sociological definition, we are all deviant from time to time. Each of us violates common social norms in certain situations.

Is being overweight an example of deviance? In the United States and many other cultures, unrealistic standards of appearance and body image place a huge strain on people, especially adult women and girls. Journalist Naomi Wolf (1992) has used the term *beauty myth* to refer to an exaggerated ideal of beauty, beyond the reach of all but a few females. The beauty myth can have unfortunate consequences. In order to shed their "deviant" image and conform to (unrealistic) societal norms, many women and girls become consumed with adjusting their appearance. Yet what is deviant in one culture may be celebrated in another. In Nigeria, for example, being fat is considered a mark of beauty. Part of the coming-of-age ritual calls for young girls to spend a month in a "fattening room." Among Nigerians, being thin at this point in the life course is considered deviant (Simmons 1998).

Deviance involves the violation of group norms, which may or may not be formalized into law. It is a comprehensive concept that includes not only criminal behavior but also many actions not subject to prosecution. The public official who takes a bribe has defied social norms, but so has the high school student who refuses to sit in an assigned seat or cuts class. Of course, deviation from norms is not always negative, let alone criminal. A member of an exclusive social club who speaks out against a traditional policy of excluding women, Blacks, and Jews from admittance is deviating from the club's norms. So is a police officer who blows the whistle on police corruption or brutality.

A person can acquire a deviant identity in many ways. Because of physical or behavioral characteristics, some people are unwillingly cast in negative social roles. Once they have been assigned a deviant role, they have trouble presenting a positive image to others, and may even experience lowered self-esteem. Whole groups of people—for instance, "short people" or "redheads"—may be labeled in this way. The interactionist Erving Goffman coined the term **stigma** to describe the labels society uses to devalue members of certain social groups (Goffman 1963; Heckert and Best 1997).

Prevailing expectations about beauty and body shape may prevent people who are regarded as ugly or obese from advancing as rapidly as their abilities permit. Both overweight and anorexic people are assumed to be weak in character, slaves to their appetites or to media images.

Because they do not conform to the beauty myth, these people may be viewed as "disfigured" or "strange" in appearance, bearers of what Goffman calls a "spoiled identity." However, what constitutes disfigurement is a matter of interpretation. Of the 1 million cosmetic procedures done every year in the United States alone, many are performed on women who would be objectively defined as having a normal appearance. And while feminist sociologists have accurately noted that the beauty myth makes many women feel uncomfortable with themselves, men too lack confidence in their appearance. The number of males who choose to undergo cosmetic procedures has risen sharply in recent years; men now account for 9 percent of such surgeries, including liposuction (Kalb 1999; Saukko 1999).

Often people are stigmatized for deviant behaviors they may no longer engage in. The labels "compulsive gambler," "ex-convict," "recovering alcoholic," and "ex-mental patient" can stick to a person for life. Goffman draws a useful distinction between a prestige symbol that calls attention to a positive aspect of one's identity, such as a wedding band or a badge, and a stigma symbol that discredits or debases one's identity, such as a conviction for child molestation. While stigma symbols may not always be obvious, they can become a matter of public knowledge. Starting in 1994 many states required convicted sex offenders to register with local police departments. Some communities publish the names and addresses, and in some instances even the pictures, of convicted sex offenders on the Web.

You are a reporter who is investigating gambling activities in your community. How do you find people react to those who engage in highly stigmatized forms of gambling? How do you see them encourage other forms of gambling?

Explaining Deviance

Why do people violate social norms? We have seen that deviant acts are subject to both informal and formal sanctions. The nonconforming or disobedient person may face disapproval, loss of friends, fines, or even imprisonment. Why, then, does deviance occur?

Early explanations for deviance blamed supernatural causes or genetic factors (such as "bad blood" or evolutionary throwbacks to primitive ancestors). In the 1800s, substantial efforts were made to identify biological factors that lead to deviance, and especially to criminal activity. While such research was discredited in the 20th century, contemporary researchers, primarily biochemists, have sought to isolate genetic factors connected to certain personality traits. Although criminality (much less deviance) is hardly a personality characteristic, researchers have focused on traits that might lead to crime, such as aggression. Of course, aggression can also lead to success in the corporate world, professional sports, and other pursuits.

The contemporary search for biological roots of criminality is but one aspect of the larger sociobiology debate. In general, sociologists reject any emphasis on genetic roots of crime and deviance. The limitations of current knowledge, the possibility of reinforcing racist and sexist assumptions, and the disturbing implications for the rehabilitation of criminals have led sociologists to draw largely on other approaches to explain deviance (Sagarin and Sanchez 1988).

FUNCTIONALIST PERSPECTIVE

According to functionalists, deviance is a common part of human existence, with positive (as well as negative) consequences for social stability. Deviance helps to define the limits of proper behavior. Children who see one parent scold the other for belching at the dinner table learn about approved conduct. The same is true of the driver who receives a speeding ticket, the department store cashier who is fired for yelling at a customer, and the college student who is penalized for handing in papers weeks overdue.

Durkheim's Legacy.   Émile Durkheim ([1895] 1964) focused his sociological investigations mainly on criminal acts, yet his conclusions have implications for all types of deviant behavior. In Durkheim's view, the punishments established within a culture (including both formal and informal mechanisms of social control) help to define acceptable behavior and thus contribute to social stability. If improper acts were not sanctioned, people might stretch their standards of what constitutes appropriate conduct. Recently, for example, the gradual intensification of violence in professional wrestling, which has gone unsanctioned, has led to much greater tolerance of what was once considered deviant behavior.

Durkheim ([1897] 1951) also introduced the term *anomie* into sociological literature to describe the loss of direction felt in a society when social control of individual behavior has become ineffective. Anomie is a state of normlessness that typically occurs during a period of profound social change and disorder, such as a time of economic collapse. People become more aggressive or depressed, which results in higher rates of violent crime and suicide. Since there is much less agreement on what constitutes proper behavior during times of revolution, sudden prosperity, or economic depression, conformity and obedience become less significant as social forces. Stating exactly what constitutes deviance also becomes much more difficult.

Merton's Theory of Deviance.   What do a mugger and a teacher have in common? Each is "working" to obtain money that can be exchanged for desired goods. As this example illustrates, behavior that violates accepted norms (such as mugging) may be performed with the same basic objectives in mind as those of people who pursue conventional lifestyles.

On the basis of this kind of analysis, sociologist Robert Merton (1968) adapted Durkheim's concept of anomie to explain why people accept or reject the goals of a society, the socially approved means of meeting those goals, or both. Merton maintained that one important cultural goal in the United States is success, measured largely in terms of money. In addition to setting this goal for people, our society offers specific instructions on how to reach it—go to school, work hard, do not quit, take advantage of opportunities, and so forth.

What happens in a society with a heavy emphasis on wealth as a basic symbol of success? Merton reasoned that people adapt in certain ways, by conforming to or deviating from such cultural expectations. In his **anomie theory of deviance,** he posited five basic forms of adaptation (see Table 4–1).

Conformity to social norms, the most common adaptation in Merton's typology, is the opposite of deviance. It involves acceptance of both the overall societal goal ("become affluent") and the approved means ("work hard"). In Merton's view, there must be some consensus regarding accepted cultural goals and legitimate means for attaining them. Without such consensus, societies could exist only as collectives of people rather than as unified cultures, and might experience continual chaos.

Of course, in a varied society such as that of the United States, conformity is not universal. For example, the means for realizing objectives are not equally distributed. People in the lower social classes often identify with the same goals as those of more powerful and affluent citizens, yet they lack equal access to high-quality education and training for skilled work. Moreover, even within a society, institutionalized means for realizing objectives vary. For instance, it is legal to gain money through roulette or poker in Nevada, but not in neighboring California.

You are a young person growing up in a poor neighborhood. You yearn for the flashy, expensive lifestyle you see on *The Apprentice* or MTV. How will you get it?

Table 4–1 Merton's Modes of Individual Adaptation

Mode	Institutionalized Means (Hard Work)	Societal Goal (Acquisition of Wealth)
Nondeviant		
Conformity	+	+
Deviant		
Innovation	–	+
Ritualism	+	–
Retreatism	–	–
Rebellion	±	±

NOTE: + indicates acceptance; – indicates rejection; ± indicates replacement with new means and goals.

SOURCE: Merton 1968:194.

The other four types of behavior represented in Table 4–1 all involve some departure from conformity. The "innovator" accepts society's goals but pursues them with means regarded as improper. For example, a professional thief who specializes in safecracking may see his criminal lifestyle as an adaptation to the goal of material success.

In Merton's typology, the "ritualist" has abandoned the goal of material success and become compulsively committed to the institutional means. Work becomes simply a way of life rather than a means to achieving success. An example is the bureaucratic official who blindly applies rules and regulations without remembering the larger goals of an organization. Such would be true of a welfare caseworker who refuses to assist a homeless family because their last apartment was in another district.

The "retreatist," as described by Merton, has basically withdrawn (or "retreated") from both the goals *and* the means of society. In the United States, drug addicts and vagrants are typically portrayed as retreatists. Some social workers worry that adolescents who are addicted to alcohol will become retreatists at an early age.

The final adaptation identified by Merton reflects people's attempts to create a new social structure. The "rebel" who feels alienated from dominant means and goals may seek a dramatically different social order. Members of a revolutionary political organization, such as the Irish Republican Army (IRA) or right-wing militia groups, can be categorized as rebels according to Merton's model.

Merton's theory, though popular, has had relatively few applications. Little effort has been made to determine to what extent all acts of deviance can be accounted for by his five modes. Moreover, while Merton's theory is useful in examining certain types of behavior, such as illegal gambling by disadvantaged "innovators," his formulation fails to explain key differences in crime rates. Why, for example, do some disadvantaged groups have lower rates of reported crime than others? Why do many people reject criminal activity as a viable alternative? Merton's theory of deviance does not answer such questions easily (Clinard and Miller 1998).

Still, Merton has made a key contribution to the sociological understanding of deviance by pointing out that deviants (such as innovators and ritualists) share a great deal with conforming people. The convicted felon may hold many of the same aspirations as people with no criminal background. Thus, the theory helps us to understand deviance as socially created behavior, rather than as the result of momentary pathological impulses.

INTERACTIONIST PERSPECTIVE

The functionalist approach to deviance explains why rule violation continues to exist in societies, despite pressure to conform and obey. However, functionalists do not indicate how a given person comes to commit a deviant act, or why on some occasions crimes do or do not occur. The emphasis on everyday behavior that is the focus of the interactionist perspective is reflected in two explanations of crime: cultural transmission and routine activities theory.

Cultural Transmission. In suburban Los Angeles, some White teenagers attempt to achieve fame in a subculture of "taggers." These young people "tag" (spray graffiti on) poles, utility boxes, bridges, and freeway signs throughout the San Fernando Valley. While law enforcement officials prefer to view them as "visual terrorists," taggers gain respect from their peers by being "up the most" on prominent walls and billboards or by displaying the flashiest styles. Even parents may tolerate or endorse such deviant behavior, declaring, "At least my kid's not shooting people. He's still alive" (Wooden 1995:124).

These teenagers demonstrate that humans *learn* how to behave in social situations, whether properly or improperly. There is no natural, innate manner in which people interact with one another. Though these simple ideas are not disputed today, such was not the case when sociologist Edwin Sutherland (1883–1950) first advanced the argument that an individual undergoes the same basic socialization process whether learning conforming or deviant acts.

Sutherland, whose ideas have been the dominating force in criminology, drew on the ***cultural transmission*** school, which emphasizes that one learns criminal behavior through social interactions. Such learning includes not only the techniques of lawbreaking (for example, how to break into a car quickly and quietly) but also the motives, drives, and rationalizations of criminals. The cultural transmission approach can also be used to explain the behavior of those who habitually abuse alcohol or drugs.

Sutherland maintained that people acquire their definitions of proper and improper behavior through interactions with a primary group and significant others. He used the term ***differential association*** to describe the process through which exposure to attitudes *favorable* to criminal acts leads to rule violations. Research suggests that this process also applies to such noncriminal deviant acts as smoking, truancy, and early sexual behavior (Jackson et al. 1986).

To what extent will a given person engage in activity regarded as proper or improper? For each individual, it will depend on the frequency, duration, and importance of two types of social interactions: those that endorse deviant behavior and those that promote acceptance of social norms. People are more likely to engage in norm-defying behavior if they are part of a group or subculture that stresses deviant values, such as a street gang.

Sutherland offers the example of a boy who is sociable, outgoing, and athletic and who lives in an area with a high delinquency rate. The youth is very likely to come into contact with peers who commit acts of vandalism, fail to attend school, and so forth, and may come to adopt such behavior. However, an introverted boy living in the same neighborhood may stay away from his peers and avoid delinquency. In another community, an outgoing and athletic boy may join a Little League baseball team or a scout troup because of his interactions with peers. Thus, Sutherland views deviant behavior as the result of the types of groups to which one belongs and the kinds of friendships one has with others (Sutherland and Cressey 1978).

According to critics, though the cultural transmission approach may explain the deviant behavior of juvenile delinquents or graffiti artists, it fails to explain the conduct of the first-time impulsive shoplifter or the impoverished person who steals out of necessity. While the theory is not a precise statement of the process through which one becomes a criminal, it does stress the paramount role of social interaction in increasing a person's motivation to engage in deviant behavior (Cressey 1960; Jackson et al. 1986; Sutherland and Cressey 1978).

Routine Activities Theory.   Another, more recent interactionist explanation stresses the requisite conditions for a crime or deviant act to occur: there must be at the same time and in the same place a perpetrator, a victim, and/or an object of property. *Routine activities theory,* proposed by Marcus Felson, contends that criminal victimization increases when motivated offenders and suitable targets converge. It goes without saying that you cannot have car theft without automobiles, but the greater availability of more valuable automobiles to potential thieves *heightens* the likelihood that such a crime will occur. Campus and airport parking lots, where vehicles may be left in isolated locations for long periods, represent a new target for crime unknown just a generation ago. Routine activity of this nature can occur even in the home. If a parent keeps a number of liquor bottles in an easily accessed place, juveniles can siphon off the contents without attracting attention to their "crime." The theory derives its name from the fact that the elements of a criminal or deviant act come together in normal, legal, and routine activities. It is interactionist because of its emphasis on everyday behavior and social interaction.

Advocates of this theory see it as a powerful explanation for the rise in crime over the last 50 years. That is, routine activity has changed to make crime more likely. Homes left vacant during the day or during long vacations are now more accessible as targets of crime. The greater presence of highly portable consumer goods, such as video equipment and computers, is another change that makes crime more likely (Cohen and Felson 1979; Felson 2002).

Some significant research supports the routine activities theory. For example, studies of the aftermath of Hurricane Andrew in Florida in 1992 show that certain crimes increased as citizens and their property became more vulnerable. Studies of urban crime have documented the existence of "hot spots," such as tourist destinations, where people are more likely to be victimized because of their routine comings and goings (Cromwell et al. 1995; Sherman et al. 1989).

LABELING THEORY

The Saints and Roughnecks were two groups of high school males continually engaged in excessive drinking, reckless driving, truancy, petty theft, and vandalism. There the similarity ended. None of the Saints was ever arrested, but every Roughneck was frequently in trouble with police and townspeople. Why the disparity in their treatment? On the basis of his observation research in their high school, sociologist William Chambliss (1973) concluded that social class played an important role in the varying fortunes of the two groups.

The Saints hid behind a facade of respectability. They came from "good families," were active in school organizations, planned on attending college, and received good grades. People generally viewed their delinquent acts as isolated cases of "sowing wild oats." By contrast, the Roughnecks had no such aura of respectability. They drove around town in beat-up cars, were generally unsuccessful in school, and aroused suspicion no matter what they did.

We can understand such discrepancies by using an approach to deviance known as *labeling theory.* Unlike Sutherland's work, labeling theory does not focus on why some individuals come to commit deviant acts. Instead, it attempts to explain why certain people (such as the Roughnecks) are *viewed* as deviants, delinquents, "bad kids," "losers," and criminals, while others whose behavior is similar (such as the Saints) are not seen in such harsh terms. Reflecting the contribution of interactionist theorists, labeling theory emphasizes how a person comes to be labeled as deviant or to accept that label. Sociologist Howard Becker (1963:9; 1964), who popularized this approach, summed it up with this statement: "Deviant behavior is behavior that people so label."

Labeling theory is also called the *societal-reaction approach,* reminding us that it is the *response* to an act, not the behavior itself, that determines deviance. For example, studies have shown that some school personnel and therapists expand educational programs designed for learning-disabled students to include those with behavioral problems. Consequently, a "troublemaker" can be improperly labeled as learning-disabled, and vice versa.

Traditionally, research on deviance has focused on people who violate social norms. In contrast, labeling theory focuses on police, probation officers, psychiatrists, judges, teachers, employers, school officials, and other regulators of social control. These agents, it is argued, play a significant role in creating the deviant identity by designating certain people (and not others) as "deviant." An important aspect of labeling theory is the recognition that some individuals or groups have the power to *define* labels and apply them to others. This view ties into the conflict perspective's emphasis on the social significance of power.

In recent years the practice of *racial profiling,* in which people are identified as criminal suspects purely on the basis of their race, has come under public scrutiny. Studies confirm the public's suspicions that in some jurisdictions, police officers are much more likely to stop African American males than White males for routine traffic violations, in the expectation of finding drugs or guns in their cars. Civil rights activists refer to these cases sarcastically as DWB violations ("Driving While Black"). After the September 11, 2001, attacks on the World Trade Center and the Pentagon, profiling took a new turn as people who appeared to be Arab or Muslim came under special scrutiny.

The labeling approach does not fully explain why certain people accept a label and others reject it. In fact, this perspective may exaggerate the ease with which societal judgments can alter our self-images. Labeling theorists do suggest, however, that how much power one has relative to others is important in determining a person's ability to resist an undesirable label. Competing approaches (including that of Sutherland) fail to explain why some deviants continue to be viewed as conformists rather than as violators of rules. According to Howard Becker (1973), labeling theory was not conceived as the *sole* explanation for deviance; its proponents merely hoped to focus more attention on the undeniably important actions of those people officially in charge of defining deviance (N. Davis 1975; compare with Cullen and Cullen 1978).

Use Your Sociological Imagination

You are a teacher. What kinds of labels freely used in educational circles might be attached to your students?

CONFLICT THEORY

Conflict theorists point out that people with power protect their own interests and define deviance to suit their own needs. Sociologist Richard Quinney (1974, 1979, 1980) is a leading exponent of the view that the criminal justice system serves the interests of the powerful. Crime, according to Quinney (1970), is a definition of conduct created by authorized agents of social control—such as legislators and law enforcement officers—in a politically organized society. Quinney and other conflict theorists argue that lawmaking is often an attempt by the powerful to coerce others into their own morality (see also Spitzer 1975).

Conflict theory helps to explain why our society has laws against gambling, drug usage, and prostitution, many of which are violated on a massive scale. (We will examine these "victimless crimes" later in the chapter.) According to the conflict school, criminal law does not represent a consistent application of societal values, but instead reflects competing values and interests. Thus, marijuana is outlawed in the United States because it is alleged to be harmful to users, yet cigarettes and alcohol are sold legally almost everywhere.

Conflict theorists also contend that the entire criminal justice system of the United States treats suspects differently on the basis of their racial, ethnic, or social class background. In fact, researchers have found that discretionary differences in the way social control is exercised put deprived African Americans and Hispanics at a disadvantage in the justice system, both as juveniles and as adults (Hawkins et al. 2000; Steffensmeier and Demuth 2000).

The perspective advanced by labeling and conflict theorists forms quite a contrast to the functionalist approach to deviance. Functionalists view standards of deviant behavior as merely reflecting cultural norms, whereas conflict and labeling theorists point out that the most powerful groups in a society can shape laws and standards and determine who is (or is not) prosecuted as a criminal. Those groups would be unlikely to apply the label "deviant" to the corporate executive whose decisions lead to large-scale environmental pollution. In the opinion of conflict theorists, agents of social control and powerful groups can generally impose their own self-serving definitions of deviance on the general public.

FEMINIST PERSPECTIVE

For many years, any husband who forced his wife to have sexual intercourse—without her consent and against her will—was not legally considered to have committed rape. Laws defined rape as pertaining only to sexual relations between people who were not married to each other. Those laws reflected the overwhelmingly male composition of state legislatures at the time.

It took repeated protests by feminist organizations to change the criminal law defining rape. Husbands in all 50 states can now be prosecuted under some or most circumstances for the rape of their wives. There remain alarming exceptions: for example, in Tennessee a husband may legally use force or coercion to rape his wife as long as no weapon is present and he has not inflicted "serious bodily harm." Despite such exceptions, the rise of the women's movement has unquestionably led to important changes in societal notions of criminality. For example, judges, legislators, and police officers now view wife battering and other forms of domestic violence as serious crimes (National Center on Women and Family Law 1996).

When it comes to crime and to deviance in general, society tends to treat women in a stereotypical fashion. For example, consider how women who have many and frequent sexual partners are more likely than men who are promiscuous to be viewed with scorn. Cultural views and attitudes toward women influence how they are perceived and labeled. In addition, feminist theorists such as Freda Adler and Meda Chesney-Lind emphasize that deviance, including crime, tends to flow from economic relationships.

Table 4–2 on page 102 summarizes the various approaches sociologists have used in studying deviance.

Crime

Crime is a violation of criminal law for which some governmental authority applies formal penalties. It represents a deviation from formal social norms administered by the state. Laws divide crimes into various categories, depending on the severity of the offense, the age of the

summingUP

Table 4-2 Approaches to Deviance

Approach	Perspective	Proponent	Emphasis
Anomie	Functionalist	Émile Durkheim Robert Merton	Adaptation to societal norms
Cultural transmission/ differential association	Interactionist	Edwin Sutherland	Patterns learned through others
Routine activities	Interactionist	Marcus Felson	Impact of the social environment
Labeling/social constructionist	Interactionist	Howard Becker	Societal response to acts
Conflict	Conflict	Howard Quinney	Dominance by authorized agents Discretionary justice
Feminist	Conflict/feminist	Freda Adler Meda Chesney-Lind	Role of gender Women as victims and perpetrators

offender, the potential punishment that can be levied, and the court that holds jurisdiction over the case.

Over 1.3 million violent crimes were reported in the United States in 2003, including more than 16,500 homicides. The key ingredients in the incidence of street crime appear to have been drug use and the widespread presence of firearms. According to the FBI, 19 percent of all reported aggravated assaults, 42 percent of reported robberies, and 67 percent of reported murders involved a firearm. Even with a recent decline in major crime in the United States, current levels exceed the levels experienced in the 1960s (Department of Justice 2003).

TYPES OF CRIME

Rather than relying solely on legal categories, sociologists classify crimes in terms of how they are committed and how society views the offenses. In this section we will examine four types of crime differentiated by sociologists: professional crime, organized crime, white-collar crime, and "victimless crimes."

Professional Crime. Although the adage "crime doesn't pay" is familiar, many people do make a career of illegal activities. A *professional criminal* (or career criminal) is a person who pursues crime as a day-to-day occupation, developing skilled techniques and enjoying a certain degree of status among other criminals. Some professional criminals specialize in burglary, safecracking, hijacking of cargo, pickpocketing, and shoplifting. Such people have acquired skills that reduce the likelihood of arrest, conviction, and imprisonment. As a result, they may have long careers in their chosen "professions."

Edwin Sutherland (1937) offered pioneering insights into the behavior of professional criminals by publishing an annotated account written by a professional thief. Unlike the person who engages in crime only once or twice, professional thieves make a business of stealing. They devote their entire working time to planning and executing crimes, and sometimes travel across the nation to pursue their "professional duties." Like people in regular occupations, professional thieves consult with their colleagues concerning their work, becoming part of a subculture of similarly occupied individuals. They exchange information on good places to burglarize, outlets for stolen goods, and ways of securing bail bonds.

Organized Crime. A 1978 government report takes three pages to define the term *organized crime.* For our purposes, we will consider **organized crime** to be the work of a group that regulates relations between various criminal enterprises involved in various illegal activities, including the smuggling and sale of drugs, prostitution, and gambling. Organized crime dominates the world of illegal business just as large corporations dominate the conventional business world. It allocates territory, sets prices for goods and services, and arbitrates internal disputes. A secret, conspiratorial activity that generally evades law enforcement, it takes over legitimate businesses, gains influence over labor unions, corrupts public officials, intimidates witnesses in criminal trials, and even "taxes" merchants in exchange for "protection" (National Advisory Commission on Criminal Justice 1976).

There has always been a global element in organized crime. But law enforcement officials and policymakers now acknowledge the emergence of a new form of organized crime, one that takes advantage of advances in electronic communications. *Transnational* organized crime includes drug and arms smuggling, money laundering, and trafficking in illegal immigrants and stolen goods, such as automobiles (Office of Justice Programs 1999).

White-Collar and Technology-Based Crime. Income tax evasion, stock manipulation, consumer fraud, bribery and extraction of "kickbacks," embezzlement, and misrepresentation in advertising—these are all examples of **white-collar crime,** illegal acts committed in the course of business activities, often by affluent, "respectable" people. Edwin Sutherland (1949, 1983) likened these crimes to organized crime because they are often perpetrated through people's occupational roles (Friedrichs 1998).

A new type of white-collar crime has emerged in recent decades: computer crime. The use of high technology allows criminals to carry out embezzlement or electronic fraud, often leaving few traces, or to gain access to a company's inventory without leaving home. In a 2004 study

"BUT IF WE GO BACK TO SCHOOL AND GET A GOOD EDUCATION, THINK OF ALL THE DOORS IT'LL OPEN TO WHITE-COLLAR CRIME."

by the FBI and the Computer Security Institute, 74 percent of companies relying on computer systems reported some type of related crime. While computer viruses were the most common, nearly one out of five companies reported embezzlement, fraud, or theft (Rantala 2004).

Sutherland (1940) coined the term *white-collar crime* in 1939 to refer to acts by individuals, but the term has been broadened recently to include offenses by businesses and corporations. *Corporate crime,* or any act by a corporation that is punishable by the government, takes many forms and includes individuals, organizations, and institutions among its victims. Corporations may engage in anticompetitive behavior, environmental pollution, tax fraud, accounting fraud, stock fraud and manipulation, the production of unsafe goods, bribery and corruption, and worker health and safety violations (Simpson 1993).

Given the economic and social costs of white-collar crime, one might expect the criminal justice system to take this problem quite seriously. Yet white-collar offenders are more likely to receive fines than prison sentences. Conviction for such illegal acts does not generally harm a person's reputation and career aspirations nearly so much as conviction for street crime would. Apparently, the label "white-collar criminal" does not carry the stigma of the label "felon convicted of a violent crime."

Conflict theorists don't find such differential labeling and treatment surprising. They argue that the criminal justice system largely disregards the white-collar crimes of the affluent, while focusing instead on crimes committed by the poor. If an offender holds a position of status and influence, his or her crime is treated as less serious, and the sanction is much more lenient (Maguire 1988).

Victimless Crimes.   White-collar and street crimes endanger people's economic or personal well-being against their will (or without their direct knowledge). By contrast, sociologists use the term *victimless crime* to describe the willing exchange among adults of widely desired, but illegal, goods and services. For example, prostitution is widely regarded as a victimless crime (Schur 1965, 1985).

As a newspaper editor, how might you treat front-page stories about corporate crime differently from those about violent crime?

Some activists are working to decriminalize many of these illegal practices. Supporters of decriminalization are troubled by the attempt to legislate a moral code of behavior for adults. In their view, it is impossible to prevent prostitution, drug abuse, gambling, and other victimless crimes. The already overburdened criminal justice system should instead devote its resources to "street crimes" and other offenses with obvious victims.

Despite the wide use of the term *victimless crime,* many people object to the notion that there is no victim other than the offender in such crimes. Excessive drinking, compulsive gambling, and illegal drug use contribute to an enormous amount of personal and property damage. A person with a drinking problem can become abusive to a spouse or children; a compulsive gambler or drug user may steal to pursue his obsession. And feminist sociologists contend that prostitution, as well as the more disturbing aspects of pornography, reinforce the misconception that women are "toys" who can be treated as objects rather than people. According to critics of decriminalization, society must not give tacit approval to conduct that has such harmful consequences.

The controversy over decriminalization reminds us of the important insights of labeling and conflict theorists presented earlier. Underlying this debate are two interesting questions: Who has the power to define gambling, prostitution, and public drunkenness as "crimes"? And who has the power to label such behaviors as "victimless"? The answer, in both cases, is generally the state legislatures, and sometimes the police and the courts.

CRIME STATISTICS

Crime statistics are not as accurate as social scientists would like. However, since they relate to an issue of grave concern to the people of the United States, they are frequently cited as if they were completely reliable. Such data do serve as an indicator of police activity, as well as the approximate level of certain crimes. Yet it would be a mistake to interpret these data as an exact representation of the incidence of crime.

Understanding Crime Statistics. Reported crime is very high in the United States, and the public continues to regard crime as a major social problem. However, there has recently been a significant decline in violent crime nationwide following many years of increases. A number of explanations have been offered, including:

- A booming economy and falling unemployment rates through most of the 1990s.
- Community-oriented policing and crime prevention programs.
- New gun control laws.
- A massive increase in the prison population, which at least prevents inmates from committing crimes outside the prison.

It remains to be seen whether this pattern will continue. But even with current declines, reported crimes remain well above those of other nations, and exceed the reported rates in the United States of just 20 years earlier. Feminist scholars draw our attention to one significant variation: the proportion of major crimes committed by women has increased. In a recent 10-year period (1993–2003), female arrests for major reported crimes increased 12 percent, while comparable male arrests declined about 7 percent (Department of Justice 2004:275).

Sociologists have several ways of measuring crime. Historically, they have relied on police data, but underreporting has always been a problem with such measures. Because members of racial and ethnic minority groups often distrust law enforcement agencies, they may not contact the police. Feminist sociologists and others have noted that many women do not report rape or spousal abuse out of fear that officials will regard the crime as their fault.

Partly because of the deficiencies of official statistics, the National Crime Victimization Survey was initiated in 1972. In compiling this report, the Bureau of Justice Statistics seeks information from law enforcement agencies, but also interviews members of over 42,000 households annually to ask if they have been victims of specific crimes during the preceding year. In general, those who conduct *victimization surveys* question ordinary people, not police officers, to determine whether they have been victims of crime. As shown in Figure 4–1, data from these surveys reveal a fluctuating crime rate, with significant declines in both the 1980s and 1990s.

Unfortunately, like other crime data, victimization surveys have particular limitations. They require that victims understand what has happened to them and be willing to disclose such information to interviewers. Fraud, income tax evasion, and blackmail are examples of crimes that are unlikely to be reported in victimization studies. Nevertheless, 92 percent of all households have been willing to cooperate with investigators for the National Crime Victimization Survey (Catalano 2004).

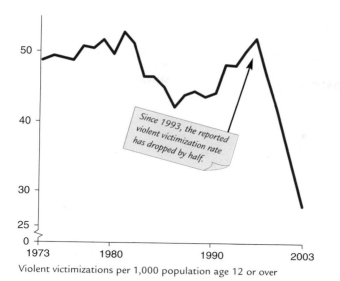

Figure 4–1
*Victimization Rates,
1973–2003* SOURCE:
Catalano 2004.

Since 1993, the reported violent victimization rate has dropped by half.

Violent victimizations per 1,000 population age 12 or over

International Crime Rates. If developing reliable crime data in the United States is difficult, making useful cross-national comparisons is even more difficult. Nevertheless, with some care, we can offer preliminary conclusions about how crime rates differ around the world.

During the 1980s and 1990s, violent crimes were much more common in the United States than in Western Europe. Murders, rapes, and robberies were reported to the police at much higher rates in the United States. Yet the incidence of certain other types of crime appears to be higher elsewhere. For example, England, Italy, Australia, and New Zealand all have higher rates of car theft than the United States (International Crime Victim Survey 2001).

Why are violent crime rates so much higher in the United States? Sociologist Elliot Currie (1985, 1998) has suggested that our society places greater emphasis on individual economic achievement than other societies. At the same time, many observers have noted that the culture of the United States has long tolerated, if not condoned, many forms of violence. Coupled with sharp disparities between poor and affluent citizens, significant unemployment, and substantial alcohol and drug abuse, all these factors combine to produce a climate conducive to crime.

Disturbing increases in violent crime are evident in other Western societies, however. For example, crime has skyrocketed in Russia since the overthrow of Communist party rule (with its strict controls on guns and criminals) in 1991. In 1988, there were fewer than 260 homicides in Moscow; now there are more than 1,000 homicides per year. Organized crime has filled a power vacuum there since the end of communism; one result is that gangland shootouts and premeditated "contract hits" have become more common. Some prominent reformist politicians have been targeted as well. Russia is the only nation in the world that incarcerates a higher proportion of its citizens than the United States. On a typical day the nation imprisons 580 per 100,000 of its adults, compared to 550 in the United States, fewer than 100 in Mexico or Britain, and only 16 in Greece (Currie 1998; Shinkai and Zvekic 1999).

Sociology Matters

Sociology matters because it explains why you accept certain social norms almost without thinking—and why you pay a price if you break those norms.

- What social norms were you expected to conform to when you became a student at your college or university? Are they similar to or different from the norms you grew up with?

- What happens to students who do not conform to accepted social norms? Is social control on your campus stricter or more lenient than social control in other parts of society?

- Is crime a problem on your campus? If so, what social forces might underlie it?

CHAPTER RESOURCES

Summary

Conformity and **deviance** are two ways in which people respond to real or imagined pressure from others. This chapter examined the mechanisms of **social control** that society uses to encourage conformity to social norms. We defined deviance and offered several theories to explain its existence. The chapter closed with a discussion of **crime** and statistics on criminal activity in the United States and other nations.

1. Stanley Milgram defined **conformity** as going along with one's peers. **Obedience,** on the other hand, means compliance with higher authorities in a hierarchical structure.

2. Some norms are so important to a society, they are formalized in **law.** Socialization is the primary source of both conformity and obedience to law.

3. **Deviance** is behavior that violates any social norm, whether it concerns conduct or personal appearance. Some forms of deviance carry a negative social **stigma,** while others are more or less accepted.

4. The sociologist Robert Merton noted that people who engage in deviant behavior share many of the same goals and values as people who conform to social norms, though they may differ in the means by which they pursue their goals. Merton's theory is called the **anomie theory of deviance.**

5. The interactionist theorist Edwin Sutherland believed that people learn criminal behavior by associating with others, an approach called **cultural transmission.** In his theory of **differential association,** Sutherland proposed that deviance results from a person's exposure to individuals who approve of criminal acts.

6. Other interactionists stress that for a crime to occur, a motivated offender must come together with a vulnerable target during the course of their usual activities, an approach called **routine activities theory.**

7. **Labeling theory** emphasizes that society brands some people who engage in a behavior as deviant, but not others, based largely on a person's social class, race, or ethnicity. This theory of deviance is called the **societal-reaction approach.**

8. Conflict theorists stress that laws and the sanctions imposed on criminals for breaking them reflect the interests of the powerful. Feminists emphasize that in crimes involving women, such as rape and prostitution, crime is defined differently, and those involved are treated differently, depending on their gender.

9. **Crime** is a violation of criminal law for which some governmental authority applies formal penalties. Sociologists differentiate among **professional crime, organized crime, white-collar crime,** and **victimless crimes** such as drug use and prostitution.

10. Crime statistics are among the least reliable social data, partly because many crimes are not reported to law enforcement agencies. Rates of violent crime are higher in the United States than in other Western societies.

www.mhhe.com/schaefersm2
Visit the Online Learning Center for *Sociology Matters* to access quizzes, review activities, and other learning tools.

Key Terms

anomie, 94

anomie theory of deviance, 95

conformity, 89

crime, 101

cultural transmission, 97

deviance, 92

differential association, 97

formal social control, 91

informal social control, 90

labeling theory, 99

law, 91

obedience, 89

organized crime, 103

professional criminal, 102

routine activities theory, 98

sanction, 88

social control, 88

societal-reaction approach, 99

stigma, 92

victimization survey, 106

victimless crime, 105

white-collar crime, 103

Stratification in the United States and Global Inequality

Understanding Stratification

Stratification by Social Class

Social Mobility

Global Inequality

Social class can be a matter of life and death. In 1912, when the British luxury liner *Titanic* hit an iceberg and sank off the coast of Newfoundland, only 705 of the 2,207 passengers and crew members—about one out of every three—survived. Faced with a shortage of lifeboats, the crew spent 45 minutes ushering first- and second-class passengers to safety before notifying third-class passengers of the need to abandon ship. By that time, most of the lifeboats were full. The result: about 62 percent of the first-class passengers lived to tell of the great maritime disaster, compared to only 25 percent of the third-class passengers (Butler 1998; Crouse 1999; Riding 1998).

The condition in which members of a society enjoy different amounts of wealth, prestige, or power is termed *social inequality.* Every society manifests some degree of social inequality. Sociologists refer to the structured ranking of entire groups of people that perpetuates unequal economic rewards and power as *stratification.* In industrial societies, these unequal rewards are evident both in people's *income*—in their salaries and wages—and in their *wealth*—in material assets such as land, stocks, and other property. But the unequal rewards of stratification can also be seen in the mortality rates of different groups, as the *Titanic*'s survivors list attests.

111

In this chapter we will examine three stratification systems, paying particular attention to the theories of Karl Marx and Max Weber. We will see how a person's social class affects his or her opportunities, including the chance to move up the social ladder. And we will look at stratification in developing countries, where multinational corporations based in developed nations have been charged with exploiting those who work in their factories.

Understanding Stratification

Not all societies are stratified in the same way. Sociologists have studied stratification in ancient as well as modern times, in Western and non-Western societies. In the following section we will compare four different general systems of stratification. Then we will discuss several theoretical approaches to stratification, its purpose and desirability.

SYSTEMS OF STRATIFICATION

Look at the four general systems of stratification examined here—slavery, castes, estates, and social classes—as ideal types useful for purposes of analysis. Any stratification system may include elements of more than one type. For example, prior to the Civil War, you could find in the southern states of the United States social classes dividing Whites as well as the institutionalized enslavement of Blacks.

To understand these systems better, it may be helpful to review the distinction between *achieved status* and *ascribed status,* discussed in Chapter 3. **Ascribed status** is a social position "assigned" to a person by society without regard for that person's unique talents or characteristics. By contrast, **achieved status** is a social position attained by a person largely through his or her own efforts. The two are closely linked. The nation's most affluent families generally inherit wealth and status, while many members of racial and ethnic minorities inherit disadvantaged status. Age and gender, as well, are ascribed statuses that influence a person's wealth and social position.

Slavery.   The most extreme form of legalized social inequality for individuals or groups is **slavery**. What distinguishes this oppressive system of stratification is that enslaved individuals are *owned* by other people, who treat these human beings as property, just as if they were household pets or appliances.

Slavery has varied in the way it has been practiced. In ancient Greece, the main source of slaves consisted of captives of war and piracy. Although succeeding generations could inherit slave status, it was not necessarily permanent. A person's status might change depending on which city-state happened to triumph in a military conflict. In effect, all citizens had the potential of becoming slaves or of being granted freedom, depending on the circumstances of history. By contrast, in the United States and Latin America, where slavery was an ascribed status, racial and legal barriers prevented the freeing of slaves.

Castes.   *Castes* are hereditary systems of rank, usually religiously dictated, that tend to be fixed and immobile. The caste system is generally associated with Hinduism in India and other countries. In India there are four major castes, called varnas. A fifth category of outcastes, referred to as untouchables, is considered to be so lowly and unclean as to have no place within this system of stratification. There are also many minor castes. Caste membership is an ascribed status (at birth, children automatically assume the same position as their parents). Each caste is quite sharply defined, and members are expected to marry within that caste.

In recent decades, industrialization and urbanization have taken their toll on India's rigid caste system. Many villagers have moved to urban areas, where their low-caste status is unknown. The anonymity of city life allows these families to take advantage of opportunities they would not otherwise have had, and eventually to move up the social ladder.

Estates.   A third type of stratification system, called *estates,* was associated with feudal societies during the Middle Ages. The **estate system,** or *feudalism,* required peasants to work land leased to them by nobles in exchange for military protection and other services. The basis for the system was the nobles' ownership of land, which was critical to their superior and privileged status. As in systems based on slavery and caste, inheritance of one's position largely defined the estate system. The nobles inherited their titles and property; the peasants were born to a subservient position in an agrarian society.

Social Classes.   A *class system* is a social ranking based primarily on economic position in which achieved characteristics can influence social mobility. In contrast to slavery and the caste and estate systems, the boundaries between classes are imprecisely defined; one can move from one stratum, or level, of society to another. Yet class systems maintain stable stratification hierarchies and patterns of class divisions, and they, too, are marked by unequal distribution of wealth and power.

Income inequality is a basic characteristic of a class system. In 2003, the median household income in the United States was $43,318. In other words, half of all households had higher incomes in that year and half had lower incomes. Yet this fact does not fully convey the income disparities in our society. In 2000, about 240,000 tax returns reported incomes in excess of $1 million. At the same time, about 20 million households reported incomes under $9,000. The people with the highest incomes, generally those heading private companies, earn well above even affluent wage earners. The compensation these CEOs receive is not necessarily linked to conventional measures of success. An analysis done in 2003 shows that the CEOs who received the largest salary increases were generally those who authorized the largest layoffs or oversaw the largest pension plan deficits (Anderson et al. 2003; Bureau of the Census 2003a:332; DeNavas-Walt et al. 2004:3).

Sociologist Daniel Rossides (1997) uses a five-class model to describe the class system of the United States: the upper class, the upper-middle class, the lower-middle class, the working class, and the lower class. Although the lines separating social classes in his model are not so sharp as the divisions between castes, he shows that members of the five classes differ significantly in ways other than just income level.

Rossides categorizes about 1 to 2 percent of the people of the United States as *upper class,* a group limited to the very wealthy. These people associate in exclusive clubs and social circles. By contrast, the *lower class,* consisting of approximately 20 to 25 percent of the population, disproportionately consists of Blacks, Hispanics, single mothers with dependent children, and people who cannot find regular work or must make do with low-paying work. This class lacks both wealth and income and is too weak politically to exercise significant power.

Both these classes, at opposite ends of the nation's social hierarchy, reflect the importance of ascribed status and achieved status. Ascribed statuses such as race and disability clearly influence a person's wealth and social position. Sociologist Richard Jenkins (1991) has researched how being disabled marginalizes a person in the labor market of the United States. People with disabilities are particularly vulnerable to unemployment, are often poorly paid, and in many cases occupy the lower rungs of the occupational ladder. Regardless of their actual performance on the job, the disabled are stigmatized as not "earning their keep." Such are the effects of ascribed status.

Sandwiched between the upper and lower classes in Rossides's model are the upper-middle class, the lower-middle class, and the working class. The *upper-middle class,* numbering about 10 to 15 percent of the population, is composed of professionals such as doctors, lawyers, and architects. They participate extensively in politics and take leadership roles in voluntary associations. The *lower-middle class,* which accounts for approximately 30 to 35 percent of the population, includes less affluent professionals (such as elementary school teachers and nurses), owners of small businesses, and a sizable number of clerical workers. While not all members of this varied class hold degrees from a college, they share the goal of sending their children there.

Rossides describes the *working class*—about 40 to 45 percent of the population—as people holding regular manual or blue-collar jobs. Certain members of this class, such as electricians, may have higher incomes than people in the lower-middle class. Yet even if they have achieved some degree of economic security, they tend to identify with manual workers and their long history of involvement in the labor movement of the United States. Of Rossides's five classes, the working class is declining noticeably in size. In the economy of the United States, service and technical jobs are replacing positions involved in the actual manufacturing or transportation of goods.

PERSPECTIVES ON STRATIFICATION

Sociologists have hotly debated stratification and social inequality and have reached varying conclusions. No theorist stressed the significance of class for society—and for social change—more strongly than Karl Marx. Marx viewed class differentiation as the crucial determinant of social, economic, and political inequality. By contrast, Max Weber questioned Marx's emphasis on the overriding importance of the economic sector and argued that stratification should be viewed as having many dimensions.

Karl Marx's View of Class Differentiation. Sociologist Leonard Beeghley (1978:1) aptly noted that "Karl Marx was both a revolutionary and a social scientist." Marx was concerned with stratification in all types of human societies, beginning with primitive agricultural tribes and continuing into feudalism. But his main focus was on the effects of economic inequality on all aspects of 19th-century Europe. The plight of the working class made him feel that it was imperative to strive for changes in the social class structure.

In Marx's view, social relations during any period of history depend on who controls the primary mode of economic production, such as land or factories. Differential access to scarce resources shapes the relationship between groups. Thus, under the estate system, most production was agricultural, and the land was owned by the nobility. Peasants had little choice but to work according to terms dictated by those who owned the land.

Using this type of analysis, Marx examined social relations within *capitalism*—an economic system in which the means of production are held largely in private hands, and the main incentive for economic activity is the accumulation of profits (Rosenberg 1991). Marx focused on the two classes that began to emerge as the estate system declined—the bourgeoisie and the proletariat. The *bourgeoisie,* or capitalist class, owns the means of production, such as factories and machinery; the *proletariat* is the working class. In capitalist societies, the members of the bourgeoisie maximize profit in competition with other firms. In the process, they exploit workers, who must exchange their labor for subsistence wages. In Marx's view, members of each class share a distinctive culture. He was most interested in the culture of the proletariat, but he also examined the ideology of the bourgeoisie, through which it justifies its dominance over workers.

According to Marx, exploitation of the proletariat will inevitably lead to the destruction of the capitalist system, because the workers will revolt. But first, the working class must develop *class consciousness*—a subjective awareness of common vested interests and the need for collective political action to bring about social change. Workers must often overcome what Marx termed *false consciousness,* or an attitude held by members of a class that does not accurately reflect its objective position. A worker with false consciousness may adopt an individualistic viewpoint toward capitalist exploitation ("*I* am being exploited by *my* boss"). By contrast, the class-conscious worker realizes that *all* workers are being exploited by the bourgeoisie and have a common stake in revolution.

For Karl Marx, class consciousness is part of a collective process in which the proletariat comes to identify the bourgeoisie as the source of its oppression. Revolutionary leaders will guide the proletariat in their class struggle. Ultimately, the proletariat will overthrow the rule of the bourgeoisie and the government (which Marx saw as representing the interests of capitalists) and eliminate private ownership of the means of production. In Marx's rather utopian view, classes and oppression will cease to exist in the postrevolutionary workers' state.

How accurate were Marx's predictions? He failed to anticipate the emergence of labor unions, whose power in collective bargaining weakens the stranglehold that capitalists maintain over workers. Moreover, as contemporary conflict theorists note, he did not foresee the extent to which political liberties and relative prosperity could contribute to "false consciousness." Many people have come to view themselves as individuals striving for improvement within "free" societies that offer substantial mobility, rather than as downtrodden members of a working class facing a collective fate. Finally, Marx did not predict that Communist party rule would be established and later overthrown in the former Soviet Union and Eastern Europe. Still, the Marxist approach to the study of class is useful in stressing the importance of stratification as a determinant of social behavior, and of the fundamental separation in many societies between two distinct groups, the rich and the poor.

Max Weber's View of Stratification.   Unlike Karl Marx, Max Weber insisted that no single characteristic (such as class) totally defines a person's position within the stratification system. Instead, writing in 1916, Weber identified three analytically distinct components of stratification: class, status, and power (Gerth and Mills 1958).

Weber used the term *class* to refer to a group of people who have a similar level of wealth and income. For example, certain workers in the United States try to support their families through minimum-wage jobs. According to Weber's definition, these wage earners constitute a class because they share the same economic position and fate. Although Weber agreed with Marx on the importance of this economic dimension of stratification, he argued that the actions of individuals and groups could not be understood *solely* in economic terms.

Weber used the term *status group* to refer to people who have the same prestige or lifestyle. An individual gains status through membership in a desirable group, such as the medical profession. But status is not the same as economic class standing. In our culture, a successful pickpocket may earn the same income as a college professor. Yet the thief is widely regarded as a member of a low-status group, whereas the professor holds high status.

For Weber, the third major component of stratification reflects a political dimension. *Power* is the ability to exercise one's will over others. In the United States, power stems from membership in particularly influential groups, such as corporate boards of directors, government bodies, and interest groups. Conflict theorists generally agree that two major sources of power—big business and government—are closely interrelated.

In Weber's view, then, each of us has not one rank in society but three. Our position in a stratification system reflects some combination of class, status, and power. Each factor influences the other two, and in fact the rankings on these three dimensions often tend to coincide. John F. Kennedy came from an extremely wealthy family, attended exclusive preparatory schools, graduated from Harvard University, and went on to become president of the United States. Like Kennedy, many people from affluent backgrounds achieve impressive status and power.

IS STRATIFICATION UNIVERSAL?

Must some members of society receive greater rewards than others? Do people need to feel socially and economically superior to others? Can social life be organized without structured inequality? These questions have been debated for centuries, especially among political activists. Utopian socialists, religious minorities, and members of recent countercultures have all attempted to establish communities that to some extent or other would abolish inequality in social relationships.

Social science research has found that inequality exists in all societies—even the simplest. For example, when anthropologist Gunnar Landtman ([1938] 1968) studied the Kiwai Papuans of New Guinea, he initially noticed little differentiation among them. Every man in the village did the same work and lived in similar housing. However, on closer inspection, Landtman observed that certain Papuans—the men who were warriors, harpooners, and sorcerers—were described as "a little more high" than others. By contrast, villagers who were female, unemployed, or unmarried were considered "down a little bit" and were barred from owning land.

Stratification is universal in that all societies maintain some form of social inequality among members. Depending on its values, a society may assign people to distinctive ranks based on their religious knowledge, skill in hunting, beauty, trading expertise, or ability to provide health care. But why has such inequality developed in human societies? And how much differentiation among people, if any, is actually essential?

Functionalist and conflict sociologists offer contrasting explanations for the existence and necessity of social stratification. Functionalists maintain that a differential system of rewards and punishments is necessary for the efficient operation of society. Conflict theorists argue that competition for scarce resources results in significant political, economic, and social inequality.

Functionalist View. Would people go to school for many years to become physicians if they could make as much money and gain as much respect working as street cleaners? Functionalists say no, which is partly why they believe that a stratified society is universal.

In the view of Kingsley Davis and Wilbert Moore (1945), society must distribute its members among a variety of social positions. It must not only make sure that these positions are filled but also see that they are staffed by people with the appropriate talents and abilities. Rewards, including money and prestige, are based on the importance of a position and the relative scarcity of qualified personnel. Yet this assessment often devalues work performed by certain segments of society, such as women's work as homemakers or in occupations traditionally filled by women, or low-status work in fast-food outlets.

Davis and Moore argue that stratification is universal and that social inequality is necessary so that people will be motivated to fill functionally important positions. But unequal rewards are not the only means of encouraging people to fill critical positions and occupations. Personal pleasure, intrinsic satisfaction, and value orientations also motivate people to enter particular careers. Functionalists agree but note that society must use some type of reward to motivate people to enter unpleasant or dangerous jobs and jobs that require a long training period. This response does not justify stratification systems in which status is largely inherited, such as slave, caste, or estate systems. Similarly, it is difficult to explain the high salaries our society offers to professional athletes or entertainers on the basis of how critical these jobs are to society's survival (Collins 1975; Kerbo 2003; Tumin 1953, 1985).

Even if stratification is inevitable, the functionalist explanation for differential rewards does not explain the wide disparity between the rich and the poor. Critics of the functionalist approach point out that the richest 10 percent of households account for 22 percent of the nation's income in Sweden, 25 percent in France, and 30 percent in the United States. In their view, the level of income inequality found in contemporary industrial societies cannot be defended—even though those societies have a legitimate need to fill certain key occupations (World Bank 2004a:60–62).

Conflict View. The writings of Karl Marx lie at the heart of conflict theory. Marx viewed history as a continuous struggle between the oppressors and the oppressed, one that would ultimately culminate in an egalitarian, classless society. In terms of stratification, he argued that the dominant class under capitalism—the bourgeoisie—manipulated the economic and political systems in order to maintain control over the exploited proletariat. Marx did not believe that stratification was inevitable, but he did see inequality and oppression as inherent in capitalism (Wright et al. 1982).

Like Marx, contemporary conflict theorists believe that human beings are prone to conflict over such scarce resources as wealth, status, and power. However, while Marx focused primarily on class conflict, more recent theorists have extended the analysis to include conflicts based on gender, race, age, and other dimensions. The British sociologist Ralf Dahrendorf has been one of the most influential contributors to the conflict approach.

Dahrendorf (1959) modified Marx's analysis of capitalist society to apply to *modern* capitalist societies. For Dahrendorf, social classes are groups of people who share common interests resulting from their authority relationships. In identifying the most powerful groups in society, he includes not only the bourgeoisie—the owners of the means of production—but also industrial managers, legislators, the judiciary, heads of the government bureaucracy, and others. In that respect, Dahrendorf has merged Marx's emphasis on class conflict with Weber's recognition that power is an important element of stratification (Cuff et al. 1990).

Conflict theorists, including Dahrendorf, contend that the powerful of today, like the bourgeoisie of Marx's time, want society to run smoothly so that they can enjoy their privileged positions. Because the status quo suits those with wealth, status, and power, they have a clear interest in preventing, minimizing, or controlling societal conflict. One way for the powerful to maintain the status quo is to define society's dominant ideology—the set of cultural beliefs and practices that supports powerful social, economic, and political interests. From a conflict perspective, society's most powerful groups and institutions control not only wealth and property, but the means of influencing people's cultural beliefs through religion, education, and the media (Abercrombie et al. 1980, 1990; Robertson 1988).

The powerful, such as leaders of government, also use limited social reforms to buy off the oppressed and reduce the danger of challenges to their dominance. For example, minimum wage laws and unemployment compensation unquestionably give some valuable assistance to needy men and women. Yet these reforms also serve to pacify those who might otherwise rebel. Of course, in the view of conflict theorists, such maneuvers can never entirely eliminate conflict, since workers will continue to demand equality, and the powerful will not give up their control of society.

Conflict theorists see stratification as a major source of societal tension and conflict. They do not agree with Davis and Moore that stratification is functional for a society or that it serves as a source of stability. Rather, conflict sociologists argue that stratification will inevitably lead to instability and social change. Table 5–1 (page 120) summarizes the conflict and functionalist perspectives on social stratification (Collins 1975; Coser 1977).

summingUP

Table 5–1 Two Major Perspectives on Social Stratification

	Functionalist	**Conflict**
Purpose of social stratification	Facilitates filling of social positions	Facilitates exploitation
Attitude toward social inequality	Necessary to some extent	Excessive and growing
Analysis of the wealthy	Talented and skilled, creating opportunities for others	Use the dominant ideology to further their own interests

Lenski's Viewpoint.   Let's return to the question posed earlier—Is stratification universal?—and consider the sociological response. Some form of differentiation is found in every culture, from the most primitive to the most advanced industrial societies of our time. Sociologist Gerhard Lenski, in his sociocultural evolution approach, described how economic systems change as their level of technology becomes more complex, beginning with hunting and gathering and culminating eventually with industrial society. In subsistence-based hunting-and-gathering societies, people focus on survival. While some inequality and differentiation is evident, a stratification system based on social class does not emerge because there is no real wealth to be claimed.

As a society advances in technology, it becomes capable of producing a considerable surplus of goods. The emergence of surplus resources greatly expands the possibilities for inequality in status, influence, and power and allows a well-defined, rigid social class system to develop. In order to minimize strikes, slowdowns, and industrial sabotage, the elites may share a portion of the economic surplus with the lower classes, but not enough to reduce their own power and privilege.

As Lenski argued, the allocation of surplus goods and services controlled by those with wealth, status, and power reinforces the social inequality that accompanies stratification systems. While this reward system may once have served the overall purposes of society, as functionalists contend, the same cannot be said for the large disparities separating the haves from the have-nots in current societies. In contemporary industrial society, the degree of social and economic inequality far exceeds the need to provide for goods and services (Lenski 1966; Nolan and Lenski 2004).

Stratification by Social Class

MEASURING SOCIAL CLASS

We assess how wealthy people are by looking at the cars they drive, the houses they live in, the clothes they wear, and so on. Yet it is not so easy to locate an individual within our social hierarchies as it would be in slavery, caste, or estate systems of stratification. To determine someone's class position, sociologists generally rely on the objective method.

Objective Method.   The *objective method* of measuring social class views class largely as a statistical category. Researchers assign individuals to social classes on the basis of criteria such as occupation, education, income, and place of residence. The key to the objective method is that the *researcher,* rather than the person being classified, identifies an individual's class position.

The first step in using this method is to decide what indicators or causal factors will be measured objectively, whether wealth, income, education, or occupation. The prestige ranking of occupations has proved to be a useful indicator of a person's class position. For one thing, it is much easier to determine accurately than income or wealth. The term *prestige* refers to the respect and admiration that an occupation holds in a society. "My daughter, the physicist" connotes something very different from "my daughter, the waitress." Prestige is independent of the particular individual who occupies a job, a characteristic that distinguishes it from esteem. *Esteem* refers to the reputation that a specific person has earned within an occupation. Therefore, one can say that the position of president of the United States has high prestige, even though it has been occupied by people with varying degrees of esteem. A hairdresser may have the esteem of his clients, but he lacks the prestige of a corporate president.

Table 5–2 (page 122) ranks the prestige of a number of occupations. In a series of national surveys, sociologists assigned prestige rankings to about 500 occupations, ranging from physician to newspaper vendor. The highest possible prestige score was 100; the lowest was 0. Physician, lawyer, dentist, and college professor were the most highly regarded occupations. Sociologists have used such data to assign prestige rankings to virtually all jobs, and have found a stability in rankings from 1925 to 1991. Similar studies in other countries have also developed useful prestige rankings for occupations (Hodge and Rossi 1964; Lin and Xie 1988; Treiman 1977).

Multiple Measures.   Another complication in measuring social class is that advances in statistical methods and computer technology have multiplied the factors used to define class under the objective method. No longer are sociologists limited to annual income and education in evaluating a person's class position. Today, studies use as criteria the value of homes, sources of income, assets, years in present occupation, neighborhoods, and considerations regarding dual careers. Adding these variables will not necessarily paint a different picture of class differentiation in the United States, but it does allow sociologists to measure class in a more complex and multidimensional way.

Whatever the technique used to measure class, the sociologist is interested in real and often dramatic differences in power, privilege, and

Table 5–2 Prestige Rankings of Occupations

Occupation	Score	Occupation	Score
Physician	86	Secretary	46
Lawyer	75	Insurance agent	45
Dentist	74	Bank teller	43
College professor	74	Nurse's aide	42
Architect	73	Farmer	40
Clergy	69	Correctional officer	40
Pharmacist	68	Receptionist	39
Registered nurse	66	Barber	36
High school teacher	66	Child care worker	35
Accountant	65	Hotel clerk	32
Airline pilot	60	Bus driver	32
Police officer and detective	60	Truck driver	30
Prekindergarten teacher	55	Salesworker (shoes)	28
Librarian	54	Garbage collector	28
Firefighter	53	Waiter and waitress	28
Social worker	52	Bartender	25
Electrician	51	Farm worker	23
Funeral director	49	Janitor	22
Mail carrier	47	Newspaper vendor	19

SOURCE: J. A. Davis et al. 2003.

opportunity in a society. The study of stratification is a study of inequality. Nowhere is this more evident than in the distribution of wealth and income.

WEALTH AND INCOME

By all measures, income in the United States is distributed unevenly. Nobel Prize–winning economist Paul Samuelson has described the situation in the following words: "If we made an income pyramid out of building blocks, with each layer portraying $500 of income, the peak would be far higher than Mount Everest, but most people would be within a few feet of the ground" (P. Samuelson and Nordhaus 2005:383).

Recent data support Samuelson's analogy. Figure 5–1 shows the distribution of U.S. income for 2003 in the form of a very tall needle-nosed pyramid. In that year those fortunate Americans who received $1 million or more in income formed a very select group representing only 0.5

percent of the population. The top 20 percent of the nation's population received incomes of $86,867 or more. In contrast, members of the bottom fifth of the nation's population received just $17,984 or less. Note the bottom-heavy nature of the income distribution: except at the base of the graph, the lower the income level, the greater the percentage of the population receiving that income (DeNavas-Walt et al. 2004:8).

There has been a modest redistribution of income in the United States over the past 70 years. From 1929 through 1970, the government's economic and tax policies shifted some income to the poor. However, in the last three decades—especially the 1980s—federal tax policies have favored the affluent. Moreover, while the salaries of highly skilled workers and professionals have continued to rise, the wages of less skilled workers have *decreased* when controlled for inflation. As a result, the Census Bureau reports that regardless of the measure used, income inequality rose substantially from 1967 to the end of the century.

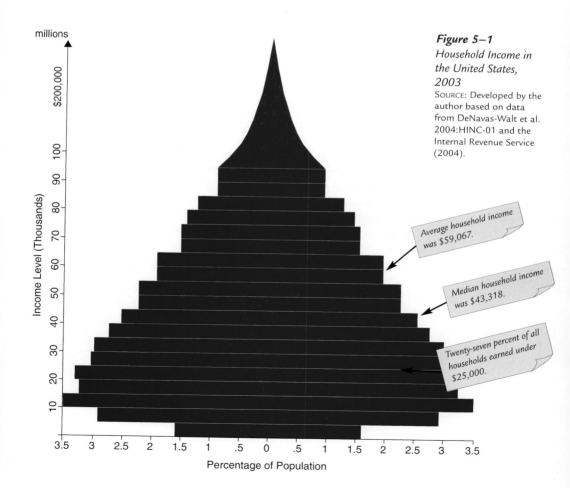

Figure 5–1

Household Income in the United States, 2003

SOURCE: Developed by the author based on data from DeNavas-Walt et al. 2004:HINC-01 and the Internal Revenue Service (2004).

Average household income was $59,067.

Median household income was $43,318.

Twenty-seven percent of all households earned under $25,000.

Survey data show that only 38 percent of people in the United States believe that government should take steps to reduce the income disparity between the rich and the poor. By contrast, 80 percent of people in Italy, 66 percent in Germany, and 65 percent in Great Britain support governmental efforts to reduce income inequality. It is not surprising, then, that many European countries provide more extensive "safety nets" to assist and protect the disadvantaged. The strong cultural value placed on individualism in the United States leads to greater potential for both economic success and failure (Lipset 1996).

In the United States, wealth is much more unevenly distributed than income. As Figure 5–2 shows, in 1997, the richest fifth of the population held 84.5 percent of the nation's wealth. Government data for that year indicate that more than 1 out of every 100 households had assets over $2.4 million, while one-fifth of all households were in debt and therefore had a negative net worth. Researchers have also found a dramatic disparity in wealth between African Americans and Whites. This disparity is evident even when educational backgrounds are held constant: the households of college-educated Whites have about three times as much wealth as the households of college-educated Blacks (Oliver and Shapiro 1995; Wolff 2002).

POVERTY

Approximately one out of every nine people in the United States lives below the poverty line established by the federal government. In 2003, 35.9 million people were living in poverty. The economic boom of the 1990s passed these people by. A Bureau of the Census report showed that one in five households had trouble meeting basic needs—everything from paying the utility bills to buying dinner.

One contributor to the United States' high poverty rate has been the large number of workers employed at minimum wage. As Figure 5–3 shows, the federal government has raised the minimum wage over the

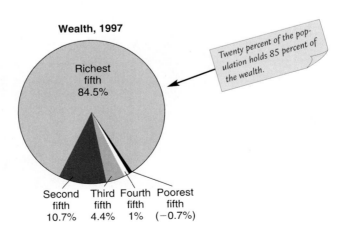

Figure 5–2

Distribution of Wealth in the United States
NOTE: *Data do not add to 100 percent due to rounding.*
SOURCE: Wolff 1999.

Wealth, 1997

Richest fifth 84.5%

Twenty percent of the population holds 85 percent of the wealth.

Second fifth 10.7% Third fifth 4.4% Fourth fifth 1% Poorest fifth (−0.7%)

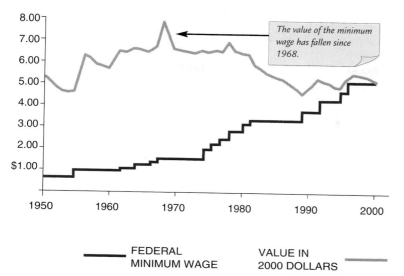

Figure 5–3

U.S. Minimum Wage Adjusted for Inflation, 1950–2002 NOTE: Some states legislate different standards. Minima as of 2005 are actually lower in two states (KS and OH) and higher in 13 states (AK, CA, CN, DE, HI, IL, MA, ME, NY, OR, RI, VT, WA) and DC. SOURCE: Bureau of the Census 2003a:425.

The value of the minimum wage has fallen since 1968.

last half century, from 75 cents in 1950 to $5.15 in 1997. But in terms of its real value, adjusted for inflation, the minimum wage has frequently failed to keep pace with the cost of living. In fact, its real value today is *lower* than it was in the late 1980s (see the figure). In this section, we'll consider just how we define "poverty" and who is included in that category.

Studying Poverty.   The efforts of sociologists and other social scientists to better understand poverty are complicated by the difficulty of defining it. This problem is evident even in government programs that conceive of poverty in either absolute or relative terms. ***Absolute poverty*** refers to a minimum level of subsistence that no family should be expected to live below. Policies concerning minimum wages, housing standards, or school lunch programs for the poor imply a need to bring citizens up to some predetermined level of existence.

One commonly used measure of absolute poverty is the federal government's *poverty line,* a money income figure adjusted annually to reflect the consumption requirements of families based on their size and composition. The poverty line serves as an official definition of which people are poor. In 2003, for example, any family of four (2 adults and 2 children) with a combined income of $18,660 or less fell below the poverty line. This definition determines which individuals and families will be eligible for certain government benefits (DeNavas-Walt et al. 2004:39).

Although by absolute standards, poverty has declined in the United States, it remains higher than in many other industrial nations. A comparatively large proportion of U.S. households are poor, meaning that members are unable to purchase basic consumer goods. If anything, this cross-national comparison understates the extent of poverty in the United States, since U.S. residents are likely to pay more for housing, health care, child care, and education than residents of other countries, where such expenses are often subsidized.

By contrast, *relative poverty* is a floating standard of deprivation by which people at the bottom of a society, whatever their lifestyles, are judged to be disadvantaged *in comparison with the nation as a whole*. Therefore, even if the poor of the 1990s are better off in absolute terms than the poor of the 1930s or 1960s, they are still seen as deserving special assistance.

In the 1990s, debate grew over the validity of the poverty line as a measure of poverty and a standard for allocating government benefits. Some critics charge that the poverty line is too low; they note that the federal government continues to use 20-year-old nutritional standards in assessing people's level of poverty. If the poverty line is too low, then government data will underestimate the extent of poverty in the United States, and many deserving poor citizens will fail to receive benefits.

Other observers dispute this view. They argue that the poverty line may actually overestimate the number of low-income people because it fails to consider noncash benefits (such as Medicare, Medicaid, food stamps, public housing, and health care and other fringe benefits provided by some employers). In response, the Bureau of the Census has considered several different definitions of poverty; they show at most a 1.4 percent lower rate. That is, if the official poverty threshold places 13 percent of the population in the category of the poor, the poverty estimate including *all* these noncash benefits would account for about 11.6 percent of the population (Brady 2003; Short et al. 1999).

Who Are the Poor?   Not only does the category of the poor defy any simple definition, but it counters the common stereotypes about poor people. For example, many people in the United States believe that the vast majority of the poor are able to work but will not. Yet many poor adults do work outside the home, although only a small proportion work full-time throughout the year. In 2003, about 30 percent of poor adults worked full-time, compared to 66 percent of all adults. Of those poor adults who do not work, most are ill or disabled, or are occupied in maintaining a home (DeNavas-Walt et al. 2004:10).

A sizable number of the poor live in urban slums, but a majority live outside those areas. Poverty is no stranger to rural areas, from Appalachia to hard-hit farming regions and Native American reservations. Table 5–3 provides additional statistical information regarding these low-income people.

Since World War II, women have constituted an increasing proportion of the poor people of the United States. Many of them are divorced or never-married mothers. In 1959, female householders accounted for 26 percent of the nation's poor; by 2003, that figure had risen to 51 percent (see Table 5–3). This alarming trend, known as the *feminization of poverty,* is evident not just in the United States but around the world.

About half of all women in the United States who are living in poverty are "in transition," coping with an economic crisis caused by the departure, disability, or death of a husband. The other half tend to be economically dependent either on the welfare system or on friends and relatives living nearby. A major factor in the feminization of poverty has been the increase in families with women as single heads of the household. In 2003, 28.0 percent of households headed by single mothers lived in poverty, compared to 12.5 percent of all people in the United States. Conflict theorists and other observers trace the higher rates of poverty among women to three distinct factors: the difficulty in finding affordable child care, sexual harassment, and sex discrimination in the labor market (see Chapter 7).

Analyses of the poor reveal that they are not a static social class. The overall composition of the poor changes continually, with some individuals and families moving above the poverty level after a year or two and others slipping below it. Still, hundreds of thousands of people remain in poverty for many years at a time. African Americans and Latinos are more likely than Whites to be "persistently poor." Over a 21-year period, 15 percent of African Americans and 10 percent of Latinos were

Table 5–3 Who Are the Poor in the United States?

Group	Percentage of the Population of the United States	Percentage of the Poor of the United States
Under 18 years old	26%	36%
18 to 64 years old	61	54
65 years and older	13	10
Whites (non-Hispanic)	83	44
Blacks	12	25
Hispanics	11	25
Asians and Pacific Islanders	4	4
Married couples and families with male householders	82	49
Families with female householders	18	51

NOTE: Data are for 2003, as reported by the Bureau of the Census in 2004. SOURCE: DeNavas-Walt et al. 2004.

persistently poor, compared to only 3 percent of Whites. Both Latinos and Blacks are less likely than Whites to leave the welfare rolls as a result of welfare reform (Mangum et al. 2003).

Explaining Poverty.   Why does poverty pervade a nation of such vast wealth? Sociologist Herbert Gans (1995) has applied functionalist analysis to this question; he argues that various segments of society actually *benefit* from the existence of the poor. Gans has identified a number of social, economic, and political functions that the poor perform for society:

- The presence of poor people means that society's dirty work—physically dirty or dangerous, underpaid and undignified, dead-end and menial jobs—will be performed at low cost.
- Poverty creates jobs for occupations and professions that "service" the poor. It creates both legal employment (public health experts, welfare caseworkers) and illegal jobs (drug dealers, numbers runners).
- The identification and punishment of the poor as deviants upholds the legitimacy of conventional social norms and mainstream values regarding hard work, thrift, and honesty.
- Within a relatively hierarchical society, the existence of poor people guarantees the higher status of the affluent. As psychologist William Ryan (1976) has noted, affluent people may justify inequality (and gain a measure of satisfaction) by "blaming the victims" of poverty for their disadvantaged condition.
- Because of their lack of political power, the poor often absorb the costs of social change. Under the policy of deinstitutionalization, mental patients released from long-term hospitals have been "dumped" primarily into low-income communities and neighborhoods. Similarly, halfway houses for rehabilitated drug abusers, often rejected by more affluent communities, tend to end up in poorer neighborhoods.

In Gans's view, then, poverty and the poor actually perform positive functions for many nonpoor groups in the United States.

LIFE CHANCES

Max Weber thought that class was closely related to one's *life chances*—that is, the opportunities people have to provide themselves with material goods, positive living conditions, and favorable life experiences (Gerth and Mills 1958). Life chances are reflected in such measures as housing, education, and health. Occupying a higher position in society improves a person's life chances and brings greater access to social rewards. Occupying a lower position forces a person to devote more energy and resources to the necessities of life.

Class position, for instance, affects a person's health in important ways. In fact, class is increasingly being viewed as an important predictor of health. The affluent avail themselves of improved health services that poor people cannot afford. The chances of a child's dying during the first year of life are much higher in poor families than among the middle class. This higher infant mortality rate results in part from the inadequate nutrition received by low-income expectant mothers. Even when they survive infancy, the poor are more likely than the affluent to suffer from serious chronic illnesses such as arthritis, bronchitis, diabetes, and heart disease. In addition, the poor are less likely to be protected from the high costs of illness by private health insurance. They may have jobs without health insurance; may work part-time and not be eligible for employee health benefits; or may simply be unable to afford the premiums (Goode 1999; DeNavas-Walt et al. 2004).

All these factors contribute to differences in the death rates of the poor and the affluent. Studies drawing on health data in the United States document the impact of class (as well as race) on mortality. Moreover, ill health among the poor only serves to increase the likelihood that the poor will remain impoverished (Huie et al. 2003; R. Mills and Bhandari 2003).

Like disease, crime can be particularly devastating when it attacks the poor. According to the 2003 National Crime Victimization Survey, people in low-income families are more likely to be assaulted, raped, or robbed than the most affluent people. Furthermore, if accused of a crime, a person with low income and status is likely to be represented by an overworked public defender. Whether innocent or guilty, the accused may sit in jail for months, unable to raise bail (Catalano 2004).

Wealth, status, and power may not ensure happiness, but they certainly provide additional ways of coping with problems and disappointments. For this reason, the opportunity for advancement is of special significance to those who are on the bottom of society looking up. These people want the rewards and privileges that are granted to high-ranking members of a culture.

Imagine a society in which there are no social classes—no differences in people's wealth, income, and life chances. What would such a society be like? Would it be stable, or would its social structure change over time?

Social Mobility

Ronald Reagan's father was a barber; Jimmy Carter began as a peanut farmer. Yet each man eventually achieved the most powerful and prestigious position in our country. The rise of a child from a poor background to the presidency—or to some other position of great prestige, power, or financial reward—is an example of social mobility. The term *social mobility* refers to the movement of individuals or groups from one position of a society's stratification system to another. But how significant—how frequent, how dramatic—is social mobility in a class society such as the United States?

OPEN VERSUS CLOSED STRATIFICATION SYSTEMS

Sociologists use the terms *open stratification system* and *closed stratification system* to indicate the degree of social mobility in a society. An **open system** implies that the position of each individual is influenced by his or her *achieved* status. Such a system encourages competition among members of society. The United States is moving toward this ideal type as the nation attempts to reduce the barriers facing women, racial and ethnic minorities, and people born in the lower social classes.

At the other extreme of social mobility is the **closed system,** which allows little or no possibility of moving up. The slavery, caste, and estate systems of stratification are examples of closed systems. In such societies, social placement is based on *ascribed* statuses that cannot be changed, such as race or family background.

TYPES OF SOCIAL MOBILITY

An airline pilot who becomes a police officer moves from one social position to another of the same rank. Each occupation has the same prestige ranking: 60 on a scale ranging from a low of 0 to a high of 100 (see Table 5–2 on page 122). Sociologists call this kind of movement **horizontal mobility.** However, if the pilot were to become a lawyer (prestige ranking of 75), he or she would experience **vertical mobility,** the movement of a person from one social position to another of a different rank. Vertical mobility can also involve moving *downward* in a society's stratification system, as would be the case if the airline pilot became a bank teller (prestige ranking of 43). Pitirim Sorokin ([1927] 1959) was the first sociologist to distinguish between horizontal and vertical mobility.

Most sociological analysis focuses on vertical social mobility. One way of examining vertical mobility is to contrast intergenerational and intragenerational mobility. **Intergenerational mobility** involves changes in the social position of children relative to their parents. Thus, a plumber whose father was a physician provides an example of downward intergenerational mobility. A film star whose parents were both factory workers illustrates upward intergenerational mobility.

Intragenerational mobility involves changes in a person's social position within his or her adult life. A woman who enters the paid labor force as a teacher's aide and eventually becomes superintendent of the school district experiences upward intragenerational mobility. A man who becomes a taxicab driver after his accounting firm goes bankrupt undergoes downward intragenerational mobility.

SOCIAL MOBILITY IN THE UNITED STATES

The belief in upward mobility is an important value in our society. Does that mean the United States is indeed the land of opportunity? Not unless such ascriptive characteristics as race, gender, and family background have ceased to be significant in determining one's future prospects. We can see the impact of these factors in the occupational structure.

Occupational Mobility.   Two sociological studies conducted a decade apart offer insight into the degree of social mobility in the nation's occupational structure (Blau and Duncan 1967; Featherman and Hauser 1978). Taken together, these investigations lead to several noteworthy conclusions. First, occupational mobility (both intergenerational and intragenerational) has been common among males. Approximately 60 to 70 percent of sons are employed in higher-ranked occupations than their fathers.

Second, although there is a great deal of social mobility in the United States, much of it covers a very short distance. That is, people who reach an occupational level different from that of their parents usually advance or fall back only one or two out of a possible eight occupational levels. Thus, the child of a laborer may become an artisan or a technician, but he or she is less likely to become a manager or professional. The odds against reaching the top are extremely high unless one begins from a relatively privileged position.

The Impact of Education.   Another conclusion of both studies is that education plays a critical role in social mobility. The impact of formal schooling on adult status is even greater than that of family background (although as we have seen, family background influences the likelihood that one will receive higher education). Furthermore, education represents an important means of intergenerational mobility. Three-fourths of college-educated men in these studies achieved some upward mobility, compared with only 12 percent of those who received no schooling (see also J. Davis 1982).

Education's impact on social mobility has diminished somewhat in the last decade, however. An undergraduate degree—a B.A. or a B.S.—serves less as a guarantee of upward mobility than it did in the past simply because more and more entrants into the job market now hold such a degree. Moreover, intergenerational mobility is declining, since there is no longer such a stark difference between generations. In earlier decades many high school–educated parents successfully sent their children to college, but today's college students are increasingly likely to have college-educated parents (Hout 1988).

The Impact of Race.   Sociologists have long documented the fact that the class system is more rigid for African Americans than it is for members of other racial groups. Black men who have good jobs, for example, are less likely than White men to see their adult children attain the same status. The cumulative disadvantage of discrimination plays a significant role in the disparity between the two groups' experience. Compared to White households, the relatively modest wealth of African

American households means that adult Black children are less likely than adult White children to receive financial support from their parents. Indeed, young Black couples are much more likely than young White couples to be assisting their parents—a sacrifice that hampers their social mobility.

The African American middle class has grown over the last few decades, due to economic expansion and the benefits of the civil rights movement of the 1960s. Yet many of these middle-class households have little savings, a fact that puts them in danger during times of crisis. Studies stretching back several decades show that downward mobility is significantly higher for Blacks than it is for Whites (Hout 1984; Sernau 2001; W. J. Wilson 1996).

The Impact of Gender.   Studies of mobility, even more than those of class, have traditionally ignored the significance of gender, but some research findings are now available that explore the relationship between gender and mobility.

Women's employment opportunities are much more limited than men's (as Chapter 7 will show). Moreover, according to recent research, women whose skills far exceed the jobs offered them are more likely than men to withdraw entirely from the paid labor force. Their withdrawal violates an assumption common to traditional mobility studies: that most people will aspire to upward mobility and seek to make the most of their opportunities.

In contrast to men, women have a rather large range of clerical occupations open to them. But modest salary ranges and small prospects for advancement limit their chance of upward mobility. Moreover, self-employment as shopkeepers, entrepreneurs, independent professionals, and the like—an important road to upward mobility for men—is more difficult for women, who find it harder to secure the necessary financing. Although sons commonly follow in the footsteps of their fathers, women are unlikely to move into their fathers' positions. Consequently, gender remains an important factor in shaping social mobility within the United States. Women in the United States (and in other parts of the world) are especially likely to be trapped in poverty, unable to rise out of their low-income status (P. Smith 1994).

Global Inequality

Adolphe Mulinowa begins his day hauling sand at a construction site in Goma, a Congolese town located just over the border with Rwanda. For an hour's work he earns 5 cents. He spends the next four hours standing by the roadside, peddling bottled gasoline to passing motorists for an additional 40 cents. Later on, Mulinowa hawks old shoes and live chickens on the street. By the end of his 12-hour workday he has accumulated 70 cents and a bag of cornmeal—enough to feed his family of eight for about a day.

Mulinowa's hand-to-mouth existence is typical of sub-Saharan Africa, where decades of civil war and government corruption have robbed many nations of their wealth and reduced citizens to a desperate struggle for survival. Of the roughly 600 million people in sub-Saharan Africa, half must get by on just 65 cents a day. Though the area that surrounds Goma is rich in fertile soil and other natural resources, from timber to essential minerals, no use is being made of them. Goma's economy is so depressed that even a college degree is no guarantee of well-being. Relatively well-educated bureaucrats have turned to taking bribes since the Congo's central government, strained by the costs of war, stopped paying their salaries (Maharaj 2004).

Goma's poverty makes a sharp contrast with the prosperity of developed countries. Though technology, the information superhighway, and innovations in telecommunications have helped to unify the world, fostering global trade and manufacturing, the profits of these new business ventures are not being shared equally. There remains a substantial disparity between the world's "have" and "have-not" nations. For example, in 2004, the average value of goods and services produced per citizen (per capita gross national income) in the industrialized countries of the United States, Japan, Switzerland, Belgium, and Norway was more than $28,000. In 13 very poor nations the value was $800 or less. In fact, the richest 1 percent of the world's population received as much income as the poorest 57 percent. Four forces are particularly responsible for the domination of the world marketplace by a few nations: the legacy of colonialism, globalization, the advent of multinational corporations, and modernization (Haub 2004; United Nations Development Programme 2001).

LEGACY OF COLONIALISM

Colonialism occurs when a foreign power maintains political, social, economic, and cultural domination over a people for an extended period. In simple terms, it is rule by outsiders. The long reign of the British Empire over much of North America, parts of Africa, and India was an example of colonial domination. The same can be said of French rule over Algeria, Tunisia, and other parts of North Africa. Relations between the colonial nation and colonized people are similar to those between the dominant capitalist class and the proletariat, as described by Karl Marx.

By the 1980s, colonialism had largely disappeared. Most of the nations that were colonies before World War I had achieved political independence and established their own governments. However, for many of these countries, the transition to genuine self-rule was not yet complete. Colonial domination had established patterns of economic exploitation that continued even after the colonies achieved their nationhood—in part because they were unable to develop their own industry and technology.

Their dependence on more industrialized nations, including their former colonial masters, for managerial and technical expertise, investment capital, and manufactured goods kept former colonies in a subservient position. Such continuing dependence and foreign domination constitute **neocolonialism.** Today neocolonialism can be seen in the factories and assembly plants that serve more industrialized nations, including Mexico's *maquiladoras* and China's electronics plants.

The economic and political consequences of colonialism and neocolonialism are readily apparent. Drawing on the conflict perspective, sociologist Immanuel Wallerstein (1974, 1979a, 2004) views the global economic system as one divided between nations that control wealth and nations from which resources are taken. Neocolonialism, he believes, allows industrialized societies to accumulate even more capital.

Wallerstein has advanced a **world-systems analysis** to describe the unequal economic and political relationships in which certain industrialized nations (among them the United States, Japan, and Germany) and their global corporations dominate the *core* of the world's economic system. At the *semiperiphery* of the system are countries with marginal economic status, such as Israel, Ireland, and South Korea. Wallerstein suggests that the poor developing countries of Asia, Africa, and Latin America are on the *periphery* of the world's economic system. Core nations and their corporations control and exploit these nations' economies, much as the old colonial empires ruled their colonies (Chase-Dunn and Grimes 1995).

The division between core and periphery nations is significant and remarkably stable. A study by the International Monetary Fund (2000) found little change over the course of the *last 100 years* for the 42 economies studied. The only changes were Japan's movement up into the group of core nations and China's movement down toward the margins of the semiperiphery nations. Yet Wallerstein (2000) speculates that the world system as we currently understand it may soon undergo unpredictable changes. The world is becoming increasingly urbanized, a trend that is gradually eliminating the large pools of low-cost workers in rural areas. In the future, core nations will have to find other ways to reduce their labor costs. The exhaustion of land and water resources through clear-cutting and other forms of pollution is also driving up the costs of production worldwide.

Wallerstein's world-systems analysis is the most widely used version of **dependency theory.** According to this theory, even as developing countries make economic advances, they remain weak and subservient to core nations and corporations in an increasingly intertwined global economy. Their weakness allows industrialized nations to continue to exploit them. In a sense, dependency theory applies the conflict perspective on a global scale.

According to world-systems analysis and dependency theory, a growing share of the human and natural resources of developing countries is being redistributed to the core industrialized nations. In part, this redistribution occurs because developing countries owe huge sums of money to industrialized nations as a result of foreign aid, loans, and trade deficits. Thus, the global debt crisis has intensified the Third World dependency begun under colonialism, neocolonialism, and multinational investment. International financial institutions are now pressuring indebted countries to take severe measures to meet their interest payments. The result is that developing nations may be forced to devalue their currencies, freeze workers' wages, increase the privatization of industry, and reduce government services and employment.

You are traveling through a developing country. What evidence do you see of neocolonialism?

GLOBALIZATION

Closely related to these problems is *globalization,* or the worldwide integration of government policies, cultures, social movements, and financial markets through trade and the exchange of ideas. While public discussion of globalization is relatively recent, intellectuals have been pondering its social consequences for a long time. Karl Marx and Friedrich Engels warned in the *Communist Manifesto* (written in 1848) of a world market that would lead to production in distant lands, sweeping away existing working relationships. Today, developments outside a country are as likely to influence people's lives as changes at home. For example, though much of the world was already in recession by September 2001, within weeks the economic repercussions of the terrorist attacks on New York and Washington, D.C., had begun to affect African game wardens and Asian taxi drivers. Some observers see globalization and its effects as the natural result of advances in communications technology, particularly the Internet and satellite transmission of the mass media. Others view it more critically, as a process that allows multinational corporations to expand unchecked. We will examine this issue more fully in the next section (Chase-Dunn et al. 2000; Feketekuty 2001; Feuer 1959; Pearlstein 2001).

Because world financial markets transcend governance by conventional nation states, international organizations such as the World Bank and the International Monetary Fund have emerged as major players in the global economy. The function of these institutions, which are heavily funded and influenced by countries such as the United States, is to encourage economic trade and development and ensure the smooth operation of international financial markets. As such they are seen as promoters of globalization and defenders primarily of the interests of core nations. Ever since the meeting of the World Trade Organization (WTO) in Seattle, Washington, in 1999, wherever leaders of the core nations have gathered, protesters have converged to draw attention to a variety of issues, including violations of workers' rights, destruction of the environment, loss of cultural identity (see Chapter 2), and discrimination against minority groups in periphery nations.

MULTINATIONAL CORPORATIONS

Worldwide corporate giants play a key role in neocolonialism. The term *multinational corporations* refers to commercial organizations that are headquartered in one country but do business throughout the world. Such private trade and lending relationships are not new; merchants have conducted business abroad for hundreds of years, trading gems, spices, garments, and other goods. However, today's multinational giants are not merely buying and selling overseas; they are also *producing* goods all over the world, from sneakers to sewing machines (Wallerstein 1974).

Moreover, today's "global factories" (factories throughout the developing world that are run by multinational corporations) now sit alongside the "global office." Multinationals based in core countries are beginning to establish reservations services, claims adjustment offices, and data processing centers in periphery nations. As service industries become more important in the international marketplace, many companies are concluding that the low costs of overseas operations more than offset the expense of transmitting information around the world.

Do not underestimate the size of these global corporations. The total revenues of many multinational businesses are equivalent to the total value of goods and services exchanged in *entire nations*. Foreign sales represent an important source of profit for multinational corporations, a fact that encourages them to expand into other countries (in many cases, the developing nations). The economy of the United States is heavily dependent on foreign commerce, much of which is conducted by multinationals. Over one-fourth of all goods and services produced in the United States has to do with either the export of goods to foreign countries or the import of goods from abroad (United States Trade Representative 2003).

Sociologists differ in their appraisal of the economic and social effects of these behemoth organizations. We'll examine two perspectives on multinational corporations, the functionalist view and the conflict view.

Functionalist View.   Functionalists believe that multinational corporations can actually help the developing nations of the world. They bring jobs and industry to areas where subsistence agriculture previously served as the only means of survival. Multinationals promote rapid development through the diffusion of inventions and innovations from industrial nations. Viewed from a functionalist perspective, the combination of skilled technology and management provided by multinationals and the relatively cheap labor available in developing nations is ideal for a global enterprise. Multinationals can take maximum advantage of technology while reducing costs and boosting profits.

The international ties of multinational corporations also facilitate the global exchange of ideas and technology, making the nations of the world more interdependent. These ties may prevent certain disputes from reaching the point of serious conflict. A country cannot afford to sever diplomatic relations, or engage in warfare, with a nation that is the head-quarters for its main business suppliers or a key outlet for its exports.

Conflict View.   Conflict theorists challenge this favorable evaluation of the impact of multinational corporations. They emphasize that multina-tionals exploit local workers to maximize profits. Starbucks—the inter-national coffee retailer based in Seattle—gets some of its coffee from farms in Guatemala. But to earn enough money to buy a pound of Starbucks coffee, a Guatemalan farmworker would have to pick 500 pounds of beans, an amount that represents five days of work (Entine and Nichols 1996).

The pool of cheap labor in the developing world prompts multina-tionals to move their factories out of core countries. An added bonus for the multinationals is the fact that the developing world discourages strong trade unions. Organized labor in industrialized countries insists on decent wages and humane working conditions, but governments seeking to attract or keep multinationals may develop a "climate for investment" that includes repressive antilabor laws—laws that restrict union activity and collective bargaining. These governments know that if labor's de-mands become too threatening, the multinational firm will simply move its plant elsewhere. Nike, for example, moved its factories from the United States to Korea to Indonesia to Vietnam in search of the lowest la-bor costs. Conflict theorists conclude that on the whole, multinational corporations have a negative social impact on workers in both industrial-ized and developing nations.

Workers in the United States and other core countries are beginning to recognize that their own interests are served by helping to organize workers in developing nations. As long as multinationals can exploit cheap labor abroad, they will be in a strong position to reduce wages and benefits in industrialized countries. With this in mind, labor unions, reli-gious organizations, campus groups, and other activists have mounted public campaigns to pressure companies such as Nike, Starbucks, Reebok, the Gap, and Wal-Mart to improve the wages and working conditions in their overseas operations (Appelbaum and Dreier 1999).

Several sociologists who have surveyed the effects of foreign invest-ment conclude that although it may initially contribute to a host nation's wealth, it eventually increases economic inequality within developing nations. In both income and ownership of land, the upper and middle classes benefit most from economic expansion; the lower classes are less likely to benefit. Multinationals invest in limited industries and restricted regions. Although certain sectors of the host nation's economy expand, such as hotels and expensive restaurants, their very expansion appears to retard growth in agriculture and other economic sectors. Moreover, multinational corporations often buy out or force out local entrepreneurs and companies, increasing a nation's economic and cultural dependence

(Bornschier et al. 1978; Chase-Dunn and Grimes 1995; Evans 1979; Wallerstein 1979b).

MODERNIZATION

Around the world, millions of people are witnessing a revolutionary transformation of their day-to-day life. Contemporary social scientists use the term ***modernization*** to describe the far-reaching process through which developing nations move from traditional or less developed institutions to those characteristic of more developed societies.

Wendell Bell (1981), whose definition of modernization we are using, notes that modern societies tend to be urban, literate, and industrial. They have sophisticated transportation and media systems. Their families tend to be organized on the nuclear family rather than the extended-family model. Members of societies that have undergone modernization shift their allegiance from traditional sources of authority, such as parents and priests, to newer authorities, such as government officials.

Many sociologists are quick to note that terms such as *modernization* and even *development* contain an ethnocentric bias. The unstated assumption behind these terms is that "they" (people living in developing countries) are struggling to become more like "us" (in the core industrialized nations). Viewed from a conflict perspective, these terms perpetuate the dominant ideology of capitalist societies.

A similar criticism has been made of ***modernization theory,*** the functionalist view that modernization and development will gradually improve the lives of people in developing nations. According to this theory, though countries develop at uneven rates, the development of peripheral countries is assisted by innovations transferred from the industrialized world. Critics of modernization theory, including dependency theorists, counter that any such technology transfer only increases the dominance of core nations over developing countries and facilitates further exploitation.

When we see all the Coca-Cola and Dunkin' Donuts signs going up in developing countries, it is easy to assume that globalization and economic change are effecting cultural change. But that is not always the case, researchers note. Distinctive cultural traditions, such as a particular religious orientation or a nationalistic identity, often persist in developing nations, and can soften the impact of modernization. Some contemporary sociologists emphasize that both industrialized and developing countries are "modern." Increasingly, researchers are viewing modernization as movement along a series of social indicators—among them degree of urbanization, energy use, literacy, political democracy, and use of birth control. Clearly, these are subjective indicators; even in industrialized nations, not everyone would agree that wider use of birth control represents "progress" (Armer and Katsillis 1992; Hedley 1992; Inglehart and Baker 2000).

Current modernization studies generally take a convergence perspective. Using the indicators just noted, researchers focus on how societies are moving closer together, despite their traditional differences. From a conflict perspective, however, the modernization of developing countries often perpetuates their dependence on—and continued exploitation by—more industrialized nations. Conflict theorists view such continuing dependence on foreign powers as a form of contemporary neocolonialism.

Sociology Matters

Sociology matters because it defines your social class, an important part of your place in the social system.

- Do wide differences in family wealth and income separate students on your campus? What about the people in your hometown? How do sociologists explain these differences?
- What is your family's social class, and what measures of social class do you base your answer on? How does your family's social class affect your life chances?
- Where do you fit in the global stratification system? How many of the products you use were made by workers in developing nations? Would your social standing be different if you couldn't afford to buy those products?

CHAPTER RESOURCES

Summary

Stratification is the structured ranking of entire groups of people in a society, so as to perpetuate **social inequality.** Worldwide, stratification can be seen in the unequal distribution of **wealth** and **income** within countries, as well as in the gap between rich and poor nations. This chapter examined four systems of stratification, including the **class system** that prevails in the United States. It considered two theoretical explanations for the existence of social inequality, as well as the relationship between stratification and **social mobility.** It closed with a discussion of stratification in developing countries.

1. All cultures manifest some degree of **social inequality** through stratification systems such as **slavery, castes,** *estates,* and **classes.**

2. Karl Marx wrote that **capitalism** created two distinct social classes, the **bourgeoisie** (owners of the means of production) and the **proletariat** (workers).

3. Max Weber identified three analytically distinct components of stratification: **class, status group,** and **power.**

4. Functionalists assert that stratification benefits society by motivating people to fill demanding positions. Conflict theorists, however, see stratification as a major source of societal tension.

5. Sociologists distinguish between **absolute poverty,** which is defined as a minimum level of subsistence, and **relative poverty,** a floating standard of deprivation that is based on comparison with society as a whole.

6. One's **life chances**—opportunities to obtain material goods, positive living conditions, and favorable life experiences—are related to one's social class. The higher a person's social class, the better one's life chances.

7. **Social mobility** is more likely to be found in an **open system** that emphasizes a person's **achieved status** than in a **closed system** that focuses on a person's **ascribed status.**

8. In 2004, the per capita gross national income of several developing countries was $800 or less. Many such countries, former colonies of developed nations, are still subject to foreign domination through the process of **neocolonialism.**

9. According to sociologist Immanuel Wallerstein, the global economic system is divided between industrialized nations that control the world's wealth, called *core nations,* and the developing nations they exploit, called *periphery nations.* Wallerstein's teaching, a version of **dependency theory,** is referred to as **world-systems analysis.**

10. Critics blame the process of **globalization**—the worldwide integration of government policies, cultures, social movements, and financial markets through trade and the exchange of ideas—for contributing to the cultural domination of periphery nations by core nations. They also charge that **multinational corporations** exploit workers in developing countries in order to maximize their profits.

www.mhhe.com/schaefersm2
Visit the Online Learning Center for *Sociology Matters* to access quizzes, review activities, and other learning tools.

Key Terms

absolute poverty, 125

achieved status, 112

ascribed status, 112

bourgeoisie, 115

capitalism, 115

caste, 113

class, 116

class consciousness, 115

class system, 113

closed system, 130

colonialism, 133

dependency theory, 134

estate system, 113

esteem, 121

false consciousness, 116

feminization of poverty, 127

globalization, 135

horizontal mobility, 130

income, 111

intergenerational mobility, 130

intragenerational mobility, 130

life chances, 128

modernization, 138

modernization theory, 138

multinational corporation, 136

neocolonialism, 134

objective method, 121

open system, 130

power, 117

prestige, 121

proletariat, 115

relative poverty, 126

slavery, 112

social inequality, 111

social mobility, 129

status group, 116

stratification, 111

vertical mobility, 130

wealth, 111

world-systems analysis, 134

Inequality by Race and Ethnicity

The Privileges of the Dominant

The Social Construction of Race and Ethnicity

Race, Ethnicity, and Minority Groups

Immigration and New Ethnic Groups

Explaining Inequality by Race and Ethnicity

Patterns of Prejudice and Discrimination

In a laboratory at the University of Colorado, Boulder, subjects in an experiment played video games as researchers recorded their moves. Presented with a rapid-fire series of pictures showing Black and White men holding various objects—cell phones, cameras, wallets, guns—subjects pressed one button if they considered a character harmless and another button to "shoot" characters they believed to be armed. Dr. Bernadette Park and her colleagues were studying people's split-second reactions to tests of decision making involving race and the potential for violence. When they analyzed the results, they found that the subjects, most of whom were White, had reacted more quickly to pictures of Black men with guns than to pictures of White men with guns. Subjects were also more likely to mistakenly shoot an unarmed Black character than an unarmed White character. The results were the same for Black subjects as for White subjects.

These results were not unusual. In a similar study at the University of Washington, Dr. Anthony G. Greenwald and his colleagues asked college students to distinguish virtual citizens and police officers from armed criminals. They found that subjects were more likely to misperceive and shoot at pictures of Black men than pictures of White men. For the last three decades, in fact, research has suggested that Americans are more likely to see Black men as being violent than White men (Correll et al. 2002; Greenwald et al. 2003).

What are the social implications of these studies? At bottom, they reveal the deep-seated effect of race on our social perceptions and even our actions. On a collective level, our racial biases underlie the societal prejudice that members of ethnic and minority groups encounter every day. In this chapter we will see how the ascribed characteristics of race and ethnicity create social privilege for some and discrimination for others. We will see that race and ethnicity are socially constructed concepts rather than genetically determined traits. Though functionalists, conflict theorists, feminists, and interactionists have offered different explanations for the unequal treatment of Whites and Blacks, all agree that prejudice and discrimination are real, on both an individual and an institutional level.

The Privileges of the Dominant

One aspect of discrimination that is often overlooked is the privileges that dominant groups enjoy at the expense of others. For instance, we tend to focus more on the difficulty women have getting ahead at work and getting a hand at home than on the ease with which men avoid household chores and manage to make their way in the world. Similarly, we concentrate more on discrimination against racial and ethnic minorities than on the advantages members of the White majority enjoy. Indeed, most White people rarely think about their "Whiteness," taking their status for granted. But sociologists and other social scientists are becoming increasingly interested in what it means to be "White," for White privilege is the other side of the proverbial coin of racial discrimination.

The feminist scholar Peggy McIntosh (1988) became interested in White privilege after noticing that most men would not acknowledge that there were privileges attached to being male—even if they would agree that being female had its disadvantages. Did White people suffer from a similar blind spot regarding their own racial privilege? she wondered. Intrigued, McIntosh began to list all the ways in which she benefited from her Whiteness. She soon realized that the list of unspoken advantages was long and significant.

McIntosh found that as a White person, she rarely needed to step out of her comfort zone, no matter where she went. If she wished to, she could spend most of her time with people of her own race. She could find a good place to live in a pleasant neighborhood, and get the foods she liked to eat in almost any grocery store. She could attend a public meeting without feeling that she did not belong, that she was different from everyone else.

McIntosh discovered, too, that her skin color opened doors for her. She could cash checks and use credit cards without suspicion, browse through stores without being shadowed by security guards. She could be seated without difficulty in a restaurant. If she asked to see the manager, she could assume he or she would be of her own race. If she needed help from a doctor or a lawyer, she could get it.

McIntosh also realized that her Whiteness made the job of parenting easier. She did not need to worry about protecting her children from people who did not like them. She could be sure that their textbooks would show pictures of people who looked like them, and that their history texts would describe White people's achievements. She knew that the television programs they watched would include White characters.

These are only some of the privileges McIntosh found she took for granted as a result of her membership in the dominant racial group in the United States. Whiteness *does* carry privileges—to a much greater extent than most White people realize. In the following section we will examine the social construction of race and ethnicity—abstract concepts that have enormous practical consequences for millions of people throughout the world.

The Social Construction of Race and Ethnicity

In the southern part of the United States, if a person had even a single drop of "Black blood," that person was defined and viewed as Black, even if he or she *appeared* to be White. Clearly, race had social significance in the South, enough so that White legislators established official standards for who was "Black" and who was "White."

The so-called one-drop rule was a vivid example of the *social construction of race*—the process by which people come to define a group as a race based in part on physical characteristics, but also on historical, cultural, and economic factors. It is an ongoing process subject to some debate, especially in a diverse society such as the United States, where each year increasing numbers of children are born to parents of different racial backgrounds.

In the 2000 census, nearly 7 million people in the United States (or about 2 percent of the population) reported that they were of two or more races. Half the people classified as multiracial were under age 18, suggesting that this segment of the population will grow in the years to come. People who claimed both White and American Indian ancestry were the largest group of multiracial residents (Tafoya et al. 2004).

This statistical finding of millions of multiracial people obscures how individuals handle their identity. The prevailing social construction of race pushes people to choose just one race, even if they acknowledge a broader cultural background. Still, many individuals, especially young adults, struggle against social pressure to choose a single identity, and instead openly embrace multiple heritages. Tiger Woods, the world's best-known professional golfer, considers himself both Asian and African American.

Ethnicity, too, is subject to social construction. Which ethnic groups are White, for instance? Do we consider Turkish and Arab Americans to be White? In the 1800s, Irish and Italian Americans were definitely viewed as non-White and were treated as such. Gradually, as other ethnic groups came to see them as White, Irish and Italian Americans became accepted members of mainstream society.

Social construction of race and ethnicity occurs throughout the world, as people in virtually all societies define their position in the social hierarchy in terms of race, ethnicity, and nationality. A dominant or majority group has the power not only to define itself legally but to define a society's values. Sociologist William I. Thomas (1923), an early critic of theories of racial and gender differences, saw that the "definition of the situation" could mold the personality of the individual. To put it another way, Thomas, writing from the interactionist perspective, observed that people respond not only to the objective features of a situation or person but also to the *meaning* that situation or person has for them. Thus, we can create false images or stereotypes that become real in their consequences. **Stereotypes** are unreliable generalizations about all members of a group that do not recognize individual differences within the group.

In the last 30 years, critics have pointed out the power of the mass media to perpetuate false racial and ethnic stereotypes. Television is a prime example: Almost all the leading dramatic roles are cast as Whites, even in urban-based programs like *Friends*. Blacks tend to be featured mainly in crime-based dramas.

We have seen how both ordinary people and powerful institutions like the media can influence our conceptions of race and ethnicity. How do sociologists conceive of race and ethnicity? The next two sections present a sociological overview of racial and ethnic groups in the United States—both the old, established groups and the new ethnic groups formed by recent immigrants.

Use Your Sociological Imagination

Using a TV remote control, how quickly do you think you could find a television show in which all the characters share your own racial or ethnic background? What about a show in which all the characters share a different ethnic background from your own—how quickly could you find one?

Race, Ethnicity, and Minority Groups

Sociologists frequently distinguish between racial and ethnic groups. The term **racial group** is used to describe a group that is set apart from others because of obvious physical differences. Whites, African Americans, and Asian Americans are all considered racial groups in the United States. While race does turn on physical differences, it is the culture of a particular society that constructs and attaches social significance to those differences, as we will see later. Unlike racial groups, an **ethnic group** is set apart from others primarily because of its national origin or distinctive cultural patterns. In the United States, Puerto Ricans, Jews, and Polish Americans are all categorized as ethnic groups (see Table 6–1).

MINORITY GROUPS

A numerical minority is any group that makes up less than half of some larger population. The population of the United States includes thousands of numerical minorities, including television actors, green-eyed people, tax lawyers, and descendants of the Pilgrims who arrived on the *Mayflower*. However, these numerical minorities are not considered to be minorities in the sociological sense; in fact, the number of people in a group does not necessarily determine its status as a social minority (or dominant group). When sociologists define a minority group, they are primarily concerned with the economic and political power, or powerlessness, of that group. A ***minority group*** is a subordinate group whose members have significantly less control or power over their own lives than the members of a dominant or majority group have over theirs.

Sociologists have identified five basic properties of a minority group—unequal treatment, physical or cultural traits, ascribed status, solidarity, and in-group marriage (Wagley and Harris 1958):

1. Members of a minority group experience unequal treatment compared to members of a dominant group. For example, the management of an apartment complex may refuse to rent to African Americans, Hispanics, or Jews. Social inequality may be created or maintained by prejudice, discrimination, segregation, or even extermination.

2. Members of a minority group share physical or cultural characteristics that distinguish them from the dominant group. Each society arbitrarily decides which characteristics are most important in defining the groups.

3. Membership in a minority (or dominant) group is not voluntary; people are born into the group. Thus, race and ethnicity are considered *ascribed* statuses.

4. Minority group members have a strong sense of group solidarity. William Graham Sumner, writing in 1906, noted that people make distinctions between members of their own group (the *in-group*) and everyone else (the *out-group*). When a group is the object of long-term prejudice and discrimination, the feeling of "us versus them" can and often does become extremely intense.

5. Members of a minority generally marry others from the same group. A member of a dominant group is often unwilling to marry into a supposedly inferior minority. In addition, the minority group's sense of solidarity encourages marriages within the group and discourages marriages to outsiders.

Table 6-1 Racial and Ethnic Groups in the United States, 2000

Classification	Number in Thousands	Percentage of Total Population
Racial groups		
Whites (includes 16.9 million White Hispanics)	211,461	75.1%
Blacks/African Americans	34,658	12.3
Native Americans, Alaskan Native	2,476	0.9
Asian Americans	10,243	3.6
Chinese	2,433	0.9
Filipinos	1,850	0.7
Asian Indians	1,679	0.6
Vietnamese	1,123	0.4
Koreans	1,077	0.4
Japanese	797	0.2
Other	1,285	0.5
Ethnic groups		
White ancestry (single or mixed)		
Germans	42,842	15.2
Irish	30,525	10.8
English	24,509	8.7
Italians	15,638	5.6
Poles	8,977	3.2
French	8,310	3.0
Jews	5,200	1.8
Hispanics (or Latinos)	35,306	12.5
Mexican Americans	23,337	8.3
Central and South Americans	5,119	1.8
Puerto Ricans	3,178	1.1
Cubans	1,412	0.5
Other	2,260	0.8
Total (all groups)	**281,422**	

NOTE: Percentages do not total 100 percent and figures under subheadings do not add up to figures under major headings because of overlap among groups (e.g., Polish American Jews or people of mixed ancestry, such as Irish and Italian). Hispanics may be of any race.

SOURCES: Brittingham and de la Cruz 2004; Bureau of the Census 2003a; Grieco and Cassidy 2001; Therrien and Ramirez 2001; United Jewish Communities 2003.

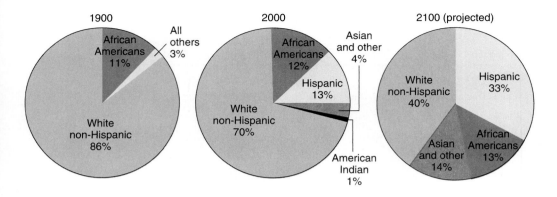

Figure 6–1

Racial and Ethnic Groups in the United States, 1900–2100 (Projected)

The racial and ethnic composition of what is today the United States is undergoing rapid change. SOURCES: Author's estimate based on Brittingham and de la Cruz 2004; Bureau of the Census 1975, 2003a; Thornton 1987.

RACE

The term *racial group* refers to those minorities (and the corresponding dominant groups) set apart from others by obvious physical differences. But what is an "obvious" physical difference? Each society determines which differences are important while ignoring other characteristics that could serve as a basis for social differentiation. In the United States, we see differences in both skin color and hair color. Yet people learn informally that differences in skin color have a dramatic social and political meaning, while differences in hair color do not.

When observing skin color, people in the United States tend to lump others rather casually into such categories as "Black," "White," and "Asian." More subtle differences in skin color often go unnoticed. However, such is not the case in other societies. In many nations of Central America and South America, people distinguish among color gradients on a continuum from light to dark skin. Brazil has approximately 40 color groupings, while in other countries people may be described as "Mestizo Hondurans," "Mulatto Colombians," or "African Panamanians." What we see as "obvious" differences, then, are subject to each society's social definitions.

The largest racial minorities in the United States are African Americans (or Blacks), Native Americans (or American Indians), and Asian Americans (Japanese Americans, Chinese Americans, and other Asian peoples). Figure 6–1 provides information about the changing population of racial and ethnic groups in the United States over the past century. It suggests that the racial and ethnic composition of the U.S. population will change more in the next hundred years than it has in the last hundred.

ETHNICITY

An ethnic group, unlike a racial group, is set apart from others because of its national origin or distinctive cultural patterns. Among the ethnic groups in the United States are peoples with a Spanish-speaking background, referred to collectively as *Latinos* or *Hispanics,* such as Puerto Ricans, Mexican Americans, Cuban Americans, and other Latin Americans. Other ethnic groups in this country include Jewish, Irish, Italian, and Norwegian Americans. While these groupings are convenient, they serve to obscure differences *within* these ethnic categories (as in the case of Hispanics) as well as to overlook the mixed ancestry of so many ethnic people in the United States.

The distinction between racial and ethnic minorities is not always clear-cut. Some members of racial minorities, such as Asian Americans, may have significant cultural differences from other groups. At the same time, certain ethnic minorities, such as Latinos, may have obvious physical differences that set them apart from other residents of the United States.

Despite categorization problems, sociologists continue to feel that the distinction between racial groups and ethnic groups is socially significant. That is because in most societies, including the United States, physical differences tend to be more visible than ethnic differences. Partly as a result of this fact, stratification along racial lines is more resistant to change than stratification along ethnic lines. Members of an ethnic minority sometimes can become, over time, indistinguishable from the majority — although the process may take generations and may never include all members of the group. By contrast, members of a racial minority find it much more difficult to blend in with the larger society and to gain acceptance from the majority. In the next section, we will examine immigration and the process through which new ethnic groups gain a foothold in the United States. We will see that established racial and ethnic groups often feel threatened by competition from the new arrivals.

Immigration and New Ethnic Groups

A significant segment of the population of the United States is made up of White ethnics whose ancestors arrived from Europe within the last 100 years. The nation's White ethnic population includes about 43 million people who claim at least partial German ancestry, 30 million Irish Americans, 16 million Italian Americans, and 9 million Polish Americans, as well as immigrants from other European nations (see Table 6–1 on page 147). Some of these people continue to live in close-knit ethnic neighborhoods, while others have largely assimilated and left the "old ways" behind.

Many White ethnics today identify only sporadically with their heritage. ***Symbolic ethnicity*** refers to an emphasis on such concerns as ethnic food or political issues rather than on deeper ties to one's ethnic heritage. This identity is reflected in the occasional family trip to an ethnic bakery, in the celebration of a ceremonial event such as St. Joseph's Day among Italian Americans, or among Irish Americans, in particular concern about the future of Northern Ireland. Except in cases in which

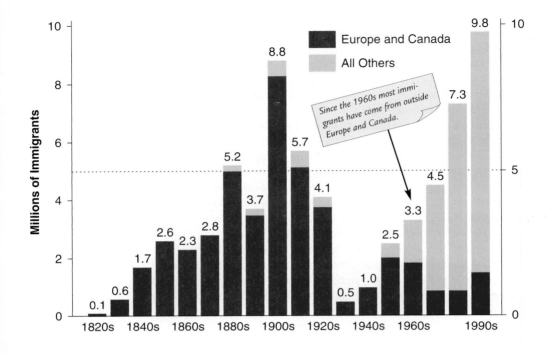

Figure 6–2
Immigration in the United States, 1820s–1990s
SOURCES: Author's estimate based on Immigration and Naturalization Service 2002:20–22; Martin and Midgley 2003:4.

new immigration reinforces old traditions, symbolic ethnicity tends to decline with each passing generation (Alba 1990; Gans 1979).

HISTORY OF IMMIGRATION

The contemporary diversity of the United States is not accidental, but reflects centuries of immigration. The United States has long had policies to determine who has preference to enter the country. Often, clear racial and ethnic biases are built into these policies. In the 1920s, U.S. policy gave preference to people from western Europe, while making it difficult for residents of southern and eastern Europe, Asia, and Africa to enter the country. During the late 1930s and early 1940s, the federal government refused to lift or loosen restrictive immigration quotas to allow Jewish refugees to escape the terror of the Nazi regime. In line with this policy, the S.S. *St. Louis,* with more than 900 Jewish refugees on board, was denied permission to land in the United States in 1939. The ship was forced to sail back to Europe, where at least a few hundred of its passengers later died at the hands of the Nazis (Morse 1967; G. Thomas and Witts 1974).

Since the 1960s, policies in the United States have encouraged the immigration of people who have relatives here, as well as of those who have needed skills. This change has significantly altered the pattern of sending nations. Previously, Europeans dominated, but for the last 40 years, immigrants have come primarily from Latin America and Asia (see Figure 6–2). This means that in the future, an ever-growing proportion of the United States will be Asian or Hispanic. To a large degree, fear and resentment of this growing racial and ethnic diversity is a key factor in opposition to immigration. Many people are very concerned that the new arrivals do not reflect the nation's cultural and racial heritage.

The long border with Mexico provides ample opportunity for illegal immigration into the United States. Throughout the 1980s, the public perception that the United States had lost control of its borders grew. Feeling pressure for immigration control, Congress ended a decade of debate by approving the Immigration Reform and Control Act of 1986. The act marked a historic change in the nation's immigration policy. For the first time, the hiring of illegal aliens was outlawed, and employers caught violating the law became subject to fines and even prison sentences. Just as significant a change was the extension of amnesty and legal status to many illegal immigrants already living in the United States.

Almost 20 years later, the act appears to have had mixed results. Substantial numbers of illegal immigrants continue to enter the country each year; an estimated 8 to 9 million are present at any given time. Increased

Though many people resent the presence of illegal immigrants in the United States, certain sectors of the U.S. economy are dependent on their labor. Illegal immigrants harvest the nation's crops, earning below-minimum wage rates that keep produce prices low.

border surveillance since September 11, 2001, has reduced their freedom to move back and forth across the border, however. Illegal immigrants to the United States are employed disproportionately in low-income jobs, making them an important part of the workforce (FAIR US 2003).

FUNCTIONS OF IMMIGRATION

Despite people's fears about it, immigration performs many valuable functions. For the receiving society, it alleviates labor shortages, such as exist in the fields of health care and technology in the United States. In 1998, Congress debated not whether individuals with technological skills should be allowed into the country, but just how much to increase the annual quota. For the sending nation, migration can relieve economies unable to support large numbers of people. Often overlooked is the large amount of money immigrants send *back* to their home nations. For example, every year, immigrants from Mexico and their children in the United States send more than $14 billion *back* to their home country (G. Thompson 2003).

Immigration can be dysfunctional as well. Although studies generally show that immigration has a positive impact on the receiving nation's economy, areas that accept high concentrations of immigrants may find it difficult to meet short-term social service needs. Furthermore, when migrants with skills or educational potential leave developing countries, it can be dysfunctional for those nations as well. No amount of payments sent back home can make up for the loss of valuable human resources from poor nations.

THE CONFLICT APPROACH TO IMMIGRATION

White ethnics and racial minorities have often been antagonistic toward one another because of economic competition—an interpretation rooted in the conflict approach to sociology. As Blacks, Latinos, and Native Americans emerge from the lower class, they compete with working-class Whites for jobs, housing, and educational opportunities. In times of high unemployment or inflation, any such competition can easily generate intense intergroup conflict.

Conflict theorists have noted how much of the debate over immigration is phrased in economic terms. The debate intensifies when the arrivals are of different racial and ethnic backgrounds from the host population. For example, Europeans often refer to "foreigners," but the term does not necessarily mean one of foreign birth. In Germany, "foreigners" refers to people of non-German ancestry, even if they were *born* in Germany; it does not refer to people of German ancestry born in another country who may choose to immigrate to their "mother country." Fear and dislike of "new" ethnic groups divide countries throughout the world.

Explaining Inequality by Race and Ethnicity

To understand how and why people make social distinctions based on race and ethnicity, we must turn to theory. All the major theoretical perspectives presume that culture, rather than biology, is the major determinant of racial-ethnic distinctions, yet they offer quite different explanations for discrimination. Viewing race from the macro level, functionalists observe that prejudice and discrimination based on race and ethnicity serve positive functions for dominant groups. In contrast, feminists and conflict theorists see the economic structure as a central factor in the exploitation of minorities. Interactionists stress the myriad ways in which everyday contact between people of different racial and ethnic backgrounds contributes to tolerance or hostility.

THE FUNCTIONALIST VIEW

What possible use could racial bigotry have for society? Functionalist theorists, while agreeing that racial hostility is hardly to be admired, point out that it indeed serves positive functions for those practicing discrimination.

Anthropologist Manning Nash (1962) has identified three functions that racially prejudiced beliefs have for the dominant group:

1. Such views provide a moral justification for maintaining an unequal society that routinely deprives a minority group of its rights and privileges. For example, southern Whites justified slavery by believing that Africans were physically and spiritually subhuman and devoid of souls (Hoebel 1949).

2. Racist beliefs discourage members of the subordinate minority from attempting to question their lowly status, which would be to question the very foundations of society.

3. Racial myths encourage support for the existing order by introducing the argument that any major societal change (such as an end to discrimination) would only bring greater poverty to the minority and lower the majority's standard of living. As a result, Nash suggests, racial prejudice grows when a society's value system (for example, one underlying a colonial empire or a regime that perpetuates slavery) is being threatened.

Although racial prejudice and discrimination may serve the interests of the powerful, such unequal treatment can also be dysfunctional for a society, and even for its dominant group. Sociologist Arnold Rose (1951) outlined four dysfunctions associated with racism:

1. A society that practices discrimination fails to use the resources of all individuals. Discrimination limits the search for talent and leadership to the dominant group.

2. Discrimination aggravates social problems such as poverty, delinquency, and crime and places the financial burden to alleviate those problems on the dominant group.

3. Society must invest a good deal of time and money to defend the barriers to full participation of all members.

4. Racial prejudice and discrimination often undercut goodwill and friendly diplomatic relations between nations.

THE CONFLICT RESPONSE

Conflict theorists would certainly agree with Arnold Rose that racial prejudice and discrimination have many harmful consequences for society. Sociologists such as Oliver Cox (1948), Robert Blauner (1972), and Herbert M. Hunter (2000) have used *exploitation theory* (also called *Marxist class theory*) to explain the basis of racial subordination in the United States. As we saw in Chapter 5, Karl Marx viewed the exploitation of the lower class as a basic part of the capitalist economic system. From a Marxist point of view, racism keeps minorities in low-paying jobs, thereby supplying the capitalist ruling class with a pool of cheap labor. Moreover, by forcing racial minorities to accept low wages, capitalists can restrict the wages of *all* members of the proletariat. Workers from the dominant group who demand higher wages can always be replaced by minorities, who have no choice but to accept low-paying jobs.

The conflict view of race relations seems persuasive in a number of instances. Japanese Americans were the object of little prejudice until they began to enter jobs that brought them into competition with Whites. The movement to keep Chinese immigrants out of the United States became most fervent during the latter half of the 19th century, when Chinese and Whites fought over dwindling work opportunities. Both the enslavement of Blacks and the extermination and removal westward of Native Americans were, to a significant extent, economically motivated.

The practice of racial profiling fits both the conflict perspective and labeling theory. *Racial profiling* may be defined as any arbitrary action initiated by an authority based on race, ethnicity, or national origin rather than a person's behavior. Generally, racial profiling occurs when law enforcement officers—customs officials, airport security personnel, and police—assume that people who fit certain descriptions are likely to be engaged in illegal activities. Skin color became a key characteristic of criminal profiles beginning in the 1980s, with the emergence of the crack cocaine market. But profiling can also involve a much more explicit use of stereotypes. For example, the federal antidrug initiative Operation Pipeline encouraged officers to look specifically for people wearing dreadlocks and for Latino men traveling together.

In 2003 President George W. Bush banned racial profiling by federal agencies, but specifically exempted security personnel. Thus, immigration officials can continue to require visitors from Arab or Muslim countries to register with the government, even though visitors from other countries are not required to register. Conflict theorists point out that in all these cases, the powerful and privileged dominant majority determines who is profiled and for what purposes (D. Harris 1999; Lightblau 2003; D. Ramirez et al. 2003).

THE INTERACTIONIST APPROACH

A Hispanic woman is transferred from a job on an assembly line to a similar position working next to a White man. At first, the White man is patronizing, assuming that she must be incompetent. She is cold and resentful; even when she needs assistance, she refuses to admit it. After a week, the growing tension between the two leads to a bitter quarrel. Yet over time, each slowly comes to appreciate the other's strengths and talents. A year after they begin working together, these two workers become respectful friends. This story is an example of what interactionists call the *contact hypothesis* in action.

The *contact hypothesis* states that interracial contact between people of equal status who are engaged in a cooperative task will cause them to become less prejudiced and to abandon previous stereotypes. People will begin to see one another as individuals and discard the broad generalizations characteristic of stereotyping. Note the phrases *equal status* and *cooperative task*. In the example just given, if the two workers had been competing for one vacancy as a supervisor, the racial hostility between them might have worsened (Allport 1979; Schaefer 2005; Sigelman et al. 1996).

In the United States, as Latinos and other minorities slowly gain access to better-paying, more responsible jobs, the contact hypothesis may take on even greater significance. The trend in our society is toward increasing contact between individuals from dominant and subordinate groups. This may be one way of eliminating—or at least reducing—racial and ethnic stereotyping and prejudice. Another may be the establishment of interracial coalitions, an idea suggested by sociologist William Julius Wilson (1999). To work, such coalitions would obviously need to be built on an equal role for all members.

Table 6–2 (page 156) summarizes the three major sociological perspectives on race. No matter what the explanation for racial and ethnic distinctions—functionalist, conflict, or interactionist—these socially constructed inequalities can have powerful consequences in the form of prejudice and discrimination. In the next section, we will see how inequality based on the ascribed characteristics of race and ethnicity can poison people's interpersonal relations, depriving whole groups of opportunities others take for granted.

Patterns of Prejudice and Discrimination

In recent years, college campuses across the United States have been the scene of bias-related incidents. Student-run newspapers and radio

summingUP

Table 6–2 Sociological Perspectives on Race

Perspective	Emphasis
Functionalist	The dominant majority benefits from the subordination of racial minorities.
Conflict	Vested interests perpetuate racial inequality through economic exploitation.
Interactionist	Cooperative interracial contacts can reduce hostility.

stations have ridiculed racial and ethnic minorities; threatening literature has been stuffed under the doors of minority students; graffiti endorsing the views of White supremacist organizations such as the Ku Klux Klan have been scrawled on university walls. In some cases, violent clashes have occurred between groups of White and Black students (Bunzel 1992; Schaefer 2005).

Prejudice is a negative attitude toward an entire category of people, often an ethnic or racial minority. If you resent your roommate because he or she is sloppy, you are not necessarily guilty of prejudice. However, if you immediately stereotype your roommate on the basis of such characteristics as race, ethnicity, or religion, that is a form of prejudice. Prejudice tends to perpetuate false definitions of individuals and groups.

Sometimes prejudice results from *ethnocentrism*—the tendency to assume that one's own culture and way of life represent the norm or are superior to all others. Ethnocentric people judge other cultures by the standards of their own group, which leads quite easily to prejudice against other cultures.

One important and widespread form of prejudice is *racism,* the belief that one race is supreme and all others are innately inferior. When racism prevails in a society, members of subordinate groups generally experience prejudice, discrimination, and exploitation. Racism can be subtle and deep-seated, as the psychological experiments described in the opening of this chapter showed. Though many Americans both White and Black condemn racism, research results suggest that racist stereotypes—such as that of the violent Black male—may be rooted in our subconscious thought processes.

DISCRIMINATORY BEHAVIOR

Prejudice often leads to *discrimination,* the denial of opportunities and equal rights to individuals and groups based on some type of arbitrary bias. Say that a White corporate president with a prejudice against Asian Americans has to fill an executive position. The most qualified candidate for the job is a Vietnamese American. If the president refuses to hire this candidate and instead selects an inferior White candidate, he or she is engaging in an act of racial discrimination.

Prejudiced *attitudes* should not be equated with discriminatory *behavior.* Although the two are generally related, they are not identical; either condition can be present without the other. A prejudiced person does not always act on his or her biases. The White president, for example, might choose—despite his or her stereotypes—to hire the Vietnamese American. That would be prejudice without discrimination. On the other hand, a White corporate president with a completely respectful view of Vietnamese Americans might refuse to hire them for executive posts, out of fear that biased clients would take their business elsewhere. In that case, the president's action would constitute discrimination without prejudice.

Discrimination persists even for the most educated and qualified minority group members from the best family backgrounds. Despite their talents and experiences, they sometimes encounter attitudinal or organizational bias that prevents them from reaching their full potential. The term **glass ceiling** refers to an invisible barrier that blocks the promotion of a qualified individual in a work environment because of the individual's gender, race, or ethnicity (Schaefer 2005; Yamagata et al. 1997).

In early 1995, the federal Glass Ceiling Commission issued the first comprehensive study of barriers to promotion in the United States. The commission found that glass ceilings continued to block women and minority group men from top management positions in the nation's industries. Although White men constitute 45 percent of the labor force today, they hold down a much higher proportion of the top positions. Even in the most diverse corporations, as listed in *Fortune* magazine in 2002, White men held over 80 percent of both the board of directors seats and the top 50 paid positions. According to the commission, the existence of this glass ceiling results principally from the fears and prejudices of many middle- and upper-level White male managers, who believe that the inclusion of women and minority group men in management circles will threaten their own prospects for advancement (Bureau of the Census 2003a:385; Department of Labor 1995a, 1995b; Hickman 2002).

INSTITUTIONAL DISCRIMINATION

Discrimination is practiced not only by individuals in one-to-one encounters but also by institutions. Social scientists are particularly concerned with the ways in which structural factors such as employment, housing, health care, and government administration maintain the social significance of race and ethnicity. **Institutional discrimination** refers to the denial of opportunities and equal rights to individuals and groups that results from the normal operations of a society. This kind of discrimination consistently affects certain racial and ethnic groups more than others.

The U.S. Commission on Civil Rights (1981:9–10) has identified various forms of institutional discrimination, including:

- Rules requiring that only English be spoken at a place of work, even when it is not a business necessity to restrict the use of other languages.

- Preferences shown by law and medical schools in the admission of children of wealthy and influential alumni, nearly all of whom are White.

- Restrictive employment-leave policies, coupled with prohibitions on part-time work, that make it difficult for the heads of single-parent families (most of whom are women) to obtain and keep jobs.

A recent example of institutional discrimination occurred in the wake of the September 11, 2001, terrorist attack on the United States. In the heat of demands to prevent terrorist takeovers of commercial airplanes, Congress passed the Aviation and Transportation Security Act, which was intended to strengthen airport screening procedures. The law stipulated that all airport screeners must be U.S. citizens. Nationally, 28 percent of all airport screeners are legal residents but not citizens of the United States; as a group, they are disproportionately Latino, Black, and Asian. Many observers noted that other airport and airline workers, including pilots, cabin attendants, and even armed National Guardsmen stationed at airports, need not be citizens. Efforts are now being made to test the constitutionality of the act. At the least, the debate over its fairness shows that even well-meant legal measures can have disastrous consequences for racial and ethnic minorities.

In some cases, even ostensibly neutral institutional standards can turn out to have discriminatory effects. African American students at a midwestern state university protested a policy under which fraternities and sororities that wished to use campus facilities for a dance were required to post $150 security deposits to cover possible damages. The Black students complained that the policy had a discriminatory impact on minority student organizations. Campus police countered that the university's policy applied to all student groups interested in using campus facilities. However, since the overwhelmingly White fraternities and sororities at the school used their own houses for dances, the policy indeed affected only African American and other minority organizations.

Attempts have been made to eradicate or compensate for discrimination in the United States. The 1960s saw the passage of many pioneering civil rights laws, including the landmark 1964 Civil Rights Act (which prohibits discrimination in public accommodations and publicly owned facilities on the basis of race, color, creed, national origin, and gender). In two important rulings in 1987, the Supreme Court held that federal prohibitions against racial discrimination protect members of all ethnic minorities—including Hispanics, Jews, and Arab Americans—even though they may be considered White.

For more than 20 years, affirmative action programs have been instituted to overcome past discrimination. ***Affirmative action*** refers to positive efforts to recruit minority members or women for jobs, promotions, and educational opportunities. Many people resent these programs, arguing that advancing one group's cause merely shifts the discrimination to another group. By giving priority to African Americans in admissions, for example, a school may overlook more qualified White candidates. In many parts of the country and many sectors of the economy, affirmative action is being rolled back, even though it was never fully implemented.

Discriminatory practices continue to pervade nearly all aspects of life in the United States today, in part because various individuals and groups actually *benefit* from them in terms of money, status, and influence. Even ex-convicts who are White are privileged in comparison to non-Whites.

A recent study by sociologist Devah Pager (2003) documents this kind of racial discrimination. Pager sent four young men out to look for an entry-level job in Milwaukee, Wisconsin. All four were 23-year-old college students, but they presented themselves as high school graduates with similar job histories. Two of the men were Black and two were White. One Black applicant and one White applicant claimed to have served 18 months in jail for a felony conviction (possession of cocaine with intent to distribute).

As one might expect, the four men's experiences with 350 potential employers were vastly different. Predictably, the White applicant with a purported prison record received only half as many callbacks as the other White applicant (17 percent compared to 34 percent). But as dramatic as the effect of his criminal record was, the effect of his race was more significant. Despite his prison record, he received slightly more callbacks than the Black applicant *with no criminal record* (17 percent compared to 14 percent). Race, it seems, was more of a concern to potential employers than a criminal background (Pager 2003).

MEASURING DISCRIMINATION

Can discrimination be measured in terms of lost income or opportunities? Doing so is a complicated process. Researchers must first confirm that prejudice exists by assessing people's attitudes toward a minority group and showing that its members are treated differently from others. Then they must find a way to assign a cost to the discrimination.

Researchers have managed to draw some tentative conclusions, however, by comparing income data for African Americans versus Whites and for men versus women. As Figure 6–3 (page 160) shows, with a median income of $46,579, White men earned 39 percent more than Black

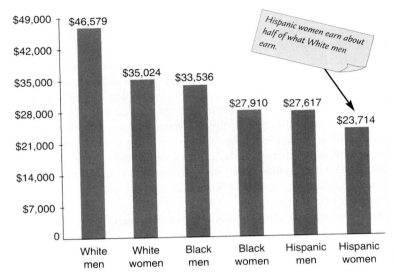

Figure 6–3
U.S. Median Income by Race, Ethnicity, and Gender, 2003
NOTE: *Median income includes all financial sources and is limited to year-round, full-time workers over 15 years of age. "White" refers to non-Hispanic.* SOURCE: DeNavas-Walt et al. 2004.

men in 2003, and nearly twice what Hispanic women earned. Black women earned significantly less than White women ($27,910 compared to $35,024), indicating that they bore a double burden because of their race and gender. The strong disparity between Black women's and White men's incomes has remained unchanged over more than 50 years. As great as this apparent inequality of income is, studies show that inequality in wealth among racial and ethnic groups is even greater (DeNavas-Walt et al. 2004; Kochhar 2004).

These differences are not entirely the result of discrimination in employment, for members of the six groups are not equally prepared to obtain high-paying jobs. Past discrimination is a significant factor in the poor educational backgrounds of minority group members. Historically, taxpayers, who are predominantly White, have been unwilling to subsidize the public education of African Americans and Hispanics at the same level as White pupils. Test results in today's inner-city schools show the continuing effect of such discriminatory spending patterns.

To address this problem, researchers have compared the median incomes of Blacks and Whites, as well as men and women, with approximately the same educational level. As Table 6–3 shows, even though workers with higher educational levels generally earn more money than others, the disparity between the races and the sexes remains. The gap between the races does narrow a bit as educational levels rise; still, both African Americans and women lag behind. In some cases, the contrast is dramatic: women with a master's degree earn $6,000 less than men who have only a baccalaureate degree ($50,163 compared to $56,502).

The income gap shown in Table 6–3 may not be caused entirely by employment discrimination. The table shows only the level of schooling obtained by workers, not the quality. Though in recent years, efforts have been made to eliminate geographical disparities in school funding, racial minorities are still more likely than Whites to attend inadequately financed schools. Inequality of educational opportunity may also affect women, since educational institutions often shepherd women into low-paid sex-segregated occupations, such as nursing and elementary education.

What is the collective effect of discrimination in employment? Economist Andrew Brimmer (1995), citing numerous government studies, estimates that if employers used African Americans' talents and abilities, based on their formal schooling, to the fullest, the nation's gross domestic product (GDP) would be about 3 or 4 percent higher each year. Estimates of the economic cost of discrimination have not changed much since the mid-1960s. The percentage of GDP lost would be even higher, of course, if economists were to include losses from the underutilization of women's and other minorities' talents. The widespread practice of steering women toward low-paid, low-level jobs, even if they are qualified for more challenging and rewarding work, has a hidden cost to society.

Table 6–3 U.S. Median Income by Race and Sex, Holding Education Constant, 2003

	Race		Sex	
	White Families	Black Families	Male	Female
Total	$61,036	$36,688	$41,939	$31,565
High School				
Nongraduate	30,841	19,956	26,468	18,938
Graduate	48,901	31,670	35,412	26,074
College				
Some college	58,178	39,214	41,348	30,142
Bachelor's degree	84,227	64,977	56,502	41,327
Master's degree	95,214	77,453	70,640	50,163
Doctorate degree	100,000	81,346	87,131	66,491

Even at the very highest levels of schooling, the income gap remains between Whites and Blacks. Education also has little apparent effect on the income gap between male and female workers.

NOTES: Figures are median income from all sources except capital gains. Included are public assistance payments, dividends, pensions, unemployment compensation, and so on. Incomes are for all workers over 25 years of age. High school graduates include those with GEDs. Data for Whites are for White non-Hispanics. "Some college" excludes associate degree holders. Black data for doctorate is author's estimate.

SOURCE: DeNavas-Walt et al. 2004: FINC-01 and PINC-03.

Sociology Matters

Sociology matters because it makes us think about why some people in our society are treated better than others.

- Do you consider yourself to be prejudiced? If not, do you think you might have some subconscious prejudices that would show up in a video game like the one described in the chapter opening? Can you think of a way to change this type of automatic response?

- Are you White? If so, what privileges, perhaps because of your race or citizenship, do you enjoy that you have always taken for granted? Can you think of a way to reduce one or more of those privileges so that others can be more equal—and would you cooperate with such an effort?

Sociology matters because it makes us more aware of prejudice and discrimination against members of minority groups.

- Are you non-White? If so, what kinds of stereotyping and discrimination have you seen non-Whites experience? Do you think racial discrimination can be reduced through cooperative contact among people of different races?

- Are you or your parents recent immigrants to the United States? If so, what is the primary basis on which others react to you—your ethnic group, race, or country of origin? Do you think you or your children will someday blend into mainstream society in the United States, and if so, what might hasten that process?

CHAPTER RESOURCES

Summary

The social dimensions of race and ethnicity are important factors in shaping people's lives. In this chapter, we defined the meaning of race and ethnicity and examined the social construction of those ascribed statuses. We discussed three theoretical perspectives on the unequal treatment of individuals based on their **racial** and **ethnic groups.** We noted some patterns of **prejudice** and **discrimination** against members of those groups, many of whom are recent immigrants. And we studied the economic effects of the unequal treatment of **minority groups.**

1. In the United States, people who are White enjoy numerous privileges that they rarely acknowledge, to themselves or to people of other races.

2. Race and ethnicity are socially constructed. The meaning people attach to the physical characteristics of certain groups, which are often expressed in **stereotypes,** gives race and ethnicity their social significance.

3. When sociologists define a **minority group,** they are concerned primarily with the economic and political power, or powerlessness, of the group.

4. A **racial group** is set apart from others by obvious physical differences, whereas an **ethnic group** is set apart primarily because of national origin or distinctive cultural patterns.

5. Over the last century, the racial and ethnic composition of immigrants to the United States has changed as the major sending nations changed. One hundred years ago, White ethnics from Europe predominated; today's immigrants come mainly from Latin America and Asia.

6. Functionalists point out that to the dominant groups in a society, discrimination against minority groups may seem to be functional. But for society as a whole, discrimination can be dysfunctional.

7. Conflict theorists stress the harmful consequences of racial subordination. They see the unequal treatment of minority groups as an integral part of capitalism, a view known as **exploitation theory.**

8. Interactionists focus on the micro level of race relations, pointing out the ways in which Whites dominate members of other racial and ethnic groups in everyday social interactions. According to their **contact hypothesis,** racial prejudice and discrimination can be reduced through cooperative contact between the races.

9. **Prejudice** is a negative attitude toward an entire group, often an ethnic or racial minority. Prejudice is often based on **ethnocentrism**—the belief that one's own culture is superior to all others—or on **racism**—the belief that one race is supreme and all others are inferior.

www.mhhe.com/schaefersm2
Visit the Online Learning Center for *Sociology Matters* to access quizzes, review activities, and other learning tools.

10. Prejudice often leads to **discrimination** against members of a minority group. Discrimination that results from the normal operations of a society is known as **institutional discrimination.**

Key Terms

affirmative action, 159

contact hypothesis, 155

discrimination, 156

ethnic group, 145

ethnocentrism, 156

exploitation theory, 154

glass ceiling, 157

institutional discrimination, 157

minority group, 146

prejudice, 156

racial group, 145

racial profiling, 154

racism, 156

stereotype, 145

symbolic ethnicity, 149

Inequality by Gender

The Social Construction of Gender

Explaining Inequality by Gender

Women: The Oppressed Majority

The Double Jeopardy of Minority Women

He works. She works. Both are physicians—a high-status occupation with considerable financial rewards. He makes $140,000. She makes $88,000.

These median earnings for physicians in the United States were released by the Census Bureau in 2004. They are typical of the results of the bureau's detailed study of occupations and income. Take air traffic controllers. He makes $67,000; she earns $56,000. Or housekeepers: he makes $19,000; she earns $15,000. What about teacher's assistants? He makes $20,000; she earns $15,000. Statisticians at the bureau looked at the median earnings for no fewer than 821 occupations ranging from dishwasher to chief executive. After adjusting for workers' age, education, and work experience, they came to an unmistakable conclusion: Across the board, there is a substantial gender gap in the median earnings of full-time workers.

Men do not always earn more than women for doing the same work. Researchers at the Census Bureau found 2 occupations out of 821 in which women typically earn about 1 percent more income than men: hazardous materials recovery and telecommunications line installation. These two occupations, however, employed less than 1 out of every 1,000 workers the bureau studied (Weinberg 2004).

In this chapter, we will see how the ascribed characteristic of gender creates privilege for men and discrimination for women. Like differences in race, differences in gender are visible. And like race and ethnicity, gender is socially constructed. Though functionalists, conflict theorists, feminists, and interactionists take different views of this subject, all agree that our society treats women and men unequally. Women may be a majority in terms of their numbers, but they are treated more like a minority group. For minority women, the intersection of gender and race creates a double jeopardy of discrimination that no other minority group faces.

The Social Construction of Gender

How do airline passengers react when the captain's voice belongs to a female? What do we make of a father who announces that he will be late for work because his son has a routine medical checkup? Consciously or unconsciously, we are likely to assume that flying a commercial plane is a *man's* job, and that most parental duties are, in fact, *maternal* duties. Gender is such a routine part of our everyday activities that we typically take it for granted, noticing only when someone deviates from conventional behavior and expectations.

Although a few people begin life with an unclear sexual identity, the overwhelming majority begin with a definite sex and quickly receive societal messages about how to behave. Many societies have established social distinctions between females and males that do not inevitably result from biological differences between the sexes (such as women's reproductive capabilities).

In studying gender, sociologists are interested in the gender-role socialization that leads females and males to behave differently. In Chapter 2, *gender roles* were defined as expectations regarding the proper behavior, attitudes, and activities of males and females. The application of traditional gender roles leads to many forms of differentiation between women and men. Both sexes are physically capable of learning to cook and sew, yet most Western societies determine that women should perform these tasks. Both men and women are capable of learning to weld and fly airplanes, but these functions are generally assigned to men.

Gender roles are evident not only in our work and behavior but in how we react to others. We are constantly "doing gender" without realizing it. If the father just mentioned sits in the doctor's office with his son in the middle of a workday, he will probably receive approving glances from the receptionist and from other patients. "Isn't he a wonderful father?" runs through their minds. But if the boy's mother leaves *her* job and sits with the son in the doctor's office, she will not receive such silent applause.

We socially construct our behavior to create or exaggerate male–female differences. For example, men and women come in a variety of heights, sizes, and ages. Yet traditional norms regarding marriage and even casual dating tell us that in heterosexual couples, the man should be older, taller, and wiser than the woman. As we will see throughout this chapter, such social norms help to reinforce and legitimize patterns of male dominance.

In recent decades, women have entered occupations and professions that were once dominated by men. Yet our society still focuses on "masculine" and "feminine" qualities, as if men and women must be evaluated in those terms. Clearly, we continue to "do gender," and the social construction of gender continues to define significantly different expectations for females and males (Husey 2003; Lindsey 2005; West and Zimmerman 1987).

GENDER-ROLE SOCIALIZATION

Male babies get blue blankets; females get pink ones. Boys are expected to play with trucks, blocks, and toy soldiers; girls receive dolls and kitchen goods. Boys must be masculine—active, aggressive, tough, daring, and dominant—but girls must be feminine—soft, emotional, sweet, and submissive. These traditional gender-role patterns have been influential in the socialization of children in the United States.

An important element in traditional views of proper "masculine" and "feminine" behavior is ***homophobia,*** or fear of and prejudice against homosexuality. Homophobia contributes significantly to rigid gender-role socialization, since many people stereotypically associate male homosexuality with femininity and lesbianism with masculinity. Consequently, men and women who deviate from traditional expectations about gender roles are often presumed to be gay. Despite the advances made by the gay liberation movement, the continuing stigma attached to homosexuality in our culture places pressure on all males (whether gay or not) to exhibit only narrow "masculine" behavior and on all females (whether lesbian or not) to exhibit only narrow "feminine" behavior (Lindsey 2005; Seidman 2002).

It is *adults,* of course, who play a critical role in guiding children into those gender roles deemed appropriate by society. Parents are normally the first and most crucial agents of socialization. But other adults, older siblings, the mass media, and religious and educational institutions also exert an important influence on gender-role socialization, in the United States and elsewhere.

WOMEN'S AND MEN'S GENDER ROLES

How does a girl come to develop a feminine self-image, while a boy develops one that is masculine? In part, they do so by identifying with females and males in their families and neighborhoods and in the media. If a young girl regularly sees female characters on television working as defense attorneys and judges, she may believe that she herself can become a lawyer. It will not hurt if the women that she knows—her mother, sister, parents' friends, or neighbors—are lawyers. But if she sees women portrayed in the media only as models, nurses, and secretaries, her identification and self-image will be quite different. Even if she does become a professional, she may secretly regret falling short of the media stereotypes—a shapely, sexy young woman in a bathing suit, or the perfect wife and mother.

Television is far from being alone in stereotyping women. Studies of children's books published in the United States in the 1940s, 1950s, and 1960s found that females were significantly underrepresented in central roles and illustrations. Virtually all female characters were portrayed as helpless, passive, incompetent, and in need of a strong male caretaker. By the 1980s, there was slightly less stereotyping in children's books, with some female characters shown to be active. Nevertheless, boys were still shown engaged in active play three times as often as girls (Kortenhaus and Demarest 1993).

Social research on gender roles reveals some persistent differences between men and women in North America and Europe. Women experience a mandate to marry and become a mother. Often, marriage is viewed as their true entry into adulthood. And they are expected not only to become mothers but to *want* to be mothers. Though marriage and parenthood play a role in men's lives, they do not appear to be as critical in a man's life course. Rather, society defines men's roles in terms of economic success. While women may achieve recognition in the labor force, it is not as important to their identity as it is for men (Brettell and Sargent 2005).

Men's roles are socially constructed in much the same way as women's roles. Family, peers, and the media all influence how a boy or a man comes to view his appropriate role in society. Robert Brannon (1976) and James Doyle (1995) have identified five aspects of the male gender role:

- Antifeminine element—show no "sissy stuff," including any expression of openness or vulnerability.
- Success element—prove one's masculinity at work and sports.
- Aggressive element—use force in dealing with others.
- Sexual element—initiate and control all sexual relations.
- Self-reliant element—keep cool and unflappable.

No systematic research has established all these elements as necessarily common to all males, but specific studies have confirmed individual elements.

Males who do not conform to the socially constructed gender role face constant criticism and even humiliation, both from children when they are boys and from adults as men. It can be agonizing to be treated as a "chicken" or a "sissy"—particularly if such remarks come from one's father or brothers. At the same time, boys who successfully adapt to cultural standards of masculinity may grow up to be inexpressive men who cannot share their feelings with others. They may be forceful and tough, but as a result they are also closed and isolated (Faludi 1999; McCreary 1994; Sheehy 1999).

To what extent do actual biological differences between the sexes contribute to these cultural differences associated with gender? This question brings us back to the debate over nature versus nurture (see Chapter 2). In assessing the alleged and real differences between men and women, it is useful to examine cross-cultural data.

A CROSS-CULTURAL PERSPECTIVE

The research of anthropologist Margaret Mead points to the importance of cultural conditioning—as opposed to biology—in defining the social roles of males and females. In *Sex and Temperament,* Mead described the typical behaviors of each sex in three different cultures in New Guinea. In the Arapesh culture, she wrote, both women and men behaved in what we would consider a feminine way. In the Mundugumor culture, on the other hand, both sexes exhibited what we would call masculine behavior. The Tchambuli completely reversed our cultural conceptions of masculine and feminine. If biology determined all differences between the sexes, then cross-cultural differences such as those Mead described would not exist. Her findings confirm the influential role of culture and socialization in gender-role differentiation. There appears to be no innate or biological reason to designate completely different gender roles for men and women (Mead [1935] 2001; 1973).

In any society, gender stratification requires not only individual socialization into traditional gender roles within the family but also the promotion and support of those roles by other social institutions, such as religion and education. Moreover, even with all major institutions socializing the young into conventional gender roles, every society has women and men who resist and successfully oppose the stereotypes: strong women who become leaders or professionals, gentle men who care for children, and so forth. It seems clear that differences between the sexes are not dictated by biology. Indeed, the maintenance of traditional gender roles requires constant social controls—and those controls are not always effective.

Explaining Inequality by Gender

THE FUNCTIONALIST VIEW

Cross-cultural studies have shown that societies dominated by men are much more common than those in which women play the decisive role. Functionalists maintain that this type of gender differentiation contributes to overall social stability. Sociologists Talcott Parsons and Robert Bales (1955), for instance, argued that to function most effectively, the family requires adults who will specialize in particular roles. They viewed the traditional arrangement of gender roles as arising out of the need to establish a division of labor between marital partners.

Parsons and Bales contended that women take the expressive, emotionally supportive role and men the instrumental, practical role, with the two complementing each other. *Instrumentality* refers to an emphasis on tasks, a focus on more distant goals, and a concern for the external relationship between one's family and other social institutions. *Expressiveness* denotes a concern for the maintenance of harmony and the internal emotional affairs of the family. According to this theory, women's interest in expressive goals frees men for instrumental tasks, and vice versa. Women become "anchored" in the family as wives, mothers, and household managers; men become anchored in the occupational world outside the home. Of course, Parsons and Bales offered this framework in the 1950s, when many more women were full-time homemakers than is true today. Though they did not explicitly endorse traditional gender roles, they implied that dividing tasks between spouses was functional for the family unit.

Given the typical socialization of women and men in the United States, the functionalist view may seem persuasive. However, it would lead us to expect girls and women with no interest in children to become baby-sitters and mothers. Similarly, males who love spending time with children might be "programmed" into careers in the business world. Such differentiation might harm the individual who does not fit into prescribed roles, while depriving society of the contributions of many talented people who are confined by gender stereotyping. Moreover, the functionalist approach does not convincingly explain why men should be categorically assigned to the instrumental role and women to the expressive role.

THE CONFLICT RESPONSE

Viewed from a conflict perspective, the functionalist approach to explaining gender distinctions masks the underlying power relations between men and women. Parsons and Bales never explicitly presented the expressive and instrumental tasks as being of unequal value to society, yet their inequality is quite evident. Although social institutions may pay lip service to women's expressive skills, men's instrumental skills are more highly rewarded, whether in terms of money or prestige. Consequently, any division of labor by gender into instrumental and expressive tasks is far from neutral in its impact on women.

Conflict theorists contend that the relationship between females and males has traditionally been one of unequal power, with men occupying the dominant position. Men may originally have become powerful in preindustrial times because their size, physical strength, and freedom from childbearing duties allowed them to dominate women physically. In contemporary societies, such considerations are not so important, yet cultural beliefs about the sexes are long established, as anthropologist Margaret Mead ([1935] 2001) and feminist sociologist Helen Mayer Hacker (1951, 1974) both stressed. Such beliefs support a social structure that places males in controlling positions.

Thus, conflict theorists see gender differences as a reflection of the subjugation of one group (women) by another group (men). If we use an analogy to Marx's analysis of class conflict (see Chapter 5), we can say that males are like the bourgeoisie, or capitalists; they control most of society's wealth, prestige, and power. Females are like the proletariat, or workers; they can acquire valuable resources only by following the dictates of their "bosses." Men's work is uniformly valued; women's work (whether unpaid labor in the home or wage labor outside the home) is devalued.

THE FEMINIST PERSPECTIVE

A significant component of the conflict approach to gender stratification draws on feminist theory. Although use of that term is comparatively recent, the critique of women's position in society and culture goes back to some of the earliest influences on sociology. Among the most important are Mary Wollstonecraft's *A Vindication of the Rights of Women* (originally published in 1792), John Stuart Mill's *The Subjection of Women* (originally published in 1869), and Friedrich Engels's *The Origin of the Family, Private Property, and the State* (originally published in 1884).

Engels, a close associate of Karl Marx, argued that women's subjugation coincided with the rise of private property during the industrial revolution. Only when people moved beyond an agrarian economy could males enjoy the luxury of leisure and withhold rewards and privileges from women. Drawing on the work of Marx and Engels, contemporary feminist theorists often view women's subordination as part of the overall exploitation and injustice they see as inherent in capitalist societies. Some radical feminist theorists, however, view the oppression of women as inevitable in *all* male-dominated societies, whether they are labeled "capitalist," "socialist," or "communist" (Feuer 1959; Tuchman 1992).

Feminist sociologists would find little to disagree with in the conflict theorists' perspective, but they are more likely to embrace a political action agenda. Also, feminists would argue that the very discussion of women and society, however well meaning, has been distorted by the exclusion of women from academic thought, including sociology. In Chapter 1 we noted the many accomplishments of Jane Addams and Ida Wells-Barnett, but they generally worked outside the discipline, focusing on what we would now call applied sociology and social work. At the time, their efforts, while valued as humanitarian, were seen as unrelated

Studies show that as many as 96 percent of all interruptions in cross-sex (male–female) conversations are initiated by men.

to the research and conclusions being reached in academic circles, which of course were male academic circles (Anderson 2003; J. Howard 1999).

Like functionalists, conflict and feminist theorists acknowledge that it is not possible to drastically change gender roles without dramatic revisions in a culture's social structure. Functionalists perceive a potential for social disorder, or at least unknown social consequences, if all aspects of traditional gender stratification are disturbed. Yet for conflict and feminist theorists, no social structure is desirable if it is maintained by oppressing a majority of its citizens. These theorists argue that gender stratification may be functional for men who hold power and privilege, but it is hardly in the interest of women.

THE INTERACTIONIST PERSPECTIVE

While functionalists and conflict theorists who study gender distinctions typically focus on macro-level social forces and institutions, interactionist researchers often concentrate on the micro level of everyday behavior. For example, interactionist studies show that men initiate up to 96 percent of all interruptions in cross-sex (male–female) conversations. Men are more likely than women to change the topic of conversation, to ignore topics chosen by members of the opposite sex, to minimize the contributions and ideas of members of the opposite sex, and to validate their own contributions. These patterns reflect the conversational (and in a sense, political) dominance of males. Moreover, even when women occupy a prestigious position, such as that of physician, they are more likely to be interrupted than their male counterparts (Ridgeway and Smith-Lovin 1999; Tannen 1990; West and Zimmerman 1983).

In certain studies, all participants are advised in advance of the overall finding that males are more likely than females to interrupt during a cross-sex conversation. After learning this information, men reduce the frequency of their interruptions, yet they continue to verbally dominate their conversations with women. At the same time, women reduce their already low frequency of interruption, along with other conversationally dominant behaviors.

These findings regarding cross-sex conversations have been frequently replicated. They have striking implications when we consider the power dynamics underlying likely cross-sex interactions—employer and job seeker, college professor and student, husband and wife, to name just a few. From an interactionist perspective, these simple, day-to-day exchanges are one more battleground in the struggle for sexual equality—as women try to "get a word in edgewise" in the midst of men's interruptions and verbal dominance (Okamoto and Smith-Lovin 2001; Tannen 1994a, 1994b).

Table 7–1 summarizes the major sociological perspectives on gender.

Women: The Oppressed Majority

Many people, both male and female, find it difficult to conceive of women as a subordinate and oppressed group. Yet take a look at the political structure of the United States: Women remain noticeably underrepresented. For example, in 2003, only 6 of the nation's 50 states had a female governor (Arizona, Delaware, Hawaii, Kansas, Michigan, and Montana).

Women have made modest progress in certain political arenas. In 1981, out of 535 members of Congress, only 21 were women: 19 in the House of Representatives and 2 in the Senate. In contrast, the Congress

summingUP

Table 7–1 Sociological Perspectives on Gender

Theoretical Perspective	Emphasis
Functionalist	Gender differentiation contributes to social stability.
Conflict	Gender inequality is rooted in the female–male power relationship.
Feminist	Women's subjugation is integral to society and social structure.
Interactionist	Gender distinctions are reflected in people's everyday behavior.

that took office in January 2003 had 71 women: 59 in the House and 12 in the Senate. Yet the leadership of Congress still remains overwhelmingly male (Center for American Women and Politics 2003).

SEXISM AND SEX DISCRIMINATION

Just as African Americans are victimized by racism, women suffer from sexism in our society. *Sexism* is the ideology that one sex is superior to the other. The term is generally used to refer to male prejudice and discrimination against women. In Chapter 6, we noted that Blacks can suffer from both individual acts of racism and institutional discrimination. *Institutional discrimination* was defined as the denial of opportunities and equal rights to individuals or groups that results from the normal operations of a society. In the same sense, women suffer from both individual acts of sexism (such as sexist remarks or acts of violence) and institutional sexism.

It is not simply that particular men in the United States are biased in their treatment of women. All the major institutions of our society—the government, the armed forces, large corporations, the media, universities, and the medical establishment—are controlled by men. In their "normal," day-to-day operations, these institutions often discriminate against women, perpetuating sexism. For example, if the central office of a nationwide bank sets a policy that single women are a bad risk for loans—regardless of their incomes and investments—the bank will discriminate against women in state after state. It will do so even at branches in which loan officers hold no personal biases concerning women, but are merely "following orders."

Our society is run by male-dominated institutions, yet with the power that flows to men come responsibility and stress. Men have higher reported rates of certain types of mental illness than women do, and a greater likelihood of death from heart attack or stroke. The pressure on men to succeed, and then to remain on top in the competitive world of work, can be especially intense. That is not to suggest that gender stratification is as damaging to men as it is to women. But the power and privilege men enjoy are no guarantee of well-being.

SEXUAL HARASSMENT

U.S. courts recognize two kinds of sexual harassment. Legally, *sexual harassment* is defined as behavior that occurs when work benefits are made contingent on sexual favors (as a quid pro quo), or when touching, lewd comments, or the appearance of pornographic material creates a hostile environment in the workplace. In 1998, the Supreme Court ruled that harassment applies to people of the same sex as well as the opposite sex. The quid pro quo type of harassment is fairly easy to identify in a court of law. But the issue of a hostile environment has become the subject of considerable debate, both in court and among the general public (Greenhouse 1998; Lewin 1998).

Sexual harassment must be understood in the context of continuing prejudice and discrimination against women. Whether it occurs in the federal bureaucracy, in the corporate world, or in universities, sexual harassment generally takes place in organizations in which White males are at the top of the hierarchy of authority and women's work is valued less than men's. One survey of the private sector found that African American women were three times more likely than White women to experience sexual harassment. From a conflict perspective, it is not surprising that women—and especially women of color—are most likely to become victims of sexual harassment. In terms of job security, these groups are typically an organization's most vulnerable employees (Jones 1988).

What would happen if the women at your school or workplace started harassing the men?

THE STATUS OF WOMEN WORLDWIDE

A detailed overview of the status of the world's women, issued by the United Nations in 2000, noted that women and men live in different worlds—worlds that differ in access to education and work opportunities, and in health, personal security, and human rights. The Hindu culture of India, for example, makes life especially harsh for widows. When Hindu women marry, they join their husband's family. If the husband dies, the widow becomes the "property" of that family. In many cases, she ends up working as an unpaid servant; in others, she is simply abandoned and left penniless. Ancient Hindu scriptures portray widows as "inauspicious," and advise that "a wise man should avoid her blessings like the poison of a snake" (Burns 1998:10). Such attitudes die slowly in the villages, where most Indians live.

According to the U.N. report, women grow half the world's food, but they rarely own land. They constitute one-third of the world's paid labor force, but are generally found in the lowest-paying jobs. Single-parent households headed by women, which appear to be on the increase in many nations, are typically found in the poorest sections of the population. The feminization of poverty has become a global phenomenon. As in the United States, women worldwide are underrepresented politically.

While acknowledging that much has been done to sharpen people's awareness of gender inequities, the U.N. report identified a number of continuing concerns:

- Despite advances in higher education, women still face major barriers when they attempt to use their educational achievements to advance in the workplace. For example, women rarely hold more than 1 to 2 percent of top executive positions.

- Women almost always work in occupations with lower status and pay than men. In both developing and developed countries, many women work as unpaid family laborers.

- Despite social norms regarding support and protection, many widows around the world receive little concrete support from extended family networks.
- In many African and a few Asian nations, traditions mandate the cutting of female genitals, typically by practitioners who fail to use sterilized instruments. The custom can lead to immediate and serious complications from infection, and eventually to long-term health problems.
- Though males outnumber females as refugees, refugee women have unique needs, such as protection against physical and sexual abuse (United Nations 2000).

Despite these challenges, women are not responding passively; they are mobilizing, individually and collectively. Given the significant underrepresentation of women in government offices and national legislatures, however, the task is difficult.

What conclusions can we draw about women's equality worldwide? First, as anthropologist Laura Nader (1986:383) has observed, even in the relatively more egalitarian nations of the West, women's subordination is "institutionally structured and culturally rationalized, exposing them to conditions of deference, dependency, powerlessness, and poverty." Though the situation of women in Sweden and the United States is significantly better than it is in Saudi Arabia and Bangladesh, women nevertheless remain in a second-class position in the world's most affluent and developed countries.

Second, there is a link between the wealth of industrialized nations and the poverty of developing countries. Viewed from a conflict perspective or through the lens of Immanuel Wallerstein's world systems analysis, the economies of developing nations are controlled and exploited by industrialized countries and multinational corporations based in those countries. Much of the exploited labor in developing nations, especially in the nonindustrial sector, is performed by women. Women workers typically toil long hours for low pay, but contribute significantly to their families' incomes (Jacobson 1993).

WOMEN IN THE WORKFORCE OF THE UNITED STATES

"Does your mother work?" "No, she's just a housewife." This once-familiar exchange reminds us of women's traditional role in the United States. That is, women's work has generally been viewed as unimportant. Several decades ago the Commission on Civil Rights (1976:1) concluded that the passage in the Declaration of Independence proclaiming that "all men are created equal" had been taken too literally for too long. That is especially true with respect to opportunities for employment.

Women's participation in the paid labor force of the United States increased steadily throughout the 20th century (see Figure 7–1). No longer

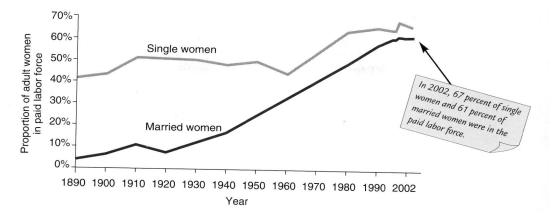

In 2002, 67 percent of single women and 61 percent of married women were in the paid labor force.

is the adult woman associated solely with the role of homemaker. Instead, millions of women—married and single, with and without children—have entered the labor force. In 2000, 60 percent of adult women in the United States held jobs outside the home, compared to 38 percent in 1960. A majority of women are now members of the paid labor force, not full-time homemakers. Among new mothers, 55 percent return to the labor force within a year of giving birth. As recently as 1971, only 31 percent of them went back to work (Bachu and O'Connell 2001; Bureau of the Census 2002a:367).

Yet women entering the job market find their options restricted in important ways. Particularly damaging is occupational segregation, or confinement to sex-typed "women's jobs." For example, in 2002, women accounted for 99 percent of all secretaries, 98 percent of all dental hygienists, and 82 percent of all librarians. Entering such sex-typed occupations places women in "service" roles that parallel the traditional gender-role standard under which housewives "serve" their husbands.

Women are *underrepresented* in occupations historically defined as "men's jobs," which often carry much greater financial rewards and prestige than women's jobs. For example, in 2002, women accounted for approximately 60 percent of the paid labor force of the United States. Yet they constituted only 11 percent of all engineers, 19 percent of all dentists, 31 percent of all physicians, and 28 percent of all computer systems analysts (see Table 7–2 on page 178).

Women from all groups and men from minority groups sometimes encounter attitudinal or organizational bias that prevents them from reaching their full potential. As we saw in Chapter 6, the term **glass ceiling** refers to an invisible barrier that blocks the promotion of a qualified individual in a work environment because of the individual's gender, race, or ethnicity. Women are doing better than minorities in landing top management positions, but they still lag well behind men. According to one

Figure 7–1
Trends in U.S. Women's Participation in the Paid Labor Force, 1890–2002

SOURCES: Bureau of the Census 1975; 2003a:390.

Table 7–2 U.S. Women in Selected Occupations, 2002

Women as Percentage of All Workers in the Occupation			
Underrepresented		**Overrepresented**	
Firefighters	3%	High school teachers	59%
Airline pilots	4	Social workers	74
Engineers	11	Cashiers	77
Clergy	14	File clerks	82
Police	18	Librarians	82
Dentists	19	Elementary teachers	83
Computer systems analysts	28	Registered nurses	93
Lawyers	29	Receptionists	97
Mail carriers	30	Child care workers	98
Physicians	31	Dental hygienists	98
College teachers	43	Secretaries	99

SOURCE: Bureau of the Census 2003a:399–401.

study, women hold only 15 percent of the seats on the boards of directors of the Fortune 1000 largest corporations in the United States. As for the Fortune 500, only six of them had female CEOs by 2003: Avon, Golden West Financial, Hewlett-Packard, Lucent, Mirant, and Xerox (D. Jones 2003; G. Strauss 2002).

One response to the glass ceiling and other gender bias in the workplace is to start your own business and work for yourself. This route to success, traditionally taken by men from immigrant and racial minority groups, has become more common among women as they have increasingly sought paid employment outside the home. According to data released in 2001, women own an impressive 5.4 million businesses in the United States. However, many of those operations are very small, self-run firms. Only 16 percent of women-owned businesses have any paid employees (Bureau of the Census 2001c).

The workplace patterns described here have one crucial result: women earn less money than men. A study done by the General Accounting Office (2002) compared managerial salaries for women and men in the 10 industries that employ 70 percent of women workers, including entertainment, insurance, retailing, public administration, and education. Women managers came closest to matching men's salaries in education, where those who worked full time earned 91 cents for every dollar received by their male counterparts. But on average, women earned only about 78 cents for every dollar earned by men. Particularly troubling was the finding that in most industries, the male–female earnings gap had actually widened between 1995 and

2000. The gap remained even after researchers adjusted their findings for variables such as education, age, and marital status. The glass ceiling is very firm.

Women, as we saw in Chapter 5, are also more likely to be poor. Female heads of households and their children account for most of the nation's poor families. Yet not all women are in equal danger of experiencing poverty. Women who are members of racial and ethnic minorities suffer from "double jeopardy"—stratification by race and ethnicity as well as by gender—as we will see later (Bureau of Labor Statistics 2002).

THE SOCIAL CONSEQUENCES OF WOMEN'S EMPLOYMENT

"What a circus we women perform every day of our lives. It puts a trapeze artist to shame." These words by the writer Anne Morrow Lindbergh apply to the lives of women today, who try to juggle both work and family. Their predicament has many social consequences. For one thing, it puts pressure on child care facilities, on public financing of day care, and even on the fast-food industry, which provides many of the meals women once prepared during the day. For another, it raises questions about the household responsibilities of male wage earners.

Who does the housework when women become productive wage earners? Studies indicate that there is a clear gender gap in the performance of housework, although the differences are narrowing. One study found women doing more housework and spending more time on child care than men, whether on a workday or a weekend (Bond et al. 1998). Another development, over the last 20 years, is women's involvement in elder care. According to a Department of Labor (1998) study, 72 percent of such caregivers are women, who typically spend around 18 hours per week looking after a parent. On and off the job, then, a woman's workday is much longer than a man's.

Sociologist Arlie Hochschild (1989, 1990) has used the phrase *second shift* to describe the double burden—work outside the home followed by child care and housework—that many women face and few men share equitably. On the basis of interviews with and observations of 52 couples over an eight-year period, Hochschild reports that wives (but not their husbands) drive home from the office while planning domestic schedules and play dates for their children—and then begin their second shift. Drawing on national studies, she concludes that women spend 15 fewer hours in leisure activities each week than their husbands. In a year, these women work an extra month of 24-hour days because of the "second shift"; over a dozen years, they work an extra year of 24-hour days. Hochschild found that the women she studied were fraying at the edges, and so were their careers and their marriages. With such reports in mind, many feminists have advocated greater governmental and corporate support for child care, more flexible family leave policies, and other reforms designed to ease the burden on the nation's families.

Most studies of gender, child care, and housework focus on the time women and men actually spend on those duties. However, sociologist Susan Walzer (1996) was interested in whether there are gender differences in the amount of time parents spend *thinking* about the care of their children. Drawing on interviews with 25 couples, Walzer found that mothers are much more involved than fathers in the invisible mental labor associated with caring for a baby. For example, while involved in work outside the home, mothers are more likely to think about their babies, and to feel guilty if they become so consumed with the demands of their jobs that they *fail* to think about their babies.

The Double Jeopardy of Minority Women

Many women experience differential treatment not just because of their gender but because of their race and ethnicity. These citizens face a "double jeopardy"—that of subordinate status twice defined. A disproportionate share of these low-status women are also impoverished due to old age, ill health, disability, and the like.

Figure 6–3 (on page 160) showed clearly the double burden that minority women bear. In 2003, White women earned slightly more income than Black men. Black women earned considerably less—$27,910 compared to $35,024 for White women and $33,536 for Black men. Hispanic women earned less than Hispanic men—$23,714 compared to $27,617. These income gaps persist despite affirmative action programs that benefit both women and minorities.

Feminists have addressed the particular needs of minority women. The question for African American women, Latinas, Asian American women, and others appears to be whether they should unite with their "brothers" against racism or challenge them for their sexism. One answer is that in a truly just society, both sexism and racism must be eradicated (Epstein 1999).

The discussion of gender roles among African Americans has always provoked controversy. Advocates of Black nationalism contend that feminism only distracts women from full participation in the Black struggle. The existence of feminist groups among Blacks, in their view, simply divides the Black community, thereby serving dominant Whites. In contrast, Black feminists such as Florynce Kennedy argue that little is to be gained by adopting or maintaining the gender-role divisions of the dominant society. African American journalist Patricia Raybon (1989) has noted that the media commonly portray Black women in a negative light: as illiterate welfare mothers or prostitutes, for example. Black feminists emphasize that it is not solely Whites and White-dominated media that focus on these negative images; Black men (most recently, some Black male rap artists) have also made degrading comments about African American women.

The plight of Latinas is usually considered part of either the Latino or the feminist movement, despite the distinctive experience of Mexican American, Cuban, Puerto Rican, and Central and South American women. In the past, these women have been excluded from decision making in the two institutions that most directly affect their daily lives: the family and the church. Especially in the lower class, the Hispanic family reflects the pervasive tradition of male domination. And of course, the Roman Catholic church relegates women to supportive roles while reserving the leadership positions for men (Browne 2001; De Andra 1996).

Activists among minority women do not agree on whether priority should be given to fighting for sexual equality or to eliminating racial and ethnic inequality. Neither can be ignored. Helen Mayer Hacker (1974:11), who pioneered research on both Blacks and women, stated before the American Sociological Association, "As a partisan observer, it is my fervent hope that in fighting the twin battles of sexism and racism, Black women and Black men will [create] the outlines of the good society for all Americans" (see also Zia 1993).

Sociology Matters

Sociology matters because it explains how we come to be feminine or masculine.

- What was your childhood idea of how a person of your gender should behave, and where did you get it? Did you ever feel confined by the gender roles you learned as a child?

- Has your concept of your gender role changed over time? If so, who or what influenced you to change your thinking and behavior? Will your children learn the same gender roles as you? Why or why not?

Sociology matters because it raises our awareness of the unequal treatment of women and men.

- Have you and a friend ever been treated differently because one of you was male and the other was female? If so, did you resent the unequal treatment? Can you think of a way to change it?

- Do you believe men and women will ever be equal? Why or why not?

Summary

Like race and ethnicity, gender has an enormous influence on people's lives. In this chapter we explained the cultural basis for gender and examined the ways in which gender defines a person's social roles. We discussed four theoretical perspectives on gender and studied the economic and social effects of prejudice and discrimination on women around the world.

1. Like race, gender is an ascribed status that is socially constructed. **Gender roles** define significantly different expectations for females and males.

2. In the United States, **homophobia**—fear of and prejudice against homosexuality—contributes to rigid gender-role socialization. Family, peers, and the media reinforce gender role stereotypes for both sexes.

3. Cross-cultural studies such as those done by Margaret Mead show that rather than being biologically determined, gender roles differ from one culture to the next.

4. Functionalists maintain that well-defined gender roles contribute to a society's stability. They stress the **instrumentality,** or emphasis on tasks, of the male role and the **expressiveness,** or emphasis on harmony, of the female role.

5. Conflict theorists stress men's dominance over women. They see women's inequality of income, wealth, prestige, and power as the result of men's deliberate subjugation of women.

6. Like conflict theorists, feminists stress the power struggle between the sexes. More than conflict theorists, they tend to see women's inequality as part of the exploitation inherent in capitalist societies.

7. Interactionist studies of interruptions in everyday conversation have shown that men interrupt women much more frequently than women interrupt men—one indication of the pervasive inequality between the sexes.

8. Women experience a special kind of prejudice known as **sexism.** They suffer institutional discrimination in the form of lower pay and restricted opportunities, as well as **sexual harassment** in school and on the job.

9. Worldwide, women are undereducated, underpaid, and over-worked. In the United States, women who work in the paid labor

force are restricted by a **glass ceiling** that blocks their promotion to higher-paying jobs. These women commonly work a **second shift** when they get home.

10. Women who belong to minority groups experience a double jeopardy: discrimination based on both their gender and their race or ethnicity.

www.mhhe.com/schaefersm2
Visit the Online Learning Center for *Sociology Matters* to access quizzes, review activities, and other learning tools.

Key Terms

expressiveness, 170

gender role, 166

glass ceiling, 177

homophobia, 167

instrumentality, 170

second shift, 179

sexism, 174

sexual harassment, 174

Social Institutions: Family and Religion

Studying Social Institutions

The Family: A Global View

Studying the Family

Religion as a Social Institution

Religious Behavior

Among the Tibetans, a woman may be married to more than one man at a time, usually brothers. This system allows sons to share the limited amount of good land they may inherit. Among the Betsileo of Madagascar, a man has multiple wives, each one living in a different village where he cultivates rice. Wherever he has the best rice field, that wife is considered his first or senior wife. Among the Yanomami of Brazil and Venezuela, it is considered proper to have sexual relations with your opposite-sex cousins if they are the children of your mother's brother or your father's sister. But if your opposite-sex cousins are the children of your mother's sister or your father's brother, the same practice is considered to be incest. What can we learn from such varied patterns of family life? Though they may seem to defy generalization, sociologists have discovered that the stunning diversity of families around the world masks similarities in their social function (Haviland et al. 2005; Kottak 2004).

Similar observations may be made about the diversity of religion around the world. When we in the United States think of religion, a variety of images may spring to mind. We may picture a solemn prayer service in a small New England town, a passionate revival meeting in the deep South, or a Hare Krishna group chanting on the streets of San Francisco. If we think of worldwide religious observances, we may imagine Islamic travelers on pilgrimage to Mecca, Orthodox Jews praying at Jerusalem's Western Wall, or an African tribe marking the birth of a child through ritual. Around the world, we find an amazing diversity in religion. Yet sociologists would stress the social functions that all religions perform.

Religion and the family are both *social institutions*—organized patterns of beliefs and behavior that are centered on basic social needs. All societies have social institutions; they may be thought of as *cultural universals*—general practices found in every culture, such as sports, food preparation, and funeral ceremonies (see Chapter 2). The fact that all societies have these cultural universals is not surprising, for they meet our needs for food, clothing, and shelter, as well as for support and reassurance, occupational training, and social order. In this chapter, we will begin by considering social institutions from the three major sociological perspectives: functionalist, conflict, and interactionist. Then we will apply those perspectives to two major social institutions, the family and religion. In Chapter 9 we will extend the analysis to three more social institutions: education, government, and the economy (Murdock 1945).

Studying Social Institutions

FUNCTIONALIST VIEW

One way to study social institutions is to examine how they fulfill essential functions. To survive, any society or relatively permanent group must accomplish five major tasks, or functional prerequisites (see Table 8–1, page 186):

1. *Replacing personnel.* Any group or society must replace personnel when they die, leave, or become incapacitated. This function is accomplished through such means as immigration, annexation of neighboring groups, acquisition of slaves, or sexual reproduction. The Shakers, a religious sect that came to the United States in 1774, are a conspicuous example of a group that has *failed* to replace personnel. Their religious beliefs commit the Shakers to celibacy; to survive, the group must recruit new members. At first, the Shakers proved quite successful in attracting members, reaching a peak of about 6,000 in the 1840s. As of 2004, however, the only Shaker community left in this country was a farm in Maine with five members—three men and two women (Sabbathday Lake 2004).

2. *Teaching new recruits.* No group or society can survive if many of its members reject the established behavior and responsibilities. Thus, finding or producing new members is not sufficient. The group or society must encourage recruits to learn and accept its values and

summingUP

Table 8–1 Five Major Functions of Institutions

Functional Prerequisite	Related Social Institutions
Replacing personnel	Family Government (immigration)
Teaching new recruits	Family (basic skills) Economy (occupations) Education (schools) Mass media Religion (sacred teachings)
Producing and distributing goods and services	Family (food preparation) Economy Government (regulations regarding labor and commerce) Health care system
Preserving order	Family (child rearing, regulation of sexual behavior) Government Religion (morals)
Providing and maintaining a sense of purpose	Government (patriotism) Religion

customs. Such learning can take place formally in schools (where learning is a manifest function) or informally, through interaction and negotiation in peer groups (where instruction is a latent function).

3. *Producing and distributing goods and services.* Any relatively permanent group or society must provide and distribute desired goods and services to its members. Each society establishes a set of rules for the allocation of financial and other resources. These rules must satisfy the needs of most members to some extent, or the society will risk the possibility of discontent, and ultimately disorder.

4. *Preserving order.* The native people of Tasmania, a large island just south of Australia, are now extinct. In the 1800s they were destroyed by the hunting parties of European conquerors, who looked on them as half-human. The Tasmanians' annihilation underscores a critical function of every group or society—preserving order and protecting itself from attack. Because the Tasmanians were unable to defend themselves against the more highly developed European technology of warfare, an entire people was wiped out.

5. *Providing and maintaining a sense of purpose.* People must feel motivated to continue as members of a group or society in order to fulfill the first four requirements. The behavior of New Yorkers after the terrorist attack on the World Trade Center on September 11, 2001, is a testament to the importance of maintaining a sense of

purpose. In the face of a crippling blow to their city, residents flocked to makeshift blood donation centers; left food, clothing, and money at firehouses and police stations; and swelled the crowds at memorial services, carrying candles, flags, and signs proclaiming their unbroken resolve.

Many aspects of a society can assist people in developing and maintaining a sense of purpose. For some people, religious values or personal moral codes are paramount; for others, patriotism or tribal identities are especially meaningful. Whatever the source, in any society there remains one common, critical reality. If an individual does not have a sense of purpose, he or she has little reason to contribute to a society's survival.

This list of functional prerequisites does not specify *how* a society and its corresponding social institutions should perform each task. For example, one society may protect itself from external attack by amassing a frightening arsenal of weaponry, while another may make a determined effort to remain neutral in world politics and to promote cooperative relationships with its neighbors. No matter what the strategy, any society or relatively permanent group must attempt to satisfy all these functional prerequisites for survival. If a society fails on even one condition, as the Tasmanians did, it runs the risk of extinction (Aberle et al. 1950; Mack and Bradford 1979).

CONFLICT VIEW

Conflict theorists do not concur with the functionalist approach to social institutions. Although theorists of both perspectives agree that institutions are organized to meet basic social needs, conflict theorists object to the implication that the outcome is necessarily efficient and socially desirable.

From a conflict perspective, the present organization of social institutions is no accident. Major institutions, such as education, help to maintain the privileges of the most powerful individuals and groups in a society, while contributing to the powerlessness of others. To give one example, public schools in the United States are financed largely through property taxes, an arrangement that allows people from more affluent areas to provide their children with better-equipped schools and better-paid teachers than people from low-income areas. As a result, children from prosperous communities are better prepared to compete academically than children from impoverished communities. The structure of the nation's educational system permits and even promotes such unequal treatment.

Conflict theorists argue that social institutions such as education are inherently conservative. Without question, it has been difficult to implement educational reforms that promote equal opportunity—whether bilingual education, school desegregation, or mainstreaming of students with disabilities. From a functionalist perspective, social change can be dysfunctional, since it often leads to instability. But from a conflict view, why should we preserve the existing social structure if it is unfair and discriminatory?

Social institutions also operate in gendered and racist environments, as conflict theorists, as well as feminists and interactionists, have pointed out. In schools, offices, and government institutions, assumptions about what people can do reflect the sexism and racism of the larger society. For instance, many people assume that women cannot make tough decisions—even those in the top echelons of corporate management. Others assume that all Black students at elite colleges represent affirmative action admissions. Inequality based on gender, economic status, race, and ethnicity thrives in such an environment—to which we might add discrimination based on age, physical disability, and sexual orientation. The truth of this assertion can be seen in routine decisions by employers on how to advertise jobs, as well as whether to provide fringe benefits such as child care and parental leave.

INTERACTIONIST VIEW

Social institutions affect our everyday behavior, whether we are driving down the street or waiting in a long shopping line. Sociologist Mitchell Duneier (1994a, 1994b) studied the social behavior of the word processors, all women, who work in the service center of a large Chicago law firm. Duneier was interested in the informal social norms that emerged in this work environment and the rich social network that the female employees had created.

The Network Center, as it is called, is a single, windowless room in a large office building where the law firm occupies seven floors. The center is staffed by two shifts of word processors, who work either from 4:00 P.M. to midnight or from midnight to 8:00 A.M. Each word processor works in a cubicle with just enough room for her keyboard, terminal, printer, and telephone. Work assignments for the word processors are placed in a central basket and completed according to precise procedures.

At first glance, we might think that these women labor with little social contact, apart from limited work breaks and occasional conversations with their supervisor. However, drawing on the interactionist perspective, Duneier learned that despite working in a large office, these women found private moments to talk (often in the halls or outside the washroom) and share a critical view of the law firm's attorneys and daytime secretaries. Indeed, the word processors routinely suggested that their assignments represented work that the "lazy" secretaries should have completed during the normal workday. One word processor in particular resented the lawyers' superior attitude, and pointedly refused to recognize or speak with any attorney who would not address her by name (Duneier 1994b).

Interactionist theorists emphasize that our social behavior is conditioned by the roles and statuses we accept, the groups we belong to, and

Use Your Sociological Imagination

Do you think that social networks might be more important to a migrant worker in California than to someone with political and social clout? Why or why not?

the institutions within which we function. For example, the social roles associated with being a judge occur within the larger context of the criminal justice system. The status of "judge" stands in relation to other statuses, such as attorney, plaintiff, defendant, and witness, as well as to the social institution of government. Although courts and jails have great symbolic importance, the judicial system derives its continued significance from the roles people carry out in their social interactions (Berger and Luckmann 1966).

The Family: A Global View

As we saw at the beginning of this chapter, there are many variations in "the family" from one culture to the next. Yet the family as a social institution exists in all cultures. Moreover, certain general principles concerning its composition, kinship patterns, and authority patterns are universal.

COMPOSITION: WHAT IS THE FAMILY?

A *family* may be defined as a set of people who are related by blood, marriage (or some other agreed-upon relationship), or adoption who share the primary responsibility for reproduction and caring for members of society. If we were to take our information on what a family is from what we see on television, we might come up with some strange scenarios. The media don't always present a realistic view of the family. Moreover, many people still think of the family in very narrow terms—as a married couple and their unmarried children living together. However, that is but one type of family, what sociologists refer to as a ***nuclear family.*** The term *nuclear family* is well chosen, since this type of family serves as the nucleus, or core, on which larger family groups are built.

Most people in the United States see the nuclear family as the preferred family arrangement. Yet by 2000, only about a third of the nation's family households fit this model. The proportion of households in the United States composed of married couples with children at home has decreased steadily over the last 30 years, and is expected to continue shrinking. At the same time, the number of female-headed households has increased (see Figure 8–1, page 190). Similar trends are evident in other industrialized nations, including Canada, Great Britain, and Japan.

A family in which relatives—such as grandparents, aunts, or uncles—live in the same home as parents and their children is known as an ***extended family.*** Although not common, such living arrangements do exist in the United States. The structure of the extended family offers certain advantages over that of the nuclear family. Crises such as death, divorce, and illness put less strain on family members, since there are more people who can provide assistance and emotional support. In addition, the extended family constitutes a larger economic unit than the nuclear

Figure 8–1
U.S. Households by
Family Type,
1940–2003

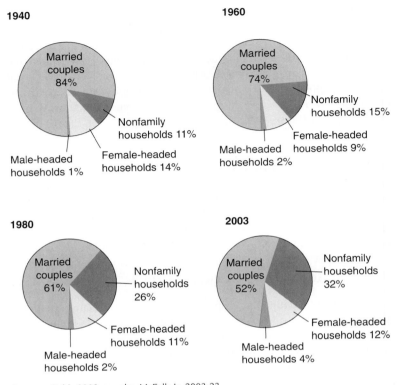

SOURCES: Fields 2003; see also McFalls Jr. 2003:23.

family. If the family is engaged in a common enterprise—a farm or small business—the additional family members may represent the difference between prosperity and failure.

In considering these differing family types, we have limited ourselves to the form of marriage that is characteristic of the United States—monogamy. The term ***monogamy*** describes a form of marriage in which one woman and one man are married only to each other. Some observers, noting the high rate of divorce in the United States, have suggested that "serial monogamy" is a more accurate description of the form that monogamy takes in the United States. In ***serial monogamy,*** a person may have several spouses in his or her life, but only one spouse at a time.

Serial monogamy is certainly more common today than it was a century ago due to a greater incidence and acceptance of divorce. In the United States and many other countries, the divorce rate began to increase in the late 1960s, but then started to level off and has even declined slightly from its highest point in U.S. history, reached in the early 1980s. The recent decline has been attributed to two factors: an increase in the age at which people first marry and an increase in the educational level of those who marry (National Marriage Project 2004:18–19).

Some cultures allow an individual to have several husbands or wives simultaneously. This form of marriage is known as *polygamy.* In fact, most societies throughout the world, past and present, have preferred polygamy to monogamy. Anthropologist George Murdock (1949, 1957) sampled 565 societies and found that some type of polygamy was the preferred form in more than 80 percent. While polygamy declined steadily through most of the 20th century and into the 21st, in 19 African nations at least 20 percent of the women are still living in polygamous unions (Seager 2003).

There are two basic types of polygamy. According to Murdock, the most common—endorsed by the majority of cultures he sampled—was *polygyny,* in which a husband may have several wives at the same time. The wives are often sisters, who are expected to hold similar values and to have experience sharing a household. In polygynous societies, relatively few men have multiple spouses. Most individuals live in monogamous families; having multiple wives is viewed as a mark of status.

The other principal variation of polygamy is *polyandry,* in which a woman may have several husbands at the same time. Such is the case in Tibet, as we saw in the chapter opening. Polyandry, however, is exceedingly rare. It is accepted in some extremely poor societies that practice female infanticide (the killing of baby girls) and thus have a relatively small number of women. Like many other societies, polyandrous cultures devalue the social worth of women.

KINSHIP PATTERNS: TO WHOM ARE WE RELATED?

Many of us can trace our roots by looking at a family tree or listening to our elders talk about their lives—and the lives of ancestors who died long before we were born. Yet a person's lineage is more than a personal history; it reflects societal patterns that govern descent. In every culture, children encounter relatives to whom they are expected to show an emotional attachment. This state of being related to others is called *kinship.* Kinship is culturally learned, rather than being totally determined by biological or marital ties. For example, adoption creates a kinship tie that is legally acknowledged and socially accepted.

The family and the kin group are not necessarily one and the same. The family is a household unit, but kin do not always live together or function as a collective body on a daily basis. Kin groups include aunts, uncles, cousins, in-laws, and so forth. In a society such as the United States, the kinship group may come together only rarely, usually for a wedding or funeral. However, kinship ties frequently create obligations and responsibilities. We may feel compelled to assist our kin, and we feel free to call upon relatives for many types of aid, including loans and baby-sitting.

How do we identify kinship groups? The principle of descent assigns people to kinship groups according to their relationship to their mother or father. There are three primary ways of determining descent. The United States follows the system of *bilateral descent,* in which both sides of a person's family are regarded as equally important. For example, no higher value is given to the brothers of one's father than to the brothers of one's mother.

Most societies—according to George Murdock, 64 percent—favor one side of the family or the other in tracing descent. *Patrilineal* (from Latin *pater,* "father") *descent* favors the father's relatives in terms of property, inheritance, and emotional ties. *Matrilineal* (from Latin *mater,* "mother") *descent* favors the mother's relatives.

New forms of reproductive technology will soon force a new way of looking at kinship. Today, a combination of biological and social processes can "create" a family member, requiring that more distinctions be made about who is related to whom (Cussins 1998).

AUTHORITY PATTERNS: WHO RULES?

Imagine that you have recently married and must begin to make decisions about the future of your new family. You and your spouse face many questions. Where will you live? How will you furnish your home? Who will do the cooking, the shopping, the cleaning? Whose friends will be invited to dinner? Each time a decision must be made, an issue is raised: Who has the power to make the decision? In simple terms, who rules the family? Conflict theorists examine these questions in the context of traditional gender distinctions, which have given men a dominant position over women.

Societies vary in the way that power is distributed within the family. If a society expects males to dominate in family decision making, it is termed a *patriarchy.* In patriarchal societies such as Iran, the eldest male frequently wields the greatest power, although wives are expected to be treated with respect and kindness. An Iranian woman's status is typically defined by her relationship to a male relative, usually as a wife or daughter. In many patriarchal societies women find it more difficult to obtain a divorce than a man does (Farr 1999). By contrast, in a *matriarchy,* women dominate in family decision making. Matriarchies are rare; they emerged among Native American tribal societies and in nations where men were absent for long periods, for warfare or food gathering.

In a third type of authority pattern, the *egalitarian family,* spouses are regarded as equals. This pattern does not mean that each decision is shared, however. Wives may hold authority in some spheres, husbands in others. Many sociologists believe the egalitarian family has begun to replace the patriarchal family as the social norm in the United States.

Clearly, there is great variation in the composition, kinship patterns, and authority patterns of families around the world. Yet as we have seen, the family fulfills certain universal social functions. In the next section, we will examine those functions from three different sociological perspectives.

Studying the Family

Do we really need the family? A century ago, Friedrich Engels ([1884] 1959), a colleague of Karl Marx, described the family as the ultimate source of social inequality because of its role in the transfer of power, property, and privilege. More recently, conflict theorists have argued that the family contributes to societal injustice, denies women opportunities that are extended to men, and limits freedom in sexual expression and mate selection. In contrast, the functionalist perspective focuses on the ways in which the family gratifies the needs of its members and contributes to social stability. The interactionist view considers the intimate, face-to-face relationships that occur in the family.

FUNCTIONALIST VIEW

The family performs six major functions, first outlined 70 years ago by sociologist William F. Ogburn (Ogburn and Tibbits 1934):

1. *Reproduction.* For a society to maintain itself, it must replace dying members. In this sense, the family contributes to human survival through its function of reproduction.

2. *Protection.* Unlike the young of other animal species, human infants need constant care and economic security. In all cultures, the family assumes the ultimate responsibility for the protection and upbringing of children.

3. *Socialization.* Parents and other kin monitor a child's behavior and transmit the norms, values, and language of their culture to the child.

4. *Regulation of sexual behavior.* Sexual norms are subject to change both over time (for instance, in the customs for dating) and across cultures (compare strict Saudi Arabia to the more permissive Denmark). Whatever the period or cultural values of a society, however, standards of sexual behavior are most clearly defined within the family circle.

5. *Affection and companionship.* Ideally, the family provides members with warm and intimate relationships, helping them to feel satisfied and secure. Of course, a family member may find such rewards outside the family—from peers, in school, at work—and may even perceive the home as an unpleasant or abusive setting. Nevertheless, we expect our relatives to understand us, to care for us, and to be there for us when we need them.

6. *Provision of social status.* We inherit a social position because of the family background and reputation of our parents and siblings. The family presents the newborn child with an ascribed status based on race and ethnicity that helps to determine his or her place within society's stratification system. Moreover, family resources affect

children's ability to pursue certain opportunities, such as higher education and special lessons.

Traditionally, the family has fulfilled a number of other functions, such as providing religious training, education, and recreation. But Ogburn argued that other social institutions have gradually assumed many of those functions. Education once took place by the family fireside; now it is the responsibility of professionals working in schools and colleges. Even the family's traditional recreational function has been transferred to outside groups such as Little Leagues, athletic clubs, and Internet chat rooms.

CONFLICT VIEW

Conflict theorists view the family not as a contributor to social stability, but as a reflection of the inequality in wealth and power that is found within the larger society. Feminist and conflict theorists note that the family has traditionally legitimized and perpetuated male dominance. Throughout most of human history—and in a wide range of societies—husbands have exercised overwhelming power and authority in the family. Not until the first wave of contemporary feminism in the United States during the mid-1800s was a substantial challenge made to the historic status of wives and children as the husband's legal property.

While the egalitarian family has become a more common pattern in the United States in recent decades—owing in good part to the activism of feminists beginning in the late 1960s and early 1970s—male dominance over the family has hardly disappeared. Sociologists have found that women are significantly more likely to leave their jobs when their husbands find better employment opportunities than men are when their wives receive desirable job offers (Bielby and Bielby 1992).

Conflict theorists also view the family as an economic unit that contributes to societal injustice. The family is the basis for transferring power, property, and privilege from one generation to the next. Although the United States is viewed widely as a land of opportunity, social mobility is restricted in important ways. Children inherit the privileged or less-than-privileged social and economic status of their parents (and in some cases, of earlier generations as well). As conflict theorists point out, the social class of parents significantly influences children's socialization experiences and the degree of protection they receive. Thus the socioeconomic status of a child's family will have a marked influence on his or her nutrition, health care, housing, educational opportunities, and in many respects, life chances as an adult.

INTERACTIONIST VIEW

Interactionists focus on the micro level of family and other intimate relationships. They are interested in how individuals interact with one another, whether they are cohabiting partners or longtime married couples. For example, in a study of both Black and White two-parent households, researchers found that when fathers are more involved with their children (reading to them, helping them with homework, or restricting their television viewing) children have fewer behavior problems, get along better with others, and are more responsible (Mosley and Thomson 1995).

Another interactionist study might examine the role of the stepparent. The increased number of single parents who remarry has sparked interest in those who are helping to raise other people's children. Studies have found that stepmothers are more likely than stepfathers to accept the blame for bad relations with their stepchildren. Interactionists theorize that stepfathers (like most fathers) may simply be unaccustomed to interacting directly with children when the mother isn't there (Bray and Kelly 1999; Furstenberg and Cherlin 1991).

FEMINIST VIEW

Because "women's work" has traditionally focused on family life, feminist sociologists have taken a strong interest in the family as a social institution. As we saw in Chapter 7, research on gender roles in child care and household chores has been extensive. Sociologists have looked particularly closely at how women's work outside the home impacts their child care and housework—duties Arlie Hochschild (1989, 1990) has referred to as the "second shift." Today, researchers recognize that for many women, the second shift includes the care of aging parents as well.

Feminist theorists have urged social scientists and social agencies to rethink the notion that families in which no adult male is present are automatically a cause for concern, or even dysfunctional. They have also contributed to research on single women, single-parent households, and lesbian couples. In the case of single mothers, researchers have focused on the resiliency of many such households, despite economic stress. According to Velma McBride Murray and her colleagues (2001) at the University of Georgia, such studies show that among African Americans, single mothers draw heavily on kinfolk for material resources, parenting advice, and social support. Considering feminist research on the family as a whole, one researcher concluded that the family is the "source of women's strength" (L. Richardson et al. 2004).

Finally, feminists stress the need to investigate neglected topics in family studies. For instance, in a small but significant number of dual-income households, the wife earns a higher income than the husband. Sociologist Suzanne Bianchi estimates that in 11 percent of marriages, the wife earns at least 60 percent of the family's income. Yet beyond individual case studies, little research has been done on how these families may differ from those in which the husband is the major breadwinner (Tyre and McGinn 2003:47).

Table 8–2 Sociological Perspectives on the Family

Theoretical Perspective	Emphasis
Functionalist	The family as a contributor to social stability Roles of family members
Conflict	The family as a perpetuator of inequality Transmission of poverty or wealth across generations
Interactionist	Relationships among family members
Feminist	The family as a perpetuator of gender roles Female-headed households

Table 8–2 summarizes the four major theoretical perspectives on the family.

Religion as a Social Institution

According to Émile Durkheim, *religion* is a unified system of beliefs and practices relative to sacred things. As a cultural universal, religion plays a basic role that includes both manifest and latent social functions. Among its *manifest* (open and stated) functions, religion defines the spiritual world and gives meaning to the divine. Religion also provides an explanation for events that seem difficult to understand, such as what lies beyond the grave. In contrast, the *latent* functions of religion are unintended, covert, or hidden. Even though the manifest function of church services is to offer a forum for religious worship, they might at the same time fulfill a latent function as a meeting ground for unmarried members.

In this section, we'll consider four functions that sociologists have stressed in their study of religion. We'll see that religion helps to integrate society and provides people with social support in time of need. We'll discuss Max Weber's view of religion as a source of social change. Finally, we'll examine the conflict perspective on religion as a means of social control. Note that for the most part, religion's impact is best understood from a macro-level viewpoint, oriented toward the larger society. The social support function is an exception: it is best viewed on the micro level, directed toward the individual.

THE INTEGRATIVE FUNCTION OF RELIGION

Émile Durkheim viewed religion as an integrative power in human society—a perspective that is reflected in functionalist thought today. Durkheim sought to answer a perplexing question: "How can human societies be held together when they are composed of individuals and social groups with diverse interests and aspirations?" In his view, religious bonds often transcend these personal and divisive forces. Durkheim acknowledged that religion is not the only integrative force; nationalism or patriotism may serve the same end.

How does religion provide this "societal glue"? Religion, whether it be Buddhism, Islam, Christianity, or Judaism (see Table 8–3), offers people meaning and purpose. It gives them certain ultimate values and ends to hold in common. Although those values and ends are subjective and not always fully accepted, they help society to function as an integrated social system. For example, funerals, weddings, bar and bat mitzvahs, and confirmations serve to integrate people into larger communities through shared beliefs and values about the ultimate questions of life.

Religion also serves to bind people together in times of crisis and confusion. Immediately after the terrorist attacks of September 11, 2001, on New York City and Washington, D.C., attendance at worship services in the United States increased dramatically. Muslim, Jewish, and Christian clerics made joint appearances to honor the dead and urge citizens not to retaliate against those who looked, dressed, or sounded different from others. The integrative power of religion can be seen, too, in the role that churches, synagogues, and mosques have traditionally played and continue to play for immigrant groups in the United States. For example, Roman Catholic immigrants may settle near a parish church that offers

summingUP

Table 8–3 Major World Religions

Faith	Current Following, in Millions (and Percent of World Population)	Primary Location of Followers Today	Founder (and Approximate Birth Date)	Important Texts (and Holy Sites)
Buddhism	360 (5.9%)	Southeast Asia, Mongolia, Tibet	Gautama Siddhartha (563 B.C.)	Triptaka (areas in Nepal)
Christianity	2,000 (33%)	Europe, North America, South America	Jesus (6 B.C.)	Bible (Jerusalem, Rome)
Hinduism	811 (13.4%)	India, Indian communities overseas	No specific founder (1500 B.C.)	Sruti and Smrti texts (seven sacred cities, including Vavansi)
Islam	1,190 (19.6%)	Middle East, Central Asia, North Africa, Indonesia	Mohammad (A.D. 570)	Qur'an or Koran (Mecca, Medina, Jerusalem)
Judaism	14 (0.2%)	Israel, United States, France, Russia	Abraham (2000 B.C.)	Torah, Talmud (Jerusalem)

services in their native language, such as Polish or Spanish. Similarly, Korean immigrants may join a Presbyterian church with many Korean American members and with religious practices like those of churches in Korea. Like other religious organizations, these Roman Catholic and Presbyterian churches help to integrate immigrants into their new homeland.

Religious conflict is evident in the United States as well, as sociologist James Davison Hunter (1991) has pointed out. In many communities, Christian fundamentalists, conservative Catholics, and Orthodox Jews have joined forces in a battle against their liberal counterparts for control of the secular culture. The battlefield is an array of familiar social issues, among them multiculturalism, child care, abortion, home schooling, gay rights, and government funding for the arts.

RELIGION AND SOCIAL SUPPORT

Most of us find it difficult to accept the stressful events of life—the death of a loved one, a serious injury, bankruptcy, divorce, and so forth. Our difficulty is especially pronounced when something "senseless" happens. How can family and friends come to terms with the death of a talented college student, not even 20 years old?

Through its emphasis on the divine and the supernatural, religion allows us to "do something" about the calamities we face. In some faiths, adherents can offer sacrifices or pray to a deity in the belief that such acts will change their earthly condition. At a more basic level, religion encourages us to view our personal misfortunes as relatively unimportant in the broader perspective of human history—or even as part of an undisclosed divine purpose. Friends and relatives of the deceased college student may see his death as being "God's will," as having some ultimate benefit that we cannot understand now. This perspective may be much more comforting than the terrifying feeling that any of us can die senselessly at any moment—that there is no divine "answer" to why one person lives a long and full life, while another dies tragically at a relatively early age.

On a more practical level, faith-based community organizations are taking on more and more responsibility for providing concrete social assistance. In fact, President George W. Bush created the Office of Faith-Based and Community Initiatives to ease regulations that prevent religious groups from competing for government funding. Sociologist William Julius Wilson (1999) has singled out faith-based organizations in 40 communities from California to Massachusetts as models of social reform. These organizations identify experienced leaders and assemble them into nonsectarian coalitions devoted to community development.

RELIGION AND SOCIAL CHANGE

When a person seems driven to work and succeed, we often attribute his or her ambition to the "Protestant work ethic." The term comes from the writings of Max Weber, who carefully examined the connection between religious allegiance and capitalist development. Weber's findings appeared in his pioneering work *The Protestant Ethic and the Spirit of Capitalism* ([1904] 1958).

Weber noted that in European nations with both Protestant and Catholic citizens, an overwhelming number of business leaders, owners of capital, and skilled workers were Protestant. In his view, this pattern was no mere coincidence. Weber pointed out that the followers of John Calvin (1509–1564), a leader of the Protestant Reformation, emphasized a disciplined work ethic, this-worldly concerns, and a rational orientation to life that he termed the ***Protestant ethic.*** One by-product of the Protestant ethic was a drive to accumulate savings that could be used for future investment. This "spirit of capitalism," to use Weber's phrase, contrasted with the moderate work hours, leisurely work habits, and lack of ambition that he saw as typical of the times (Winter 1977; Yinger 1974).

Few books on the sociology of religion have aroused as much commentary and criticism as Weber's work. It has been hailed as one of the most important theoretical works in the field and an excellent example of macro-level analysis. Like Durkheim, Weber demonstrated that religion is not solely a matter of intimate personal belief. Rather, the collective nature of religion has social consequences for society as a whole.

Weber provided a convincing description of the origins of European capitalism. But the capitalist economic system has since been adopted by non-Calvinists in many parts of the world. Contemporary studies done in the United States show little or no difference in achievement orientation between Roman Catholics and Protestants. Apparently, the "spirit of capitalism" has become a generalized cultural trait (Greeley 1989).

Conflict theorists caution that Weber's theory—even if it is accepted—should not be regarded as applicable to mature capitalism, as reflected in the rise of multinational corporations. Marxists would disagree with Weber not on the origins of capitalism, but on its future. Unlike Marx, Weber believed that capitalism could endure indefinitely as an economic system. He added, however, that the decline of religion as an overriding force in society opened the way for workers to express their discontent more vocally (Collins 1980).

RELIGION AND SOCIAL CONTROL: A CONFLICT VIEW

Karl Marx thought that religion *impeded* social change by encouraging oppressed people to focus on other-worldly concerns rather than on their immediate poverty or exploitation. Marx described religion as an "opiate" that was particularly harmful to oppressed peoples. He felt that religion often drugged the masses into submission by offering a consolation for their harsh lives on earth: the hope of salvation in an ideal afterlife. For example, during the period of slavery in the United States, White masters forbade Blacks to practice native African religions. Instead, they encouraged them to adopt Christianity, which taught that obedience would lead to salvation and eternal happiness. Viewed from a conflict perspective, Christianity may have pacified certain slaves and blunted the rage that often fuels rebellion (McGuire 1997; Yinger 1970).

Marx acknowledged that religion plays an important role in propping up the existing social structure. Religious values, as already noted, reinforce other social institutions and the social order as a whole. From Marx's perspective, however, religion's promotion of social stability only helps to perpetuate patterns of social inequality. According to Marx, the dominant religion reinforces the interests of those in power (Harap 1982).

Consider, for example, India's traditional caste system. Castes define the social structure of that society, at least among the Hindu majority. The caste system was almost certainly the creation of the priesthood, but it also serves the interests of India's political rulers by granting a certain religious legitimacy to social inequality.

Like the Hindu faith, contemporary Christianity reinforces traditional patterns of behavior that call for the subordination of the less powerful. The role of women in the church is an example of uneven distribution of power. Assumptions about gender roles leave women in a subservient position both within Christian churches and at home. In fact, women find it as difficult to achieve leadership positions in many churches as they do in large corporations. Like Marx, conflict theorists argue that to whatever extent religion actually does influence social behavior, it reinforces existing patterns of dominance and inequality.

From the Marxist perspective, religion functions as an "agent of depoliticization" (J. Wilson 1978). In simpler terms, religion keeps people from seeing their lives and societal conditions in political terms—for example, by obscuring the overriding significance of conflicting economic interests. Marxists suggest that by inducing a "false consciousness" among the disadvantaged, religion lessens the possibility of collective political action, which can end capitalist oppression and transform society.

Religion is not the only social institution whose functions have been the subject of controversy among theorists. Conflict theorists charge that schools, too, discriminate in favor of the powerful and against the disadvantaged, as we will see in Chapter 9.

The social support that religious groups provide is suddenly withdrawn from your community. How will your life or the lives of others change? What will happen if religious groups stop pushing for social change?

Religious Behavior

All religions have certain elements in common, yet those elements are expressed in the distinctive manner of each faith. These patterns of religious behavior, like other patterns of social behavior, are of great interest to sociologists—especially interactionists—since they underscore the relationship between religion and society.

Religious beliefs, religious rituals, and religious experience all help to define what is sacred and to differentiate the sacred from the profane. Let's examine these three dimensions of religious behavior, as seen through the eyes of interactionists.

BELIEF

Some people believe in life after death, in supreme beings with unlimited powers, or in supernatural forces. **Religious beliefs** are statements to which members of a particular religion adhere. These views can vary dramatically from one religion to the next.

The Adam and Eve account of creation found in Genesis, the first book of the Old Testament, is an example of a religious belief. Many people in the United States strongly adhere to this biblical explanation of creation, and even insist that it be taught in public schools. These people, known as creationists, are worried by the secularization of society, and oppose teaching that directly or indirectly questions biblical scripture. Worldwide, the strength of religious beliefs varies dramatically. In general, spirituality is not as strong in industrialized nations as it is in developing nations. The United States is an exception to the trend toward secularization, in part because the government encourages religious expression (without explicitly supporting it) by allowing religious groups to claim charitable status, and even to receive federal aid for activities such as educational services. And although belief in God is relatively weak in formerly communist states such as Russia, surveys show a growth in spirituality in communist countries over the last 10 years.

RITUAL

Religious rituals are practices required or expected of members of a faith. Rituals usually honor the divine power (or powers) worshiped by believers; they also remind adherents of their religious duties and responsibilities. Rituals and beliefs can be interdependent; rituals generally affirm beliefs, as in a public or private statement confessing a sin. Like any social institution, religion develops distinctive norms to structure people's behavior. Moreover, sanctions are attached to religious rituals, whether rewards (bar mitzvah gifts) or penalties (expulsion from a religious institution for violation of norms).

In the United States, rituals may be very simple, such as saying grace at a meal or observing a moment of silence to commemorate someone's death. Yet certain rituals, such as the process of canonizing a saint, are quite elaborate. Most religious rituals in our culture focus on services conducted at houses of worship. Attendance at a service, silent and spoken prayers, communion, and singing of spiritual hymns and chants are common forms of ritual behavior that generally take place in group settings. From an interactionist perspective, these rituals serve as important face-to-face encounters in which people reinforce their religious beliefs and their commitment to their faith.

For Muslims, a very important ritual is the *hajj,* a pilgrimage to the Grand Mosque in Mecca, Saudi Arabia. Every Muslim who is physically and financially able is expected to make this trip at least once. Each year

2 million pilgrims go to Mecca during the one-week period indicated by the Islamic lunar calendar. Muslims from all over the world make the *hajj,* including those in the United States, where many tours are arranged to facilitate the trip.

EXPERIENCE

In the sociological study of religion, the term ***religious experience*** refers to the feeling or perception of being in direct contact with the ultimate reality, such as a divine being, or of being overcome with religious emotion. A religious experience may be rather slight, such as the feeling of exaltation a person receives from hearing a choir sing Handel's "Hallelujah Chorus." But many religious experiences are more profound, such as a Muslim's experience on a *hajj.* In his autobiography, the late African American activist Malcolm X (1964:338) wrote of his *hajj* and how deeply moved he was by the way that Muslims in Mecca came together across race and color lines. For Malcolm X, the color blindness of the Muslim world "proved to me the power of the One God."

Another profound religious experience, for many Christians, is being "born again"—that is, at a turning point in one's life, making a personal commitment to Jesus. According to a 2003 national survey, 42 percent of people in the United States claim they have had a born-again Christian experience at some time in their lives. An earlier survey found that Southern Baptists (75 percent) were the most likely to report such experiences; in contrast, only 21 percent of Catholics and 24 percent of Episcopalians stated that they had been born again. The collective nature of religion, as emphasized by Durkheim, is evident in these statistics. The beliefs and rituals of a particular faith can create an atmosphere either friendly or indifferent to this type of religious experience. Thus, a Baptist would be encouraged to come forward and share such experiences with others, whereas an Episcopalian who claims to have been born again would receive much less interest (Newport 2004).

Table 8–4 summarizes the three major sociological perspectives on religion.

Table 8–4 Sociological Perspectives on Religion

Theoretical Perspective	Emphasis
Functionalist	Religion as a source of social integration and unification Religion as a source of social support for individuals
Conflict	Religion as a potential obstacle to structural social change
Interactionist	Individual religious expression through belief, ritual, and experience

summing**UP**

Sociology Matters

Sociology matters because it explains the purposes and functions of our most basic social institutions.

- Do you see the institutions of the family and religion differently now that you have read this chapter? Did anything you learned surprise you?

- The family and religion are two social institutions whose authority has declined over the last century. Why do you think they have lost some of their importance? Do you think our society is weaker or stronger as a result?

Sociology matters because it helps us to look at familiar social institutions from new and different perspectives.

- Which of the four major perspectives on the family strikes you as the most meaningful? Why?

- Which of the four major perspectives would be most helpful to you in studying religion?

CHAPTER RESOURCES

Summary

The social institutions of the **family** and **religion** are cultural universals, found in various forms in all human cultures. Functionalists stress the essential tasks social institutions perform, but conflict theorists charge that social institutions strengthen the powerful at the expense of the powerless. This chapter examined **kinship** and the family around the world; four sociological perspectives on the family; the social functions of religion; and various aspects of religious behavior.

1. To survive, a society must perform five essential functions: it must replace its personnel, teach new recruits, produce and distribute goods and services, preserve order, and provide people with a sense of purpose. Social institutions perform these essential functions.

2. The **extended family,** common in the past, offers certain advantages over today's **nuclear family.** Some sociologists think that in

the United States, the **egalitarian family** has become the norm, replacing the older *patriarchal family.*

3. All cultures determine kinship in one of three ways: by descent from both parents, a method called **bilateral descent;** by descent from the father only, called **patrilineal descent;** or by descent from the mother only, called **matrilineal descent.**

4. William F. Ogburn outlined six basic functions of the family: reproduction, protection, socialization, regulation of sexual behavior, companionship, and the provision of social status.

5. Conflict theorists charge that male dominance of the family contributes to social injustice and denies women opportunities that are extended to men. Like feminists, they see the family's role in socializing children as the primary source of sexism.

6. Émile Durkheim stressed the social impact of religion in attempting to understand individual religious behavior within the context of the larger society.

7. Religion helps to integrate a diverse society and provides social support in time of need. It can serve as a source of social change and a means of social control.

8. Max Weber saw a connection between capitalism and religious allegiance, which he termed the **Protestant ethic.**

9. Karl Marx charged that religion reinforces the control of those in power, discouraging collective political action to end capitalist oppression.

10. Religious behavior is expressed through religious **belief, ritual,** and **experience.** These three dimensions of religious behavior help to define the sacred and differentiate it from the profane.

www.mhhe.com/schaefersm2
Visit the Online Learning Center for *Sociology Matters* to access quizzes, review activities, and other learning tools.

Key Terms

bilateral descent, 192

egalitarian family, 192

extended family, 189

family, 189

kinship, 191

matriarchy, 192

matrilineal descent, 192

monogamy, 190

nuclear family, 189

patriarchy, 192

patrilineal descent, 192

polyandry, 191

polygamy, 191

polygyny, 191

Protestant ethic, 199

religion, 196

religious belief, 201

religious experience, 202

religious ritual, 201

serial monogamy, 190

Social Institutions: Education, Government, and the Economy

Sociological Perspectives on Education

Education: Schools as Formal Organizations

Government: Authority and Power

Economic Systems

Economic Transformation

In the United States today, nearly 6 out of 10 people ages 3 to 34 are in school. Seven out of 10 adults are in the labor force. Of those who are employed, 21 million work for national, state, or local governments, whose combined payroll totals over $61 billion. Clearly, the three social institutions of education, government, and the economy have a profound impact on our daily lives. These institutions also have a significant effect on one another. For example, government data released in 2004 show that the typical college graduate earns over $51,000 a year, compared to about $27,000 a year for a high school graduate. Higher education confers significant economic benefits (Bureau of the Census 2003a:150, 312, 385; Stoops 2004).

In the last chapter we learned that a *social institution* is an organized pattern of beliefs and behavior centered on basic social needs. We saw that two institutions, the family and religion, meet our need for support and a sense of purpose. In this chapter we will concentrate on the three institutions of education, government, and the economy, which are devoted to fulfilling our need for learning, for social order, and for the goods and services that sustain life. We will begin with a discussion of three sociological perspectives on education, followed by a consideration of schools as formal organizations. Then we will examine government as the source of legitimate authority and power.

205

We'll look at three different models of the power structure in the United States. Next, we'll compare two major economic systems, capitalism and socialism. The chapter will close with a discussion of the economic transformation our society is currently undergoing.

Sociological Perspectives on Education

Education is a formal process of learning in which some people consciously teach while others adopt the social role of learner. Besides being a major industry in the United States, education is the social institution that formally socializes members of our society. In the last few decades, increasing proportions of people have obtained high school diplomas, college degrees, and advanced professional degrees. For example, the proportion of people 25 years of age or over with a high school diploma increased from 41 percent in 1960 to more than 85 percent in 2003. Those with a college degree rose from 8 percent in 1960 to about 27 percent in 2003. The functionalist, conflict, and interactionist perspectives offer distinctive views of this increasingly important social institution (Stoops 2004).

FUNCTIONALIST VIEW

Like other social institutions, education has both manifest (open, stated) and latent (hidden) functions. The most basic *manifest* function of education is the transmission of knowledge. Schools teach students how to read, speak foreign languages, and repair automobiles. Another important manifest function is the bestowal of status. Because many believe this function is performed inequitably, we will consider it later, in the section on the conflict view of education.

In addition to these manifest functions, schools perform a number of *latent* functions: transmitting culture, promoting social and political integration, maintaining social control, and serving as an agent of change.

Transmitting Culture. As a social institution, education performs a rather conservative function—transmitting the dominant culture. Schooling exposes each generation of young people to the existing beliefs, norms, and values of their culture. In our society, we learn respect for social control and reverence for established institutions, such as religion, the family, and the presidency. Of course, this statement is true of many other cultures as well. While schoolchildren in the United States are hearing about the accomplishments of George Washington and Abraham Lincoln, British children are hearing about the distinctive contributions of Queen Elizabeth I and Winston Churchill.

Sometimes nations may reassess the ways in which they transmit culture. Recently South Koreans began to question the content of their school curriculum. South Korean schools teach traditional Confucian values, with a focus on rote memorization. The emphasis is on accumulating facts rather than on reasoning logically. Entrance to college turns on a highly competitive exam that tests students' knowledge of facts. Once in college, students have virtually no opportunity to change their educational programs, and their instruction continues to emphasize memorization. The combination of an economic crisis and growing complaints about the educational process has caused government officials to reevaluate the nation's educational structure. Moreover, growth in juvenile crime, although low by our standards, has led the government to introduce a new civic education program emphasizing honesty and discipline (Woodard 1998).

Promoting Social and Political Integration. Many institutions require students in their first year or two of college to live on campus, to foster a sense of community among diverse groups. Education serves the latent function of promoting social and political integration by transforming a population composed of diverse racial, ethnic, and religious groups into a society whose members share—to some extent—a common identity. Historically, schools in the United States have played an important role in socializing the children of immigrants into the norms, values, and beliefs of the dominant culture. From a functionalist perspective, the common identity and social integration fostered by education contribute to societal stability and consensus (Touraine 1974).

In the past, the integrative function of education was most obvious in its emphasis on promoting a common language. Immigrant children were expected to learn English. In some instances, they were even forbidden to speak their native languages on school grounds. More recently, bilingualism has been defended both for its educational value and as a means of encouraging cultural diversity. However, critics argue that bilingualism undermines the social and political integration that education has traditionally promoted.

Maintaining Social Control. In performing the manifest function of transmitting knowledge, schools go far beyond teaching skills like reading, writing, and mathematics. Like other social institutions, such as the family and religion, education prepares young people to lead productive and orderly lives as adults by introducing them to the norms, values, and sanctions of the larger society.

Through the exercise of social control, schools teach students various skills and values essential to their future positions in the labor force. They learn punctuality, discipline, scheduling, and responsible work habits, as well as how to negotiate the complexities of a bureaucratic organization. As a social institution, education reflects the interests of both the family and another social institution, the economy. Students are trained for what is ahead, whether it be the assembly line or a physician's office. In effect, then, schools serve as a transitional agent of social control, bridging the gap between parents and employers in the life cycle of most individuals (Bowles and Gintis 1976; M. Cole 1988).

Serving as an Agent of Change.   So far, we have focused on the conservative functions of education—on its role in transmitting the existing culture, promoting social and political integration, and maintaining social control. Yet education can also stimulate or bring about desired social change. Sex education classes were introduced in public schools in response to a soaring pregnancy rate among teenagers. Affirmative action in admissions—giving priority to females or minorities—has been endorsed as a means of countering racial and sexual discrimination. Project Head Start, an early childhood program that serves more than 905,000 children annually, has sought to compensate for the disadvantages in school readiness experienced by children from low-income families (Bureau of the Census 2002a:357).

Education also promotes social change by serving as a meeting ground where students can share their distinctive beliefs and traditions. In 2002, there were 582,867 foreign students in the United States, of whom 72 percent were from developing nations. Cross-cultural exchanges between these visitors and citizens of the United States ultimately broaden the perspective of both the hosts and their guests. The same is certainly true when students from the United States attend schools in Europe, Latin America, Africa, or the Far East (Institute of International Education 2004).

CONFLICT VIEW

Conflict theorists view education as an instrument of elite domination. They point to the sharp inequalities that exist in the educational opportunities available to different racial and ethnic groups. The year 2004 marked the 50th anniversary of the Supreme Court's landmark decision *Brown v. Board of Education,* which declared unconstitutional the segregation of public schools. Yet today, African Americans are still 11 percent less likely than Whites, and Latinos 36 percent less likely than Whites, to have completed high school. Furthermore, Black and Latino schoolchildren continue to underperform White schoolchildren on nationally standardized tests (Hurn 1985; National Center for Education Statistics 2004).

Conflict theorists also argue that the educational system socializes students into values dictated by the powerful, that schools stifle individualism and creativity in the name of maintaining order, and that the level of change they promote is relatively insignificant. From a conflict perspective, the inhibiting effects of education are particularly apparent in the "hidden curriculum" and the differential way in which status is bestowed on students.

The Hidden Curriculum. Schools are highly bureaucratic organizations, as we will see later. Many teachers rely on rules and regulations to maintain order. Unfortunately, the need for control and discipline can take precedence over the learning process. Teachers may focus on obedience to the rules as an end in itself, in which case students and teachers alike become victims of what Philip Jackson (1968) has called the *hidden curriculum* (see also Margolis 2001; B. Smith 2004).

The term **hidden curriculum** refers to standards of behavior that are deemed proper by society and are taught subtly in schools. According to this curriculum, children must not speak until the teacher calls on them, and must regulate their activities according to the clock or bells. In addition, they are expected to concentrate on their own work rather than to assist other students who learn more slowly. A hidden curriculum is evident in schools around the world. For example, Japanese schools offer guidance sessions that seek to improve the classroom experience and develop healthy living skills. In effect, these sessions instill values and encourage behavior useful in the Japanese business world, such as self-discipline and openness to group problem solving and decision making (Okano and Tsuchiya 1999).

Credentialism. Fifty years ago, a high school diploma was the minimum requirement for entry into the paid labor force of the United States. Today, a college diploma is virtually the bare minimum. This change reflects the process of *credentialism*—a term used to describe an increase in the lowest level of education needed to enter a field.

In recent decades, the number of occupations that are viewed as professions has risen. Credentialism is one symptom of this trend. Employers and occupational associations typically contend that such changes are a logical response to the increasing complexity of many jobs. However, in many cases, employers raise the degree requirements for a position simply because all applicants have achieved the existing minimum credential (D. Brown 2001; Hurn 1985).

Conflict theorists observe that credentialism may reinforce social inequality. Applicants from poor and minority backgrounds are especially likely to suffer from the escalation of qualifications, since they lack the financial resources needed to obtain degree after degree. In addition, upgrading of credentials serves the self-interest of the two groups most responsible for this trend. Educational institutions profit from prolonging the investment of time and money that people make by staying in school. Moreover, current jobholders have a stake in raising occupational requirements, since credentialism can increase the status of an occupation and lead to demands for higher pay. Max Weber anticipated this possibility as early as 1916, concluding that the "universal clamor for the creation of educational certificates in all fields makes for the formation of a privileged stratum in businesses and in offices" (Gerth and Mills 1958: 240–241; Hurn 1985).

Use Your Sociological Imagination

How would you react if the job you have or plan to pursue suddenly required a higher-level degree? If suddenly the requirements were lowered?

Bestowal of Status. Conflict theorists are far more critical of the *differential* way in which education bestows status. They stress that schools sort pupils according to their social class backgrounds. Although the educational system helps certain poor children to move into middle-class professional positions, it denies most disadvantaged children the same educational opportunities afforded to children of the affluent. In this way, schools tend to preserve social class inequalities in each new generation (Giroux 1988; Pinkerton 2003).

Even a single school can reinforce class differences by putting students in tracks. The term *tracking* refers to the practice of placing students in specific curriculum groups on the basis of their test scores and other criteria. Tracking begins very early, often in reading groups during first grade. Most recent research on such ability groupings raises questions about its effectiveness, especially for low-ability students. Tracks can reinforce the disadvantages that children from less affluent families may face if they haven't been exposed to reading materials, computers, and other forms of educational stimulation during their early childhood years. It is estimated that about 60 percent of elementary schools in the United States and about 80 percent of secondary schools use some form of tracking (Hallinan 2003; Sadker and Sadker 2003).

Tracking and differential access to higher education are evident in many nations around the world. Japan's educational system mandates equality in school funding and insists that all schools use the same textbooks. Nevertheless, only the more affluent Japanese families can afford to send their children to *juku,* or cram schools. These afternoon schools prepare high school students for examinations that determine admission into prestigious colleges (Efron 1997).

Treatment of Women in Education. The educational system of the United States, like many other social institutions, has long been characterized by discriminatory treatment of women. In 1833, Oberlin College became the first institution of higher learning to admit female students—some 200 years after the first men's college was established. But Oberlin's administrators believed that women should aspire to become wives and mothers, not lawyers and intellectuals. In addition to attending classes, female students washed men's clothing, cared for their rooms, and served them at meals. In the 1840s, Lucy Stone, then an Oberlin undergraduate and later one of the nation's most outspoken feminist leaders, refused to write a commencement address because it would have been read to the audience by a male student.

In the 20th century, sexism in education showed up in many ways—in textbooks with negative stereotypes of women, counselors' pressure on female students to prepare for "women's work," and unequal funding for women's and men's athletic programs. But perhaps nowhere was educational discrimination more evident than in the employment of teachers. The positions of university professor and college administrator, which hold relatively high status in the United States, were generally filled by men. Public school teachers, who earn much lower salaries, were largely female.

Women have made great strides in one area: the proportion of women who continue their schooling. Women's access to graduate education and to medical, dental, and law schools has increased dramatically in the last few decades as a result of the Education Act of 1972, which forbade discrimination against women in education.

INTERACTIONIST VIEW

The labeling approach suggests that if we treat people in particular ways, they may fulfill our expectations. Children who are labeled as "trouble-makers" may come to view themselves as delinquents. Similarly, a dominant group's stereotyping of racial minorities may limit their opportunities to break away from expected roles.

Can the labeling process operate in the classroom? Psychologist Robert Rosenthal and school principal Lenore Jacobson (1968) documented what they referred to as a *teacher-expectancy effect*—the impact that a teacher's expectations about a student's performance may have on the student's actual achievements. This effect is especially evident in the lower grades (through grade three).

In their experiment, children in a San Francisco elementary school were administered a verbal and reasoning pretest. Rosenthal and Jacobson then *randomly* selected 20 percent of the sample and designated them as "spurters"—children of whom teachers could expect superior performance. On a later verbal and reasoning test, the spurters scored significantly higher than before. Moreover, teachers evaluated them as more interesting, more curious, and better-adjusted than their classmates. These results were striking. Apparently, teachers' perceptions that the students were exceptional led to noticeable improvements in their performance.

Studies in the United States have revealed that teachers wait longer for an answer from a student they believe to be a high achiever and are more likely to give such children a second chance. In one experiment, teachers' expectations were even shown to have an impact on students' athletic achievements. Teachers obtained better athletic performance—as measured in the number of sit-ups or push-ups performed—from those students of whom they *expected* higher numbers (Babad and Taylor 1992).

Table 9–1 on page 212 summarizes the three major theoretical perspectives on education.

Education: Schools as Formal Organizations

Mid-20th-century educators would be amazed at the scale of schools in the United States as we head into the 21st century. California's public

summingUP

Table 9–1 Sociological Perspectives on Education

Theoretical Perspective	Emphasis
Functionalist	Transmission of the dominant culture Social and political integration Maintenance of social control Promotion of desirable social change
Conflict	Domination by the elite through unequal access to schooling Hidden curriculum Credentialism Differential bestowal of status
Interactionist	Teacher-expectancy effect

school system, the largest in the nation, currently enrolls as many children as there were in the entire country's secondary schools in 1950 (Bureau of the Census 1975:368; 2003a).

In many respects, today's schools are similar to factories, hospitals, and business firms when viewed as formal organizations. Like those other organizations, schools do not operate autonomously; they are influenced by the market of potential students. This market orientation is especially true of private schools, but could have broader impact if acceptance of voucher plans and other school choice programs increases. The parallels between schools and other formal organizations will become more apparent as we examine the bureaucratic nature of schools, teaching as an occupational role, and student subcultures (Daugherty and Hammack 1992).

BUREAUCRATIZATION OF SCHOOLS

A single teacher simply cannot transmit culture and skills to children of varying ages or prepare them for many diverse occupations. The growing number of students being served by individual schools and school systems, as well as the greater degree of specialization required by a technologically complex society, have combined to bureaucratize schools.

Max Weber noted five basic characteristics of bureaucracy, all of which are evident in the vast majority of schools, whether at the elementary, secondary, or college level.

1. *Division of labor.* Specialized experts teach particular age levels and specific subjects. For example, public elementary and secondary schools now employ instructors whose sole responsibility is to work with children with learning disabilities or physical impairments. In a college sociology department, one professor may specialize in the sociology of religion, another in marriage and the family, and a third in industrial sociology.

2. *Hierarchy of authority.* Each employee of a school system is responsible to a higher authority. Teachers must report to principals and assistant principals and may also be supervised by department heads. Principals are answerable to a superintendent of schools, and the superintendent is hired and fired by a board of education. Even the students are hierarchically organized by grade and within clubs and organizations.

3. *Written rules and regulations.* Teachers and administrators must conform to numerous rules and regulations in the performance of their duties. This bureaucratic requirement can become dysfunctional; the time invested in completing forms could instead be spent in preparing lessons or conferring with students.

4. *Impersonality.* The university has been portrayed as a giant, faceless bureaucracy that cares little for the uniqueness of the individual. As class sizes have swelled at schools and universities, it has become more difficult for teachers to give personal attention to each student. In fact, bureaucratic norms may actually encourage teachers to treat all students in the same way, despite the fact that students have distinctive personalities and learning needs.

5. *Employment based on technical qualifications.* At least in theory, the hiring of teachers and college professors is based on professional competence and expertise. Promotions are normally dictated by written personnel policies; people who excel may be granted life-long job security through tenure. Teachers have achieved these protections partly because of the bargaining power of unions (Borman and Spring 1984; Tyler 1985).

Functionalists take a generally positive view of the bureaucratization of education. Teachers can master the skills needed to work with a specialized clientele, since they no longer are expected to cover a broad range of instruction. The chain of command within schools is clear. Students are presumably treated in an unbiased fashion because of uniformly applied rules. Finally, security of position protects teachers from unjustified dismissal. In general, then, functionalists maintain that bureaucratization of education increases the likelihood that students, teachers, and administrators will be dealt with fairly—that is, on the basis of rational, equitable criteria.

In contrast, conflict theorists argue that the trend toward more centralized education has had harmful consequences for disadvantaged people. The standardization of educational curricula, including textbooks, generally reflects the values, interests, and lifestyles of the most powerful groups in our society, and may ignore those of racial and ethnic minorities. In addition, the disadvantaged, more so than the affluent, will find it difficult to sort through complex educational bureaucracies and to organize effective lobbying groups. In the view of conflict theorists, then,

Use Your Sociological Imagination

What would your school be like if it were less bureaucratic?

low-income and minority parents are likely to have even less influence over citywide and statewide educational administrators than they have over local school officials (Bowles and Gintis 1976; Katz 1971).

Finally, some schools can seem overwhelmingly bureaucratic, with the effect of stifling rather than nourishing intellectual curiosity in students. This problem has led many parents and policymakers to push for school choice programs—that is, allowing parents to choose the school that suits their children's needs, forcing schools to compete for their "customers."

TEACHERS: EMPLOYEES AND INSTRUCTORS

Whether they instruct preschoolers or graduate students, teachers are employees of formal organizations with bureaucratic structures. There is an inherent conflict in serving as a professional within a bureaucracy. The organization follows a hierarchy of authority and expects adherence to its rules, but professionalism demands individual responsibility of the practitioner. This conflict is very real for teachers, who experience all the positive and negative consequences of working in bureaucracies.

A teacher undergoes many perplexing stresses every day. While teachers' academic assignments have become more specialized, the demands on their time remain diverse and contradictory. Order is needed to establish an environment in which students can actually learn, yet there is a conflict inherent in serving as an instructor and a disciplinarian at the same time. Burnout is one result of such stresses: 20 percent of new teachers quit the profession within three years (*Education Week* 2000). Another stress on teachers is the threat of violence. Many observers sense that the nation's schools have been the scene of increasingly violent misbehavior in recent years, although those concerns may be overblown.

Given these difficulties, does teaching remain an attractive profession in the United States? In 2003, 5.3 percent of first-year college students indicated that they were interested in becoming elementary school teachers, and 4.4 percent, high school teachers. These figures are dramatically lower than the 13 percent of first-year male students and 38 percent of first-year female students who held such occupational aspirations in 1968 (Astin et al. 1994; Sax et al. 2003:30).

Undoubtedly, economic considerations enter into students' feelings about the attractiveness of teaching. In 2002, the average salary for all public elementary and secondary school teachers in the United States was $44,367, placing teachers somewhere near the average of all wage earners in the nation. In most other industrial countries, teachers' salaries are higher in relation to the general standard of living (F. H. Nelson and Drown 2003).

STUDENT SUBCULTURES

An important latent function of education relates directly to student life: Schools provide for students' social and recreational needs. Education helps toddlers and young children to develop interpersonal skills that are essential during adolescence and adulthood. During the high school and college years, students may meet future husbands and wives and may establish lifelong friendships.

When people observe high schools, community colleges, or universities from the outside, students appear to constitute a cohesive, uniform group. However, the student subculture is actually much more complex and diverse. High school cliques and social groups may crop up based on race, social class, physical attractiveness, placement in courses, athletic ability, and leadership roles in the school and community. In his classic community study of "Elmtown," August B. Hollingshead (1975) found some 259 distinct cliques in a single high school. The cliques, whose average size was five, were centered on the school itself, on recreational activities, and on religious and community groups.

Amid these close-knit and often rigidly segregated cliques, gay and lesbian students are particularly vulnerable. Peer group pressure to conform is intense at this age. Although coming to terms with one's sexuality is difficult for all adolescents, for those whose sexual orientation does not conform to societal expectations it can be downright dangerous. According to a study by the Massachusetts Department of Education (2000), students who describe themselves as gay, lesbian, or bisexual are significantly more likely than others to attempt suicide, miss classes, and be threatened or injured by other students.

We can find a similar diversity at the college level. Burton Clark and Martin Trow (1966) and more recently, Helen Lefkowitz Horowitz (1987) have identified some distinctive subcultures among college students. Here are four ideal types of subculture that came out of their analyses:

1. The *collegiate* subculture focuses on having fun and socializing. These students define what constitutes a "reasonable" amount of academic work (and what amount of work is "excessive," leading to the label of "grind"). Members of the collegiate subculture have little commitment to academic pursuits.

2. The *academic* subculture identifies with the intellectual concerns of the faculty and values knowledge for its own sake.

3. The *vocational* subculture is interested primarily in career prospects, and views college as a means of obtaining the academic degrees essential for advancement.

4. The *nonconformist* subculture is hostile to the college environment and seeks out ideas that may or may not relate to college studies. Members may find outlets for their thinking through campus publications or issue-oriented groups.

Each college student is exposed to these competing subcultures and must determine which (if any) seems most in line with his or her feelings and interests.

The typology used by these researchers reminds us that school is a complex social organization—almost like a community with different neighborhoods. Of course, these four subcultures are not the only ones evident on college campuses in the United States. For example, one might find subcultures of Vietnam veterans or former full-time homemakers at community colleges and four-year commuter institutions.

Sociologist Joe R. Feagin has studied a distinctive collegiate subculture: Black students at predominantly White universities. These students must function academically and socially within a setting where there are few Black faculty members or Black administrators, where harassment of Blacks by campus police is common, and where the curricula place little emphasis on Black contributions. Feagin (1989:11) suggests that "for minority students life at a predominantly White college or university means long-term encounters with *pervasive whiteness*." In Feagin's view, African American students at such institutions experience both blatant and subtle racial discrimination, which has a cumulative impact that can seriously damage the students' confidence (see also Feagin et al. 1996). Once again, conflict theorists would point out that social institutions—in this case, higher education—tend to reinforce the power of the dominant group at the expense of the disadvantaged. In the next section, we will study the exercise of power in another social institution, government.

Government: Authority and Power

A society does not exist in a vacuum. Someone or some group makes important decisions about how to use resources and how to allocate goods, whether it be a tribal chief, a parliament, or a dictator. A cultural universal common to all societies, then, is the exercise of authority and power. The struggle for authority and power inevitably involves *politics,* which political scientist Harold Lasswell (1936) tersely defined as "who gets what, when, and how." In their study of politics and government, sociologists are concerned with social interactions among individuals and groups and their impact on the larger political and economic order.

Power lies at the heart of a political system. According to Max Weber, *power* is the ability to exercise one's will over others. To put it another way, whoever can control the behavior of others is exercising power. Power relations can involve large organizations, small groups, or even people in an intimate association.

There are three basic sources of power in any political system—force, influence, and authority. *Force* is the actual or threatened use of coercion to impose one's will on others. When leaders imprison or even execute political dissidents, they are applying force; so, too, are terrorists when they seize or bomb an embassy or assassinate a political leader. *Influence,* on the other hand, refers to the exercise of power through a process of persuasion. A citizen may change his or her position regarding a Supreme Court nominee because of a newspaper editorial, the expert testimony of a law school dean before the Senate Judiciary Committee, or a stirring speech at a rally by a political activist. In each case, sociologists would view such efforts to persuade people as examples of influence. Now let's take a look at the third source of power, *authority.*

TYPES OF AUTHORITY

The term ***authority*** refers to power that has been institutionalized and is recognized by the people over whom it is exercised. Sociologists commonly use the term in connection with those who hold legitimate power through elected or publicly acknowledged positions. A person's authority is limited by the constraints of a particular social position. Thus, a referee has the authority to decide whether a penalty should be called during a football game, but has no authority over the price of tickets to the game.

Max Weber ([1913–1922] 1947) developed a system for classifying authority that has become one of the most useful and frequently cited contributions of early sociology. Weber identified three ideal types of authority: traditional, legal-rational, and charismatic. He did not insist that only one type characterizes a given society or organization. All can be present in a single society, but their relative importance will vary. Sociologists have found Weber's typology valuable in understanding different manifestations of legitimate power.

Traditional Authority.   Until the middle of the last century, Japan was ruled by a revered emperor, whose absolute power was passed down from generation to generation. In a political system based on ***traditional authority,*** legitimate power is conferred by custom and accepted practice. A king or queen is accepted as ruler of a nation simply by virtue of inheriting the crown; a tribal chief rules because that is the accepted practice. The ruler may be loved or hated, competent or destructive; in terms of legitimacy, that does not matter. For the traditional leader, authority rests in custom, not in personal characteristics, technical competence, or even written law. People accept such authority because "this is how things have always been done." Traditional authority is absolute when the ruler has the ability to determine a society's laws and policies.

Legal-Rational Authority.   The U.S. Constitution gives Congress and our president the authority to make and enforce laws and policies. Power made legitimate by law—by the written rules and regulations of a political system—is known as ***legal-rational authority.*** Generally, in societies based on legal-rational authority, leaders are thought to have specific fields of competence and authority, but are not thought to be endowed with divine inspiration, as in certain societies with traditional forms of authority.

Charismatic Authority.   Joan of Arc was a simple peasant girl in medieval France, yet she was able to rally the French people and lead them into battle against English invaders. How was this possible? As Weber observed, power can be legitimized by an individual's *charisma*. The term ***charismatic authority*** refers to power made legitimate by a leader's exceptional personal or emotional appeal to his or her followers. Charisma lets a person lead or inspire without relying on set rules or traditions. In fact, charismatic authority is derived more from the beliefs of followers than from the actual qualities of leaders. So long as people *perceive* a leader to have qualities that set him or her apart from ordinary citizens, that leader's authority will remain secure and often unquestioned.

Unlike traditional rulers, charismatic leaders often become well-known by breaking with established institutions and advocating dramatic changes in the social structure and economic system. Their strong hold over their followers enables them to build protest movements that challenge the dominant norms and values of a society. Thus, charismatic leaders such as Jesus, Joan of Arc, Mahatma Gandhi, Malcolm X, and Martin Luther King all used their power to press for changes in accepted social behavior. But so did Adolf Hitler, whose charismatic appeal turned people toward violent and destructive ends in Nazi Germany.

Observing from an interactionist perspective, sociologist Carl Couch (1996) points out that the growth of the electronic media has facilitated the development of charismatic authority. During the 1930s and 1940s, the heads of state of the United States, Great Britain, and Germany all used radio to issue direct appeals to citizens. In recent decades, television has allowed leaders to "visit" people's homes and communicate with them. Time and again, Saddam Hussein rallied the Iraqi people through shrewd use of television appearances. In both Taiwan and South Korea in 1996, troubled political leaders facing reelection campaigns spoke frequently to national audiences and exaggerated military threats from neighboring China and North Korea, respectively. And in 2004, during his successful re-election campaign, President George W. Bush would land before camera crews in the *Marine One* helicopter, dramatically reinforcing his image as Commander-in-Chief.

Though Weber distinguished between traditional, legal-rational, and charismatic authority as ideal types, in reality, individual leaders and political systems often combine two or more of these forms. Presidents Franklin D. Roosevelt, John F. Kennedy, and Ronald Reagan wielded power largely through legal-rational authority. At the same time, they were unusually charismatic leaders who commanded the personal loyalty of large numbers of citizens.

Use Your Sociological Imagination

What would our government be like if it were founded on traditional rather than legal-rational authority? What difference would it make to the average citizen?

WHO RULES IN THE UNITED STATES?

Who really holds power in the United States? Do "we the people" genuinely run the country through our elected representatives? Or is it true that behind the scenes, a small elite controls both our government and our economic system? It is difficult to determine the location of power in a society as complex as the United States. In exploring this critical question, social scientists have developed two basic views of our nation's power structure: the power elite and the pluralist models.

Power Elite Models. Karl Marx believed that 19th-century representative democracy was essentially a sham. He argued that industrial societies were dominated by relatively small numbers of people who owned factories and controlled natural resources. In Marx's view, government officials and military leaders were servants of this capitalist class and followed their wishes. Therefore, any key decisions made by politicians inevitably reflected the interests of the dominant bourgeoisie. Like others who hold to an *elite model* of power relations, Marx believed that society is ruled by a small group of individuals who share a common set of political and economic interests.

Mills's Model. Sociologist C. Wright Mills took this model a step further in his pioneering work *The Power Elite* ([1956] 2000b). Mills described a small group of military, industrial, and government leaders who controlled the fate of the United States. Power rested in the hands of a few, both inside and outside government—the *power elite.*

A pyramid illustrates the United States' power structure in Mills's model (see Figure 9–1a, page 220). At the top are the corporate rich, leaders of the executive branch of government, and heads of the military (whom Mills called the "warlords"). These are the power elite. Directly below are local opinion leaders, members of the legislative branch of government, and leaders of special-interest groups. Mills thought these individuals and groups would basically follow the wishes of the dominant power elite. At the bottom of the pyramid are the unorganized, exploited masses.

This power elite model is similar to the work of Karl Marx in many respects. The most striking difference is that Mills believed that the economically powerful coordinate their maneuvers with the military and political establishments, to serve their common interests. Yet, reminiscent of Marx, Mills argued that the corporate rich were perhaps the most powerful element of the power elite (first among "equals"). And of course, the powerless masses at the bottom of Mills's power elite model certainly bring to mind Marx's portrait of the oppressed workers of the world, who have "nothing to lose but their chains."

A fundamental element in Mills's thesis is that the power elite operates as a self-conscious, cohesive unit. Although not necessarily diabolical or ruthless, the elite comprises similar types of people who interact with one another regularly and have essentially the same political and economic interests. Mills's power elite is not a conspiracy, but rather a community of interest and sentiment among a small number of influential people (A. Hacker 1964).

Figure 9–1
Power Elite Models

THE POWER ELITE

a. C. Wright Mills's model, 1956

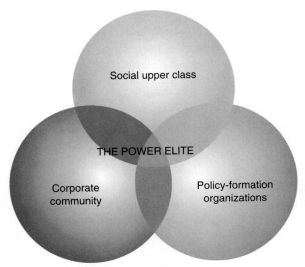

b. G. William Domhoff's model, 1998

SOURCE: Domhoff 2001:96.

Admittedly, Mills failed to clarify when the elite opposes protests and when it tolerates them; he also failed to provide detailed case studies to substantiate the interrelationship among members of the power elite. Nevertheless, his challenging theory forced scholars to look more critically at the democratic political system of the United States.

Domhoff's Model.   More recently, sociologist G. William Domhoff (2001) has agreed with Mills that a powerful elite runs the United States. He finds that it is still largely White, male, and upper class, as he wrote in his book with Richard L. Zweigenhaft (1998), *Diversity in the Power Elite*. But Domhoff stresses the role played both by elites of the corporate community and by leaders of policy-formation organizations, such as chambers of commerce and labor unions. Many of the people in both groups belong to the social upper class.

While these groups overlap (see Figure 9–1b), they do not necessarily agree on specific policies. Domhoff notes that in the electoral arena, two different coalitions have exercised influence. A *corporate-conservative coalition* has played a large role in both political parties and has generated support for particular candidates through direct-mail appeals. It is opposed by a *liberal-labor coalition* based in unions, local environmental organizations, a segment of the minority group community, liberal churches, and the university and arts communities (Zweigenhaft and Domhoff 1998).

The Pluralist Model.   Several social scientists insist that in the United States, power is more widely shared than the elite models indicate. In their view, a *pluralist model* more accurately describes the nation's political system. According to the *pluralist model,* many competing groups within the community have access to government officials, so that no single group is dominant.

The pluralist model suggests that a variety of groups play a significant role in decision making. Typically, pluralists make use of intensive case studies or community studies based on observation research. One of the most famous—an investigation of decision making in New Haven, Connecticut—was reported by Robert Dahl in his book *Who Governs?* (1961). Dahl found that although the number of people involved in any important decision was rather small, community power was nonetheless diffuse. Few political actors exercised decision-making power on all issues. One individual or group might be influential in a battle over urban renewal but at the same time have little impact over educational policy. Several other studies of local politics, in such communities as Chicago and Oberlin, Ohio, further document the absence of monolithic power structures on the local level of government.

The pluralist model, however, has not escaped serious questioning. Domhoff (1978, 2001) reexamined Dahl's study of decision making in New Haven and argued that Dahl and other pluralists had failed to show that elites prominent in local decision making belonged to a larger national ruling class. In addition, studies of community power, such as Dahl's work in New Haven, can examine decision making only on issues that become part of the political agenda. They fail to address the possible power of elites to keep certain matters that threaten their dominance entirely *out* of the realm of government debate.

Dianne Pinderhughes (1987) has criticized the pluralist model for failing to account for the exclusion of African Americans from the political process. Drawing on her studies of Chicago politics, Pinderhughes points out that the residential and occupational segregation of Blacks and their long political disenfranchisement violate the logic of pluralism—which would hold that such a substantial minority should always have been influential in community decision making. This critique applies to many cities across the United States where other large racial and ethnic minorities, among them Asian Americans, Puerto Ricans, and Mexican Americans, are relatively powerless (Watts 1990).

The power struggles that underlie government and politics, no matter what model a social scientist uses to analyze them, have a great deal to do with the distribution of a society's economic resources. In the next sections of this chapter we will study the economy, both in theory and in its practical implications for tomorrow's workforce.

Economic Systems

The economy fulfills the basic social function of producing and distributing goods and services (see Table 8–1 on page 186). But how is this seemingly amorphous social institution organized? A society's *economic system* for producing, distributing, and consuming goods and services will depend on both its level of development and its political ideology. In this section, we will consider the two basic economic systems associated with contemporary industrial societies: capitalism and socialism. In theory, these two economic systems conform perfectly to certain ideals, such as private or collective ownership. However, real economic systems rarely measure up to the ideal types on which they are based. To a greater or lesser extent, most economic systems today incorporate some elements of both capitalism and socialism.

CAPITALISM

In preindustrial societies, land was the source of virtually all wealth. The Industrial Revolution changed all that. It required that certain individuals and institutions be willing to take substantial risks in order to finance new inventions, machinery, and business enterprises. Eventually, bankers, industrialists, and other holders of large sums of money replaced landowners as the most powerful economic force. These people invested their funds in the hope of realizing even greater profits in factories and business firms.

The transition to private ownership of business was accompanied by the emergence of the capitalist economic system. *Capitalism* is an economic system in which the means of production are held largely in private hands, and the main incentive for economic activity is the accumulation of profits. In practice, capitalist systems vary in the degree to which the government regulates private ownership and economic activity (Rosenberg 1991).

Immediately following the Industrial Revolution, the prevailing form of capitalism was what is termed *laissez-faire* ("let them do"). Under the principle of laissez-faire, as expounded and endorsed by British economist Adam Smith (1723–1790), businesses could compete freely, with minimal government intervention. They retained the right to regulate themselves, operating essentially without fear of government interference (Smelser 1963).

Two centuries later, capitalism has taken on a somewhat different form. Private ownership and maximization of profits still remain the most significant characteristics of capitalist economic systems. However, in contrast to the era of laissez-faire, today's form of capitalism features extensive government regulation of economic relations. Without restrictions, business firms can mislead consumers, endanger the safety of their workers, and even defraud investors—all in the pursuit of greater profits. That is why the government of a capitalist nation often monitors prices, sets safety standards for industries, protects the rights of consumers, and regulates collective bargaining between labor unions and management. Yet in a capitalist system, government rarely takes over ownership of an entire industry.

Contemporary capitalism also differs from laissez-faire in another important respect: it tolerates monopolistic practices. A *monopoly* exists when a single business firm controls the market. Domination of an industry allows the firm to effectively control a commodity by dictating pricing, standards of quality, and availability. Buyers have little choice but to yield to the firm's decisions; there is no other place to purchase the product or service. Monopolistic practices violate the ideal of free competition cherished by Adam Smith and other supporters of laissez-faire capitalism.

Some capitalistic nations, such as the United States, attempt to outlaw monopolies through antitrust legislation. Such laws are meant to prevent any business from taking over so much of an industry that it gains control of the market. The U.S. government approves of monopolies only in certain exceptional cases, such as the utility and transportation industries. Even then, regulatory agencies scrutinize these officially approved monopolies to protect the public. The protracted legal battle between the Justice Department and Microsoft, owner of the dominant operating system for personal computers, illustrates the uneasy relationship between government and virtual private monopolies in capitalistic countries.

Conflict theorists point out that although *pure* monopolies are not a basic element of the U.S. economy, competition is much more restricted than one might expect in what is called a *free enterprise system*. In numerous industries, a few companies dominate the field and prevent new enterprises from entering the marketplace.

SOCIALISM

Socialist theory was refined in the writings of Karl Marx and Friedrich Engels. These European radicals were disturbed by the exploitation of the working class that emerged during the Industrial Revolution. In their view, capitalism forced large numbers of people to exchange their labor for low wages. The owners of industry profited from workers' labor primarily because they paid workers less than the value of the goods produced.

As an ideal type, a socialist economic system attempts to eliminate such economic exploitation. Under *socialism,* the means of production and distribution in a society are collectively rather than privately owned. The basic objective of the economic system is to meet people's needs rather than to maximize profits. Socialists reject the laissez-faire philosophy that free competition benefits the general public. Instead, they believe that the central government, acting on behalf of the people, should make basic economic decisions. Therefore, government ownership of all major industries—including steel production, automobile manufacturing, and agriculture—is a major feature of socialism as an ideal type.

In practice, socialist economic systems vary in the extent to which they tolerate private ownership. For example, in Great Britain, a nation with some aspects of both a socialist and a capitalist economy, passenger airline service is concentrated in the government-owned corporation British Airways. Yet private airline companies are allowed to compete with British Airways.

Socialist societies differ from capitalist nations in their commitment to social service programs. For example, the U.S. government provides health care and health insurance to the elderly and poor through the Medicare and Medicaid programs. In contrast, socialist countries typically offer government-financed medical care to *all* citizens. In theory, the wealth of the people as a collectivity is used to provide health care, housing, education, and other key services to each individual and family.

Marx believed that the socialist state would eventually "wither away" and evolve into a *communist* society. As an ideal type, **communism** refers to an economic system in which all property is communally owned and no social distinctions are made on the basis of people's ability to produce. In recent decades, the Soviet Union, the People's Republic of China, Vietnam, Cuba, and the nations of Eastern Europe were popularly thought of as communist economic systems. However, this viewpoint represents an incorrect usage of a term with sensitive political connotations. All nations known as communist in the 20th century have actually fallen far short of the ideal type.

By the early 1990s, Communist parties were no longer ruling the nations of Eastern Europe. The first major challenge to Communist rule came in 1980, when Poland's Solidarity movement—led by Lech Walesa and backed by many workers—questioned the injustices of that society. Though martial law forced Solidarity underground, the movement eventually negotiated the end of Communist party rule, in 1989. Over the next two years, Communist parties were overthrown by popular uprisings in the Soviet Union and throughout Eastern Europe. The former Soviet Union, Czechoslovakia, and Yugoslavia were then subdivided to accommodate ethnic, linguistic, and religious differences within those areas.

As of 2005, China, Cuba, North Korea, and Vietnam remained socialist societies ruled by Communist parties. Even in those countries, however, capitalism was making inroads. In that year, fully 25 percent of China's production originated in the private business sector. Indeed, at the Chinese Communist party's 80th anniversary celebration in 2001, President Jiang Zemin asked the party to formally welcome private business owners as members.

As we have seen, capitalism and socialism serve as ideal types. In reality, the economy of each industrial society—including the United States, the European Union, and Japan—contains certain elements of both capitalism and socialism. Whatever the differences—whether a country more closely fits the ideal type of capitalism or socialism—all industrial societies rely chiefly on mechanization in the production of goods and services. And all economies, whether capitalist or socialist, change as a result of social and technological advances. In the next section, we will examine some of the economic trends that are transforming the United States at the beginning of the 21st century.

The U.S. economy has become predominantly socialistic rather than capitalistic. What do you as a worker have now that you did not have before? What do you lack?

Economic Transformation

As advocates of the power elite model point out, the trend in capitalist societies has been toward concentration of ownership by giant corporations, especially multinational ones. For example, there were 7,032 mergers in 2002 alone, involving $1.2 trillion in business. The U.S. economy is changing in important ways, in part because it is increasingly intertwined with and dependent on the global economy. In 2002, foreign companies acquired 336 U.S. firms valued together at $68 billion (Bureau of the Census 2003a:571).

In the following sections, we will examine two developments in the global economy that have interested sociologists: the changing face of the workforce and deindustrialization. As these trends show, any change in the economy inevitably has social and political implications, and soon becomes a concern of policymakers.

THE CHANGING FACE OF THE WORKFORCE

The workforce in the United States is constantly changing. During World War II, when men were mobilized to fight abroad, women entered the workforce in large numbers. And with the rise of the civil rights

Figure 9–2

Racial and Ethnic Composition of the U.S. Labor Force, 1980 and 2020 (projection)

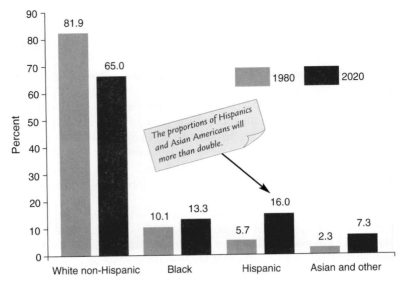

SOURCE: Toossi 2002:24.

movement, minorities found numerous job opportunities open to them. The active recruitment of women and minorities into the workplace, known as *affirmative action,* has helped minorities to climb the occupational ladder.

While predictions are not always reliable, sociologists and labor specialists foresee a workforce increasingly composed of women and racial and ethnic minorities. In 1960 there were twice as many men in the labor force as women. During the period from 1980 to 2020, three women are expected to enter the labor force for every two men. It's possible that by 2020 the female workforce may be only 3 percent smaller than the male workforce. The dynamics for minority groups in the workforce are even more dramatic. The number of Black, Latino, and Asian American workers continues to increase at a rate faster than the number of White workers, as Figure 9–2 shows (Toossi 2002:24).

More and more, the workforce reflects the diversity of the population as ethnic minorities enter the labor force and immigrants and their children move from marginal jobs or employment in the informal economy to positions of greater visibility and responsibility. The impact of this changing labor force is not merely statistical. A more diverse workforce means that relationships between workers are more likely to cross gender, racial, and ethnic lines. Interactionists note that people will find themselves supervising and being supervised by people very different from themselves. In response to these changes, 75 percent of businesses have instituted some type of cultural diversity training program (Melia 2000).

DEINDUSTRIALIZATION

What happens when a company decides it is more profitable to move its operations out of a long-established community to another part of the country, or out of the country altogether? People lose jobs; stores lose customers; the local government's tax base declines and it cuts services. This devastating process has occurred again and again over the last decade or so.

The term *deindustrialization* refers to the systematic, widespread withdrawal of investment in basic aspects of productivity, such as factories and plants. Giant corporations that deindustrialize are not necessarily refusing to invest in new economic opportunities. Rather, the targets and locations of investment change, and the need for labor decreases as technology continues to automate production. First, plants may relocate from the central city to the suburbs. The next step may be a move from suburban areas of the Northeast and Midwest to southern states, where labor laws place more restrictions on unions. Finally, a corporation may simply relocate *outside* the United States to a country with lower wages. General Motors, for example, decided to build a multibillion-dollar plant in Spain rather than in Kansas City (Lynn 2003).

Although deindustrialization often involves relocation, in some instances it takes the form of corporate restructuring, as companies seek to reduce costs in the face of growing worldwide competition. When a restructuring occurs, the impact on the bureaucratic hierarchy of formal organizations can be significant. A large corporation may choose to sell off or entirely abandon less productive divisions and eliminate layers of management viewed as unnecessary. Wages and salaries may be frozen and fringe benefits cut—all in the name of "restructuring." Increasing reliance on automation also spells the end of work as we have known it.

The term *downsizing* was introduced in 1987 to refer to reductions taken in a company's workforce as part of deindustrialization. Viewed from a conflict perspective, the unprecedented attention given to downsizing in the mid-1990s reflected the continuing importance of social class in the United States. Conflict theorists note that job loss has long been a feature of deindustrialization among blue-collar workers. But when large numbers of middle-class managers and other white-collar employees with substantial incomes began to be laid off, suddenly the media began expressing great concern over downsizing (Richtel 2000; Safire 1996; R. Samuelson 1996a, 1996b).

The latest version of downsizing is the outsourcing of service jobs at U.S. companies to workers in foreign countries. U.S. firms have outsourced certain types of work for generations. For example, moderate-sized businesses such as furniture stores and commercial laundries have long contracted for, or outsourced, their delivery services to domestic carriers. The new trend toward "offshoring" carries this practice one step further, by transferring work to foreign contractors. Now, even large

companies are turning to overseas firms, many of them located in developing countries. Offshoring has become the latest tactic in the time-worn business strategy of raising profits by reducing costs.

Originally, companies transferred manufacturing jobs to foreign factories, where wage rates were much lower. But the transfer of work from one country to another is no longer limited to manufacturing. Office and professional jobs are being exported, too, thanks to advanced telecommunications and the growth of skilled, English-speaking labor forces in developing nations with relatively low wage scales. The trend includes even those jobs that require considerable training, such as accounting and financial analysis, computer programming, claims adjustment, telemarketing, and hotel and airline reservations. Today, when you call a toll-free number to reach a customer service representative, chances are the person who answers the phone will not be speaking from the United States.

Estimates are that 3.3 million white-collar jobs worth an annual payroll of $136.4 billion will have moved overseas by the year 2015. Admittedly, that is only a small fraction of service-sector jobs. But more and more, increases in overseas outsourcing are being accompanied by job reductions at home. Middle-class workers *and voters* are alarmed by the trend. While moving high-tech work to India does help to lower costs, the impact on those technical and service workers who have been displaced is clearly devastating. Economists argue for assistance to laid-off workers but against broad-based efforts to block outsourcing (Brainard and Litan 2004; Drezner 2004).

The social costs of deindustrialization and downsizing cannot be overemphasized. Plant closings lead to substantial unemployment in a community, which can have a devastating impact on both the micro and macro levels. On the micro level, the unemployed person and his or her family must adjust to a loss of spending power. Painting or re-siding the house, buying health insurance or saving for retirement, even thinking about having another child must be put aside. Both marital happiness and family cohesion may suffer as a result. Although many dismissed workers eventually reenter the paid labor force, they must often accept less desirable positions with lower salaries and fewer benefits (DePalma 2002). Unemployment and underemployment are tied to many social problems discussed throughout this textbook, among them the need for child care, the controversy over welfare, and immigration issues.

Sociology Matters

Sociology matters because it prompts us to look critically at the social institutions that shape our lives.

- What was the hidden curriculum in the primary and secondary schools you attended? Were students assigned to tracks? Do you think the teachers' expectations had an effect on students' academic achievement?

- Do you know anyone who has lost a job because a factory closed, an office was downsized, or jobs were sent to a foreign country? Do the cost savings U.S. consumers get when jobs are sent overseas make up for the losses to U.S. workers?

Sociology matters because it highlights the struggle between the powerful and the powerless:

- Analyze your school or workplace in terms of power and authority. Who governs it, and by what kind of authority? Which model (power elite, pluralist) best fits its power structure?

- Do you consider the division of power and authority in the United States to be fair and just? If not, which social institution do you think is most in need of reform? How would you work to change it?

CHAPTER RESOURCES

Summary

Like the family and religion, the social institutions of **education,** government, and the economy are cultural universals, found in various forms in all human cultures. This chapter examined three sociological perspectives on education; schools as formal organizations; forms of **authority** and **power** in government; two basic **economic systems;** and two trends that are transforming the U.S. economy.

1. Functionalists stress that schools perform *latent* as well as *manifest functions.* Their latent (hidden) functions include the transmission of culture, the promotion of social and political integration, the maintenance of social control, and the advancement of social change.

2. Conflict theorists note that schools have a **hidden curriculum** that supports conventional social standards. They charge that schools track students according to their social class and perpetuate the unequal treatment of women.

3. Interactionists have noted a **teacher-expectancy effect,** in which teachers' assumptions about students' abilities may affect students' academic performance.

4. Today, most schools in the United States are organized in a bureaucratic fashion. Weber's five basic characteristics of bureaucracy are all evident in schools.

5. Schools are complex social organizations. Teachers suffer from the stress of role conflict—that of being both an educator and a disciplinarian—that is inherent in their job. Students are divided into many subcultures on the basis of their interests and experiences, gender, race, age, and sexual orientation.

6. There are three basic sources of **power** in any political system: **force, influence,** and **authority.** Max Weber identified three ideal types of authority: **traditional, legal-rational,** and **charismatic.**

7. Advocates of the **elite model** of the nation's power structure see the United States as being ruled by a small group of individuals, called the **power elite,** who share common political and economic interests. Advocates of the **pluralist model** believe that power is shared more widely among conflicting groups.

8. Though capitalist **economic systems** vary in the degree to which government regulates economic activity, all emphasize the two fundamental principles of **capitalism,** private ownership and the profit motive.

9. Socialist economic systems, in contrast, aim to eliminate economic exploitation and meet people's needs through government regulation and even ownership. Marx believed that **communism** would evolve naturally out of **socialism.**

10. The U.S. economy is changing. More and more women and minority group members are entering the workforce; at the same time, workers are struggling to adjust to the effects of **deindustrialization, downsizing,** and the outsourcing of jobs to foreign countries.

www.mhhe.com/schaefersm2
Visit the Online Learning Center for *Sociology Matters* to access quizzes, review activities, and other learning tools.

Key Terms

authority, 217

capitalism, 222

charismatic authority, 218

communism, 224

credentialism, 209

deindustrialization, 227

downsizing, 227

economic system, 222

education, 206

elite model, 219

force, 216

hidden curriculum, 209

influence, 216

laissez-faire, 223

legal-rational authority, 217

monopoly, 223

pluralist model, 221

politics, 216

power, 216

power elite, 219

socialism, 224

teacher-expectancy effect, 211

tracking, 210

traditional authority, 217

CHAPTER 10

Population, Community, Health, and the Environment

Demography: The Study of Population

How Did Communities Originate?

Urbanization and Its Consequences

Health and Illness: Sociological Perspectives

Social Epidemiology

The Environment: The World and Our Place in It

Imagine that on January 1, 2000, explorers discovered a new mini-continent, about the size of California, in the Pacific Ocean. We can use this imaginary land mass, which we will call Populandia, to illustrate the world's population growth. What would happen if from January 1 onward, we transplanted the natural increase in the world's population—that is, all those babies born above and beyond the number needed to replace those people who have died—to Populandia?

According to the best estimates, a jumbo jet carrying at least 280 newborns would arrive at Populandia International Airport every 2 minutes. By the end of the first day (January 1, 2000), 204,224 people would reside in Populandia—about as many as currently live in Baltimore, Maryland. Five years later, at the beginning of the year 2005, the population would have climbed to over 453 million, making Populandia the world's third largest nation—more populous than either the United States or Indonesia (*Intercom* 1978; United Nations Population Division 2004a).

The striking growth of our hypothetical continent of Populandia suggests the pressure that the natural increase in population is placing on our planet. Population growth has a direct impact on the quality of life in our communities. It threatens our health and strains the capacity of our environment to support us. Anyone who is concerned about these issues must be concerned about population growth. This chapter begins with the debate about the threat of overpopulation, a subject that has occupied some of the world's best minds since the end of the 18th century. To better understand this debate, we will learn some basic concepts that researchers have developed in their study of population. Then we will look at communities, health, and the environment from a sociological perspective, noting their interdependence and their connection to population issues.

Demography: The Study of Population

Population issues engage the attention of both natural and social scientists. The biologist explores the nature of reproduction and casts light on factors that affect *fertility,* the level of reproduction in a society. The medical pathologist examines and analyzes trends in the causes of death. Geographers, historians, and psychologists also have distinctive contributions to make to our understanding of population. Sociologists, more than these other researchers, focus on the *social* factors that influence population rates and trends.

Sociologists are keenly aware that various elements of population — such as fertility and *mortality* (the number of deaths) — are profoundly affected by the norms, values, and social patterns of a society. Fertility is influenced by people's age of entry into sexual unions and by their use of contraception — both of which, in turn, reflect the social and religious values that guide a particular culture. Mortality is shaped by a nation's level of nutrition, acceptance of immunization, and provisions for sanitation, as well as its general commitment to health care and health education.

The formal term for the scientific study of population is *demography.* Demographers draw on several components of population, including size, composition, and territorial distribution, to understand the social consequences of population change. They study geographical variations and historical trends in their effort to develop population forecasts. They also analyze the structure of a population — the age, gender, race, and ethnicity of its members. This type of analysis was popularized by Thomas Malthus.

MALTHUS'S THESIS AND MARX'S RESPONSE

The Reverend Thomas Robert Malthus (1766–1834) was educated at Cambridge University and spent his life teaching history and political economy. He strongly criticized two major institutions of his time — the church and slavery — yet his most significant legacy for contemporary scholars is his still-controversial *Essays on the Principle of Population,* published in 1798.

Essentially, Malthus held that the world's population was growing more rapidly than the available food supply. He argued that food supply increases in an arithmetic progression (1, 2, 3, 4, and so on), whereas population expands by a geometric progression (1, 2, 4, 8, and so on). According to his analysis, the gap between food supply and population will continue to grow over time. Even though the food supply will increase, it will not increase nearly enough to meet the needs of an expanding world population.

Malthus advocated population control to close the gap between rising population and food supply, yet he explicitly denounced artificial means of birth control because they were not sanctioned by religion. For Malthus, one appropriate way to control population was to postpone marriage. He argued that couples must take responsibility for the number of children they choose to bear; without such restraint, the world would face widespread hunger, poverty, and misery (Malthus et al. [1824] 1960; Petersen 1979).

Karl Marx strongly criticized Malthus's views on population. Marx pointed to the nature of economic relations in Europe's industrial societies as the central problem. He could not accept the Malthusian notion that rising world population, rather than capitalism, was the cause of social ills. In Marx's opinion, there was no special relationship between world population and the supply of resources (including food). If society is well ordered, he reasoned, increases in population should lead to greater wealth, not to hunger and misery.

Of course, Marx did not believe that capitalism operated under these ideal conditions. He maintained that capitalism devoted resources to the financing of buildings and tools rather than to more equitable distribution of food, housing, and other necessities of life. Marx's work is important to the study of population because he linked overpopulation to the unequal distribution of resources. His concern with the writings of Malthus also testifies to the importance of population in political and economic affairs.

The insights of Malthus and Marx regarding population issues have since been incorporated in what is termed the *neo-Malthusian view.* Paul Ehrlich (1968; Ehrlich and Ehrlich 1990), author of *The Population Bomb,* and other neo-Malthusians agree with Malthus that world population growth is outstretching natural resources. However, in contrast to the British theorist, they insist that birth control measures are needed to regulate population increases. Their condemnation of developed nations, which despite their low birthrates consume a disproportionately large share of world resources, is founded on Marxist thought. While they are rather pessimistic about the future, these theorists stress that birth control and sensible use of resources are essential responses to rising world population (Tierney 1990; Weeks 2005; for a critique, see Commoner 1971).

STUDYING POPULATION TODAY

The relative balance of births and deaths is no less important today than it was during the lifetime of Malthus and Marx. The suffering that Malthus spoke of is certainly a reality for many people of the world, who are chronically hungry and poor. Malnutrition remains the largest contributing factor to illness and death among children in developing countries. Almost 18 percent of these children will die before age five—a rate over 11 times higher than in developed nations. Warfare and large-scale migration intensify problems of population and food supply. For example, recent strife in Bosnia, Iraq, and Sudan caused very uneven distribution of food supplies, leading to regional concerns about malnutrition and even starvation. Combating world hunger may require reducing human births, dramatically increasing the world's food supply, or perhaps both at the same time (World Bank 2000b:277).

In the United States and most other countries, the census is the primary mechanism for collecting population information. A *census* is an enumeration, or counting, of a population. The Constitution of the United States requires that a census be held every 10 years to determine congressional representation. This periodic investigation is supplemented by *vital statistics,* or records of births, deaths, marriages, and divorces that are gathered through a registration system maintained by governmental units. In addition, other governmental surveys provide up-to-date information on commercial developments, educational trends, industrial expansion, agricultural practices, and the status of such groups as children, the elderly, racial minorities, and single parents.

In administering a nationwide census and conducting other types of research, demographers employ many of the skills and techniques described in Chapter 1, including questionnaires, interviews, and sampling. The precision of population projections depends on the accuracy of a series of estimates that demographers must make. First, they must determine past population trends and establish a base population as of the date for which the forecast begins. Next, birthrates and death rates must be established, along with estimates of future fluctuations. In projecting a nation's population trends, demographers must consider migration as well, since a significant number of individuals may enter and leave a country.

ELEMENTS OF DEMOGRAPHY

Demographers communicate population facts with a language derived from the basic elements of human life—birth and death. The *birthrate* (or more specifically, the *crude birthrate*) is the number of live births per 1,000 population in a given year. In 2004, for example, there were 14 live births per 1,000 people in the United States. The birthrate provides information on the actual reproductive patterns of a society.

One way demographers can project future growth in a society is to make use of the *total fertility rate (TFR).* The TFR is the average number of children born alive to any woman, assuming that she conforms to current fertility rates. The TFR reported for the United States in 2004 was 2.0 live births per woman—not high compared to over 8 births per woman in a developing country such as Niger.

Mortality, like fertility, is measured in several different ways. The *death rate* (also known as the *crude death rate*) is the number of deaths per 1,000 population in a given year. In 2004, the United States had a death rate of 8.0 per 1,000 population. The *infant mortality rate* is the number of deaths of infants under one year of age per 1,000 live births in a given year. This particular measure serves as an important indicator of a society's level of health care; it reflects prenatal nutrition, delivery procedures, and infant screening measures. The infant mortality rate also functions as a useful indicator of future population growth, since those infants who survive to adulthood will contribute to further population increases.

Another general measure of health used by demographers is *life expectancy,* or the median number of years a person can be expected to live under current mortality conditions. This figure is usually reported as life expectancy *at birth.* At present, Japan reports a life expectancy at birth of 82 years—slightly higher than the United States' figure of 77 years. By contrast, life expectancy at birth is less than 35 in several developing nations, including Zambia.

The *growth rate* of a society is the difference between births and deaths, plus the difference between *immigrants* (those who enter a country to establish permanent residence) and *emigrants* (those who leave a country permanently) per 1,000 population. For the world as a whole, the growth rate is simply the difference between births and deaths per 1,000 population, since worldwide immigration and emigration must of necessity be equal. In 2004, the United States had a growth rate of 0.6 percent, compared with an estimated 1.3 percent for the entire world (Haub 2004).

What do these growth rates suggest about the world's future? Was Malthus right when he wrote that the world's population will inevitably outstrip our ability to feed ourselves? Before we attempt to answer this question, let's take a look at how agricultural production has changed over time. The next section will present a brief history of communities, including their methods of production, from the early days of civilization to the present.

How Did Communities Originate?

EARLY COMMUNITIES

A *community* is a unit of social organization, either spatial or political, that gives people a sense of belonging. How did this social arrangement come into being? For most of human history, people used very basic tools and knowledge to survive. They satisfied their need for an adequate food supply through hunting, foraging for fruits or vegetables, fishing, and herding. In comparison with later industrial societies, early civilizations were much more dependent on the physical environment and much less able to alter that environment to their advantage. Perhaps that is why early peoples banded together in nomadic groups in the first known communities.

The emergence of horticultural societies, in which people actually cultivated food rather than merely gathering fruits and vegetables, led to many dramatic changes in human social organization. It was no longer necessary to move from place to place in search of food. Because people had to remain in specific locations to cultivate crops, more stable and enduring communities began to develop. As agricultural techniques became more and more sophisticated, a cooperative division of labor involving both family members and others developed. It gradually became possible for people to produce more food than they actually needed for themselves. They could give food, perhaps as part of an exchange, to others who might be involved in nonagricultural labor.

This transition from subsistence to surplus represented a critical step in the emergence of cities. Eventually, people produced enough goods to cover both their own needs and those of people not engaged in agricultural tasks. The surplus was limited to agricultural products at first, but gradually it evolved to include all types of goods and services. Residents of a city came to rely on community members who provided craft products and means of transportation, gathered information, and so forth (Nolan and Lenski 2004).

With these social changes came an even more elaborate division of labor, as well as greater opportunity for differential rewards and privileges. So long as everyone was engaged in the same tasks, stratification was limited to such factors as gender, age, and perhaps the ability to perform the task (a skillful hunter could win unusual respect from the community). However, the surplus allowed for expansion of goods and services, leading to greater differentiation, a hierarchy of occupations, and social inequality. Therefore, surplus was a precondition not only for the establishment of cities but for the division of members of a community into social classes (see Chapter 5). The ability to produce goods for other communities, then, marked a fundamental shift in human social organization.

PREINDUSTRIAL CITIES

Archaeologists estimate that beginning about 10,000 B.C., permanent settlements free from dependence on crop cultivation had emerged. By today's standards, these early communities would barely qualify as cities. The Mesopotamian city of Ur had a population of about 10,000 and was limited to roughly 220 acres of land, including the canals, the temple, and the harbor. The *preindustrial city,* as it is termed, generally had only a few thousand residents. Its society was characterized by a relatively closed class system and limited social mobility. Status in these early cities was usually based on ascribed characteristics such as family background, and education was limited to members of the elite. All the residents relied on perhaps 100,000 farmers as well as their own part-time farming to provide them with the needed agricultural surplus.

Why were early cities so small and relatively few in number? Several key factors restricted urbanization:

- *Reliance on animal power (both humans and beasts of burden) as a source of energy for economic production.* Dependence on muscle power limited humans' ability to use and alter the environment.

- *Modest levels of surplus produced by the agricultural sector.* Between 50 and 90 farmers may have been required to support one city resident (K. Davis [1949] 1995).

- *Problems in transportation and storage of food and other goods.* Even an excellent crop could easily be lost as a result of such difficulties.

- *Hardships of migration to the city.* For many peasants, migration was physically impossible. A few weeks of travel was out of the question without more sophisticated techniques of food storage.

- *Dangers of city life.* Concentrating a society's population in a small area left it open to attack from outsiders, as well as more susceptible to extreme damage from plagues and fires.

Gideon Sjoberg (1960) examined the available information on early urban settlements in medieval Europe, India, and China. He identified three preconditions of city life: advanced technology in both agricultural and nonagricultural areas, a favorable physical environment, and a well-developed social organization. For Sjoberg, the criteria for defining a "favorable" physical environment were variable. Proximity to coal and iron helps only if a society knows how to *use* those natural resources. Similarly, proximity to a river is particularly beneficial only if a culture has the means to transport water efficiently to the fields for irrigation and to the cities for consumption. Specialized social roles were important because cities brought people together in new ways through the exchange of goods and services. A well-developed social organization ensured that these relationships were clearly defined and acceptable to all.

INDUSTRIAL AND POSTINDUSTRIAL CITIES

Imagine the results of harnessing the energy in air, water, and other natural resources to do society's work. Just as advances in agricultural technology once led to dramatic changes in community life, so did the process of industrialization. The *Industrial Revolution,* which began in the middle of the 18th century, focused on the application of nonanimal sources of power to labor tasks. Industrialization had a wide range of effects on people's lifestyles, as well as on the structure of communities. Emerging urban settlements became centers not only of industry but of banking, finance, and industrial management.

The factory system that developed during the Industrial Revolution led to a much more refined division of labor than existed in early preindustrial cities. In turn, the many new jobs it created produced a complex set of relationships among workers. Thus, the *industrial city* was not merely more populous than its preindustrial predecessors; it was based on very different principles of social organization. Sjoberg outlined the contrasts between preindustrial and industrial cities: see Table 10–1.

In comparison with preindustrial cities, industrial cities had a more open class system and more mobility. After initiatives in industrial cities by women's rights groups, labor unions, and other political activists, formal education gradually became available to children from poor and working-class families. While ascribed characteristics such as gender, race, and ethnicity remained important, a talented or skilled individual had more opportunity to better his or her social position than in the past. In these and other respects, the industrial city was genuinely a different world from the preindustrial urban community.

Table 10–1 Comparing Types of Cities

Preindustrial Cities (through 18th century)	Industrial Cities (18th through mid-20th century)	Postindustrial Cities (beginning late 20th century)
Closed class system—pervasive influence of social class at birth	Open class system—mobility based on achieved characteristics	Wealth based on ability to obtain and use information
Economic realm controlled by guilds and a few families	Relatively open competition	Corporate power dominates
Beginnings of division of labor in creation of goods	Elaborate specialization in manufacturing of goods	Sense of place fades, transnational networks emerge
Pervasive influence of religion on social norms	Influence of religion limited to certain areas as society becomes more secularized	Religion becomes more fragmented; greater openness to new religious faiths
Little standardization of prices, weights, and measures	Standardization enforced by custom and law	Conflicting views of prevailing standards
Population largely illiterate, communication by word of mouth	Emergence of communication through posters, bulletins, and newspapers	Emergence of extended electronic networks
Schools limited to elites and designed to perpetuate their privileged status	Formal schooling open to the masses and viewed as a means of advancing the social order	Professional, scientific, and technical personnel become increasingly important

SOURCES: Based on E. Phillips 1996:132–135; Sjoberg 1960:323–328.

*summing***UP**

In the latter part of the 20th century, a new type of urban community emerged. The ***postindustrial city*** is a city in which global finance and the electronic flow of information dominate the economy. Production is decentralized and often takes place outside urban centers, but control is centralized in multinational corporations whose influence transcends urban and even national boundaries. Social change is a constant feature of the postindustrial city. Economic and spatial restructuring seems to occur each decade, if not more frequently. In the postindustrial world, cities are forced into increasing competition with one another for economic opportunities, which deepens the plight of the urban poor (Phillips 1996; D. Smith and Timberlake 1993).

Sociologist Louis Wirth (1928, 1938) argued that a relatively large and permanent settlement leads to distinctive patterns of social behavior, which he called ***urbanism.*** He identified three critical factors that contribute to urbanism: the size of the population, population density, and the heterogeneity (variety) of the population. A frequent result of urbanism, according to Wirth, is that residents become insensitive to events around them and restrict their attention to the primary groups to which they are emotionally attached.

In most parts of the world today, populations are concentrating more and more in urban areas. What are the effects of urbanization on the people who congregate in cities? In the following section, we will see how urbanization shapes both the neighborhoods Americans live or do not live in and the economic well-being of people in developing countries.

Use Your Sociological Imagination

What would the ideal city of the future look like? Describe its architecture, public transportation, neighborhoods, schools, and workplaces. What kinds of people would live and work there?

Urbanization and Its Consequences

The 1990 census was the first to demonstrate that more than half the U.S. population lives in urban areas of 1 million or more residents. In only three states (Mississippi, Vermont, and West Virginia) do more than half the residents live in rural areas. Clearly, urbanization has become a central aspect of life in the United States (Bureau of the Census 1991).

Urbanization can be seen throughout the rest of the world, too. In 1900, only 10 percent of the world's people lived in urban areas, but by 2005, that proportion had risen to around 50 percent. By the year 2025, the number of city dwellers could reach 5 billion (Koolhaas et al. 2001:3; United Nations Population Division 2004b).

During the 19th and early 20th centuries, rapid urbanization occurred primarily in European and North American cities. Since World War II, however, an urban "explosion" has hit the world's developing countries. Such rapid growth is evident in the rising number of "squatter settlements," outlying areas occupied by the very poor.

The trend toward urbanization is so important, some sociologists have devoted their careers to the study of its effects. In the following sections we will examine two contrasting perspectives on urbanization, a

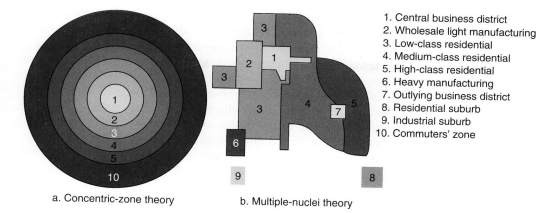

1. Central business district
2. Wholesale light manufacturing
3. Low-class residential
4. Medium-class residential
5. High-class residential
6. Heavy manufacturing
7. Outlying business district
8. Residential suburb
9. Industrial suburb
10. Commuters' zone

a. Concentric-zone theory   b. Multiple-nuclei theory

Figure 10–1
Ecological Theories of Urban Growth

SOURCE: Harris and Ullman 1945:13.

functionalist view called *urban ecology* and a conflict view called the *new urban sociology.*

FUNCTIONALIST VIEW: URBAN ECOLOGY

Human ecology is concerned with the interrelationships between people and their spatial setting and physical environment. Human ecologists have long been interested in how the physical environment shapes people's lives (for example, rivers can serve as a barrier to residential expansion) as well as in how people influence the surrounding environment (for example, air-conditioning has accelerated the growth of major metropolitan areas in the Southwest). *Urban ecology* focuses on such relationships as they emerge in urban areas. Although the urban ecological approach examines social change in cities, it is nevertheless functionalist in its orientation because it emphasizes that different elements in urban areas contribute to social stability.

Early urban ecologists such as Robert Park (1916, 1936) and Ernest Burgess (1925) concentrated on city life, but drew on the approaches used by ecologists in studying plant and animal communities. With few exceptions, today's urban ecologists trace their work back to the **concentric-zone theory** Burgess devised in the 1920s (see Figure 10–1*a*). Using Chicago as an example, Burgess proposed a theory for describing land use in industrial cities. At the center, or nucleus, of such a city is the central business district. Large department stores, hotels, theaters, and financial institutions occupy this highly valued land. Surrounding this urban center are other zones that contain other types of land use. According to this theory, the city grows over time by spreading outward from the center.

Note that the creation of zones is a *social* process, not the result of nature alone. Families and business firms compete for the most valuable land; those possessing the most wealth and power generally win. Thus the concentric-zone theory is a dynamic model of urban growth. As urban growth proceeds, each zone moves even farther from the central business district. Yet while the theory allows for outward growth of cities, it does not provide for major restructuring, as happens when a dying central business district gives way to the pull of outlying centers of commerce and technology. In such cases, the theory assumes a greater degree of stability than actually exists.

Because of its functionalist orientation and its emphasis on stability, the concentric-zone theory tended to understate or ignore certain tensions apparent in metropolitan areas. For example, urban ecologists viewed the growing use by the affluent of land in a city's peripheral areas uncritically, while some described the arrival of African Americans in White neighborhoods in the 1930s in terms such as "invasion" and "succession." Moreover, the urban ecological perspective gave little thought to gender inequities, such as the establishment of men's softball and golf leagues in city parks, without any programs for women. Consequently, the urban ecological approach has been criticized for its failure to address issues of gender, race, and class.

By the middle of the 20th century, urban populations had spread beyond traditional city limits. No longer could urban ecologists focus exclusively on *growth* in the central city, for large numbers of urban residents were abandoning the cities to live in suburban areas. In response to the emergence of more than one focal point in some metropolitan areas, Chauncy D. Harris and Edward Ullman (1945) presented the ***multiple-nuclei theory*** (see Figure 10–1b). In their view, all urban growth does not radiate outward from a central business district. Instead, a metropolitan area may have many centers of development, each of which reflects a particular urban need or activity. Thus, a city may have a financial district, a manufacturing zone, a waterfront area, an entertainment center, and so forth. Certain types of business firms and certain types of housing will naturally cluster around each distinctive nucleus (Schwab 1993).

The rise of suburban shopping malls is a vivid example of the phenomenon of multiple nuclei within metropolitan areas. Initially, all major retailing was located in the city's central business district. Each residential neighborhood had its own grocers, bakers, and butchers, but people traveled to the center of the city to make major purchases at department stores. However, as metropolitan areas expanded and the suburbs became more populous, an increasing number of people began to shop nearer their homes. Today, the suburban mall is a significant retailing and social center in communities across the United States.

In a refinement of the multiple-nuclei theory, contemporary urban ecologists have begun to study what journalist Joel Garreau (1991) has called "edge cities." These communities, which have grown up on the outskirts of major metropolitan areas, are economic and social centers with identities of their own. By any standard of measurement—height of buildings, amount of office space, presence of medical or leisure-time facilities, or of course, population—edge cities qualify as independent cities rather than as large suburbs.

Whether metropolitan areas include edge cities or multiple nuclei, more and more of them are characterized by spread-out development and unchecked growth. In recent years, Las Vegas has been the most dramatic example. With a new house built every 20 minutes, by 2004 the city had mushroomed from 38 to 235 square miles. The social consequences of such rapid growth are equally dramatic, from a shortage of affordable housing and an inadequate number of food pantries to an overstretched water supply, poor health care delivery, and impossible traffic. Today's cities are very different from the preindustrial cities of a thousand years ago (D. Murphy 2004).

CONFLICT VIEW: NEW URBAN SOCIOLOGY

Contemporary sociologists point out that metropolitan growth is not governed by waterways and rail lines, as a purely ecological interpretation might suggest. From a conflict perspective, communities are human creations that reflect people's needs, choices, and decisions—though some people have more influence over those decisions than others. Drawing on conflict theory, proponents of an approach that has come to be called the *new urban sociology* consider the interplay of local, national, and worldwide forces and their effect on local space, with special emphasis on the impact of global economic activity (Gottdiener and Hutchison 2000).

New urban sociologists note that urban ecologists typically have avoided examining the social forces, largely economic in nature, that have guided urban growth. For example, central business districts may be upgraded or abandoned, depending on whether urban policymakers grant substantial tax exemptions to developers. The suburban boom in the post–World War II era was fueled by federal housing policies that channeled investment capital into the construction of single-family homes rather than affordable rental housing in the cities. Similarly, while some observers suggest that the growth of sun-belt cities results from a "good business climate," new urban sociologists counter that the term is a euphemism for hefty state and local government subsidies and anti-labor policies (Gottdiener and Feagin 1988; M. Smith 1988).

The new urban sociology draws generally on the conflict perspective, and more specifically on sociologist Immanuel Wallerstein's *world-systems analysis* (see Chapter 5). Wallerstein argues that certain industrialized nations (among them, the United States, Japan, and Germany) hold a dominant position at the *core* of the global economic system. The poor developing countries of Asia, Africa, and Latin America occupy the *periphery* of the global economy, where they are controlled and exploited by core industrialized nations. Through world-systems analysis, new urban sociologists consider urbanization from a global perspective. They view cities not as independent and autonomous entities, but rather as the outcome of decision-making processes directed or influenced by a society's dominant classes and by core industrialized nations. New urban sociologists note that the rapidly growing cities of the world's developing countries were shaped first by colonialism and then by a global economy controlled by core nations and multinational corporations (Gottdiener and Feagin 1988; D. Smith 1995).

The urban ecologists of the 1920s and 1930s were not ignorant of the role that the larger economy played in urbanization, but their theories emphasized the impact of local rather than national or global forces. In contrast, through a broad, global emphasis on social inequality and social conflict, new urban sociologists explore such topics as the existence of a homeless population, the power of multinational corporations, and deindustrialization. Developers, builders, and investment bankers, they suggest, are not especially interested in urban growth when it means providing housing for middle- or low-income people. This lack of interest contributes to the problem of homelessness. Urban elites counter that the nation's housing shortage and the plight of the homeless are not their fault—and insist that they do not have the capital needed to construct and support such housing. But affluent people *are* interested in growth and *can* somehow find capital to build new shopping centers, office towers, and ballparks. Why, then, can't they provide the capital for affordable housing, ask new urban sociologists?

Part of the answer is that developers, bankers, and other powerful real estate interests view housing in quite a different manner from tenants and most homeowners. For a tenant, an apartment is shelter, housing, a home. But for developers and investors—many of them large (and sometimes multinational) corporations—an apartment is simply a housing investment. These financiers and owners are concerned primarily with maximizing profit, not with solving social problems (Feagin 1983; Gottdiener and Hutchison 2000).

As we have seen throughout this textbook—in studying such varied issues as deviance, race and ethnicity, and gender—no single theoretical approach offers the only valuable perspective. Both urban ecology and the new urban sociology offer significantly different ways of viewing urbanization, both of which enrich our understanding of this complex phenomenon. Clearly, however, urbanization does affect the well-being of those who live in our cities, including their health and quality of life. In the following two sections, we will discuss the concepts of health and illness from a sociological perspective, as well as the distribution of health care and the relative health of different social groups.

Health and Illness: Sociological Perspectives

In the preamble to its 1946 constitution, the World Health Organization defined **health** as a "state of complete physical, mental, and social well-being, and not merely the absence of disease and infirmity" (Leavell and Clark 1965:14). Imagine a continuum with health on one end and death on the other. In this definition, the "healthy" end of our continuum represents an ideal rather than a precise condition. Along the continuum, people define themselves as "healthy" or "sick" on the basis of criteria established by themselves, relatives, friends, coworkers, and medical practitioners. Because health is relative, we can view it in a social context and consider how it varies in different situations or cultures (Twaddle 1974; Wolinsky 1980).

Who controls definitions of health and illness in our society, and for what ends? Why is it that you may consider yourself sick or well when others do not agree? What are the consequences of viewing yourself (or being viewed) as ill or disabled? In this section, by drawing on four sociological perspectives—functionalism, conflict theory, interactionism, and labeling theory—we will gain insight into the social context that shapes definitions of health and the treatment of illness.

FUNCTIONALIST APPROACH

Illness entails breaks in our social interactions both at work and at home. From a functionalist perspective, then, "being sick" must be controlled so that not too many people are released from their societal responsibilities at any one time. Functionalists contend that an overly broad definition of illness would disrupt the workings of a society.

"Sickness" requires that one take on a social role, even if temporarily. The *sick role* refers to societal expectations about the attitudes and behavior of a person viewed as being ill. Sociologist Talcott Parsons (1951, 1975), well known for his contributions to functionalist theory, has outlined the behavior required of people considered "sick." They are exempted from their normal, day-to-day responsibilities and generally do not suffer blame for their condition. Yet they are obligated to try to get well, which may include seeking competent professional care. Attempting to get well is particularly important in the world's developing countries. Modern, automated industrial societies can absorb a greater degree of illness or disability than horticultural or agrarian societies, where the availability of workers is far more critical (Conrad 2000).

According to Parsons's theory, physicians function as "gatekeepers" for the sick role. They either verify a patient's condition as "illness" or designate the patient as "recovered." The ill person becomes dependent on the doctor, who can control valuable rewards (not only treatment of illness, but excused absences from work and school). Parsons suggests that the doctor–patient relationship is somewhat like that between parent and child. Like a parent, the physician helps the patient to enter society as a full and functioning adult (Segall 1976).

The concept of the sick role is not without criticism. First, patients' judgments regarding their own state of health may be related to their gender, age, social class, and ethnic group. For example, younger people may fail to detect warning signs of a dangerous illness, while the elderly may focus too much on the slightest physical malady. Second, the sick role may be more applicable to people experiencing short-term illnesses than to those with recurring, long-term illnesses. Finally, even simple factors, such as whether or not a person is employed, seem to affect willingness to assume the sick role—as does the impact of socialization into a particular occupation or activity. For example, beginning in childhood, athletes learn to define certain ailments as "sports injuries" and therefore do not regard themselves as "sick." Nonetheless, sociologists continue to rely on Parsons's model for functionalist analysis of the relationship between illness and societal expectations of the sick (Curry 1993).

CONFLICT APPROACH

Conflict theorists observe that the medical profession has assumed a pre-eminence that extends well beyond whether to excuse a student from school or an employee from work. Sociologist Eliot Freidson (1970:5) has likened the position of medicine today to that of state religions yesterday—it has an officially approved monopoly of the right to define health and illness and to treat illness. Conflict theorists use the term *medicalization of society* to refer to the growing role of medicine as a major institution of social control (Conrad and Schneider 1992; McKinlay and McKinlay 1977; Zola 1972, 1983).

The Medicalization of Society.   Social control involves techniques and strategies for regulating behavior in order to enforce the distinctive norms and values of a culture. Typically, we think of informal social control as occurring within families and peer groups, and of formal social control as being carried out by authorized agents such as police officers, judges, school administrators, and employers. However, viewed from a conflict perspective, medicine is not simply a "healing profession"; it is a regulating mechanism as well.

How does medicine manifest its social control? First, the field has greatly expanded its domain of expertise in recent decades. Physicians now examine a wide range of issues, among them sexuality (including homosexuality), old age, anxiety, obesity, child development, alcoholism, and drug addiction. Society tolerates such expansion of the boundaries of medicine in the hope that these experts can bring new "miracle cures" to complex human problems, just as they have to the control of certain infectious diseases.

The social significance of this expanding medicalization is that once a problem is viewed using a *medical model*—once medical experts become influential in proposing and assessing relevant public policies—it becomes more difficult for "common people" to join the discussion and exert influence on decision making. It also becomes more difficult to view these issues as being shaped by social, cultural, or psychological factors, rather than simply by physical or medical factors (Caplan 1989; Conrad and Schneider 1992; Starr 1982).

Second, medicine serves as an agent of social control by retaining absolute jurisdiction over many health care procedures. It has even attempted to guard its jurisdiction by placing health care professionals such as chiropractors and nurse-midwives outside the realm of acceptable medicine. Despite the fact that midwives first brought professionalism to child delivery, they have been portrayed as having invaded the "legitimate" field of obstetrics in both the United States and Mexico. Nurse-midwives have sought licensing as a way to achieve professional respectability, but physicians continue to exert power to ensure that midwifery remains a subordinate occupation (Friedland 2000).

Inequities in Health Care.   The medicalization of society is but one concern of conflict theorists. As we have seen throughout this textbook, when analyzing any issue, conflict theorists seek to determine who benefits, who suffers, and who dominates at the expense of others. From a conflict perspective, there are glaring inequities in health care delivery in the United States. For example, poor and rural areas tend to be underserved, because medical services concentrate where people are numerous and/or wealthy.

Similarly, from a global perspective, there are obvious inequities in health care delivery. Today, the United States has about 28 physicians per 1,000 people, while African and Asian nations have fewer than 1 per 1,000. This situation is only worsened by the ***brain drain***—the immigration to the United States and other industrialized nations of skilled workers, professionals, and technicians who are desperately needed in their home countries. As part of the brain drain, physicians, nurses, and other health care professionals have come to the United States from developing countries such as India, Pakistan, and various African states. Conflict theorists view such emigration out of the Third World as yet another way in which the world's core industrialized nations enhance their quality of life at the expense of developing countries. One way the developing countries suffer is in lower life expectancy. In Africa and much of Latin America and Asia, life expectancy is far lower than in industrialized nations (United Nations Development Programme 2004).

Conflict theorists emphasize that inequities in health care resources have clear life-and-death consequences. For example, in 2004, the infant mortality rate in the African nation of Sierra Leone ranged as high as 180 infant deaths per 1,000 live births. In contrast, Japan's infant mortality rate was only 3.0 deaths per 1,000 live births, and Iceland's was only 2.4. From a conflict perspective, the dramatic differences in infant mortality rates around the world reflect, at least in part, unequal distribution of health care resources based on the wealth or poverty of various communities and nations (Haub 2004).

In 2004, the United States had a rate of 6.7 infant deaths per 1,000 live births, although the estimated rate in some poor, inner-city neighborhoods exceeds 30 deaths per 1,000 live births. Despite the wealth of the United States, at least 39 nations have *lower* infant mortality rates, among them Canada, Great Britain, and Japan. Conflict theorists point out that unlike the United States, these countries offer some form of government-supported health care for all citizens, which typically leads to greater availability and use of prenatal care (Haub 2004).

INTERACTIONIST APPROACH

From an interactionist point of view, patients are not passive; often, they actively seek the services of a health care practitioner. In examining health, illness, and medicine as a social institution, then, interactionists engage in micro-level study of the roles played by health care professionals and patients. Interactionists are particularly interested in how physicians learn to play their occupational role. According to Brenda L. Beagan (2001), the technical language students learn in medical school becomes the basis for the script they follow as novice physicians. The familiar white coat is their costume—one that helps them to appear confident and professional at the same time that it identifies them as doctors to patients and other staff members. Beagan found that many medical students struggle to project the appearance of competence they think their role demands.

Sometimes patients play an active role in health care by *failing* to follow a physician's advice. For example, some patients stop taking medications long before they should. Some take an incorrect dosage on purpose, and others never even fill their prescriptions. Such noncompliance results in part from the prevalence of self-medication in our society; many people are accustomed to self-diagnosis and self-treatment. On the other hand, patients' active involvement in their health care can sometimes have very *positive* consequences. Some patients read books about preventive health care techniques, attempt to maintain a healthful and nutritious diet, carefully monitor any side effects of medication, and adjust the dosage based on perceived side effects. Finally, physicians may *change* their approach to a patient at the patient's request.

LABELING APPROACH

Labeling theory helps us to understand why certain people are viewed as deviants, "bad kids," or criminals, whereas others whose behavior is similar are not. Labeling theorists also suggest that the designation "healthy" or "ill" generally involves social definition by others. Just as police officers, judges, and other regulators of social control have the power to define certain people as criminals, health care professionals (especially physicians) have the power to define certain people as "sick." Moreover, like labels that suggest nonconformity or criminality, labels associated with illness commonly reshape how others treat us and how we see ourselves. Our society attaches serious consequences to labels that suggest less-than-perfect physical or mental health (Becker 1963; C. Clark 1983; Schwartz 1987).

A historical example illustrates perhaps the ultimate extreme in labeling social behavior as a sickness. In the 19th century, as enslavement of Africans in the United States came under increasing attack, medical authorities provided new rationalizations for the oppressive practice. Noted physicians published articles stating that the skin color of Africans deviated from "healthy" white skin coloring because Africans suffered from congenital leprosy. Moreover, the continuing efforts of enslaved Africans to escape from their White masters were classified as an example of the "disease" of drapetomania (or "crazy runaways"). The prestigious *New Orleans Medical and Surgical Journal* suggested that the remedy for this "disease" was to treat slaves kindly, as one might treat children. Apparently, medical authorities would not entertain the view that it was healthy and sane to flee slavery or join in a slave revolt (Szasz 1971).

By the late 1980s, the power of another label—"person with AIDS"—had become quite evident. This label often functions as a master status that overshadows all other aspects of a person's life. Once someone is told that he or she has tested positive for HIV, the virus associated with AIDS, that person is forced to confront immediate and difficult questions: Should I tell my family members, my sexual partner(s), my friends, my coworkers, my employer? How will these people respond? The public's intense fear of this disease has led to prejudice and discrimination—even social ostracism—against those who have (or are suspected of having) AIDS. A person who has AIDS must deal not only with the serious medical consequences of the disease, but with the distressing social consequences associated with the label.

According to labeling theorists, we can view a variety of life experiences as illnesses or not. Recently, premenstrual syndrome, posttraumatic disorders, and hyperactivity have been "labeled" medically recognized disorders. In addition, disagreements have arisen in the medical community over whether chronic fatigue syndrome constitutes a medical illness.

Probably the most noteworthy medical example of labeling is the case of homosexuality. For years, psychiatrists classified being gay or lesbian not as a lifestyle, but as a mental disorder subject to treatment. This official sanction by the psychiatric profession became an early target of the growing gay and lesbian rights movement in the United States. In 1974, members of the American Psychiatric Association voted to drop homosexuality from the standard manual on mental disorders (Adam 1995; Monteiro 1998).

The four sociological approaches just described share certain common themes. First, any person's health or illness is more than an organic condition, since it is subject to the interpretation of others. The impact of culture, family and friends, and the medical profession means that health and illness are not purely biological occurrences but sociological occurrences as well. Second, since members of a society (especially industrial societies) share the same health care delivery system, health is a group and societal concern. Although health may be defined as the complete well-being of an individual, it is also the result of the social environment, as the next section will show (Cockerham 2001).

Social Epidemiology

Social epidemiology is the study of the distribution of disease, impairment, and general health status across a population. The first epidemiologists concentrated on the scientific study of epidemics, focusing on how the diseases started and spread. Contemporary social epidemiology is much broader in scope, concerned not only with epidemics but with nonepidemic diseases, injuries, drug addiction and alcoholism, suicide, and mental illness. The field draws on the work of a wide variety of scientists and researchers, among them physicians, sociologists, public health officials, biologists, veterinarians, demographers, anthropologists, psychologists, and meteorologists. Recently, epidemiologists at the federal government's Centers for Disease Control and Prevention took on the new role of tracking bioterrorism. In 2001 they mobilized to trace the anthrax outbreak and prepare for any terrorist use of smallpox or other lethal microbes that could start an epidemic.

Researchers in social epidemiology commonly use two concepts: *incidence* and *prevalence*. **Incidence** refers to the number of new cases of a specific disorder occurring within a given population during a stated period, usually a year. For example, the incidence of AIDS in the United States in 2001 was 43,158 cases. In contrast, **prevalence** refers to the total number of cases of a specific disorder that exist at a given time. The prevalence of AIDS in the United States through December 2002 was about 385,000 cases. The statistics become more worrisome if we consider HIV infection as well as AIDS. Among people ages 15 to 49, the prevalence of HIV/AIDS, expressed as a percentage of the U.S. population, stood at 0.6 percent by the end of 2003. Worldwide, the rate was about 1.1 percent, but in at least 20 nations, including Haiti, Kenya, and South Africa, it was estimated at more than 5 percent. In Swaziland, over 38 percent of the population was either infected with HIV or suffering from AIDS (Bureau of the Census 2003a:132; Centers for Disease Control and Prevention 2003; Haub 2004).

When incidence figures are presented as rates, or as the number of reports of a disorder per 100,000 people, they are called **morbidity rates.** (The term **mortality rate,** you will recall, refers to the incidence of *death* in a given population.) Sociologists find morbidity rates useful because they reveal that a specific disease occurs more frequently among one segment of a population than another. As we shall see, social class, race, ethnicity, gender, and age can all affect a population's morbidity rates. In 1999, the U.S. Department of Health and Human Services, recognizing the inequality inherent in U.S. morbidity and mortality rates, launched the Campaign for 100% Access and Zero Health Disparities, an ambitious undertaking (Bureau of Primary Health Care 2004).

SOCIAL CLASS

Social class is clearly associated with differences in morbidity and mortality rates. Studies in the United States and other countries have consistently shown that people in the lower classes have higher rates of mortality and disability. A study published in 1998, for instance, documents the impact of class on mortality. The authors concluded that Americans whose family incomes were less than $10,000 could expect to die seven years sooner than those with incomes of at least $25,000 (Bureau of the Census 2000a:135).

Why is class linked to health? Crowded living conditions, substandard housing, poor diet, and stress all contribute to the ill health of many low-income people in the United States. In certain instances, poor education may lead to a lack of awareness of measures necessary to maintain good health. Financial strains are certainly a major factor in the health problems of less affluent people.

Another reason for the link between class and health is that the poor—many of whom belong to racial and ethnic minorities—are less able than others to afford quality medical care. As Figure 10–2 shows, the affluent are more likely than the poor to have health insurance, either because they can afford it or because they have jobs that provide it.

Another factor in the link between class and health is evident in the workplace: The occupations of people in the working and lower classes of

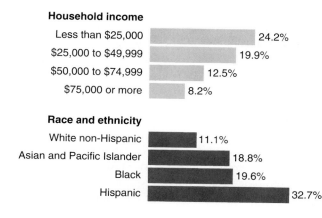

Household income

Less than $25,000 — 24.2%
$25,000 to $49,999 — 19.9%
$50,000 to $74,999 — 12.5%
$75,000 or more — 8.2%

Race and ethnicity

White non-Hispanic — 11.1%
Asian and Pacific Islander — 18.8%
Black — 19.6%
Hispanic — 32.7%

Figure 10–2

Percentage of People without Health Insurance, 2003

SOURCE: DeNavas-Walt et al. 2004:15.

the United States tend to be more dangerous than those of more affluent citizens. Miners, for example, risk injury or death from explosions and cave-ins; they are also vulnerable to respiratory diseases such as black lung. Workers in textile mills who are exposed to toxic substances may contract a variety of illnesses, including one commonly known as *brown lung disease.* In recent years, the nation has learned of the perils of asbestos poisoning, a particular worry for construction workers (R. Hall 1982).

In the view of Karl Marx and contemporary conflict theorists, capitalist societies such as the United States care more about maximizing profits than they do about the health and safety of industrial workers. As a result, government agencies do not take forceful action to regulate workplace conditions, and workers suffer many preventable job-related injuries and illnesses. Research also shows that the lower classes are more vulnerable to environmental pollution than the affluent, as we will see shortly.

RACE AND ETHNICITY

Health profiles of many racial and ethnic minorities reflect the social inequality evident in the United States. Research shows that the lower classes and members of racial and ethnic minorities are more vulnerable to environmental pollution than affluent citizens. Class plays a role, but race is more oppressive: though upwardly mobile Whites can generally escape from pollution centers, even well-off Blacks tend to be restricted in their residential mobility. The poor economic and environmental conditions of groups such as African Americans, Hispanics, and Native Americans are manifested in high morbidity and mortality rates. It is true that some afflictions, such as sickle-cell anemia among Blacks, have a clear genetic basis, but in most instances, environmental factors contribute to the differential rates of disease and death.

In many respects, the mortality rates for African Americans are distressing. Compared with Whites, Blacks have higher death rates from heart disease, pneumonia, diabetes, and cancer. The death rate from strokes is twice as high among African Americans. Such epidemiological findings reflect in part the fact that a higher proportion of Blacks are found among the nation's lower classes. According to the National Center for Health Statistics (2004), Whites can expect to live 77.7 years. In contrast, life expectancy for Blacks is 72.2 years.

As noted earlier, infant mortality is regarded as a primary indicator of health care. There is a significant gap in the United States between the infant mortality rates of African Americans and Whites: Generally, the rate of infant deaths is more than twice as high among Blacks. African Americans account for 15 percent of all live births in the nation but 30 percent of infant deaths. Puerto Ricans and Native Americans have infant mortality rates that are lower than those of African Americans but higher than those of Whites (Mathews et al. 2002).

Another reason for the disparity in mortality rates is differential treatment of patients by the medical establishment. The media often focus on obvious forms of racism, such as hate crimes, while overlooking the more insidious forms in social institutions like the medical establishment. In one study of differential treatment, researchers analyzed the records of about 40,000 Medicare beneficiaries. In comparing White and Black patients of the *same* social class with *similar* medical conditions, they found that White patients were 40 percent more likely to undergo a life-saving procedure known as cardiac catheterization (Budrys 2003; Caesar and Williams 2002; Smedley et al. 2002).

Drawing on the conflict perspective, sociologist Howard Waitzkin (1986) suggests that racial tensions contribute to the medical problems of Blacks. In his view, the stress resulting from racial prejudice and discrimination helps to explain the higher rates of hypertension found among African Americans (and Hispanics) compared with Whites. Hypertension—twice as common in Blacks as in Whites—is believed to be a critical factor in Blacks' high mortality rates from heart disease, kidney disease, and stroke (Morehouse Medical Treatment Effectiveness Center 1999).

Some Mexican Americans, as well as many other Latinos, adhere to cultural beliefs that make them less likely to use the established medical system. Most Hispanics probably use folk healers, or *curanderos,* infrequently, but perhaps 20 percent rely on home remedies. They may interpret their illnesses according to traditional Latino folk practices, or *curanderismo*—a form of holistic health care and healing. Curanderismo influences how one approaches health care and even how one defines illness. Some illnesses are defined according to folk beliefs, such as *susto* (fright sickness) and *atague* (or fighting attack). Because these complaints often have biological bases, sensitive medical practitioners need to deal with them carefully and diagnose and treat illnesses accurately (Council on Scientific Affairs 1999; Trotter and Chavira 1997).

GENDER

A large body of research indicates that in comparison with men, women experience a higher prevalence of many illnesses, though they tend to live longer. There are variations—for example, men are more likely to have parasitic diseases, whereas women are more likely to become diabetic—but as a group, women appear to be in poorer health than men.

The apparent inconsistency between the ill health of women and their greater longevity deserves an explanation, and researchers have advanced a theory. Women's lower rate of cigarette smoking (reducing their risk of heart disease, lung cancer, and emphysema), lower consumption of alcohol (reducing their risk of auto accidents and cirrhosis of the liver), and lower rate of employment in dangerous occupations explain about one-third of their greater longevity than men. Moreover, some clinical studies suggest that the differences in morbidity may actually be less pronounced than the data show. Researchers argue that women are much more likely than men to seek treatment, to be diagnosed as having a disease, and thus to have their illness reflected in the data examined by epidemiologists.

From a conflict perspective, women have been particularly vulnerable to the medicalization of society, with everything from birth to beauty being treated in an increasingly medical context. Such medicalization may contribute to women's higher morbidity rates compared to those of men. Ironically, even though women have been especially affected by medicalization, medical researchers have often excluded women from clinical studies. Female physicians and researchers charge that sexism lies at the heart of such research practices, and insist there is a desperate need for studies of female subjects (Bates 1999; McDonald 1999; Vidaver et al. 2000).

AGE

Health is the overriding concern of the elderly. Most older people in the United States report having at least one chronic illness, but only some of those conditions are potentially life threatening or require medical care. At the same time, health problems can affect the quality of life of older people in important ways. Almost half of older people in the United States are troubled by arthritis, and many have visual or hearing impairments that can interfere with the performance of everyday tasks.

Older people are also especially vulnerable to certain types of mental health problems. Alzheimer's disease, the leading cause of dementia in the United States, afflicts an estimated 4 million older people. While some individuals with Alzheimer's exhibit only mild symptoms, the risk of severe problems resulting from the disease rises substantially with age. Only 10 percent of people age 65 or over have symptoms of Alzheimer's, but the figure rises to 48 percent of people age 85 and over (Alzheimer's Association 1999).

Not surprisingly, older people in the United States use health services more often than younger people. In 2001, people age 15 to 24 visited physicians an average of 2.4 times a year, compared to 8.4 annual visits for those 75 and over. Similar discrepancies show up in rates of hospitalization. Twenty-two percent of people hospitalized in the United States were age 75 and over, while people age 15 to 24 accounted for only 9.6 percent of those hospitalized. The disproportionate use of the health care system by older people is a critical factor in all discussions about the cost of health care and possible reforms of the health care system (Bureau of the Census 2003a:120, 124).

In sum, to achieve the goal of 100 percent access and zero health disparities, federal health officials must overcome inequities that are rooted not just in age, but in social class, race and ethnicity, and gender. If that were not enough, they must also deal with a geographical disparity in health care resources. Dramatic differences in the availability of physicians, hospitals, and nursing homes exist from one state to another and between urban and rural areas within the same state.

The disparity in health resources that exists from one place to another, both within the United States and throughout the globe, is only one way in which our environment can affect our well-being. Our quality of life, whether in the cities, the suburbs, or rural areas, is closely related to the environment. In the final section of this chapter, we will see how human despoliation of the environment can have a negative effect not only on our natural surroundings, but on the health of whole communities.

The Environment: The World and Our Place in It

Urban sprawl has been encroaching on the fields and forests that surround U.S. cities, replacing them with residential developments and malls. The new construction disturbs wildlife and threatens the water supply, and the cars residents drive to work every day choke the highways, contributing to air pollution and global warming.

Like suburban residents, business owners are reluctant to acknowledge the effects of these activities on the environment, particularly their contribution to global warming. The gradual warming of the world's temperature, many scientists believe, is caused by "greenhouse gases" like carbon monoxide, which are produced by the fuel-burning factories and vehicles on which a developed economy depends. The United States, home to just 5 percent of the world's population, produces a staggering 25 percent of the world's greenhouse gases (Andrews 2001).

In 1997, at an international environmental conference in Kyoto, Japan, the United States signed the Kyoto protocol, an agreement that calls for a worldwide reduction in greenhouse gases. But in March 2001, the United States withdrew support for the protocol, indicating that it was not in the nation's best interest. The decision reflected the complexity of global environmental concerns. Unlike many developing nations, the United States had already taken several measures designed to improve the energy efficiency of cars and factories and reduce their noxious emissions. Further reductions in greenhouse gases, U.S. officials had begun to realize, would mean restricting output at the nation's factories. With an economic recession looming in the United States, President George W. Bush backed away from the nation's commitment to improve the global environment.

World leaders were swift to condemn the United States for walking away from the protocol, but U.S. business interests applauded the action. Furthermore, although U.S. citizens saw global warming as a serious problem, in 2001, only 48 percent of them said they would be willing to pay 25 cents more per gallon of gasoline to address the issue. Faced with the cost of environmental protection—lower production and higher prices—Americans shrank from supporting the protocol (Gelbspan 2002; Paul 2001).

Despite public unwillingness to confront the cost, environmental problems are real. With each passing year, we learn more about the environmental damage caused by burgeoning population levels and consumption patterns. Though environmental disasters are still comparatively rare, we can see the superficial signs of despoliation almost everywhere. Our air, our water, and our land are being polluted, whether we live in St. Louis, Mexico City, or Lagos, Nigeria. In the sections that follow, we will survey these problems and see what sociologists have to say about them.

ENVIRONMENTAL PROBLEMS: AN OVERVIEW

In recent decades the world has witnessed some serious environmental disasters. For example, Love Canal, a neighborhood near Niagara Falls in New York State, was declared a disaster area in 1978 because of chemical contamination. In the 1940s and 1950s, a chemical company had disposed of waste products on the site, where a housing development and a school were later built. The metal drums that held the chemical wastes eventually rusted, and toxic chemicals with noxious odors began seeping into residents' yards and basements. Investigations revealed that the company knew as early as 1958 that toxic chemicals were seeping into homes and a school playground. After repeated protests in the late 1970s, 239 families living in Love Canal had to be relocated.

In 1986, a series of explosions set off a catastrophic nuclear reactor accident at Chernobyl, a part of Ukraine (in what was then the Soviet Union). The accident killed at least 32,000 people. Some 300,000 residents had to be evacuated after the area became uninhabitable for 19 miles in any direction. High levels of radiation were found as far as 30 miles from the reactor site, and radioactivity levels climbed well above normal as far away as Sweden and Japan. According to one estimate, the Chernobyl accident and the resulting nuclear fallout may ultimately result in 100,000 excess cancer cases worldwide (Shcherbak 1996).

While Love Canal, Chernobyl, and other environmental disasters grab the headlines, it is the silent, day-to-day deterioration of the environment that ultimately poses a devastating threat to humanity. While we cannot examine all our environmental problems in detail, two broad areas of concern stand out: air and water pollution.

Air Pollution. More than 1 billion people on the planet are exposed to potentially health-damaging levels of air pollution (World Resources Institute 1998). Unfortunately, in cities around the world, residents have come to accept smog and polluted air as "normal." In urban areas, air pollution is caused primarily by emissions from automobiles, and secondarily by emissions from electric power plants and heavy industries. Urban smog not only limits visibility; it can lead to health problems as uncomfortable as eye irritation and as deadly as lung cancer. Such problems are especially severe in developing countries. The World Health Organization estimates that up to 700,000 premature deaths *per year* could be prevented if pollutants were brought down to safer levels (Carty 1999).

People are capable of changing their behavior, yet they are unwilling to make such changes permanent. During the 1984 Olympic games in Los Angeles, residents were asked to carpool and stagger their work hours to relieve traffic congestion and improve the quality of the air the athletes would breathe. These behavioral changes resulted in a remarkable 12 percent drop in ozone levels. However, when the Olympians left, residents reverted to their normal behavior, and the ozone levels climbed (Nussbaum 1998).

Water Pollution. Throughout the United States, dumping of waste materials by industries and local governments has polluted streams, rivers, and lakes. Consequently, many bodies of water have become unsafe for drinking, fishing, and swimming. Around the world, pollution of the oceans is an issue of growing concern. Such pollution results from regular waste dumping, and is made worse by fuel leaks and occasional oil spills from shipping. In a dramatic accident in 1989, the oil tanker *Exxon Valdez* ran aground in Prince William Sound, Alaska. The tanker's cargo of 11 million gallons of crude oil spilled into the sound and washed onto the shore, contaminating 1,285 miles of shoreline. About 11,000 people joined in a cleanup effort that cost over $2 billion. ExxonMobil is still fighting court-ordered settlements that would partially cover the cost of the cleanup (Sunstein et al. 2003; Zarembo 2003).

Less dramatic than large-scale accidents or disasters, but more common in many parts of the world, are problems with the basic water supply. Worldwide, over 1 billion people lack safe and adequate drinking water, and 2.4 billion have no acceptable means of sanitation—a problem that further threatens the quality of water supplies. The health costs of unsafe water are enormous (United Nations 2003).

What are the basic causes of our growing environmental problems? Neo-Malthusians such as Paul Ehrlich and Anne Ehrlich see world population growth as the central factor in environmental deterioration. They argue that population control is essential to preventing widespread starvation and environmental decay. Barry Commoner, a biologist, counters that the primary cause of environmental ills is the increasing use of technological innovations that are destructive to the world's environment—among them plastics, detergents, synthetic fibers, pesticides, herbicides, and chemical fertilizers. In the following sections we will contrast the functionalist and conflict approaches to the study of environmental issues (Commoner 1971, 1990; Ehrlich 1968; Ehrlich and Ehrlich 1990; Ehrlich and Ellison 2002).

HUMAN ECOLOGY

Earlier, we noted that ***human ecology*** is concerned with interrelationships between people and their environment. As Barry Commoner

(1971:39) has stated, "Everything is connected to everything else." Human ecologists focus both on how the physical environment shapes people's lives and on how people influence the surrounding environment.

In an application of the human ecological perspective, sociologist Riley Dunlap suggests that the natural environment serves three basic functions for humans, as it does for the many animal species (Dunlap 1993; Dunlap and Catton 1983):

1. *The environment provides the resources essential for life.* These include air, water, and materials used to create shelter, transportation, and other necessities. If human societies exhaust these resources—for example, by polluting the water supply or cutting down rain forests—the consequences can be dire.

2. *The environment serves as a waste repository.* More so than other living species, humans produce a huge quantity and variety of waste products—bottles, boxes, papers, sewage, and garbage, to name just a few. Various types of pollution have become more common because human societies are generating more wastes than the environment can safely absorb.

3. *The environment "houses" our species.* It is our home, our living space, the place where we reside, work, and play. At times we take this home for granted, but not when day-to-day living conditions become unpleasant and difficult. If our air is "heavy," if our tap water turns brown, if toxic chemicals seep into our neighborhoods, we remember why it is vital to live in a healthful environment.

Dunlap (1993) points out that these three functions of the environment actually compete with one another. Human use of the environment for one of these functions will often strain its ability to fulfill the other two. For example, with world population continuing to rise, we have an increasing need to raze forests or farmland and build housing developments. But each time we do so, we are reducing the amount of land that provides food, lumber, or habitat for wildlife.

This tension between the three essential functions of the environment brings us back to the human ecologists' view that "everything is connected to everything else." In facing the environmental challenges of the 21st century, government policymakers and environmentalists must determine how they can fulfill human societies' pressing needs (for example, for food, clothing, and shelter) while at the same time preserving the environment as a source of resources, a waste repository, and our home.

A CONFLICT VIEW OF ENVIRONMENTAL ISSUES

In Chapter 5 we drew on world-systems analysis to show how a growing share of the human and natural resources of developing countries is being redistributed to the core industrialized nations. This process only intensifies the destruction of natural resources in poorer regions of the world. From a conflict perspective, less affluent nations are being forced to exploit their mineral deposits, forests, and fisheries in order to meet their debt obligations to industrialized nations. The poor turn to the only means of survival available to them: They plow mountain slopes, burn tropical forests, and overgraze grasslands (Livernash and Rodenburg 1998).

Brazil exemplifies this interplay between economic troubles and environmental destruction. Each year more than 11,000 square miles of the Amazon rain forest are cleared for crops and livestock through burning. The elimination of the rain forest affects worldwide weather patterns, heightening the gradual warming of the earth. These socioeconomic patterns, with their harmful environmental consequences, are evident not only in Latin America but in many regions of Africa and Asia.

Conflict theorists are well aware of the environmental implications of land use policies in the Third World, but they contend that focusing on the developing countries is ethnocentric. Who, they ask, is more to blame for environmental deterioration: the poverty-stricken and "food-hungry" populations of the world or the "energy-hungry" industrialized nations (G. Miller 1972:117)? These theorists point out that Western industrialized nations account for only 25 percent of the world's population but are responsible for 85 percent of worldwide consumption. Take the United States alone: A mere 5 percent of the world's people consume more than half the world's nonrenewable resources and more than one-third of all the raw materials produced. Such data lead conflict theorists to charge that the most serious threat to the environment comes from "affluent megaconsumers and megapolluters" (Bharadwaj 1992; G. Miller 1972).

Allan Schnaiberg (1994) refines this analysis by criticizing the focus on affluent consumers as the cause of environmental troubles. In his view, the capitalist system's "treadmill of production" is the real culprit, because of its inherent need to build ever-expanding profits. This treadmill necessitates an increasing demand for products, the purchase of natural resources at minimal cost, and the manufacturing of products as quickly and cheaply as possible—no matter what the long-term environmental consequences.

ENVIRONMENTAL JUSTICE

Kennedy Heights, a new subdivision of Houston, attracted buyers in the late 1960s with its tidy brick façade homes and bucolic street names. But what the mostly Black buyers were not told was that developers had constructed the homes on oil pits abandoned by Gulf Oil decades earlier. After suffering periodic contamination of their water supply and a variety of illnesses, including high rates of cancer and lupus, Kennedy Heights residents filed a class-action suit against Chevron, the company that had acquired Gulf Oil. This case of environmental pollution was compounded by charges of "environmental racism," based on Gulf Oil documents prepared in 1967 that targeted the area "for Negro residential and commercial development" (Verhovek 1997).

While the Kennedy Heights case is still making its tortuous way through the courts, some headway is being made in promoting *environmental justice,* a legal strategy based on claims that racial minorities and the lower classes are subjected disproportionately to environmental hazards. In 1998, Shintech, a chemical company, dropped plans to build a plastics plant in an impoverished Black community in Mississippi. Opponents of the plant had filed a civil rights complaint with the Environmental Protection Agency (EPA). EPA administrator Carol Browner praised Shintech's decision: "The principles applied to achieve this solution should be incorporated into any blueprint for dealing with environmental justice issues in communities across the nation" (Associated Press 1998:18).

Following reports from the EPA and other organizations documenting discriminatory location of hazardous waste sites, in 1994 President Bill Clinton issued an executive order that requires all federal agencies to ensure that low-income and minority communities have access to better information about their environment, as well as an opportunity to participate in shaping government policies that affect their communities' health. Initial efforts to implement the policy have aroused widespread opposition because of the delays it imposes in establishing new industrial sites. Some observers question the wisdom of an order that slows economic development of areas in dire need of employment opportunities. But others note that such businesses employ few unskilled or less skilled workers, and only make the environment less livable (Cushman 1998; Goldman and Fitton 1994).

Sociology Matters

Sociology matters because it explains the connection between population patterns and the community in which you live.

- What kind of community—urban, suburban, or rural—do you live in? Is your community growing, or has its population been declining? What is responsible for the growth or decline of your community?

- Examine the city nearest you from the point of view of an urban sociologist. Is its economy industrial or postindustrial? Which theory describes its growth better, the concentric-zone theory or the multiple-nuclei theory? Does the city have any global economic ties?

Sociology matters because it highlights the relationship between your race, ethnicity, and social class and your quality of life.

- Evaluate the health of the people in your community: Do you think it is better than average, average, or worse than average? How many people in your community have low incomes or are members of minority groups? How many lack health care or health insurance?

- Describe your community's environment. Does it present any health hazards? If so, could some of the health problems in your community be related to those hazards?

CHAPTER RESOURCES

Summary

The size, composition, and distribution of the world's population have an important influence on our **communities,** our **health,** and our environment. This chapter introduced **demography,** the scientific study of population. We followed the growth of communities from prehistory through the present, and considered urbanization from both the functionalist and conflict perspectives. We studied the relationship between people's health, their geographic distribution, and the social groups to which they belong. And we acknowledged the connection between our health and the environment we live in.

1. Thomas Robert Malthus suggested that the world's population was growing more rapidly than the available food supply, and that the gap between the two would increase over time. But Karl Marx saw capitalism, rather than rising population, as the main cause of the world's social ills.

2. The primary tool for obtaining **vital statistics** on the population of the United States and most other countries is the **census.**

3. Stable **communities** first developed when humans became farmers, and their surplus production allowed others to live in **preindustrial cities.** Thousands of years later, the mechanization of production ushered in the era of the **industrial city,** a large population center dominated by factories. In the twentieth century, globalization and

the electronic flow of information gave rise to the **postindustrial city,** characterized by corporate offices rather than factories.

4. **Urban ecology** is a functionalist view of urbanization that focuses on the interrelationships between city dwellers and their environment. Urban ecologists developed two theories of urban growth, the **concentric-zone theory** and the **multiple-nuclei theory.**

5. **New urban sociology,** a conflict view of urbanization, focuses on the interplay of local, national, and global economic forces and their effect on cities throughout the world. This school of thought draws on Immanuel Wallerstein's **world-systems analysis.**

6. Functionalists, conflict theorists, and labeling theorists all see medicine as an institution of social definition and control. Functionalists see doctors as gatekeepers to the **sick role;** conflict theorists see them as proponents of the medicalization of society.

7. **Social epidemiology** is the study of the distribution of disease, disability, and **health** across a population. Epidemiological studies have shown that lower-class people have higher rates of mortality and disability than upper-class people. Similarly, racial and ethnic minorities have higher rates of morbidity and mortality than Whites.

8. From the perspective of **human ecology,** the natural environment serves three basic functions: It provides essential resources, serves as a waste repository, and houses our species. Thus, air and water pollution threatens our health and well-being.

9. Conflict theorists charge that the most serious threat to the environment comes from Western industrialized nations, which consume a disproportionate amount of the world's resources.

10. Racial minorities tend to be exposed more than other groups to environmental hazards, a social pattern that has prompted calls for **environmental justice.**

www.mhhe.com/schaefersm2
Visit the Online Learning Center for *Sociology Matters* to access quizzes, review activities, and other learning tools.

Key Terms

birthrate, 235

brain drain, 247

census, 235

community, 236

concentric-zone
theory, 241

curanderismo, 253

death rate, 236

demography, 233

environmental
justice, 260

fertility, 233

growth rate, 236

health, 244

human ecology, 241,
257

incidence, 250

industrial city, 239

infant mortality rate,
236

life expectancy, 236

morbidity rate, 250

mortality rate, 250

multiple-nuclei
theory, 242

new urban sociology,
243

postindustrial city, 240

preindustrial city, 237

prevalence, 250

sick role, 245

social epidemiology,
250

total fertility rate
(TFR), 236

urban ecology, 241

urbanism, 240

vital statistics, 235

world-systems
analysis, 243

Social Movements, Social Change, and Technology

Social Movements

Theories of Social Change

Resistance to Social Change

Technology and the Future

Technology and Society

In 1998, a rap star named Chuck D stiffed the music industry by posting his recordings on the Internet, instead of releasing them on his usual label. The next year Napster, the website that allowed computer owners to download popular music for free, was born. Together, these two events spelled trouble for the music industry. Soon thousands of music lovers were bypassing Sam Goody's and Wal-Mart, swapping their favorite tunes online instead. Panicked, recording executives rushed to challenge the illegal downloads in court, and eventually squashed the free-for-all. But that wasn't the end of downloading. The music industry eventually bowed to the inevitable and began to market the latest tracks online. Music fans downloaded them on their tiny Apple iPods, which by 2004 could hold over 10,000 songs (Apple 2004; Spar 2001).

This well-known episode in popular culture is an example of the social change that often follows the introduction of a new technology, such as the World Wide Web. *Social change* may be defined as significant alteration over time in behavior patterns and culture (Moore 1967). Clearly, Chuck D's distribution of his digitized music over the Web changed both the way people behaved—how they selected, obtained, and listened to popular music—and the cultural institution that is the music business. In this chapter, we will examine the process of social change, with special emphasis on the impact of technological advances. We will begin with social movements, which often spearhead social change. Then we will consider different sociological perspectives on change, and note how vested interests attempt to block it. Finally, we will look at the role of technology in spurring social change, from Web surfing and the outsourcing of service jobs to sex selection and genetic engineering.

Social Movements

Social movements are the most powerful source of social change. Although such factors as physical environment, population, technology, and social inequality also serve as sources of change, it is the *collective* effort of individuals organized in social movements that ultimately leads to change.

Sociologists use the term ***social movements*** to refer to organized collective activities to bring about or resist fundamental change in an existing group or society (Benford 1992). Herbert Blumer (1955:19) recognized the special importance of social movements when he defined them as "collective enterprises to establish a new order of life."

In many nations, including the United States, social movements have had a dramatic impact on the course of history and the evolution of social structure. Consider the actions of abolitionists, suffragists, civil rights workers, and activists opposed to the war in Vietnam. Members of each social movement stepped outside traditional channels for bringing about social change and yet had a noticeable influence on public policy. Equally dramatic collective efforts in Eastern Europe helped to topple Communist regimes in a largely peaceful manner, in nations that many observers had felt were "immune" to such social change (Ramet 1991).

Though social movements imply the existence of conflict, we can also analyze their activities from a functionalist perspective. Even when unsuccessful, social movements contribute to the formation of public opinion. Initially, the ideas of Margaret Sanger and other early advocates of birth control were viewed as "radical," yet contraceptives are now widely available in the United States. Moreover, functionalists view social movements as training grounds for leaders of the political establishment. Such heads of state as Cuba's Fidel Castro and South Africa's Nelson Mandela came to power after serving as leaders of revolutionary movements. Poland's Lech Walesa, Russia's Boris Yeltsin, and Czech playwright Vaclav Havel led protest movements against Communist rule and later became leaders of their countries' governments.

How and why do social movements emerge? Obviously, people are often discontented with current conditions. But what causes them to organize at a particular moment in a collective effort to work for change? In this section we will examine two different explanations for why people mobilize. We will acknowledge the often underestimated role of gender in social movements, and study recent changes in the character of social movements.

THE RELATIVE DEPRIVATION APPROACH

Those members of a society who feel most frustrated and disgruntled by the social and economic conditions of their lives are not necessarily "worst off" in an objective sense. Social scientists have long recognized that what is most significant is how people *perceive* their situation. Karl Marx pointed out that although the misery of the workers was important in reflecting their oppressed state, so was their position *relative* to the capitalist ruling class (Marx and Engels [1847] 1955).

The term **relative deprivation** is defined as the conscious feeling of a negative discrepancy between legitimate expectations and present actualities (J. Wilson 1973). In other words, life isn't as good as you hoped it would be. Such a state may be characterized by scarcity rather than complete lack of necessities (as we saw in the distinction between absolute and relative poverty in Chapter 5). A relatively deprived person is dissatisfied because he or she feels downtrodden relative to some appropriate reference group. Thus, blue-collar workers who live in two-family houses with little lawn space—though they are hardly at the bottom of the economic ladder—may nevertheless feel deprived in comparison with corporate managers and professionals who live in lavish and exclusive suburbs.

In addition to the feeling of relative deprivation, two other elements must be present before discontent will be channeled into a social movement. People must feel that they have a *right* to their goals, that they deserve better than what they have. For example, the struggle against European colonialism in Africa intensified when growing numbers of Africans decided that it was legitimate for them to have political and economic independence. At the same time, the disadvantaged group must perceive that it cannot attain its goals through conventional means. This belief may or may not be correct. Whichever is the case, the group will not mobilize into a social movement unless people share the perception that they can end their relative deprivation only through collective action (Morrison 1971).

Critics of this approach have noted that an increase in feelings of deprivation is not always necessary before people are moved to act. In addition, this approach fails to explain why certain feelings of deprivation are transformed into social movements, whereas in other similar situations, no collective effort is made to reshape society. Consequently, in recent years, sociologists have given increasing attention to the forces needed to bring about the emergence of social movements (Alain 1985; Finkel and Rule 1987; Orum 1989).

THE RESOURCE MOBILIZATION APPROACH

It takes more than desire to start a social movement. It helps to have money, political influence, access to the media, and personnel. The term **resource mobilization** refers to the ways in which a social movement utilizes such resources. The success of a movement for change will depend in good part on what resources it has and how effectively it mobilizes them (see also Gamson 1989; Staggenborg 1989a, 1989b).

Sociologist Anthony Oberschall (1973:199) has argued that to sustain social protest or resistance, there must be an "organizational base and continuity of leadership." As people become part of a social movement, norms develop to guide their behavior. Members of the movement may be expected to attend regular meetings of organizations, pay dues, recruit new adherents, and boycott "enemy" products or speakers. They may be expected to adopt special language or new words for familiar terms. In recent years, social movements have been responsible for such new terms of self-reference as *Blacks* and *African Americans* (used to replace *Negroes*), *senior citizens* (used to replace *old folks*), *gays* (used to replace *homosexuals*), and *people with disabilities* (used to replace *the handicapped*).

Leadership is a central factor in the mobilization of the discontented into social movements. Often, a movement will be led by a charismatic figure, such as Dr. Martin Luther King Jr. As Max Weber described it in 1904, *charisma* is that quality of an individual that sets him or her apart from ordinary people. Of course, charisma can fade abruptly, which accounts for the fragility of certain social movements (Morris 2000).

Yet many social movements do persist over long periods because their leadership is well organized and ongoing. Ironically, as Robert Michels (1915) noted, political movements that fight for social change eventually take on bureaucratic forms of organization. Leaders tend to dominate the decision-making process without directly consulting followers. The bureaucratization of social movements is not inevitable, however. More radical movements that advocate major structural change in society and embrace mass actions tend not to be hierarchical or bureaucratic (Fitzgerald and Rodgers 2000).

Why do certain individuals join a social movement, whereas others in similar situations do not? Some people are recruited to join. Karl Marx recognized the importance of recruitment when he called on workers to become *aware* of their oppressed status and develop a shared class consciousness. Marx held that the development of a social movement (specifically, the revolt of the proletariat) would require leaders to sharpen the awareness of the oppressed. They would need to help workers to overcome **false consciousness,** or attitudes that did not reflect workers' objective position, in order to organize a revolutionary movement. Similarly, sociologists who take the resource mobilization approach point out that one of the challenges women's liberation activists of the late 1960s and early 1970s faced was to convince women that they were being deprived of their rights and of socially valued resources.

Unlike the relative deprivation approach, the resource mobilization perspective focuses on the strategic difficulties facing social movements. Moreover, any movement for fundamental change will almost certainly arouse opposition. Effective mobilization will depend in part, then, on how the movement deals with resistance to its activities.

Today, technology facilitates the mobilization of resources for social change. Virtual social movements can develop quickly on the Web without the face-to-face contact of protest marches and petition drives. Chinese dissidents, Mexican Zapatistas, and members of the environmentalist organization Greenpeace are just a few of the organizations that have mounted virtual social movements on the Web.

Sociologists are just beginning to study virtual social movements. Roberta Garner looked at 542 websites that could be regarded as "ideological postings," ranging in content from ultrapatriotism and White racism to religious extremism, regional separatism, and militant environmentalism. Garner found that some sites in her sample, which was not random, represented the interests of a group or organization, while others reflected the opinions of isolated individuals. Like conventional social movements, these websites served as an alternative source of information, bypassing mainstream sources of opinion such as newspaper editorials. Because no gatekeeper barred these sites from the Web, they enjoyed the appearance of legitimacy (Garner 1999; Zook 1996).

GENDER AND SOCIAL MOVEMENTS

Sociologists point out that gender is an important element in understanding the development of social movements. In our male-dominated society, women find it difficult to assume leadership positions in social movement organizations. While women often serve disproportionately as volunteers in these movements, their work is not always recognized, nor are their voices as easily heard as men's. Moreover, gender bias causes the real extent of women's influence to be overlooked. Traditional examinations of the sociopolitical system tend to focus on such male-dominated corridors of power as legislatures and corporate boardrooms, to the neglect of more female-dominated domains, such as households, community-based groups, or faith-based networks. But efforts to influence family values, child rearing, relationships between parents and schools, and spiritual values are clearly significant to a culture and society (Ferree and Merrill 2000; Noonan 1995).

Scholars of social movements now realize that gender can affect even the way we view organized efforts to bring about or resist change. For example, an emphasis on using rationality and cold logic to achieve goals helps to obscure the importance of passion and emotion in successful social movements. Calls for a more serious study of the role of emotion are frequently seen as applying only to the women's movement, because emotion is traditionally thought of as feminine. Yet it would be difficult to find any movement, from labor battles to voting rights to animal rights, in which passion was not part of the consensus-building force (Ferree and Merrill 2000; Taylor 1995).

NEW SOCIAL MOVEMENTS

Beginning in the late 1960s, European social scientists observed a change in both the composition and the targets of emerging social movements. In the past, traditional social movements had focused on economic issues, often led by labor unions or by people who shared the same occupation. However, many social movements that have become active in recent decades—including the contemporary women's movement, the peace movement, and the environmental movement—do not have the social class roots typical of the labor protests in the United States and Europe over the past century (Tilly 1993).

The term *new social movements* refers to organized collective activities that address values and social identities, as well as improvements in the quality of life. These movements may be involved in developing collective identities. Many have complex agendas that go beyond a single issue, and even cross national boundaries. Educated, middle-class people are significantly represented in some of these new social movements, such as the women's movement and the movement for lesbian and gay rights.

New social movements generally do not view government as their ally in the struggle for a better society. While they typically do not seek to overthrow the government, they may criticize, protest, or harass public officials. Researchers have found that members of new social movements show little inclination to accept established authority, even scientific or technical authority. This characteristic is especially evident in the environmental and anti–nuclear power movements, whose activists present their own experts to counter those of government or big business (Garner 1996; Polletta and Jasper 2001; Scott 1990).

The environmental movement is one of many new movements that have adopted a worldwide focus. In their efforts to reduce air and water pollution, curtail global warming, and protect endangered animal species, environmental activists have realized that establishing strong regulatory measures within a single country is not sufficient. Similarly, labor union leaders and human rights advocates cannot adequately address exploitative sweatshop conditions in a developing country if a multinational corporation can simply move the factory to another country where workers are paid even less. Whereas traditional social movements tend to emphasize resource mobilization on a local level, new social movements take a broader, global perspective on social and political activism.

Table 11–1 on page 270 summarizes the sociological approaches that have contributed to social movement theory. Each approach has added to our understanding of the development of social movements. But in a larger sense, what causes social change? In the next section, we will see how sociologists have used some of the major theoretical perspectives to analyze and interpret the process of social change.

summingUP

Table 11–1 Contributions to Social Movement Theory

Approach	Emphasis
Relative deprivation approach	Social movements are especially likely to arise when rising expectations are frustrated.
Resource mobilization approach	The success of social movements depends on which resources are available and how effectively they are used.
New social movement theory	Social movements arise when people are motivated by value issues and social identity questions.

Theories of Social Change

A new millennium provides the occasion to offer explanations of *social change,* which we have defined as a significant alteration over time in behavior patterns and culture. Such explanations are clearly a challenge in the diverse and complex world we inhabit today. Nevertheless, theorists from several disciplines have sought to analyze social change. In some instances, they have examined historical events to arrive at a better understanding of contemporary changes. We will review three theoretical approaches to change—evolutionary, functionalist, and conflict theory— and then take a look at global social change today.

EVOLUTIONARY THEORY

The pioneering work of Charles Darwin (1809–1882) in biological evolution contributed to 19th-century theories of social change. Darwin's approach stresses a continuing progression of successive life forms. For example, human beings came at a later stage of evolution than reptiles and represent a more complex form of life. Social theorists seeking an analogy to this biological model originated ***evolutionary theory,*** in which society is viewed as moving in a definite direction. Early evolutionary theorists generally agreed that society was progressing inevitably to a higher state. As might be expected, they concluded in ethnocentric fashion that their own behavior and culture were more advanced than those of earlier civilizations.

Auguste Comte (1798–1857), a founder of sociology, was an evolutionary theorist of social change. He saw human societies as moving forward in their thinking from mythology to the scientific method. Similarly, Émile Durkheim ([1893] 1933) maintained that society progressed from simple to more complex forms of social organization.

The writings of Comte and Durkheim are examples of ***unilinear evolutionary theory.*** This approach contends that all societies pass through the same successive stages of evolution and inevitably reach the same end. The English sociologist Herbert Spencer (1820–1903) took a similar approach: Spencer likened society to a living body whose interrelated parts were moving toward a common destiny. However, contemporary evolutionary theorists such as Gerhard Lenski are more likely to see social change as being multilinear than to rely on the more limited unilinear perspective. *Multilinear evolutionary theory* holds that change can occur in several ways, and does not inevitably lead in the same direction (Haines 1988; Turner 1985).

Multilinear theorists recognize that human culture has evolved along a number of lines. For example, the theory of demographic transition graphically demonstrates that in developing nations, population change has not necessarily followed the model evident in industrialized nations. Sociologists today hold that events do not necessarily follow in a single or even several straight lines, but instead are subject to disruptions—a topic we will consider later, in our discussion of global social change.

FUNCTIONALIST THEORY

Functionalist sociologists focus on what *maintains* a system, not on what changes it. This statement might seem to suggest that functionalists can offer little of value to the study of social change. Yet as the work of sociologist Talcott Parsons demonstrates, functionalists have made a distinctive contribution to this area of sociological investigation.

Parsons (1902–1979), a leading proponent of functionalist theory, viewed society as being in a natural state of equilibrium. By "equilibrium," he meant that society tends toward a state of stability or balance. Parsons would view even prolonged labor strikes or civilian riots as temporary disruptions in the status quo rather than as significant alterations in social structure. Therefore, according to his *equilibrium model,* as changes occur in one part of society, adjustments must be made in other parts. If adjustments are not made, society's equilibrium will be threatened.

Taking an evolutionary approach, Parsons (1966) maintained that four processes of social change are inevitable. The first, *differentiation,* refers to the increasing complexity of social organization. The change from "medicine man" to physician, nurse, and pharmacist is an illustration of differentiation in the field of health. This process is accompanied by *adaptive upgrading,* through which social institutions become more specialized. The division of physicians into obstetricians, internists, surgeons, and so forth is an example of adaptive upgrading.

The third process identified by Parsons is the *inclusion* of groups into society that were once excluded because of such factors as gender, race, and social class background. Medical schools have practiced inclusion by admitting increasing numbers of women and African Americans. Finally, Parsons suggested that societies experience *value generalization,* the development of new values that tolerate and legitimate a greater range of activities. The acceptance of preventive and alternative medicine is an example of value generalization: our society has broadened its view of health care. All four processes identified by Parsons stress consensus—societal agreement on the nature of social organization and values (Johnson 1975; Wallace and Wolf 1980).

Though Parsons's approach explicitly incorporates the evolutionary notion of continuing progress, the dominant theme in his model is balance and stability. Society may change, but it remains stable through new forms of integration. For example, in place of the kinship ties that provided social cohesion in the past, society develops laws, judicial processes, and new values and belief systems.

Functionalists assume that social institutions will not persist unless they continue to contribute to society's well-being. This assumption leads functionalists to conclude that altering institutions will threaten societal equilibrium. Critics note that the functionalist approach virtually disregards the use of coercion by the powerful to maintain the illusion of a stable, well-integrated society (Gouldner 1960).

CONFLICT THEORY

The functionalist perspective minimizes the significance of change. It emphasizes the persistence of social life and sees change as a means of maintaining social equilibrium (or balance). In contrast, conflict theorists contend that social institutions and practices persist because powerful groups have the ability to maintain the status quo. Change has crucial significance, since it is needed to correct social injustices and inequalities.

Karl Marx accepted the evolutionary argument that societies develop along a particular path. However, unlike Comte and Spencer, he did not view each successive stage as an inevitable improvement over the previous one. Society, according to Marx, proceeds through a series of stages, each of which exploits a class of people. Ancient society exploited slaves; the estate system of feudalism exploited serfs; modern capitalist society exploits the working class. Ultimately, through a socialist revolution led by the proletariat, human society will move toward the final stage of development: a classless communist society, or "community of free individuals," as Marx described it in *Das Kapital* in 1867 (see Bottomore and Rubel 1956:250).

As we have seen, Marx had an important influence on the development of sociology. His thinking offered insights into such institutions as the economy, the family, religion, and government. The Marxist view of social change is appealing because it does not restrict people to a passive role in responding to inevitable cycles or changes in material culture. Rather, Marxist theory offers a tool to those who wish to seize control of the historical process and gain their freedom from injustice. In contrast to functionalists' emphasis on stability, Marx argues that conflict is a normal and desirable aspect of social change. In fact, change must be encouraged as a means of eliminating social inequality (Lauer 1982).

Had he lived to see it, Karl Marx would have viewed the repetitive and monotonous work of data entry as a form of exploitation of the working class.

"Keystroke! ... Keystroke!... Keystroke!"

One conflict sociologist, Ralf Dahrendorf (1959), has noted that the contrast between the functionalist perspective's emphasis on stability and the conflict perspective's focus on change reflects the contradictory nature of society. Human societies are stable and long-lasting, yet they also experience serious conflict. Dahrendorf found that the functionalist and conflict approaches were ultimately compatible, despite their many areas of disagreement. Indeed, Parsons spoke of new functions that result from social change, and Marx recognized the need for change so that societies could function more equitably.

GLOBAL SOCIAL CHANGE

We are living at a truly dramatic time in history to consider global social change. Maureen Hallinan (1997), in her presidential address to the American Sociological Association, asked those present to consider just a few of the recent political events: the collapse of communism; terrorist attacks in various parts of the world, including the United States; the dismantling of the welfare system in the United States; revolution and famine in Africa and Eastern Europe; the spread of AIDS; and the computer revolution. Just a few months after her remarks came the first verification of the cloning of a complex animal, Dolly the sheep.

In this era of massive social, political, and economic change, is it possible to predict change? Some technological changes seem obvious, but the collapse of Communist governments in the former Soviet Union and

Eastern Europe in the early 1990s took people by surprise. Prior to the Soviet collapse, however, sociologist Randall Collins (1986, 1995), a conflict theorist, had observed a crucial sequence of events that most observers had missed. In seminars as far back as 1980, and in a book published in 1986, Collins had argued that Soviet expansionism had resulted in an overextension of resources, including disproportionate spending on military forces. Such an overextension will strain a regime's stability. Moreover, geopolitical theory suggests that nations in the middle of a geographic region, such as the Soviet Union, tend to fragment into smaller units over time. Collins predicted that the coincidence of social crises on several frontiers would precipitate the collapse of the Soviet Union.

And that is just what happened. In 1979, the success of the Iranian revolution had led to an upsurge of Islamic fundamentalism in nearby Afghanistan, as well as in Soviet republics with substantial Muslim populations. At the same time, resistance to Communist rule was growing, both throughout Eastern Europe and within the Soviet Union itself. Collins had predicted that the rise of a dissident form of communism within the Soviet Union might facilitate the breakdown of the regime. Beginning in the late 1980s, Soviet leader Mikhail Gorbachev chose not to use military power and other types of repression to crush dissidents in Eastern Europe. Gorbachev offered plans for democratization and social reform of Soviet society, and seemed willing to reshape the Soviet Union into a loose federation of somewhat autonomous states. But in 1991, six republics on the western periphery declared their independence, and within months the entire Soviet Union had formally disintegrated into Russia and a number of other independent nations.

In her address, Hallinan (1997) cautioned that we need to move beyond restrictive models of social change—both the linear view of evolutionary theory and the assumptions about equilibrium within functionalist theory. She and other sociologists have looked to the "chaos theory" advanced by mathematicians to see erratic events as an integral part of change. Hallinan noted that upheavals and major chaotic shifts do occur, and that sociologists must learn to predict their occurrence, as Collins did with the collapse of the Soviet Union. Imagine, for instance, the dramatic nonlinear social change that will result from major innovations in communications and biotechnology, a topic we will discuss later in this chapter.

Resistance to Social Change

Efforts to promote social change are likely to meet with resistance. In the midst of rapid scientific and technological innovation, many people become frightened by the demands of an ever-changing society. Moreover, certain individuals and groups have a stake in maintaining the status quo.

Social economist Thorstein Veblen (1857–1929) coined the term **vested interests** to refer to those people or groups who will suffer in the event of social change. For example, the American Medical Association (AMA) has taken strong stands against national health insurance and the professionalization of midwifery. National health insurance could limit the income of physicians, and a rise in the status of midwives could threaten the preeminent position of doctors as the nation's deliverers of babies. In general, those with a disproportionate share of society's wealth, status, and power, such as members of the American Medical Association, have a vested interest in preserving the status quo (Starr 1982; Veblen 1919).

ECONOMIC AND CULTURAL FACTORS

Economic factors play an important role in resistance to social change. For example, meeting high standards for the safety of products and workers can be expensive for manufacturers. Conflict theorists argue that in a capitalist economic system, many firms are not willing to pay the price of meeting strict safety standards. They may resist social change by cutting corners or by pressuring the government to ease regulations.

Communities, too, protect their vested interests, often in the name of "protecting property values." The cry "not in my backyard" is often heard when people protest landfills, prisons, nuclear power facilities, and even bike trails and group homes for people with developmental disabilities. The targeted community may not challenge the need for the facility, but may simply insist that it be located elsewhere. The "not in my backyard" attitude has become so common that it is almost impossible for policymakers to find acceptable locations for such facilities as hazardous waste dumps (Jasper 1997).

Like economic factors, cultural factors frequently shape resistance to change. William F. Ogburn (1922) distinguished between material and nonmaterial aspects of culture. *Material culture* includes inventions, artifacts, and technology; *nonmaterial culture* encompasses ideas, norms, communications, and social organization. In music, for instance, the instruments musicians play and the CDs they record are aspects of material culture; their style of playing, such as rap, and the rules of pitch and rhythm they follow are aspects of nonmaterial culture. Ogburn pointed out that one cannot devise methods for controlling and utilizing a new technology before its introduction. Thus, nonmaterial culture typically must respond to changes in material culture. Ogburn introduced the term **culture lag** to refer to the period of maladjustment when the nonmaterial culture is still struggling to adapt to new material conditions. One example of culture lag is the questions that have been raised by the rapid, uncontrolled growth of the Internet—whether to regulate it, and if so, to what degree.

In certain cases, changes in material culture can strain the relationships between social institutions. For example, new means of birth control have been developed in recent decades. Large families are no longer economically necessary, nor are they commonly endorsed by social norms. But certain religious faiths, among them Roman Catholicism, continue to extol large families and to disapprove most methods of limiting family size, such as contraception and abortion. This gap in values represents a lag between aspects of material culture (technology) and nonmaterial culture (religious beliefs). Conflicts may emerge between religion and other social institutions, such as government and the educational system, over the dissemination of birth control and family-planning information (Riley et al. 1994a, 1994b).

RESISTANCE TO TECHNOLOGY

Technological innovations are examples of changes in material culture that have often provoked resistance. The *Industrial Revolution,* which took place largely in England during the period 1760 to 1830, was a scientific revolution focused on the application of nonanimal sources of power to labor tasks. As the revolution proceeded, societies relied more and more on new inventions that facilitated agricultural and industrial production, and on new sources of energy such as steam. In some industries, the introduction of power-driven machinery reduced the need for factory workers and made it easier for factory owners to cut wages.

Strong resistance to the Industrial Revolution emerged in some countries. In England, beginning in 1811, masked craft workers took extreme measures: They raided factories and destroyed some of the new machinery. The government hunted these rebels, known as *Luddites,* and banished or hung them. In a similar effort in France, angry workers threw their wooden shoes (*sabots*) into factory machinery to destroy it, giving rise to the term *sabotage.* While the resistance of the Luddites and the French workers was short-lived and unsuccessful, they have come to symbolize resistance to technology over the last two centuries.

Are we now in the midst of a second Industrial Revolution, with a contemporary group of Luddites resisting? Many sociologists believe that we are living in a *postindustrial society.* When this era began is difficult to pinpoint exactly. Generally, it is viewed as having begun in the 1950s, when for the first time the majority of workers in industrial societies became involved in services rather than in the actual manufacturing of goods (D. Bell 1999; Fiala 1992).

Just as the Luddites resisted the Industrial Revolution, people in many countries have resisted postindustrial technological changes. The term *neo-Luddites* refers to those who are wary of technological innovations and who question the incessant expansion of industrialization, the increasing destruction of the natural and agrarian world, and the "throw it away" mentality of contemporary capitalism, with its resulting pollution of the environment. Neo-Luddites insist that whatever the presumed benefits, industrial and postindustrial technologies have distinctive social costs, and may represent a danger to the future of both the human species and our planet (Bauerlein 1996; Rifkin 1995; Sale 1996; Snyder 1996).

Use Your Sociological Imagination

You are a neo-Luddite who wants to destroy the Internet. How will you do it? Are your motives the same as or different from those of the Luddites?

Such concerns are worth remembering as we turn to our technological future and its possible impact on social change.

Technology and the Future

Technology is cultural information about how to use the material resources of the environment to satisfy human needs and desires. Technological advances—the airplane, the automobile, the television, the atomic bomb, and more recently the computer, the fax machine, and the cellular phone—have brought striking changes in our cultures, our patterns of socialization, our social institutions, and our day-to-day social interactions. Technological innovations are, in fact, emerging and being accepted with remarkable speed. For example, scientists at Monsanto estimated in 1998 that the amount of genetic information used in practical applications will double every year. Part of the reason for this explosion in the use of new technologies is that they are becoming cheaper. In 1974, it cost $2.5 million to determine the chemical structure of a single gene; less than 25 years later that cost was just $150 (Belsie 1998).

The technological knowledge with which we work today represents only a tiny portion of the knowledge that will be available in the year 2050. We are witnessing an information explosion as well: The number of volumes in major libraries in the United States doubles every 14 years. Individuals, institutions, and societies will face unprecedented challenges in adjusting to the technological advances still to come. In the following sections, we will examine various aspects of our technological future and consider their overall impact on social change, including the strains they will bring. We will focus in particular on recent developments in computer technology and biotechnology (Cetron and Davies 1991; Wurman 1989).

COMPUTER TECHNOLOGY

The last decade has witnessed an explosion of computer technology in the United States and around the world. Its effects are particularly noteworthy with regard to the Internet, the world's largest computer network. Estimates are that by 2005, the Internet will reach 1.1 billion computer users, compared to just 50 million in 1996 (Global Reach 2004).

The Internet evolved from a computer system built in 1962 by the U.S. Defense Department, to enable scholars and military researchers to continue their government work even if part of the nation's communications system were destroyed by a nuclear attack. Until recently, it was difficult to gain access to the Internet without holding a position at a university or a government research laboratory. Today, however, virtually anyone can reach the Internet with a phone line, a computer, and a modem. People buy and sell cars, trade stocks, auction off items, research new medical remedies, vote, and track down long-lost friends online—to mention just a few of the thousands of possibilities (Reddick and King 2000).

Unfortunately, not everyone can get onto the information highway, especially not the less affluent. Moreover, this pattern of inequality is global. The core nations that Immanuel Wallerstein described in his *world-systems analysis* have a virtual monopoly on information technology; the periphery nations of Asia, Africa, and Latin America depend on them both for technology and for the information it provides. For example, North America, Europe, and a few industrialized nations in other regions possess almost all the world's *Internet hosts*—computers that are connected directly to the worldwide network. The same is true for newspapers, telephones, televisions, and even radios. Low-income periphery nations have an average of only 30 telephone lines per 1,000 people, compared to 593 per 1,000 in high-income nations. The disparity is even greater for cell phones: low-income nations have an average of 10 cell phones per 1,000 people, compared to 609 per 1,000 in high-income nations (World Bank 2003b).

Recently, however, some developing nations have begun to benefit from the ease with which information—particularly business information—can be transferred around the world instantaneously. In semiperiphery countries like India, where a growing segment of the workforce speaks English and is computer literate, multinational corporations have been opening new offices, creating well-paid service and professional jobs that boost the local economy. This outgrowth of the trend toward globalization has had a negative impact on the U.S. job market. More and more, increases in overseas outsourcing are being accompanied by job reductions at home. Estimates are that by the year 2015, 3.3 million white-collar jobs worth an estimated annual payroll of $136.4 billion will have moved overseas. The impact on those technical and service workers who have been displaced is clearly devastating.

BIOTECHNOLOGY

Sex selection of fetuses, genetically engineered organisms, cloning of sheep and cows—these have been among the significant yet controversial scientific advances in the field of biotechnology in recent years. George Ritzer's concept of McDonaldization applies to the entire area of biotechnology. Just as the fast-food concept has permeated society, no phase of life now seems exempt from therapeutic or medical intervention. In fact, sociologists view many aspects of biotechnology as an extension of the trend toward the medicalization of society, discussed in Chapter 10. Through genetic manipulation, the medical profession is expanding its turf still further (Clarke et al. 2003).

Today's biotechnology holds itself out as totally beneficial to human beings, but it is in constant need of monitoring. As we will see in the following sections, biotechnological advances have raised many difficult ethical and political questions (D. Weinstein and Weinstein 1999).

Sex Selection.   Advances in reproductive and screening technology have effectively become techniques for sex selection. In the United States, the prenatal test called amniocentesis has been used for more than 25 years to ascertain the presence of certain genetic defects that require medical attention prior to birth. Such tests can also identify the sex of the fetus, as can ultrasound scans. This outcome has had profound social implications.

In many societies, young couples planning to have only one child will want to ensure that the child is a boy, because their culture places a premium on a male heir. In such instances, advances in fetal testing may lead to abortion if the fetus is found to be female. Fetal testing clinics in Canada currently advertise that they can tell parents the sex of a fetus. Such advertising is targeted particularly at Asian Indian communities in both Canada and the United States. But in the United States, the preference for a male child is hardly limited to people from India. In one study, when asked what sex they would prefer for an only child, 86 percent of men and 59 percent of women said they wanted a boy. Moreover, through fetal testing, couples today routinely learn the sex of their child (M. Hall 1993; Sohoni 1994).

Sex selection is also possible in connection with a procedure called *in vitro fertilization*. In this procedure, which is intended to help infertile couples conceive a child, an egg is fertilized in a test tube and then implanted in the mother's womb. Couples who use this expensive procedure can now obtain a genetic analysis of the embryo before it is implanted. While the purpose of the analysis is to confirm that an embryo will be free from genetic defects, the results can also be used to select an embryo of the desired sex (Gezari 2002).

From a functionalist perspective, we can view sex selection as an adaptation of the basic family function of regulating reproduction. However, conflict theorists emphasize that sex selection may intensify the male dominance of our society and undermine the advances women have made in entering careers formerly restricted to men.

Genetic Engineering.   Even more grandiose than sex selection — and not necessarily improbable — is the possibility of altering human behavior through genetic engineering. Fish and plant genes have already been mixed to create frost-resistant potato and tomato crops; more recently, human genes have been implanted in pigs to provide humanlike kidneys for organ transplants.

One of the latest developments in genetic engineering is gene therapy. Geneticists working with mouse fetuses have managed to disable genes that carry an undesirable trait and replace them with genes carrying a desirable trait. Such advances raise staggering possibilities for altering animal and human life forms. Still, gene therapy remains highly experimental, and must be considered a long, long shot (Kolata 1999).

The debate over genetic engineering escalated in 1997 when scientists in Scotland announced that they had cloned a sheep. After many unsuccessful attempts, they had finally been able to replace the genetic material of a sheep's egg with DNA from an adult sheep, creating a lamb that was a clone of the adult. The very next year, Japanese researchers successfully cloned cows. These developments raised the possibility that in the near future, scientists may be able to clone human beings.

In 1997, President Bill Clinton banned any federal support for human cloning and urged private laboratories to abide by a voluntary moratorium until the ethical issues could be carefully considered. Six years later, no federal law on human cloning had been drafted, no less passed. However, state legislatures have grappled with the issue. As of mid-2003, only California specifically allowed human cloning, while Iowa and South Dakota explicitly banned it (Brainard 2003).

William F. Ogburn probably could not have anticipated such scientific developments when he wrote of culture lag 70 years earlier. However, the successful cloning of sheep illustrates again how quickly material culture can change, and how nonmaterial culture moves more slowly in absorbing such changes.

While cloning grabs the headlines, controversy has been growing concerning genetically modified (GM) food. This issue arose in Europe but has since spread to other parts of the world, including the United States. The idea behind the technology is to increase food production and make agriculture more economical. But critics use the term *Frankenfood* (as in "Frankenstein") to refer to everything from breakfast cereals made from genetically engineered grains to "fresh" GM tomatoes. They object to tampering with nature, and are concerned about the possible health effects of GM food. Supporters of genetically modified food include not just biotech companies, but those who see the technology as a way to help feed the burgeoning populations of Africa and Asia (Golden 1999).

Another form of biotechnology with a potentially wide-ranging impact is the Human Genome Project. This effort involves teams of scientists around the world in sequencing and mapping all the 30,000 to 40,000 human genes in existence, which are collectively known as the *human genome.* Supporters say that the resulting knowledge could revolutionize doctors' ability to treat and even prevent disease. But sociologists worry about the ethical implications of such research.

Bioterrorism.   Because biotechnology has generally been seen as a benefit to society, critics have been concerned mostly with the possibility of unintended negative consequences. Yet scientists have long recognized that chemical and biological agents can be used intentionally as weapons of mass destruction. Combatants in World War I used mustard gas, and nerve gas was used shortly thereafter. Today as many as 26 nations appear to have stockpiled chemical weapons, and another 10 have developed biological weapons programs.

More disturbing still is the prospect that terrorists might develop their own biological or chemical weapons, which are not difficult or expensive to make. The deaths that occurred as a result of anthrax contamination of the U.S. mails in 2001, shortly after the attacks on the Pentagon and World Trade Center, underscored the relative ease with which biotechnology can be used for hostile purposes. In fact, between 1975 and August 2000, terrorists created 342 incidents involving biological or chemical agents. Only about a third of those events were real attacks, and most caused few injuries and even fewer deaths. Yet because chemical and biological weapons are easy to use, these agents, which have come to be known as the poor person's nuclear bomb, are a source of increasing concern to governments the world over (Henry L. Stimson Center 2001; J. Miller et al. 2001; Mullins 2001; White 2002).

These are but a few aspects of technological change that raise questions about the future. Sociologists are not fortune-tellers; the focus of the discipline is to examine the society around us rather than to project decades ahead. But sociologists have no problem in asserting that social change (and technological change) is a given in our world. And so, they remind us, is resistance to change. We cannot know what is ahead. But the sociological imagination—with its probing and theorizing and its careful empirical studies—can assist us in understanding the past and present and in anticipating and adjusting to the future.

Try to imagine the world 100 years from now. On balance, is it a world in which technology contributes to or threatens people's well-being? In what ways?

Technology and Society

An automated teller machine (ATM) that identifies a person by his or her facial structure; a small device that sorts through hundreds of odors to ensure the safety of a chemical plant; a cell phone that recognizes its owner's voice—these are real-life examples of technology that were so much science fiction a few short decades ago. Today's computer chip not only can think but can see, smell, and hear, too (Salkever 1999).

Such technological advances can dramatically transform the material culture. The word processor, pocket calculator, photocopying machine, and compact disc player have largely eliminated the typewriter, adding machine, mimeograph, and turntable—all of which were once technological advances themselves. Moreover, technological change can reshape *nonmaterial* culture. In the following sections, we will examine the effects of technological advances on culture and social interaction, social control, and stratification and inequality.

CULTURE AND SOCIAL INTERACTION

In Chapter 2, we emphasized that language is the foundation of every culture. From a functionalist perspective, language can bring members of a society together and promote cultural integration. However, from a conflict perspective, the use of language can intensify divisions between groups and societies—just look at the battles over language in the United States, Canada, and many other societies.

How will social interaction be transformed by the growing availability of electronic forms of communication? Will people turn to e-mail, websites, and faxes rather than to telephone conversations and face-to-face meetings? Certainly, the technological shift to the telephone reduced letter writing as a means of maintaining kinship and friendship ties. For this reason, some people worry that computers and other forms of electronic communication may be socially isolating. Sociologist Sherry Turkle (1999) has warned that some individuals may become so gratified by their online lives that they may lose touch with their families, friends, and work responsibilities.

Yet Turkle (1995, 1999) has also found some positive effects from Internet usage. Over a 10-year period, she made anonymous visits to chat rooms and multiuser domains (MUDs), which allow people to assume new identities in role-playing games. She also conducted face-to-face interviews with more than 1,000 people who communicate by e-mail and participate actively in MUDs. Distinguishing between users' on-screen personae and their real identities, Turkle concluded that many MUD users' lives were enhanced by the opportunity to engage in role playing and "become someone else." A new sense of self had emerged, she wrote, that was "decentered and multiple." In making this observation, Turkle was expanding on George Herbert Mead's notion of self (Nass and Moon 2000).

One obvious form of online role playing is gender switching. In a 1999 study, researchers found that 40 percent of their subjects had presented themselves online as a member of the opposite sex. Yet gender switching does not appear to dominate online communication. Even among the gender-switched, the majority of subjects spent only about 10 percent of their time online disguised as the opposite sex (Roberts and Parks 1999).

If electronic communication can facilitate social interaction within a community—if it can create ties among people in different communities or even countries who "meet" in chat rooms or MUDs—then has it created a new interactive world known as cyberspace? The term *cyberspace* was introduced in 1984 by William Gibson, a Canadian science fiction writer. He came up with the term after he walked by a video arcade and noticed the intensity of the players hunched over their screens. Gibson felt that video game enthusiasts "develop a belief that there's some kind of actual space behind the screen. Some place that you can't see but you know is there" (Elmer-DeWitt 1995:4; Turkle 2004).

The emergence of cyberspace can be viewed as yet another step away from Ferdinand Tönnies's concept of the familiar, intimate *Gemeinschaft* and toward the comparatively impersonal *Gesellschaft*—yet another way in which social cohesion is being eroded in contemporary society. Critics of electronic communication question whether nonverbal communication, voice inflections, and other forms of interpersonal interaction will be lost as people turn to e-mail and chat rooms (P. Schaefer 1995; Schellenberg 1996).

But while some people think that by opening up the world to cyberspace interaction, we may have reduced face-to-face interaction, others have reached a different conclusion. Researchers surveyed more than 2,000 households nationwide to assess the impact of the Internet on the everyday lives of its users. Parents reported that they often surfed the Web together with their children, and that the Internet had had little effect on their children's interactions with friends. Researchers concluded that about two-thirds of the people in the United States are using the Internet more than ever, without sacrificing their social lives (Cha 2000; P. Howard et al. 2001; Nie 2001).

SOCIAL CONTROL

A data entry employee pauses to say hello to a colleague. A checker at the supermarket takes a moment to banter with a customer. A telephone representative takes too much time helping callers. Each of these situations is subject to computer surveillance. Given the absence of strong protective legislation, employees in the United States are subject to increasing and pervasive supervision by computer.

Supervisors have always scrutinized the performance of workers, but with so much work now being handled electronically, the possibilities for surveillance have risen dramatically. According to a 2001 study, one-third of the online workforce is under continuous electronic surveillance. With Big Brother watching and listening in more and more, the danger is that electronic monitoring will become a substitute for effective management, or worse, lead to perceptions of unfairness and intrusiveness (T. Levin et al. 2002; Schulman 2001).

In recent years, a new type of corporate surveillance has emerged. A number of Internet sites have been highly critical of the operations of various corporations. On McSpotlight, one could find attacks on nutritional practices at McDonald's; on Up Against the Wal, one could study advice on how to fight the opening of a new Wal-Mart store. The Internet sites of such "anticorporate vigilantes" are generally protected by the First Amendment, but powerful corporations are carefully monitoring them in an attempt to counteract their activities (Neuborne 1996).

Technological advances have also created the possibility for a new type of white-collar crime: computer crime. It is now possible to gain access to a computer without leaving home, and to carry out embezzlement or electronic fraud without leaving a trace. One report released in 2000 put cybercrime losses by big business at $10 billion in the United States alone. Typically, discussions of computer crime focus on computer theft and on problems caused by "hackers," but widespread use of computers has facilitated many new ways of participating in deviant behavior. Consequently, greatly expanded police resources may be needed to deal with online child molesters, prostitution rings, software pirates, con artists, and other types of computer criminal. There is now a Computer Crime and Intellectual Property section of the Justice Department. The consensus of the heads of the section is that these cases are increasing and becoming more difficult to solve (Piller 2000).

Not all the technological advances relevant to social control have been electronic in nature. DNA data banks have given police a powerful weapon in solving crimes; they have also opened the way to freeing wrongfully convicted citizens. From 1993 through May 2004, 15 death row inmates were released on the basis of DNA evidence. Efforts are under way to make such testing and other forms of DNA evidence as easily available as fingerprinting. While appropriate safeguards must be devised, the creation of DNA data banks has the potential to revolutionize law enforcement in the United States—especially in the prosecution of sex crimes, for which biological evidence is telling (Death Penalty Information Center 2004b).

Another connection between technology and social control is the use of computer databases and electronic verification of documents to reduce illegal immigration into the United States, especially from Muslim nations. While they are concerned about the issue of illegal entry, many Arab Americans, Hispanics, and Asian Americans nevertheless believe that *their* privacy, rather than that of Whites, is most likely to be infringed by government authorities. In the next section we will consider more fully how technological changes can intensify stratification and inequality based on race, ethnicity, and other factors.

STRATIFICATION AND INEQUALITY

"Today we stand at the brink of becoming two societies, one largely white and plugged in and the other black and unplugged." That is how Black historian Henry Lewis Gates Jr. starkly describes today's "digital divide" (Gates 1999: A15). Stratification is a continuing theme in sociology. Thus far, there is little evidence to suggest that technology will reduce inequality; in fact, it may only intensify it. Technology is costly, so it generally cannot be introduced to everyone simultaneously. Who gets access first? Conflict theorists contend that as we travel further and further along the electronic frontier through advances such as the Internet, the disenfranchised poor may become isolated from mainstream society in an "information ghetto," just as racial and ethnic minorities have traditionally been subjected to residential segregation (DiMaggio et al. 2001).

Available data show clear differences in the use of computers based on class, race, and ethnicity. A national study released in 2001 estimated that only 14 percent of households earning less than $15,000 had access to the Internet, compared to 79 percent of those with incomes of $75,000 or more. Moreover, 56 percent of Asian American households and 46 percent of White households used the Internet, compared with 24 percent of Hispanic and African American households (see Figure 11–1).

This issue goes beyond individual interest or lack of interest in computers. Accessibility is a major concern. According to a study by the Consumer Federation of America and the National Association for the Advancement of Colored People (NAACP), accessibility to computer networks through fiber-optic corridors (the "information superhighway") may bypass poor neighborhoods and minority populations. The researchers concluded that regional telephone companies' plans for these advanced communications networks target affluent areas, and may lead to an exclusionary "electronic redlining" that resembles discrimination in fields such as banking, real estate, and insurance (Lieberman 1999; Lohr 1994).

Industry executives counter that they have repeatedly stated their intention to deploy the information superhighway to *all* areas. Congress has proposed regulatory legislation to ensure equal access to the information superhighway by mandating the wiring of schools, libraries, and hospitals. And several communities, such as Manchester, New Hampshire, and Oakland, California, have recently arranged for computer hookups in publicly built low-income housing.

The issue of technology and inequality is especially sensitive when viewed in a cross-cultural perspective. Although industrialization has dramatically improved many workers' standard of living, it has allowed elites to amass untold wealth. Moreover, the activities of multinational corporations have increased the inequality between industrialized core nations such as the United States, Germany, and Japan and peripheral developing countries.

Use Your Sociological Imagination

One hundred years from now, how might society have changed? Will people be as free as they are today? Will the differences among social classes be more or less pronounced than they are now? What about the differences among nations, races, religions, and ethnic groups?

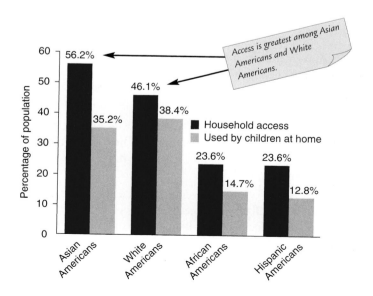

Figure 11–1

Internet Access in the United States, 2000

SOURCE: Newburger 2001:3–4

Access is greatest among Asian Americans and White Americans.

Sociology Matters

Sociology matters because it helps you to understand the social change you encounter.

- Have you had any experience working in a social movement? If so, what kind of social change were you hoping to support? What resources did the movement try to mobilize? Who were the vested interests who opposed the movement?

- Have you yourself experienced culture lag, or have you observed it in others? If so, what kind of change caused the lag—was it a new technology, or some other kind of change? Did you notice a generational difference in the way people responded to the change? Did you see any open resistance to it?

- Have new technologies helped you in any significant way, and if so, how? On balance, do you see new technologies as a benefit or a threat to society? Explain.

CHAPTER RESOURCES

Summary

Social movements are a form of collective behavior that promotes **social change,** or a significant alteration over time in behavior patterns and culture. This chapter examined social movements, sociological theories of social change, resistance to social change, and the impact of **technology** on social change.

1. A group will not mobilize into a **social movement** unless its members believe they can end their **relative deprivation** only through collective action.

2. The success of a social movement depends in good part on effective **resource mobilization.** Increasingly, social movements are using **technology**—including the Internet—to mobilize their resources.

3. Early advocates of the **evolutionary theory** of social change believed that society was progressing steadily and inevitably toward a higher state.

4. Talcott Parsons, a leading advocate of functionalist theory, thought that **social change** would always return society to a natural state of equilibrium, or balance. Conflict theorists see change more as a necessity in correcting social injustices and inequities.

5. In general, those with a disproportionate share of society's wealth, status, and power, called **vested interests,** will resist social change and attempt to preserve the status quo.

6. A period of maladjustment, called **culture lag,** occurs when a non-material culture strains to adapt to new material conditions.

7. The Internet, the world's largest computer network, has revolutionized communications and commercial activity around the world. Though developing nations typically have little access to new technologies, some semiperiphery nations have begun to benefit from the outsourcing of service and professional jobs once done in core nations.

8. Advances in biotechnology have raised difficult ethical questions about genetic engineering and the sex selection of fetuses. Increasing reliance on biotechnology has also raised concern about the threat of bioterrorism.

9. New computer and video technologies have facilitated the supervision, control, and even domination of workers and citizens by employers and the government.

10. Conflict theorists fear that the disenfranchised poor, who cannot afford new technologies, may be isolated from mainstream society in an "information ghetto."

www.mhhe.com/schaefersm2
Visit the Online Learning Center for *Sociology Matters* to access quizzes, review activities, and other learning tools.

Key Terms

culture lag, 275

equilibrium model, 271

evolutionary theory, 270

false consciousness, 267

Luddite, 276

multilinear evolutionary theory, 271

new social movement, 269

relative deprivation, 266

resource mobilization, 266

social change, 264

social movement, 265

technology, 277

unilinear evolutionary theory, 270

vested interests, 274

Glossary

Numbers following the definitions indicate pages where the terms were identified. Consult the index for further page references.

Absolute poverty: A standard of poverty based on a minimum level of subsistence that no family should be expected to live below. (125)

Achieved status: A social position attained by a person largely through his or her own efforts. (67, 112)

Affirmative action: Positive efforts to recruit minority group members or women for jobs, promotions, and educational opportunities. (159)

Agrarian society: The most technologically advanced form of preindustrial society, in which members are engaged primarily in the production of food but increase their crop yield through such technological innovations as the plow. (75)

Anomie: Durkheim's term for the loss of direction felt in a society when social control of individual behavior has become ineffective. (94)

Anomie theory of deviance: A theory developed by Robert Merton that explains deviance as an adaptation either of socially prescribed goals or of the norms governing their attainment, or both. (95)

Anticipatory socialization: Processes of socialization in which a person "rehearses" for future positions, occupations, and social relationships. (55)

Applied sociology: The use of the discipline of sociology with the specific intent of yielding practical applications for human behavior and organizations. (29)

Argot: Specialized language used by members of a subculture. (44)

Ascribed status: A social position "assigned" to a person by society without regard for the person's unique talents or characteristics. (66, 112)

Authority: Power that has been institutionalized and is recognized by the people over whom it is exercised. (217)

Basic sociology: Sociological inquiry conducted with the objective of gaining a more profound knowledge of the fundamental aspects of social phenomena. Also known as *pure sociology.* (29)

Bilateral descent: A kinship system in which both sides of a person's family are regarded as equally important. (192)

Birthrate: The number of live births per 1,000 population in a given year. Also known as the *crude birthrate.* (235)

Bourgeoisie: Karl Marx's term for the capitalist class, or the owners of the means of production. (115)

Brain drain: The immigration to the United States and other industrialized nations of skilled workers, professionals, and technicians who are desperately needed in their home countries. (247)

Bureaucracy: A component of formal organization in which rules and hierarchical ranking are used to achieve efficiency. (78)

Capitalism: An economic system in which the means of production are held largely in private hands, and the main incentive for economic activity is the accumulation of profits. (115, 222)

Caste: A hereditary system of rank, usually religiously dictated, that tends to be fixed and immobile. (113)

Causal logic: The relationship between a condition or variable and a particular consequence, with one event leading to the other. (20)

Census: An enumeration, or counting, of a population. (235)

Charismatic authority: Max Weber's term for power made legitimate by a leader's exceptional personal or emotional appeal to his or her followers. (218)

Class: A term used by Max Weber to refer to a group of people who have a similar level of wealth and income. (116)

Class consciousness: In Karl Marx's view, a subjective awareness of common vested interests and the need for collective political action to bring about social change. (115)

Classical theory: An approach to the study of formal organizations in which workers are viewed as being motivated almost entirely by economic rewards. (82)

Class system: A social ranking based primarily on economic position in which achieved characteristics can influence social mobility. (113)

Clinical sociology: The use of the discipline of sociology with the specific intent of altering social relationships or restructuring social institutions. (29)

Closed system: A social system in which there is little or no possibility of individual mobility. (130)

Code of ethics: The standards of acceptable behavior developed by and for members of a profession. (27)

Collective decision making: The active involvement of employee problem-solving groups in corporate management. (83)

Colonialism: The maintenance of political, social, economic, and cultural domination over a people by a foreign power for an extended period. (133)

Communism: As an ideal type, an economic system in which all property is communally owned and no social distinctions are made on the basis of people's ability to produce. (224)

Community: A spatial or political unit of social organization that gives people a sense of belonging. (236)

Concentric-zone theory: A theory of urban growth devised by Ernest Burgess that sees growth in terms of a series of rings radiating from the central business district. (241)

Conflict perspective: A sociological approach that assumes that social behavior is best understood in terms of conflict or tension between competing groups. (14)

Conformity: Going along with peers—individuals of our own status, who have no special right to direct our behavior. (89)

Contact hypothesis: An interactionist perspective that states that interracial contact between people of equal status engaged in a cooperative task will reduce prejudice. (155)

Content analysis: The systematic coding and objective recording of data, guided by some rationale. (27)

Control group: Subjects in an experiment who are not introduced to the independent variable by the researcher. (26)

Control variable: A factor held constant to test the relative impact of an independent variable. (23)

Correlation: A relationship between two variables in which a change in one coincides with a change in the other. (21)

Counterculture: A subculture that conspicuously and deliberately opposes certain aspects of the larger culture. (46)

Credentialism: An increase in the lowest level of education needed to enter a field. (209)

Crime: A violation of criminal law for which some governmental authority applies formal penalties. (101)

Cultural relativism: The viewing of people's behavior from the perspective of their own culture. (48)

Cultural transmission: A school of criminology that argues that criminal behavior is learned through social interactions. (97)

Cultural universal: A general practice found in every culture. (36)

Culture: The totality of learned, socially transmitted customs, knowledge, material objects, and behavior. (34)

Culture lag: Ogburn's term for the period of maladjustment when the nonmaterial culture is still struggling to adapt to new material conditions. (38, 275)

Culture shock: The feeling of surprise and disorientation that people experience when they witness cultural practices different from their own. (46)

Curanderismo: Traditional Latino folk practices for holistic health care and healing. (253)

Death rate: The number of deaths per 1,000 population in a given year. Also known as the *crude death rate.* (236)

Degradation ceremony: An aspect of the resocialization process within total institutions, in which people are subjected to humiliating rituals. (56)

Deindustrialization: The systematic, widespread withdrawal of investment in basic aspects of productivity, such as factories and plants. (227)

Demography: The scientific study of population. (233)

Dependency theory: An approach to global stratification that contends that industrialized nations exploit developing countries for their own gain. (134)

Dependent variable: The variable in a causal relationship that is subject to the influence of another variable. (20)

Deviance: Behavior that violates the standards of conduct or expectations of a group or society. (92)

Differential association: A theory of deviance proposed by Edwin Sutherland that holds that violation of rules results from exposure to attitudes favorable to criminal acts. (97)

Diffusion: The process by which a cultural item spreads from group to group or society to society. (37)

Discovery: The process of making known or sharing the existence of some aspect of reality. (36)

Discrimination: The denial of opportunities and equal rights to individuals and groups based on some type of bias. (156)

Dominant ideology: A set of cultural beliefs and practices that helps to maintain powerful social, economic, and political interests. (43)

Downsizing: Reductions taken in a company's workforce as part of deindustrialization. (227)

Dramaturgical approach: A view of social interaction popularized by Erving Goffman that examines people as if they were theatrical performers. (54)

Economic system: The social institution through which goods and services are produced, distributed, and consumed. (222)

Education: A formal process of learning in which some people consciously teach while others adopt the social role of learner. (206)

Egalitarian family: An authority pattern in which spouses are regarded as equals. (192)

Elite model: A view of society as ruled by a small group of individuals who share a common set of political and economic interests. (219)

Environmental justice: A legal strategy based on claims that racial minorities and the lower classes are subjected disproportionately to environmental hazards. (260)

Equilibrium model: Talcott Parsons's functionalist view of society as tending toward a state of stability or balance. (271)

Estate system: A system of stratification under which peasants were required to work land leased to them by nobles in exchange for military protection and other services. Also known as *feudalism.* (113)

Esteem: The reputation that a specific person has earned within an occupation. (121)

Ethnic group: A group that is set apart from others primarily because of its national origin or distinctive cultural patterns. (145)

Ethnocentrism: The tendency to assume that one's own culture and way of life represent the norm or are superior to all others. (47, 156)

Ethnography: The study of an entire social setting through extended, systematic observation. (25)

Evolutionary theory: A theory of social change that holds that society is moving in a definite direction. (270)

Experiment: An artificially created situation that allows the researcher to manipulate variables. (26)

Experimental group: Subjects in an experiment who are exposed to an independent variable introduced by a researcher. (26)

Exploitation theory: A Marxist theory that views racial subordination in the United States as a manifestation of the class system inherent in capitalism. (154)

Expressiveness: Concern for the maintenance of harmony and the internal emotional affairs of the family. (170)

Extended family: A family in which relatives—such as grandparents, aunts, or uncles—live in the same home as parents and their children. (189)

False consciousness: A term used by Karl Marx to describe an attitude held by members of a class that does not accurately reflect its objective position. (116, 267)

Family: A set of people related by blood, marriage (or some other agreed-upon relationship), or adoption who share the primary responsibility for reproduction and caring for members of society. (189)

Feminist perspective: A sociological approach that views inequity in gender as central to all behavior and organization. (16)

Feminization of poverty: A trend in which women constitute an increasing proportion of the poor people of the United States. (127)

Fertility: The level of reproduction in a society. (233)

Folkway: A norm governing everyday social behavior whose violation raises comparatively little concern. (40)

Force: The actual or threatened use of coercion to impose one's will on others. (216)

Formal norm: A norm that generally has been written down and specifies strict punishment of violators. (39)

Formal organization: A group designed for a special purpose and structured for maximum efficiency. (78)

Formal social control: Control carried out by authorized agents, such as police officers, physicians, school administrators, employers, military officers, and managers of movie theaters. (91)

Functionalist perspective: A sociological approach that emphasizes the way that parts of a society are structured to maintain its stability. (13)

Gemeinschaft: A term used by Ferdinand Tönnies to describe a small, close-knit community, often found in a rural area, in which strong personal bonds unite members. (74)

Gender role: Expectations regarding the proper behavior, attitudes, and activities of males or females. (57, 166)

Generalized other: A term used by George Herbert Mead to refer to the attitudes, viewpoints, and expectations of society as a whole that a child takes into account in his or her behavior. (53)

Gesellschaft: A term used by Ferdinand Tönnies to describe a community, often urban, that is large and impersonal, with little commitment to the group or consensus on values. (74)

Glass ceiling: An invisible barrier that blocks the promotion of a qualified individual in a work environment because of the individual's gender, race, or ethnicity. (157, 177)

Globalization: The worldwide integration of government policies, cultures, social movements, and financial markets through trade and the exchange of ideas. (36, 135)

Goal displacement: Within a bureaucracy, overzealous conformity to official regulations. (81)

Group: Any number of people with similar norms, values, and expectations who interact on a regular basis. (70)

Growth rate: The difference between births and deaths, plus the difference between immigrants and emigrants, per 1,000 population. (236)

Hawthorne effect: The unintended influence of observers or experiments on subjects of research. (26)

Health: As defined by the World Health Organization, a state of complete physical, mental, and social well-being, and not merely the absence of disease and infirmity. (244)

Hidden curriculum: Standards of behavior that are deemed proper by society and are taught subtly in schools. (209)

Homophobia: Fear of and prejudice against homosexuality. (167)

Horizontal mobility: The movement of an individual from one social position to another of the same rank. (130)

Horticultural society: A preindustrial society in which people plant seeds and crops rather than merely subsist on available foods. (75)

Human ecology: An area of study concerned with the interrelationships between people and their spatial setting and physical environment. (241, 257)

Human relations approach: An approach to the study of formal organizations that emphasizes the role of people, communication, and participation within a bureaucracy and tends to focus on informal groups. (82)

Hunting-and-gathering society: A preindustrial society in which people rely on whatever foods and fibers are readily available in order to survive. (75)

Hypothesis: A speculative statement about the relationship between two or more variables. (20)

Ideal type: A construct or model that serves as a measuring rod against which actual cases can be evaluated. (10, 79)

Impression management: A term used by Erving Goffman to refer to the altering of the presentation of the self in order to create distinctive appearances and satisfy particular audiences. (54)

Incidence: The number of new cases of a specific disorder occurring within a given population during a stated period, usually a year. (250)

Income: Salaries and wages. (111)

Independent variable: The variable in a causal relationship that when altered, causes or influences a change in a second variable. (20)

Industrial city: A city characterized by relatively large size, open competition, an open class system, and elaborate specialization in the manufacturing of goods. (239)

Industrial society: A society that depends on mechanization to produce its goods and services. (76)

Infant mortality rate: The number of deaths of infants under one year of age per 1,000 live births in a given year. (236)

Influence: The exercise of power through a process of persuasion. (216)

Informal norm: A norm that generally is understood but is not precisely recorded. (40)

Informal social control: Control that people use casually to enforce norms. (90)

In-group: Any group or category to which people feel they belong. (71)

Innovation: The process of introducing a new idea or object to a culture through discovery or invention. (36)

Institutional discrimination: The denial of opportunities and equal rights to individuals and groups that results from the normal operations of a society. (157)

Instrumentality: An emphasis on tasks, a focus on more distant goals, and a concern for the external relationship between one's family and other social institutions. (170)

Interactionist perspective: A sociological approach that generalizes about everyday forms of social interaction. (16)

Intergenerational mobility: Changes in the social position of children relative to their parents. (130)

Interview: A face-to-face or telephone questioning of a respondent to obtain desired information. (24)

Intragenerational mobility: Changes in a person's social position within his or her adult life. (130)

Invention: The combination of existing cultural items into a form that did not exist before. (36)

Kinship: The state of being related to others. (191)

Labeling theory: Theory that attempts to explain why certain people are viewed as deviants. (99)

Laissez-faire: A form of capitalism in which businesses compete freely, with minimal government intervention in the economy. (223)

Language: An abstract system of word meanings and symbols for all aspects of culture; includes gestures and other nonverbal communication. (38)

Latent function: Unconscious or unintended function; hidden purpose. (14)

Law: Governmental social control. (40, 91)

Legal-rational authority: Max Weber's term for power made legitimate by law. (217)

Life chances: Max Weber's term for people's opportunities to provide themselves with material goods, positive living conditions, and favorable life experiences. (128)

Life-course approach: A research orientation in which sociologists and other social scientists look closely at the social factors that influence people throughout their lives, from birth to death. (55)

Life expectancy: The median number of years a person can be expected to live under current mortality conditions. (236)

Looking-glass self: A concept used by Charles Horton Cooley that emphasizes the self as the product of our social interactions with others. (51)

Luddites: Rebellious craft workers in nineteenth-century England who destroyed new factory machinery as part of their resistance to the industrial revolution. (276)

Manifest function: Open, stated, and conscious function. (14)

Master status: A status that dominates others and thereby determines a person's general position within society. (68)

Material culture: The physical or technological aspects of our daily lives. (38)

Matriarchy: A society in which women dominate in family decision making. (192)

Matrilineal descent: A kinship system that favors the relatives of the mother. (192)

McDonaldization: The process through which the principles of the fast-food restaurant have come to dominate certain sectors of society, both in the United States and throughout the world. (37)

Minimal hierarchy: A relatively flat organizational structure designed to increase workers' access to those in authority. (83)

Minority group: A subordinate group whose members have significantly less control or power over their own lives than the members of a dominant or majority group have over theirs. (146)

Modernization: The far-reaching process through which developing nations move from traditional or less developed institutions to those characteristic of more developed societies. (138)

Modernization theory: A functionalist approach that proposes that modernization and development will gradually improve the lives of people in developing nations. (138)

Monogamy: A form of marriage in which one woman and one man are married only to each other. (190)

Monopoly: Control of a market by a single business firm. (223)

Morbidity rate: The incidence of disease in a given population. (250)

Mores: Norms deemed highly necessary to the welfare of a society. (40)

Mortality rate: The incidence of death in a given population. (250)

Multilinear evolutionary theory: A theory of social change that holds that change can occur in several ways, and does not inevitably lead in the same direction. (271)

Multinational corporation: Commercial organization that is headquartered in one country but does business throughout the world. (136)

Multiple-nuclei theory: A theory of urban growth developed by Harris and Ullman that views growth as emerging from many centers of development, each of which reflects a particular urban need or activity. (242)

Natural science: The study of the physical features of nature and the ways in which they interact and change. (4)

Neocolonialism: Continuing dependence of former colonies on foreign countries. (134)

New social movement: Organized collective activities that address values and social identities, as well as improvements in the quality of life. (269)

New urban sociology: An approach to urbanization that considers the interplay of local, national, and worldwide forces and their effect on local space, with special emphasis on the impact of global economic activity. (243)

Nonmaterial culture: Customs, beliefs, philosophies, governments, and patterns of communication, as well as ways of using material objects. (38)

Nonverbal communication: The sending of messages through the use of posture, facial expressions, and gestures. (17)

Norm: An established standard of behavior maintained by a society. (39)

Nuclear family: A married couple and their unmarried children living together. (189)

Obedience: Compliance with higher authorities in a hierarchical structure. (89)

Objective method: A technique for measuring social class that assigns individuals to classes on the basis of criteria such as occupation, education, income, and place of residence. (121)

Observation: A research technique in which an investigator collects information through direct participation in and/or closely watching a group or community under study. (25)

Open system: A social system in which the position of each individual is influenced by his or her achieved status. (130)

Operational definition: An explanation of an abstract concept that is specific enough to allow a researcher to assess the concept. (19)

Organized crime: The work of a group that regulates relations between various criminal enterprises involved in various illegal activities. (103)

Out-group: A group or category to which people feel they do not belong. (71)

Patriarchy: A society in which men dominate in family decision making. (192)

Patrilineal descent: A kinship system that favors the father's relatives. (192)

Personality: The individual characteristics, attitudes, needs, and behaviors that set one person apart from another. (34)

Peter principle: A principle of organizational life originated by Laurence J. Peter, according to which every employee within a hierarchy tends to rise to his or her level of incompetence. (81)

Pluralist model: A view of society in which many competing groups within the community have access to government officials, so that no single group is dominant. (221)

Politics: In Harold D. Lasswell's words, "who gets what, when, and how." (216)

Polyandry: A form of polygamy in which a woman can have several husbands at the same time. (191)

Polygamy: A form of marriage in which an individual may have several husbands or wives simultaneously. (191)

Polygyny: A form of polygamy in which a husband may have several wives at the same time. (191)

Postindustrial city: A city in which global finance and the electronic flow of information dominate the economy. (240)

Postindustrial society: A society whose economic system is engaged primarily in the processing and control of information. (76)

Postmodern society: A technologically sophisticated society that is preoccupied with consumer goods and media images. (77)

Power: The ability to exercise one's will over others. (117, 216)

Power elite: A term used by C. Wright Mills for a small group of military, industrial, and government leaders who control the fate of the United States. (219)

Preindustrial city: A city with only a few thousand residents that is characterized by a relatively closed class system and limited social mobility. (237)

Prejudice: A negative attitude toward an entire category of people, often an ethnic or racial minority. (156)

Prestige: The respect and admiration that an occupation holds in a society. (121)

Prevalence: The total number of cases of a specific disorder that exist at a given time. (250)

Primary group: A small group characterized by intimate, face-to-face association and cooperation. (70)

Professional criminal: A person who pursues crime as a day-to-day occupation. (102)

Proletariat: Karl Marx's term for the working class in a capitalist society. (115)

Protestant ethic: Max Weber's term for the disciplined work ethic, this-worldly concerns, and rational orientation to life emphasized by John Calvin and his followers. (199)

Qualitative research: Research that relies on what scientists see in the field or naturalistic settings more than on statistical data. (25)

Quantitative research: Research that collects and reports data primarily in numerical form. (25)

Questionnaire: A printed research form used to obtain desired information from a respondent. (24)

Racial group: A group that is set apart from others because of obvious physical differences. (145)

Racial profiling: Any arbitrary action initiated by an authority based on race, ethnicity, or national origin rather than on a person's behavior. (154)

Racism: The belief that one race is supreme and all others are innately inferior. (156)

Random sample: A sample for which every member of the entire population has the same chance of being selected. (21)

Reference group: Any group that individuals use as a standard in evaluating themselves and their own behavior. (71)

Relative deprivation: The conscious feeling of a negative discrepancy between legitimate expectations and present actualities. (266)

Relative poverty: A floating standard of deprivation by which people at the bottom of a society, whatever their lifestyles, are judged to be disadvantaged in comparison with the nation as a whole. (126)

Reliability: The extent to which a measure produces consistent results. (22)

Religion: According to Émile Durkheim, a unified system of beliefs and practices relative to sacred things. (196)

Religious belief: A statement to which members of a particular religion adhere. (201)

Religious experience: The feeling or perception of being in direct contact with the ultimate reality, such as a divine being, or of being overcome with religious emotion. (202)

Religious ritual: A practice required or expected of members of a faith. (201)

Research design: A detailed plan or method for obtaining data scientifically. (24)

Resocialization: The process of discarding former behavior patterns and accepting new ones as part of a transition in one's life. (55)

Resource mobilization: The ways in which a social movement utilizes such resources as money, political influence, access to the media, and personnel. (266)

Rite of passage: A ritual marking the symbolic transition from one social position to another. (54)

Role conflict: The situation that occurs when incompatible expectations arise from two or more social positions held by the same person. (69)

Role strain: The situation that occurs when the same social position imposes conflicting demands and expectations. (69)

Role taking: The process of mentally assuming the perspective of another in order to respond from that imagined viewpoint. (52)

Routine activities theory: The theory that criminal victimization increases when motivated offenders and suitable targets converge. (98)

Sample: A selection from a larger population that is statistically representative of that population. (21)

Sanction: Penalty or reward for conduct concerning a social norm. (41, 88)

Science: The body of knowledge obtained by methods based on systematic observation. (4)

Scientific management approach: Another name for the *classical theory* of formal organizations. (82)

Scientific method: A systematic, organized series of steps that ensures maximum objectivity and consistency in researching a problem. (18)

Secondary analysis: A variety of research techniques that make use of previously collected and publicly accessible information and data. (27)

Secondary group: A formal, impersonal group in which there is little social intimacy or mutual understanding. (71)

Second shift: The double burden—work outside the home followed by child care and housework—that many women face and few men share equitably. (179)

Self: According to George Herbert Mead, a distinct identity that sets one apart from others. (51)

Serial monogamy: A form of marriage in which a person may have several spouses in his or her life, but only one spouse at a time. (190)

Sexism: The ideology that one sex is superior to the other. (174)

Sexual harassment: Behavior that occurs when work benefits are made contingent on sexual favors. (174)

Sick role: Societal expectations about the attitudes and behavior of a person viewed as being ill. (245)

Significant other: A term used by George Herbert Mead to refer to those individuals who are most important in the development of the self, such as parents, friends, and teachers. (53)

Slavery: A system of enforced servitude in which some people are legally owned by other people. (112)

Social change: Significant alteration over time in behavior patterns and culture. (264)

Social control: Techniques and strategies for preventing deviant behavior in any society. (88)

Social epidemiology: The study of the distribution of disease, impairment, and general health status across a population. (250)

Social inequality: A condition in which members of a society have different amounts of wealth, prestige, or power. (111)

Social institution: An organized pattern of beliefs and behavior centered on basic social needs. (72)

Social interaction: The ways in which people respond to one another. (64–65)

Socialism: An economic system in which the means of production and distribution are collectively rather than privately owned. (224)

Socialization: The process through which people learn the attitudes, values, and actions appropriate for members of a particular culture. (34)

Social mobility: The movement of individuals or groups from one position of a society's stratification system to another. (129)

Social movement: Organized collective activities to bring about or resist fundamental change in an existing group or society. (265)

Social network: A series of social relationships that links a person directly to others, and through them indirectly to still more people. (72)

Social role: A set of expectations for people who occupy a given social position or status. (68)

Social science: The study of various aspects of human society. (4)

Social structure: The way in which a society is organized into predictable relationships. (65)

Societal-reaction approach: Another name for *labeling theory*. (99)

Society: A fairly large number of people who live in the same territory, are relatively independent of people outside it, and participate in a common culture. (35)

Sociobiology: The systematic study of the biological bases of human social behavior. (50)

Sociocultural evolution: The process of change and development in human societies that results from cumulative growth in their stores of cultural information. (75)

Sociological imagination: An awareness of the relationship between an individual and the wider society. (3)

Sociology: The systematic study of social behavior and human groups. (2)

Status: A term used by sociologists to refer to any of the full range of socially defined positions within a large group or society. (66)

Status group: A term used by Max Weber to refer to people who have the same prestige or lifestyle, independent of their class positions. (116)

Stereotype: Unreliable generalization about all members of a group that does not recognize individual differences within the group. (145)

Stigma: The labels society uses to devalue members of certain social groups. (92)

Stratification: The structured ranking of entire groups of people that perpetuates unequal economic rewards and power in a society. (111)

Subculture: A segment of society that shares a distinctive pattern of mores, folkways, and values that differs from the pattern of the larger society. (44)

Survey: A study, generally in the form of an interview or questionnaire, that provides researchers with information about how people think and act. (24)

Symbol: Gesture, object, or language that forms the basis of human communication. (52)

Symbolic ethnicity: An emphasis on such concerns as ethnic food or political issues rather than on deeper ties to one's ethnic heritage. (149)

Teacher-expectancy effect: The impact that a teacher's expectations about a student's performance may have on the student's actual achievements. (211)

Technology: Cultural information about how to use the material resources of the environment to satisfy human needs and desires. (37, 75, 277)

Telecommuter: An employee who works full-time or part-time at home rather than in an outside office, and who is linked to supervisor and colleagues through computer terminals, phones, and fax machines. (83)

Theory: In sociology, a set of statements that seeks to explain problems, actions, or behavior. (7)

Total fertility rate (TFR): The average number of children born alive to any woman, assuming that she conforms to current fertility rates. (236)

Total institution: A term coined by Erving Goffman to refer to institutions that regulate all aspects of a person's life under a single authority, such as prisons, the military, mental hospitals, and convents. (55)

Tracking: The practice of placing students in specific curriculum groups on the basis of their test scores and other criteria. (210)

Traditional authority: Legitimate power conferred by custom and accepted practice. (217)

Trained incapacity: The tendency of workers in a bureaucracy to become so specialized that they develop blind spots and fail to notice obvious problems. (80)

Unilinear evolutionary theory: A theory of social change that holds that all societies pass through the same successive stages of evolution and inevitably reach the same end. (270)

Urban ecology: An area of study that focuses on the interrelationships between urban residents and their environment. (241)

Urbanism: A term used by Wirth to describe distinctive patterns of social behavior evident among city residents. (240)

Validity: The degree to which a scale or measure truly reflects the phenomenon under study. (22)

Value: Collective conception of what is considered good, desirable, and proper—or bad, undesirable, and improper—in a culture. (42)

Variable: A measurable trait or characteristic that is subject to change under different conditions. (20)

Verstehen: The German word for "understanding" or "insight"; used by Max Weber to stress the need for sociologists to take into account the subjective meanings people attach to their actions. (10)

Vertical mobility: The movement of a person from one social position to another of a different rank. (130)

Vested interests: Veblen's term for those people or groups who will suffer in the event of social change and who have a stake in maintaining the status quo. (274)

Victimization survey: Questioning ordinary people, not police officers, to determine whether they have been victims of crime. (106)

Victimless crime: The willing exchange among adults of widely desired, but illegal, goods and services. (105)

Vital statistics: Records of births, deaths, marriages, and divorces gathered through a registration system maintained by governmental units. (235)

Wealth: An inclusive term encompassing all a person's material assets, including land, stocks, and other types of property. (111)

White-collar crime: Illegal acts committed in the course of business activities. (103)

Work team: A team of employees assigned to address specific tasks or issues in the workplace. (83)

World-systems analysis: Immanuel Wallerstein's view of the global economic system as divided between certain industrialized nations that control wealth and developing countries that are controlled and exploited. (134, 243)

References

Abercrombie, Nicholas, Bryan S. Turner, and Stephen Hill, eds. 1990. *Dominant Ideologies.* Cambridge, MA: Unwin Hyman.

Abercrombie, Nicholas, Stephen Hill, and Bryan S. Turner. 1980. *The Dominant Ideology Thesis.* London: George Allen and Unwin.

Aberle, David E., A. K. Cohen, A. K. Davis, M. J. Leng, Jr., and F. N. Sutton. 1950. "The Functional Prerequisites of a Society." *Ethics* 60 (January):100–111.

Adam, Barry D. 1995. *The Rise of a Gay and Lesbian Movement.* Rev. ed. New York: Twayne.

Addams, Jane. 1910. *Twenty Years at Hull-House.* New York: Macmillan.

———. 1930. *The Second Twenty Years at Hull-House.* New York: Macmillan.

Adler, Patricia A., Peter Adler, and John M. Johnson. 1992. "Street Corner Society Revisited." *Journal of Contemporary Ethnography* 21 (April):3–10.

Alain, Michel. 1985. "An Empirical Validation of Relative Deprivation." *Human Relations* 38(8):739–749.

Alba, Richard. 1990. *Ethnic Identity: The Transformation of White America.* New Haven: Yale University Press.

Alfino, Mark, John S. Caputo, and Robin Wynyard. 1998. *McDonaldization Revisited: Critical Essays on Consumer Culture.* Westport, CT: Praeger.

Allen, Bern P. 1978. *Social Behavior: Fact and Falsehood.* Chicago: Nelson-Hall.

Allport, Gordon W. 1979. *The Nature of Prejudice.* 25th anniversary ed. Reading, MA: Addison-Wesley.

Alzheimer's Association. 1999. "Statistics/Prevalence." Accessed January 10, 2000 (http://www.alz.org/facts/stats.htm).

American Sociological Association. 1997. *Code of Ethics.* Washington, DC: American Sociological Association. Available (www.asanet.org/members/ecoderev.html).

Andersen, Margaret. 2003. *Thinking about Women: Sociological Perspectives on Sex and Gender.* 6th ed. Boston: Allyn and Bacon.

Anderson, Sarah, John Cavanagh, Chris Hartman, and Scott Klinger. 2003. *Executive Excess 2003: CEOs Win, Workers and Tax Payers Lose.* Boston: United for a Fair Economy.

Andrews, Edmund L. 2001. "Frustrated Europeans Set to Battle U.S. on Climate." *New York Times,* July 16, p. A3.

Appelbaum, Richard, and Peter Dreier. 1999. "The Campus Anti-Sweatshops Movement." *The American Prospect* (September/October), pp. 71–78.

Apple. 2004. *iPod The Best Just Got Better.* Accessed October 4, 2004 (www.apple.com/ipod).

Armer, J. Michael, and John Katsillis. 1992. "Modernization Theory." Pp. 1299–1304 in *Encyclopedia of Sociology,* vol. 4, edited by Edgar F. Borgatta and Marie L. Borgatta. New York: Macmillan.

Associated Press. 1998. "Environmental Test Case Averted." *Christian Science Monitor,* September 21, p. 18.

Astin, Alexander, Sarah A. Parrott, William S. Korn, and Linda J. Sax. 1994. *The American Freshman: Thirty Year Trends.* Los Angeles: Higher Education Research Institute.

Azumi, Koya, and Jerald Hage. 1972. *Organizational Systems.* Lexington, MA: Heath.

Babad, Elisha Y., and P. J. Taylor. 1992. "Transparency of Teacher Expectancies Across Language, Cultural Boundaries." *Journal of Educational Research* 86:120–125.

Bachu, Amara, and Martin O'Connell. 2001. "Fertility of American Women: June 2000." *Current Population Reports,* ser. P-20, no. 543. Washington, DC: U.S. Government Printing Office.

Bates, Colleen Dunn. 1999. "Medicine's Gender Gap." *Shape,* October.

Bauerlein, Monika. 1996. "The Luddites Are Back." *Utne Reader* (March/April):24, 26.

BBC. 2004. *Has TV changed Bhutan?* Accessed July 21, 2004 (www.buddhistnews.tv/current/bhutan-180604.php).

Beagan, Brenda L. 2001. "'Even If I Don't Know What I'm Doing I Can Make It Look Like I Know What I'm Doing': Becoming a Doctor in the 1990s." *Canadian Review of Sociology and Anthropology* 38:275–292.

Beck, Allen J., et al. 2000. *Correctional Populations in the United States, 1997.* Washington, DC: Bureau of Justice Statistics.

Becker, Howard. 1963. *The Outsiders: Studies in the Sociology of Deviance.* New York: Free Press.

———, ed. 1964. *The Other Side: Perspectives on Deviance.* New York: Free Press.

———. 1973. *The Outsiders: Studies in the Sociology of Deviance.* Rev. ed. New York: Free Press.

Beeghley, Leonard. 1978. *Social Stratification in America: A Critical Analysis of Theory and Research.* Santa Monica, CA: Goodyear.

Bell, Daniel. 1999. *The Coming of Post-Industrial Society: A Venture in Social Forecasting.* With new foreword. New York: Basic Books.

Bell, Wendell. 1981. "Modernization." Pp. 186–187 in *Encyclopedia of Sociology.* Guilford, CT: DPG Publishing.

Belsie, Laurent. 1998. "Genetic Research Data Will Double Annually." *Christian Science Monitor,* July 30, p. B4.

Benford, Robert D. 1992. "Social Movements." Pp. 1880–1887 in *Encyclopedia of Sociology,* vol. 4, edited by Edgar F. Borgatta and Marie Borgatta. New York: Macmillan.

Berger, Peter, and Thomas Luckmann. 1966. *The Social Construction of Reality.* New York: Doubleday.

Bharadwaj, Lakshmik. 1992. "Human Ecology." Pp. 848–867 in *Encyclopedia of Sociology,* vol. 2, edited by Edgar E. Borgatta and Marie L. Borgatta. New York: Macmillan.

Bielby, William T., and Denise D. Bielby. 1992. "I Will Follow Him: Family Ties, Gender-Role Beliefs, and Reluctance to Relocate for a Better Job." *American Journal of Sociology* 97 (March):1241–1267.

Black, Donald. 1995. "The Epistemology of Pure Sociology." *Law and Social Inquiry* 20 (Summer):829–870.

Blau, Peter M., and Otis Dudley Duncan. 1967. *The American Occupational Structure.* New York: Wiley.

Blauner, Robert. 1972. *Racial Oppression in America.* New York: Harper and Row.

Blumer, Herbert. 1955. "Collective Behavior." Pp. 165–198 in *Principles of Sociology,* 2d ed., edited by Alfred McClung Lee. New York: Barnes and Noble.

Bond, James T., Ellen Galinsky, and Jennifer E. Swanberg. 1998. *The 1997 National Study of Changing Work Force.* New York. Families and Work Institute.

Borman, Kathryn M., and Joel H. Spring. 1984. *Schools in Central Cities: Structure and Process.* New York: Longman.

Bornschier, Volker, Christopher Chase-Dunn, and Richard Rubinson. 1978. "Cross-National Evidence of the Effects of Foreign Investment and Aid on Economic Growth and Inequality: A Survey of Findings and a Reanalysis." *American Journal of Sociology* 84 (November):651–683.

Bottomore, Tom, and Maximilien Rubel, ed. 1956. *Karl Marx: Selected Writings in Sociology and Social Philosophy.* New York: McGraw-Hill.

Bowles, Samuel, and Herbert Gintis. 1976. *Schooling in Capitalistic America: Educational Reforms and the Contradictions of Economic Life.* New York: Basic Books.

Brady, David. 2003. "Rethinking the Sociological Measurement of Poverty." *Social Forces* 81 (March): 715–752.

Brainard, Jeffrey. 2003. "Cloning Debate Moves to the States." *Chronicle of Higher Education* 49 (March 28): A22–A23.

Brainard, Lael and Robert E. Litam. 2004. "'Offshoring' Service Jobs: Bane or Boom—and What to Do?" *Brookings Institute* Policy Brief (April), pp. 1–8.

Brannigan, Augustine. 1992. "Postmodernism." Pp. 1522–1525 in *Encyclopedia of Sociology,* vol. 3, edited by Edgar F. Borgatta and Marie L. Borgatta. New York: Macmillan.

Brannon, Robert. 1976. "Ideology, Myth, and Reality: Sex Equality in Israel." *Sex Roles* 6:403–419.

Bray, James H., and John Kelly. 1999. *Step-families: Love, Marriage, and Parenting in the First Decade.* New York: Broadway Books.

Brettell, Caroline B. and Carolyn F. Sargent. 2005. *Gender in Cross-Cultural Perspective,* 4th ed. Upper Saddle River, NJ: Prentice Hall.

Brimmer, Andrew F. 1995. "The Economic Cost of Discrimination against Black Americans." Pp. 9–29 in *Economic Perspectives in Affirmative Action,* edited by Margaret C. Simms. Washington, DC: Joint Center for Political and Economic Studies.

Brittingham, Angela, and G. Patricia de la Cruz. 2004. *Ancestry: 2000.* Census Brief C2KBR–35. Washington, DC: U.S. Government Printing Office.

Brown, David K. 2001. "The Social Sources of Educational Credentialism: Status Cultures, Labor Markets, and Organizations." *Sociology of Education* 74 (Extra Issue): 19–34.

Browne, Irene. 2001. *Latinas and African Women at Work: Race, Gender and Economic Inequality.* New York: Russell Sage Foundation.

Budrys, Grace. 2003. *Unequal Health: How Inequality Contributes to Health and Illness.* Lanham, MD: Rowman and Littlefield.

Bulle, Wolfgang F. 1987. "Crossing Cultures?" *Southeast Asian Mainland.* Atlanta: Centers for Disease Control.

Bunzel, John H. 1992. *Race Relations on Campus: Stanford Students Speak.* Stanford, CA: Portable Stanford.

Bureau of the Census. 1975. *Historical Statistics of the United States, Colonial Times to 1970.* Washington, DC: U.S. Government Printing Office.

———. 1991. "Half of the Nation's Population Lives in Large Metropolitan Areas." Press release, February 21.

———. 2000a. *Statistical Abstract of the United States, 2000.* Washington, DC: U.S. Government Printing Office.

———. 2000b. "National Population Projections." Internet release of January 13. Accessed May 11 (www.census.gov/population/www/projection/natsum-T3html).

———. 2001a. *Statistical Abstract of the United States, 2001.* Washington, DC: U.S. Government Printing Office.

———. 2001b. *1997 Revenues for Women-Owned Businesses Show Continued Growth.* News release of April 4. Washington, DC: U.S. Government Printing Office.

———. 2002. *Statistical Abstract of the United States, 2002.* Washington, DC: U.S. Government Printing Office.

Bureau of Labor Statistics. 2002. "Number of Jobs Held, Labor Market Activity, and Earnings Growth Among Young Baby Boomers." News Release of August 27 (http://www.bls.gov/nls).

———. 2004b. "Current Labor Statistics." Accessed January 28, 2004 (http://www.bls.gov/opub/mlr/mlrhome.htm).

Bureau of Primary Health Care. 2004a. Home page. Accessed January 18 (www.bphc.hrsa.gov/bphcfactsheet.htm).

——— 2004. *Quality and Culture.* Accessed October 4 (http://bphc.hrsa.gov/quality/cultural.htm).

Burgess, Ernest W. 1925. "The Growth of the City." Pp. 47–62 in *The City,* edited by Robert E. Park, Ernest W. Burgess, and Roderick D. McKenzie. Chicago: University of Chicago Press.

Burns, John R. 1998. "Once Widowed in India, Twice Scorned." *New York Times,* March 29, p. A1.

Butler, Daniel Allen. 1998. *"Unsinkable": The Full Story.* Mechanicsburg, PA: Stackpole Books.

Caesar, Lena G. and David R. Williams. 2002. *The ASHA Leader Online: Socioculture and the Delivery of Health Care: Who Gets What and Why.* Accessed December 1, 2002 (www.asha.org).

Caplan, Ronald L. 1989. "The Commodification of American Health Care." *Social Science and Medicine* 28 (11):1139–1148.

Carpenter, Susan. 2000. "Full of Fight." *Los Angeles Times,* November 29, pp. E1, E3.

Carty, Win. 1999. "Greater Dependence on Cars Leads to More Pollution in World's Cities." *Population Today* 27 (December):1–2.

Castells, Manuel. 2001. *The Internet Galaxy: Reflections on the Internet, Business, and Society.* New York: Oxford University Press.

Catalano, Shannan. 2004. *Criminal Victimization 2003.* Washington, DC: U.S. Government Printing Office.

CBS News. 1998. "Experimental Prison." *Sixty Minutes.* June 30.

Center for American Women and Politics. 2003. *Women in the U.S. Congress 2003. Statewide Elective Executive Women 2003.* New Brunswick, NJ: CAWP.

Centers for Disease Control and Prevention. 2003. "A Glance at the HIV Epidemic." Accessed February 23, 2003 (www.cdc.gov).

Cetron, Marvin J., and Owen Davies. 1991. "Trends Shaping the World." *Futurist* 20 (September–October):11–21.

Cha, Ariena Eunjung. 2000. "Painting a Portrait of Dot-Camaraderie." *The Washington Post,* October 26, pp. E1, E10.

Chambliss, Wilham. 1973. "The Saints and the Roughnecks." *Society* 11 (November/December):24–31.

Chase-Dunn, Christopher, and Peter Grimes. 1995. "World-Systems Analysis." Pp. 387–417 in *Annual Review of Sociology,* 1995, edited by John Hagan. Palo Alto, CA: Annual Reviews.

Chase-Dunn, Christopher, Yukio Kawano, and Benjamin D. Brewer. 2000. "Trade Globalization Since 1795: Waves of Integration in the World System." *American Sociological Review* 65 (February):77–95.

China Daily. 2004. *Starbucks Takes Aim at China Chain.* Accessed July 21, 2004 (www2.chinadaily.com.cn).

Clark, Burton, and Martin Trow. 1966. "The Organizational Context." Pp. 17–70 in *The Study of College Peer Groups,* edited by Theodore M. Newcomb and Everett K. Wilson. Chicago: Aldine.

Clark, Candace. 1983. "Sickness and Social Control." Pp. 346–365 in *Social Interaction: Readings in Sociology,* 2d ed., edited by Howard Robboy and Candace Clark. New York: St. Martin's.

Clarke, Adele E., Janet K. Shim, Laura Maro, Jennifer Ruth, Fusket, and Jennifer R. Fishman. 2003. "Bio Medicalization: Technoscientific Transformations of Health, Illness, and U.S. Biomedicine." *American Sociological Review* 68 (April): 161–194.

Clinard, Marshall B., and Robert F. Miller. 1998. *Sociology of Deviant Behavior.* 10th ed. Fort Worth: Harcourt Brace.

Cockerham, William C. 2001. *Medical Sociology.* 8th ed. Upper Saddle River, NJ: Prentice Hall.

Cohen, Lawrence E., and Marcus Felson. 1979. "Social Change and Crime Rate Trends: A Routine Activities Approach." *American Sociological Review* 44:588–608.

Cole, Mike. 1988. *Bowles and Ginitis Revisited: Correspondence and Contradiction in Educational Theory.* Philadelphia: Falmer.

Collins, Randall. 1975. *Conflict Sociology: Toward an Explanatory Sociology.* New York: Academic.

———. 1980. "Weber's Last Theory of Capitalism: A Systematization." *American Sociological Review* 45 (December):925–942.

———. 1986. *Weberian Sociological Theory.* New York: Cambridge University Press.

———. 1995. "Prediction in Macrosociology: The Case of the Soviet Collapse." *American Journal of Sociology* 100 (May):1552–1593.

Commission on Civil Rights. 1976. *A Guide to Federal Laws and Regulations Prohibiting Sex Discrimination.* Washington, DC: U.S. Government Printing Office.

————. 1981. *Affirmative Action in the 1980s: Dismantling the Process of Discrimination.* Washington, DC: U.S. Government Printing Office.

Commoner, Barry. 1971. *The Closing Circle.* New York: Knopf.

————. 1990. *Making Peace with the Planet.* New York: Pantheon.

Conrad, Peter, ed. 2000. *The Sociology of Health and Illness: Cultural Perspectives.* 6th ed. New York: Worth.

————, and Joseph W. Schneider. 1992. *Deviance and Medicalization: From Badness to Sickness.* Expanded ed. Philadelphia: Temple University Press.

Cooley, Charles. H. 1902. *Human Nature and the Social Order.* New York: Scribner.

Cooper, Richard T. 1998. "Jobs Outside High School Can Be Costly, Report Finds." *Los Angeles Times,* November 6, p. A1.

Correll, Joshua et al. 2002. "The Police Officer's Dilemma: Using Ethnicity to Disambiguate Potentially Threatening Individuals." *Journal of Personal and Social Psychology* 83 (6):1314–1329.

Coser, Lewis. 1977. *Masters of Sociological Thought: Ideas in Historical and Social Context.* 2d ed. New York: Harcourt, Brace and Jovanovich.

Couch, Carl. 1996. *Information Technologies and Social Orders.* Edited with an introduction by David R. Maines and Shing-Ling Chien. New York: Aldine de Gruyter.

Council on Scientific Affairs. 1999. "Hispanic Health in the United States." *Journal of the American Medical Association* 265 (January 9):248–252.

Cox, Oliver C. 1948. *Caste Class and Race: A Study in Social Dynamics.* Detroit: Wayne State University Press.

Cressey, Donald R. 1960. "Epidemiology and Individual Contact: A Case from Criminology." *Pacific Sociological Review* 3 (Fall):47–58.

Cromwell, Paul F., James N. Olson, and D'Aunn Wester Avarey. 1995. *Breaking and Entering: An Ethnographic Analysis of Burglary.* Newbury Park, CA: Sage.

Crouse, Kelly. 1999. "Sociology of the Titanic." *Teaching Sociology Listserv.* May 24.

Cuff, E. C., W. W. Sharrock, and D. W. Francis, eds. 1990. *Perspectives in Sociology.* 3d ed. Boston: Unwin Hyman.

Cullen, Francis T., Jr., and John B. Cullen. 1978. *Toward a Paradigm of Labeling Theory,* Ser. 58. Lincoln: University of Nebraska Studies.

Currie, Elliot. 1985. *Confronting Crime: An American Challenge.* New York: Pantheon.

————. 1998. *Crime and Punishment in America.* New York: Metropolitan Books.

Curry, Timothy Jon. 1993. "A Little Pain Never Hurt Anyone: Athletic Career Socialization and the Normalization of Sports Injury." *Symbolic Interaction* 26 (Fall):273–290.

Cushman, John H., Jr. 1998. "Pollution Policy Is Unfair Burden, States Tell E.P.A." *New York Times,* May 10, pp. 1, 20.

Cussins, Choris M. 1998. In *Cyborg Babies: From Techno-Sex to Techno-Tots,* edited by Robbie Davis-Floyd and Joseph Dumit. New York: Routledge.

Dahl, Robert A. 1961. *Who Governs?* New Haven, CT: Yale University Press.

Dahrendorf, Ralf. 1959. *Class and Class Conflict in Industrial Sociology.* Stanford, CA: Stanford University Press.

Daugherty, Kevin, and Floyd M. Hammack. 1992. "Education Organizations." Pp. 525, 541 in *Encyclopedia of Sociology,* vol. 2, edited by Edgar F. Borgatta and Marie L. Borgatta. New York: Macmillan.

Davis, James. 1982. "Up and Down Opportunity's Ladder." *Public Opinion* 5 (June/July):11–15, 48–51.

Davis, James A., Tom W. Smith, and Peter V. Marsden. 2003. *General Social Surveys, 1972–2002: Cumulative Codebook.* Chicago: NORC.

Davis, Kingsley. 1937. "The Sociology of Prostitution." *American Sociological Review* 2 (October):744–755.

———. 1940. "Extreme Social Isolation of a Child." *American Journal of Sociology* 45 (January):554–565.

———. 1947. "A Final Note on a Case of Extreme Isolation." *American Journal of Sociology* 52 (March):432–437.

———. [1949] 1995. *Human Society.* Reprint. New York: Macmillan.

———, and Wilbert E. Moore. 1945. "Some Principles of Stratification." *American Sociological Review* 10 (April):242–249.

Davis, Nanette J. 1975. *Sociological Constructions of Deviance: Perspectives and Issues in the Field.* Dubuque, IA: Wm. C. Brown.

De Andra, Roberto M. 1996. *Chicanas and Chicanos in Contemporary Society.* Boston: Allyn and Bacon.

Death Penalty Information Center. 2004a. "Cases of Innocence 1973-Present." Accessed May 31 (www.deathpenaltyinfo.org/article.php?scid=6&did=109).

Deegan, Mary Jo, ed. 1991. *Women in Sociology: A Bio-Biographical Sourcebook.* Westport, CT: Greenwood.

DeNavas-Walt, Carmen, Bernadette D. Procter, and Robert J. Mills. 2004. "Income, Poverty, and Health Insurance in the United States: 2003. Current Population Reports." Ser. P60 No. 226. Washington, DC: U.S. Government Printing Office.

DePalma, Anthony. 1999. "Rules to Protect a Culture Make for Confusion." *New York Times,* July 14, pp. B1, B2.

———. 2002. "White-Collar Layoffs, Downsized Dreams." *New York Times,* December 5, pp. A1, A38.

Department of Justice. 2002a. *Crime in the United States 2002.* Washington, DC: U.S. Government Printing Office.

———. 2003. *Crime in the United States 2003. Uniform Crime Reports.* Washington, DC: U.S. Government Printing Office.

Department of Labor. 1995a. *Good for Business: Making Full Use of the Nation's Capital.* Washington, DC: U.S. Government Printing Office.

———. 1995b. *A Solid Investment: Making Full Use of the Nation's Human Capital.* Washington, DC: U.S. Government Printing Office.

———. 1998. "Work and Elder Care: Facts for Caregivers and Their Employers." Accessed November 20 (www.dol.gov/dol/wb/public/wbpubs/elderc.htm).

DiMaggio, Paul, Eszter Hargittai, W. Russell Neuman, and John P. Robinson. 2001. "Social Implications of the Internet." Pp. 307–336 in *Annual Review of Sociology, 2001,* edited by Karen S. Cook and John Hogan. Palo Alto, CA: Annual Reviews.

Domhoff, G. William. 1978. *Who Really Rules? New Haven and Community Power Reexamined.* New Brunswick, NJ: Transaction.

———. 2001. *Who Rules America?* 4th ed. New York: McGraw-Hill.

Downie, Andrew. 2000. "Brazilian Girls Turn to a Doll More Like Them." *Christian Science Monitor,* January 20. Accessed January 20 (www.csmonitor.com/durable/2000/01/20/fpls3-csm.shtml).

Doyle, James A. 1995. *The Male Experience.* 3d ed. Dubuque, IA: Brown & Benchmark.

Drezner, Daniel W. 2004. "The Outsourcing Bogeyman." *Foreign Affairs 03* (May/June), pp. 22–34.

Duneier, Mitchell. 1994a. "On the Job, but behind the Scenes." *Chicago Tribune,* December 26, pp. 1, 24.

———. 1994b. "Battling for Control." *Chicago Tribune,* December 28, pp. 1, 8.

Dunlap, Riley E. 1993. "From Environmental to Ecological Problems." Pp. 707–738 in *Introduction to Social Problems,* edited by Craig Calhoun and George Ritzer. New York: McGraw-Hill.

———, and William R. Catton, Jr. 1983. "What Environmental Sociologists Have in Common." *Sociological Inquiry* 53 (Spring):113–135.

Durkheim, Émile. [1912] 2001. *The Elementary Forms of Religious Life.* A new translation by Carol Cosman. New York: Oxford University Press.

———. [1893] 1933. *Division of Labor in Society.* Translated by George Simpson. Reprint, New York: Free Press.

———. [1897] 1951. *Suicide.* Translated by John A. Spaulding and George Simpson. Reprint, New York: Free Press.

———. [1895] 1964. *The Rules of Sociological Method.* Translated by Sarah A. Solovay and John H. Mueller. Reprint, New York: Free Press.

The Economist. 2004. "Veil of Tears." January 15.

Education Week. 2000. "Who Should Teach? The States Decide." *Education Week Online* 19 (18):89. Available (www.edweek.org).

Efron, Sonni. 1997. "In Japan, Even Tots Must Make the Grade." *Los Angeles Times,* February 16, pp. A1, A17.

Ehrlich, Paul R. 1968. *The Population Bomb.* New York: Ballantine.

———, and Anne H. Ehrlich. 1990. *The Population Explosion.* New York: Simon and Schuster.

———, and Katherine Ellison. 2002. "A Looming Threat We Won't Face." *Los Angeles Times,* January 20, p. M6.

Ekman, Paul, Wallace V. Friesen, and John Bear. 1984. "The International Language of Gestures." *Psychology Today* 18 (May):64–69.

Elmer-DeWitt, Philip. 1995. "Welcome to Cyberspace." *Time* 145 (Special Issue, Spring):4–11.

Engels, Friedrich. [1884] 1959. "The Origin of the Family, Private Property and the State." Pp. 392–394, excerpted in *Marx and Engels: Basic Writings on Politics and Philosophy,* edited by Lewis Feuer. Garden City, NY: Anchor.

England, Paula. 1999. "The Impact of Feminist Thought on Sociology." *Contemporary Sociology* 28 (May):263–268.

Entine, Jon, and Martha Nichols. 1996. "Blowing the Whistle on Meaningless 'Good Intentions.'" *Chicago Tribune,* June 20, sec. 1, p. 21.

Epstein, Cynthia Fuchs. 1999. "The Major Myth of the Women's Movement." *Dissent* (Fall):83–111.

Etzioni, Amitai. 1964. *Modern Organization.* Englewood Cliffs, NJ: Prentice Hall.

Evans, Peter. 1979. *Dependent Development.* Princeton, NJ: Princeton University Press.

FAIR US. 2003. "Issue Brief." Accessed August 24. (www.fairus.org/html/newsroom/html).

Faludi, Susan. 1999. *Stiffed: The Betrayal of the American Man.* New York: William Morrow.

Farr, Grant M. 1999. *Modern Iran.* New York: McGraw-Hill.

Feagin, Joe R. 1983. *The Urban Real Estate Game: Playing Monopoly with Real Money.* Englewood Cliffs, NJ: Prentice Hall.

————. 1989. *Minority Group Issues in Higher Education: Learning from Qualitative Research.* Norman, OK: Center for Research on Minority Education, University of Oklahoma.

————, Harnán Vera, and Nikitah Imani. 1996. *The Agony of Education: Black Students at White Colleges and Universities.* New York: Routledge.

Featherman, David L., and Robert M. Hauser. 1978. *Opportunity and Change.* New York: Aeodus.

Feketekuty, Geza. 2001. "Globalization—Why All the Fuss?" P. 191 in *2001 Britannica Book of the Year.* Chicago: Encyclopedia Britannica.

Felson, Marcus. 2002. *Crime and Everyday Life.* 3d ed. Thousand Oaks, CA: Pine Forge Press.

Ferree, Myra Marx, and David A. Merrill. 2000. "Hot Movements, Cold Cognition: Thinking about Social Movements in Gendered Frames." *Contemporary Society* 29 (May):454–462.

Feuer, Lewis S., ed. 1959. *Karl Marx and Friedrich Engels: Basic Writings on Politics and Philosophy.* Garden City, NY: Doubleday.

Fiala, Robert. 1992. "Postindustrial Society." Pp. 1512–1522 in *Encyclopedia of Sociology,* vol. 3, edited by Edgar F. Borgatta and Marie L. Borgatta. New York: Macmillan.

Fields, Jason. 2003. "Children's Living Arrangements and Characteristics: March 2002." *Current Population Reports,* ser. P–20, no. 547. Washington, DC: U.S. Government Printing Office.

Finkel, Steven E., and James B. Rule. 1987. "Relative Deprivation and Related Psychological Theories of Civil Violence: A Critical Review." *Research in Social Movements* 9:47–69.

Fitzgerald, Kathleen J., and Diane M. Rodgers. 2000. "Radical Social Movement Organization: A Theoretical Model." *The Sociological Quarterly* 41 (No. 4):573–592.

Flacks, Richard. 1971. *Youth and Social Change.* Chicago: Markham.

Freidson, Eliot. 1970. *Profession of Medicine.* New York: Dodd, Mead.

Fridlund, Alan J., Paul Erkman, and Harriet Oster. 1987. "Facial Expressions of Emotion; Review of Literature 1970–1983." Pp. 143–224 in *Nonverbal Behavior and Communication,* 2d ed., edited by Aron W. Seigman and Stanley Feldstein. Hillsdale, NJ: Lawrence Erlbaum Associates.

Friedland, Jonathon. 2000. "An American in Mexico Champions Midwifery as a Worthy Profession." *Wall Street Monitor,* February 15, pp. A1, A12.

Friedrichs, David O. 1998. "New Directions in Critical Criminology and White Collar Crime." Pp. 77–91 in *Cutting the Edge,* edited by Jeffrey Ross. Westport, CT: Praeger.

Furstenberg, Frank, and Andrew Cherlin. 1991. *Divided Families: What Happens to Children When Parents Part.* Cambridge, MA: Harvard University Press.

Gamson, Joshua. 1989. "Silence, Death, and the Invisible Enemy: AIDS Activism and Social Movement 'Newness.'" *Social Problems* 36 (October):351–367.

Gans, Herbert J. 1979. *Deciding What's News: A Study of CBS Evening News, NBC Nightly News, Newsweek and Time.* New York: Parthenon.

———. 1995. *The War against the Poor: The Underclass and Antipoverty Policy.* New York: Basic Books.

Garfinkel, Harold. 1956. "Conditions of Successful Degradation Ceremonies." *American Journal of Sociology* 61 (March):420–424.

Garner, Roberta. 1996. *Contemporary Movements and Ideologies.* New York: McGraw-Hill.

———. 1999. "Virtual Social Movements." Presented at Zaldfest: A conference in honor of Mayer Zald. September 17, Ann Arbor, MI.

Garreau, Joel. 1991. *Edge City: Life on the New Frontier.* New York: Doubleday.

Gates, Henry Louis, Jr. 1999. "One Internet, Two Nations." *New York Times,* October 31, p. A15.

Gauette, Nicole. 1998. "Rules for Raising Japanese Kids." *Christian Science Monitor,* October 14, pp. B1, B6.

Gecas, Victor. 1982. "Socialization." Pp. 1863–1872 in *Encyclopedia of Sociology,* vol. 4, edited by Edgar F. Borgatta and Marie L. Borgatta. New York: Macmillan.

Gelbspan, Ross. 2002. "Beyond Kyoto Lite." *The American Prospect* (February 25):26–27.

General Accounting Office. 2002. *A New Look through the Glass Ceiling: Where Are the Women?* Washington, DC: General Accounting Office.

Gerth, H. H., and C. Wright Mills. 1958. *From Max Weber: Essays in Sociology.* New York: Galaxy.

Gezari, Vanessa. 2002. "Sex Testing Used to Call Girls." *Chicago Tribune,* November 10, p. 4.

Giordano, Peggy C., Stephen A. Cernkovich, and Alfred DeMaris. 1993. "The Family and Peer Relations of Black Adolescents." *Journal of Marriage and Family* 55 (May):277–287.

Giroux, Henry A. 1988. *Schooling and the Struggle for Public Life: Critical Pedagogy in the Modern Age.* Minneapolis: University of Minnesota Press.

Global Reach. 2004. *Global Internet Statistics (by Language).* Accessed March 31 (www.global-reach.biz/globstats/erol.html).

Goffman, Erving. 1959. *The Presentation of Self in Everyday Life.* New York: Doubleday.

———. 1961. *Asylums: Essays on the Social Situation of Mental Patients and Other Inmates.* Garden City, NY: Doubleday.

———. 1963. *Stigma: Notes on Management of Spoiled Identity.* Englewood Cliffs, NJ: Prentice Hall.

Golden, Frederic. 1999. "Who's Afraid of Frankenfood?" *Time,* November 29, pp. 49–50.

Goldman, Benjamin A., and Laura Fitton. 1994. *Toxic Wastes and Race Revisited: An Update of the 1987 Report on the Racial and Social Economic Characteristics of Communities with Hazardous Waste.* Washington, DC: Center for Policy Alternatives, United Church of Christ Commission for Racial Justice, and NAACP.

Goode, Erica. 1999. "For Good Health, It Helps to Be Rich and Important." *New York Times,* June 1, pp. 1, 9.

Gottdiener, Mark, and Joe R. Feagin. 1988. "The Paradigm Shift in Urban Sociology." *Urban Affairs Quarterly* 24 (December):163–187.

Gottdiener, Mark, and Ray Hutchison. 2000. *The New Urban Sociology.* 2d ed. New York: McGraw-Hill.

Gouldner, Alvin. 1960. "The Norm of Reciprocity." *American Sociological Review* 25 (April):161–177.

Gramsci, Antonio. 1929. *Selections from the Prison Notebooks.* Antonio Gramsci. Edited and translated by Quintin Hoare and Geoffrey Nowell Smith. London: Lawrence and Wishort.

Greeley, Andrew M. 1989. "Protestant and Catholic: Is the Analogical Imagination Extinct?" *American Sociological Review* 54 (August):485–502.

Greenhouse, Linda. 1998. "High Court Ruling Says Harassment Includes Same Sex." *New York Times,* March 5, pp. A1, A17.

Greenwald, Anthony G., Mark A. Oakes, and Hunter Hoffman. 2003. "Targets of Discrimination: Effects of Race on Responses to Weapons Holders." *Journal of Experimental Social Psychology.*

Grieco, Elizabeth M., and Rachel C. Cassidy. 2001. "Overview of Race and Hispanic Origin." *Current Population Reports,* ser. CENBR/01-1. Washington, DC: U.S. Government Printing Office.

Guardian. 2003. "Fast Forward into Trouble." (June 14).

Guterman, Lila. 2000. "Why the 25-Year-Old Battle over Sociobiology Is More Than Just 'An Academic Sideshow.'" *Chronicle of Higher Education,* July 7, pp. A17–A18.

Hacker, Andrew. 1964. "Power to Do What?" Pp. 134–146 in *The New Sociology,* edited by Irving Louis Horowitz. New York: Oxford University Press.

Hacker, Helen Mayer. 1951. "Women as a Minority Group." *Social Forces* 30 (October):60–69.

———. 1974. "Women as a Minority Group, Twenty Years Later." Pp. 124–134 in *Who Discriminates against Women?* edited by Florence Denmark. Beverly Hills, CA: Sage.

Haines, Valerie A. 1988. "Is Spencer's Theory an Evolutionary Theory?" *American Journal of Sociology* 93 (March):1200–1223.

Hall, Kay. 1999. "Work from Here." *Computer User* 18 (November):32.

Hall, Mimi. 1993. "Genetic-Sex-Testing a Medical Mine Field." *USA Today,* December 20, p. 6A.

Hall, Robert H. 1982. "The Truth about Brown Lung." *Business and Society Review* 40 (Winter 1981–82):15–20.

Hallinan, Maureen T. 1997. "The Sociological Study of Social Change." *American Sociological Review* 62 (February):1–11.

———. 2003. "Ability Grouping and Student Learning." Pp. 95–140 in *Brookings Papers on Education Policy,* edited by Diane Ravitch. Washington, DC: Brookings Institute Press.

Haney, Craig, Curtis Banks, and Philip Zimbardo. 1973. "Interpersonal Dynamics in a Simulated Prison." *International Journal of Criminology and Penology* 1 (February):69–97.

Harap, Louis. 1982. "Marxism and Religion: Social Functions of Religious Belief." *Jewish Currents* 36 (January):12–17, 32–35.

Harris, Chauncy D., and Edward Ullman. 1945. "The Nature of Cities." *Annals of the American Academy of Political and Social Science* 242 (November):7–17.

Harris, David A. 1999. *Driving While Black: Racial Profiling on Our Nation's Highways.* New York: American Civil Liberties Union.

Harris, Judith Rich. 1998. *The Nurture Assumption: Why Children Turn Out the Way They Do.* New York: Free Press.

Haub, Carl. 2004. *2004 World Population Data Sheet.* Washington, DC: Population Reference Bureau.

Haviland, William A. 2003. *Cultural Anthropology.* 10th ed. Belmont, CA: Wadsworth.

———, Harald E. L. Prins, Dana Walrath, and Bunny McBride. 2005. *Cultural Anthropology—The Human Challenge.* New York: McGraw-Hill.

Hawkins, Darnell F., et al. 2000. "Race, Ethnicity, and Serious and Violent Juvenile Offending." *Juvenile Justice Bulletin,* June, p. 107.

Heckert, Druann, and Amy Best. 1997. "Ugly Duckling to Swan: Labeling Theory and the Stigmatization of Red Hair." *Symbolic Interaction* 20 (4):365–384.

Hedley, R. Alan. 1992. "Industrialization in Less Developed Countries." Pp. 914–920 in *Encyclopedia of Sociology,* vol. 2, edited by Edgar F. Borgatta and Marie L. Borgatta. New York: Macmillan.

Henry L. Stimson Center. 2001. "Frequently Asked Questions: Likelihood of Terrorists Acquiring and Using Chemical or Biological Weapons." Accessed December 28, 2001 (www.stimson.org/cwc/acquse.htm#seek).

Hickman, Jonathan. 2002. "America's 50 Best Corporations for Minorities." *Fortune* 146 (July 8), pp. 110–120.

Hochschild, Arlie Russell. 1990. "The Second Shift: Employed Women Are Putting in Another Day of Work at Home." *Utne Reader* 38 (March/April):66–73.

———, with Anne Machung. 1989. *The Second Shift: Working Parents and the Revolution at Home.* New York: Viking Penguin.

Hodge, Robert W., and Peter H. Rossi. 1964. "Occupational Prestige in the United States, 1925–1963." *American Journal of Sociology* 70 (November):286–302.

Hoebel, E. Adamson. 1949. *Man in the Primitive World: An Introduction to Anthropology.* New York: McGraw-Hill.

Hoffman, Lois Wladis. 1985. "The Changing Genetics/Socialization Balance." *Journal of Social Issues* 41 (Spring):127–148.

Hollingshead, August B. 1975. *Elmtown's Youth and Elmtown Revisited.* New York: Wiley.

Homans, George C. 1979. "Nature versus Nurture: A False Dichotomy." *Contemporary Sociology* 8 (May):345–348.

Horowitz, Helen Lefkowitz. 1987. *Campus Life.* Chicago: University of Chicago Press.

Hout, Michael. 1984. "Occupational Mobility of Black Men: 1962 to 1973." *American Sociological Review* 49 (June):308–322.

———. 1988. "More Universalism, Less Structural Mobility: The American Occupational Structure in the 1980s." *American Journal of Sociology* 91 (May):1358–1400.

Howard, Judith A. 1999. "Border Crossings between Women's Studies and Sociology." *Contemporary Sociology* 28 (September):525–528.

Howard, Philip E., Lee Rainie, and Steve Jones. 2001. "Days and Nights on the Internet." *American Behavioral Scientist* 45 (November):383–404.

Hughes, Everett. 1945. "Dilemmas and Contradictions of Status." *American Journal of Sociology* 50 (March):353–359.

Huie, Stephanie A. Bond, Patrick M. Krueger, Richard G. Rogers, and Robert A. Hummer. 2003. "Wealth, Race, and Morality." *Social Science Quarterly* 84 (September): 667–684.

Hunter, Herbert, ed. 2000. *The Sociology of Oliver C. Cox: New Perspectives: Research in Race and Ethnic Relations,* vol. 2. Stamford, CT: JAI Press.

Hunter, James Davison. 1991. *Culture Wars: The Struggle to Define America.* New York: Basic Books.

Hurn, Christopher J. 1985. *The Limits and Possibilities of Schooling.* 2nd ed. Boston: Allyn and Bacon.

Hussey, Mark. 2003. *Masculinities: Interdisciplinary Readings.* Upper Saddle River, NJ: Prentice Hall.

Immigration and Naturalization Service. 2002. *1999 Statistical Yearbook of the Immigration and Naturalization Service.* Washington, DC: U.S. Government Printing Office.

Inglehart, Ronald, and Wayne E. Baker. 2000. "Modernization, Cultural Change, and the Persistence of Traditional Values." *American Sociological Review* 65 (February):19–51.

Institute of International Education. 2004. *Open Doors: Foreign Student 2002/2003 and American Students Study Abroad.* Accessed April 5, 2004 (www.opendoors.iienetwork.org).

Intercom. 1978. "Populandia: A Country Is Born." *Intercom* 6 (January):9.

Internal Revenue Service. 2004. *Selected Income and Tax Items from Inflation-Indexed Individual Tax Returns, 1990–2001.* Statistics of Income (Spring): 200–212.

International Crime Victim Survey. 2001. *Nationwide Surveys in the Industrialized Countries.* Accessed June 13 (http://ruijis.leidenuniv.nl/group/jfer/www/icvs/index.htm).

International Monetary Fund. 2000. *World Economic Outlook: Asset Prices and the Business Cycle.* Washington, DC: International Monetary Fund.

Jackson, Elton F., Charles R. Tittle, and Mary Jean Burke. 1986. "Offense-Specific Models of the Differential Association Process." *Social Problems* 33 (April):335–356.

Jackson, Philip W. 1968. *Life in Classrooms.* New York: Holt.

Jacobson, Jodi. 1993. "Closing the Gender Gap in Development." Pp. 61–79 in *State of the World,* edited by Lester R. Brown. New York: Norton.

Jasper, James M. 1997. *The Art of Moral Protest: Culture, Biography, and Creativity in Social Movements.* Chicago: University of Chicago Press.

Jenkins, Richard. 1991. "Disability and Social Stratification." *British Journal of Sociology* 42 (December):557–580.

Jobtrak.com. 2000. "Jobtrak.com's Poll Finds That Students and Recent Grads Only Plan to Stay with Their First Employer No Longer Than Three Years." Press release January 6. Accessed June 29 (http://static. jobtrak.com/mediacenter/press_polls/poll_010600.html).

Johnson, Benton. 1975. *Functionalism in Modern Sociology: Understanding Talcott Parsons.* Morristown, NJ: General Learning.

Jones, Del. 2003. "Few Women in Fortune 500s Top Tier." *USA Today,* January 27, pp. B1, B2.

Jones, James T., IV. 1988. "Harassment Is Too Often Part of the Job." *USA Today,* August 8, p. 5D.

Juhasz, Anne McCreary. 1989. "Black Adolescents' Significant Others." *Social Behavior and Personality* 17 (2):211–214.

Kaiser Family Foundation/*The San Jose Mercury News.* 2003. *Growing Up Wind: Survey on Youth and the Internet in Silicon Valley.* Accessed January 14, 2004 (www.KFF.org).

Kalb, Claudia. 1999. "Our Quest to Be Perfect." *Newsweek* 131 (August 9):52–59.

Katovich, Michael A. 1987. Correspondence. June 1.

Katz, Michael. 1971. *Class, Bureaucracy, and the Schools: The Illusion of Educational Change in America.* New York: Praeger.

Kerbo, Harold R. 2003. *Social Stratification and Inequality: Class Conflict in Historical, Comparative, and Global Perspective,* 5th ed. New York: McGraw-Hill.

Kochhar, Rakesh. 2004. *The Wealth of Hispanic Households: 1996 to 2002.* Washington, DC: Pew Hispanic Center.

Kolata, Gina. 1999. *Clone: The Road to Dolly and the Path Beyond.* New York: William Morrow.

Komarovsky, Mirra. 1991. "Some Reflections on the Feminist Scholarship in Sociology." Pp. 1–25 in *Annual Review of Sociology,* edited by W. Richard Scott and Judith Blake. Palo Alto, CA: Annual Reviews.

Koolhaas, Rem, et al. 2001. *Mutations.* Barcelona, Spain: Actar.

Kortenhaus, Carole M., and Jack Demarest. 1993. "Gender Role Stereotyping in Children's Literature: An Update." *Sex Roles* 28 (3/4):219–232.

Kottak, Conrad. 2004. *Anthropology: The Explanation of Human Diversity.* New York: McGraw-Hill.

Landtman, Gunnar. [1938] 1968. *The Origin of Inequality of the Social Class.* New York: Greenwood (original edition 1938, Chicago: University of Chicago Press).

Lang, Eric. 1992. "Hawthorne Effect." Pp. 793–794 in *Encyclopedia of Sociology,* vol. 2, edited by Edgar F. Borgatta and Marie L. Borgatta. New York: Macmillan.

Lasswell, Harold D. 1936. *Politics: Who Gets What, When, How.* New York: McGraw-Hill.

Lauer, Robert H. 1982. *Perspectives on Social Change.* 3d ed. Boston: Allyn and Bacon.

Leavell, Hugh R., and E. Gurney Clark. 1965. *Preventive Medicine for the Doctor in His Community: An Epidemiologic Approach.* 3d ed. New York: McGraw-Hill.

Leinwand, Donna. 2000. "20% Say They Used Drugs with Their Mom and Dad." *USA Today,* August 24, pp. 1A, 2A.

Lengermann, Patricia Madoo, and Jill Niebrugge-Brantley. 1998. *The Women Founders: Sociology and Social Theory, 1830–1930.* Boston: McGraw-Hill.

Lenski, Gerhard. 1966. *Power and Privilege: A Theory of Social Stratification.* New York: McGraw-Hill.

———, Jean Lenski, and Patrick Nolan. 1995. *Human Societies: An Introduction to Macrosociology.* 7th ed. New York: McGraw-Hill.

Levin, Thomas Y., Ursula Frohne and Peter Weibel (eds.). 2002. *Ctrl Space: Rhetorics of Surveillance from Bentham to Big Brother.* Cambridge, MA: MIT Press.

Lewin, Tamar. 1998. "Debate Centers on Definition of Harassment." *New York Times,* March 22, pp. A1, A20.

Lewis, David Levering. 1994. *W. E. B. DuBois: Biography of a Race, 1868–1919.* New York: Holt.

———. 2000. *W. E. B. DuBois: The Fight for Equality and the American Century, 1919–1963.* New York: Holt.

Lieberman, David. 1999. "On the Wrong Side of the Wires." *USA Today,* October 11, pp. B1, B2.

Lightblau, Eric. 2003. "Bush Issues Racial Profiling Ban but Exempts Security Awareness." *New York Times,* June 18, pp. A1, A14.

Lin, Na, and Wen Xie. 1988. "Occupational Prestige in Urban China." *American Journal of Sociology* 93 (January):793–832.

Lin, Nan. 1999. "Social Networks and Status Attainment." Pp. 467–487 in *Annual Review of Sociology 1999,* edited by Karen S. Cook and John Hagen. Palo Alto, CA: Annual Reviews.

Lindsey, Linda L. 2005. *Gender Roles: A Sociological Perspective.* Upper Saddle River, NJ: Prentice Hall.

Lipset, Seymour Martin. 1996. *American Exceptionalism: A Double-Edged Sword.* New York: Norton.

Lipson, Karen. 1994. "'Nell' Not Alone in the Wilds." *Los Angeles Times,* December 19, pp. F1, F6.

Livernash, Robert, and Eric Rodenburg. 1998. "Population Change, Resources, and the Environment." *Population Bulletin* 53 (March).

Lohr, Steve. 1994. "Data Highway Ignoring Poor, Study Charges." *New York Times,* May 24, pp. A1, D3.

Lukacs, Georg. 1923. *History and Class Consciousness.* London: Merlin.

Lynn, Barry C. 2003. "Trading with a Low-Wage Tiger." *The American Prospect* 14 (February):10–12.

Lyotard, Jean François. 1993. *The Postmodern Explained: Correspondence, 1982–1985.* Minneapolis: University of Minnesota Press.

Mack, Raymond W., and Calvin P. Bradford. 1979. *Transforming America: Patterns of Social Change.* 2d ed. New York: Random House.

Maguire, Brendan. 1988. "The Applied Dimension of Radical Criminology: A Survey of Prominent Radical Criminologists." *Sociological Spectrum* 8 (2):133–151.

Maharaj, Davan. 2004. "When the Push for Survival Is a Full-Time Job." *Los Angeles Times,* July 11, pp. A1, A10.

Malcolm X, with Alex Haley. 1964. *The Autobiography of Malcolm X.* New York: Grove.

Malthus, Thomas Robert, Julian Huxley, and Frederick Osborn. [1824] 1960. *Three Essays on Population.* Reprint. New York: New American Library.

Mangum, Garth L., Stephen L. Mangum, and Andrew M. Sum. 2003. *The Persistence of Poverty in the United States.* Baltimore: Johns Hopkins University Press.

Margolis, Eric, ed. 2001. *The Hidden Curriculum in Higher Education.* New York: Routledge.

Martin, Marvin. 1996. "Sociology Adapting to Changes." *Chicago Tribune,* July 21, sec. 18, p. 20.

Martin, Philip, and Elizabeth Midgley. 2003. "Immigration: Shaping and Reshaping America. *Population Bulletin* 58 (June).

Martin, Susan E. 1994. "Outsider within the Station House: The Impact of Race and Gender on Black Women Politics." *Social Problems* 41 (August):383–400.

Martineau, Harriet. 1896. "Introduction" to the translation of *Positive Philosophy* by Auguste Comte. London: Bell.

———. [1837] 1962. *Society in America.* Edited, abridged, with an introductory essay by Seymour Martin Lipset. Reprint. Garden City, NY: Doubleday.

Marx, Karl, and Friedrich Engels. [1847] 1955. *Selected Work in Two Volumes.* Reprint, Moscow: Foreign Languages Publishing House.

Massachusetts Department of Education. 2000. *Learning Support Service Progress: Safe Schools Program for Gay and Lesbian Students.* Accessed July 19, 2001 (www.doe.mass.edu/lss/program/ssch.html).

Mathews, T. J., Marian F. MacDorman, and Fay Menacker. 2002. "Infant Mortality Statistics from the 1999 Period Linked Birth/Infant Death Data Set." *National Vital Statistics Reports* 50 (January 30).

Matsushita, Yoshiko. 1999. "Japanese Kids Call for a Sympathetic Ear." *Christian Science Monitor,* January 20, p. 15.

Mayer, Karl Ulrich, and Urs Schoepflin. 1989. "The State and the Life Course." Pp. 187–209 in *Annual Review of Sociology,* 1989, edited by W. Richard Scott and Judith Blake. Palo Alto, CA: Annual Reviews.

McCreary, D. 1994. "The Male Role and Avoiding Femininity." *Sex Roles* 31:517–531.

McDonald, Kim A. 1999. "Studies of Women's Health Produce a Wealth of Knowledge on the Biology of Gender Differences." *Chronicle of Higher Education* 45 (June 25):A19, A22.

McFalls, Joseph A., Jr. 2003. "Population: A Lively Introduction." *Population Bulletin* 53 (September).

McGuire, Meredith B. 1997. *Religion: The Social Context.* 4th ed. Belmont, CA: Wadsworth.

McIntosh, Peggy. 1988. "White Privilege and Male Privilege: A Personal Account of Coming to See Correspondence through Work and Women's Studies." *Working Paper* No. 189. Wellesley, MA: Wellesley College Center for Research on Women.

McKinlay, John B., and Sonja M. McKinlay. 1977. "The Questionable Contribution of Medical Measures to the Decline of Mortality in the United States in the Twentieth Century." *Milbank Memorial Fund Quarterly* 55 (Summer):405–428.

Mead, George H. 1934. In *Mind, Self and Society,* edited by Charles W. Morris. Chicago: University of Chicago Press.

———. 1964a. In *On Social Psychology,* edited by Anselm Strauss. Chicago: University of Chicago Press.

———. 1964b. "The Genesis of the Self and Social Control." Pp. 267–293 in *Selected Writings: George Herbert Mead,* edited by Andrew J. Reck. Indianapolis: Bobbs-Merrill.

Mead, Margaret. 1973. "Does the World Belong to Men—or to Women?" *Redbook* 141 (October):46–52.

————. [1935] 2001. *Sex and Temperament in Three Primitive Societies.* New York: Perennial, HarperCollins.

Melia, Marilyn Kennedy. 2000. "Changing Times." *Chicago Tribune,* January 2, sec. 17, pp. 12–15.

Merton, Robert K. 1968. *Social Theory and Social Structure.* New York: Free Press.

————, and Alice S. Kitt. 1950. "Contributions to the Theory of Reference Group Behavior." Pp. 40–105 in *Continuities in Social Research: Studies in the Scope and Methods of the American Soldier,* edited by Robert K. Merton and Paul L. Lazarsfeld. New York: Free Press.

Michels, Robert. 1915. *Political Parties.* Glencoe, IL: Free Press (reprinted 1949).

Microquest. 2002. *Microquest Special Report: Diversity Programs on Fortune 1000 Boards.* Novato, CA: Microquest.

Milgram, Stanley. 1963. "Behavioral Study of Obedience." *Journal of Abnormal and Social Psychology* 67 (October):371–378.

————. 1975. *Obedience to Authority: An Experimental View.* New York: Harper and Row.

Miller, David L., and Richard T. Schaefer. 1993. "Feeding the Hungry: The National Food Bank System as a Non-Insurgent Social Movement." Presented at the annual meeting of the Midwest Sociological Society, Chicago.

Miller, G. Tyler, Jr. 1972. *Replenish the Earth: A Primer in Human Ecology.* Belmont, CA: Wadsworth.

Miller, Judith, Stephen Engelberg, and William J. Broad. 2001. *Germs: Biological Weapons and America's Secret War.* New York: Simon and Schuster.

Mills, C. Wright. [1959] 2000a. *The Sociological Imagination. 40th Anniversary Edition: New Afterword by Todd Gitlin.* New York: Oxford University Press.

————. [1956] 2000b. *The Power Elite.* A New Edition. Afterword by Alan Wolfe. New York: Oxford University Press.

Mills, Robert J. 2001. "Health Insurance Coverage: 2000." *Current Population Reports,* ser. P. 60, no. 215. Washington, DC: U.S. Government Printing Office.

————, and Shailesh Bhandari. 2003. "Health Insurance Coverage in the United States: 2002." *Current Population Reports,* ser. P. 60, no. 223. Washington, DC: U.S. Government Printing Office.

Monteiro, Lois A. 1998. "Ill-Defined Illnesses and Medically Unexplained Symptoms Syndrome." *Footnotes* 26 (February):3, 6.

Moore, Wilbert E. 1967. *Order and Change: Essays in Comparative Sociology.* New York: Wiley.

————. 1968. "Occupational Socialization." Pp. 861–883 in *Handbook of Socialization Theory and Research,* edited by David A. Goslin. Chicago: Rand McNally.

Morehouse Medical Treatment Effectiveness Center. 1999. *A Synthesis of the Literature: Racial and Ethnic Differences in Access to Medical Care.* Menlo Park, CA: Henry J. Kaiser Family Foundation.

Morris, Aldon. 2000. "Reflections on Social Movement Theory: Criticisms and Proposals." *Contemporary Sociology* 29 (May):445–454.

Morrison, Denton E. 1971. "Some Notes toward Theory on Relative Deprivation, Social Movements, and Social Change." *American Behavioral Scientist* 14 (May/June):675–690.

Morse, Arthur D. 1967. *While Six Million Died: A Chronicle of American Apathy.* New York: Ace.

Mosley, J., and E. Thomson. 1995. Pp. 148–165 in *Fatherhood: Contemporary Theory, Research and Social Policy,* edited by W. Marsiglo. Thousand Oaks, CA: Sage.

Mullins, Marcy E. 2001. "Bioterrorism Impacts Few." *USA Today,* October 18, p. 16A.

Mumola, Christopher J. 2000. *Incarcerated Parents and Their Children.* Washington, DC: U.S. Government Printing Office.

Murdock, George P. 1945. "The Common Denominator of Cultures." Pp. 123–142 in *The Science of Man in the World Crisis,* edited by Ralph Linton. New York: Columbia University Press.

———. 1949. *Social Structure.* New York: Macmillan.

———. 1957. "World Ethnographic Sample." *American Anthropologist* 59 (August):664–687.

Murphy, Dean E. 2004. "Desert's Promised Land: Long Odds for Las Vegas Newcomers." *New York Times,* May 30, pp. A1, A16.

Murray, Velma McBride, Amanda Willert, and Diane P. Stephens. 2001. "The Half-Full Glass: Resilient African American Single Mothers and Their Children." *Family Focus,* June, pp. F4–F5.

Nader, Laura. 1986. "The Subordination of Women in Comparative Perspective." *Urban Anthropology* 15 (Fall/Winter):377–397.

Nash, Manning. 1962. "Race and the Ideology of Race." *Current Anthropology* 3 (June):285–288.

Nass, Clifford, and Youngme Moon. 2000. "Machines and Mindlessness: Social Responses to Computers." *Journal of Social Issues* 56 (No. 1):81–103.

National Advisory Commission on Criminal Justice. 1976. *Organized Crime.* Washington, DC: U.S. Government Printing Office.

National Center for Education Statistics. 2004. *The Condition of Education 2004.* Washington, DC: U.S. Government Printing Office.

National Center for Health Statistics. 2004. *Fast Stats A to Z.* Accessed October 4 (www.cdc.gov/nchs/fastats).

National Center on Women and Family Law. 1996. *Status of Marital Rape Exemption Statutes in the United States.* New York: National Center on Women and Family Law.

National Marriage Project. 2004. *The State of Our Unions: The Social Health of Marriage in America.* New Brunswick, NJ: The National Marriage Project.

Nelson, F. Howard and Rachel Drown. 2003. *Survey and Analysis of Teacher Salary Trends 2002.* Washington, DC: American Federation of Teachers.

Neuborne, Ellen. 1996. "Vigilantes Stir Firms' Ire with Cyber-antics." *USA Today,* February 28, pp. A1, A2.

Newburger, Eric C. 2001. "Home Computers and Internet Use in the United States: August 2000." *Current Population Reports,* ser. P. 23, no. 207. Washington, DC: U.S. Government Printing Office.

Newport, Frank. 2004. "A Look at Americans and Religion." Accessed April 14, 2004 (www.gallup.com).

Nie, Norman H. 2001. "Sociability, Interpersonal Relations, and the Internet." *American Behavioral Scientist* 45 (November):420–435.

Nolan, Patrick, and Gerhard Lenski. 2004. *Human Societies: An Introduction to Macrosociology.* 9th ed. Boulder, CO: Paradigm.

Noonan, Rita K. 1995. "Women against the State: Political Opportunities and Collective Action Frames in Chile's Transition to Democracy." *Sociological Forum* 10:81–111.

Nussbaum, Daniel. 1998. "Bad Air Days." *Los Angeles Times Magazine,* July 19, pp. 20–21.

Oberschall, Anthony. 1973. *Social Conflict and Social Movements.* Englewood Cliffs, NJ: Prentice Hall.

Office of Justice Programs. 1999. "Transnational Organized Crime." *NCJRS Catalog* 49 (November/December):21.

Ogburn, William F. 1922. *Social Change with Respect to Culture and Original Nature.* New York: Huebsch (reprinted 1966, New York: Dell).

———, and Clark Tibbits. 1934. "The Family and Its Functions." Pp. 661–708 in *Recent Social Trends in the United States,* edited by Research Committee on Social Trends. New York: McGraw-Hill.

Okamoto, Dina G., and Lynn Smith-Lovin. 2001. "Changing the Subject: Gender, Status, and the Dynamics of Topic Change." *American Sociological Review* 66 (December):852–873.

Okano, Kaori, and Motonori Tsuchiya. 1999. *Education in Contemporary Japan: Inequality and Diversity.* Cambridge: Cambridge University Press.

Oliver, Melvin L., and Thomas M. Shapiro. 1995. *Black Wealth/White Wealth: New Perspectives on Racial Inequality.* New York: Routledge.

Orum, Anthony M. 1989. *Introduction to Political Sociology: The Social Anatomy of the Body Politic.* 3d ed. Englewood Cliffs, NJ: Prentice Hall.

Ouchi, William. 1981. *Theory Z: How American Businesses Can Meet the Japanese Challenge.* Reading, MA: Addison-Wesley.

Pager, Devah. 2003. "The Mark of a Criminal Record." *American Journal of Sociology* 108 (March): 937–975.

Park, Robert E. 1916. "The City: Suggestions for the Investigation of Human Behavior in the Urban Environment." *American Journal of Sociology* 20 (March):577–612.

———. 1936. "Succession, an Ecological Concept." *American Sociological Review* 1 (April):171–179.

Parsons, Talcott. 1951. *The Social System.* New York: Free Press.

———. 1966. Societies: *Evolutionary and Comparative Perspectives.* Englewood Cliffs, NJ: Prentice Hall.

———. 1975. "The Sick Role and the Role of the Physician Reconsidered." *Milbank Medical Fund Quarterly Health and Society* 53 (Summer): 257–278.

———, and Robert Bales. 1955. *Family: Socialization and Interaction Process.* Glencoe, IL: Free Press.

Paul, Pamela. 2001. "Turning Up the Heat." *American Prospect* 23 (July):22–23.

Pearlstein, Steven. 2001. "Coming Soon (Maybe): Worldwide Recession." *Washington Post National Weekly Edition* 19 (November 12):18.

Perrow, Charles. 1986. *Complex Organizations.* 3d ed. New York: Random House.

Peter, Laurence J., and Raymond Hull. 1969. *The Peter Principle.* New York: Morrow.

Petersen, William. 1979. *Malthus.* Cambridge, MA: Harvard University Press.

Phillips, E. Barbara. 1996. *City Lights: Urban–Suburban Life in the Global Society.* New York: Oxford University Press.

Piller, Charles. 2000. "Cyber-Crime Loss at Firms Doubles to $10 Billion." *Los Angeles Times,* May 22, pp. C1, C4.

Pinderhughes, Dianne. 1987. *Race and Ethnicity in Chicago Politics: A Reexamination of Pluralist Theory.* Urbana: University of Illinois Press.

Pinkerton, James P. 2003. "Education: A Grand Compromise." *Atlantic Monthly* 291 (January/February):115–116.

Polletta, Francesca, and James M. Jasper. 2001. "Collective Identity and Social Movements." Pp. 283–305 in *Annual Review of Sociology, 2001,* edited by Karen S. Cook and Leslie Hogan. Palo Alto, CA: Annual Review of Sociology.

Population Reference Bureau. 1996. "Speaking Graphically." *Population Today* 24 (June/July):b.

Proctor, Bernadette D., and Joseph Dalaker. 2002. "Poverty in the United States: 2001." *Current Population Reports,* ser. P. 60, no. 219. Washington, DC: U.S. Government Printing Office.

——— . 2002. "Poverty in the United States: 2002." *Current Population Reports,* ser. P. 60, no. 222. Washington, DC: U.S. Government Printing Office.

Quinney, Richard. 1970. *The Social Reality of Crime.* Boston: Little, Brown.

——— . 1974. *Criminal Justice in America.* Boston: Little, Brown.

——— . 1979. *Criminology.* 2d ed. Boston: Little, Brown.

——— . 1980. *Class, State and Crime.* 2d ed. New York: Longman.

Ramet, Sabrina. 1991. *Social Currents in Eastern Europe: The Source and Meaning of the Great Transformation.* Durham, NC: Duke University Press.

Ramirez, Roberta R. and G. Patricia de la Cruz. 2003. "The Hispanic Population in the Current United States: March 2002." *Current Population Reports,* ser. P. 20, no. 545. Washington, DC: U.S. Government Printing Office.

Rantala, Ramona R. 2004. "Cybercrime against Businesses." *Bureau of Justice Statistics Technical Report.* March.

Raybon, Patricia. 1989. "A Case for 'Severe Bias.'" *Newsweek* 114 (October 2):11.

Reddick, Randy, and Elliot King. 2000. *The Online Student: Making the Grade on the Internet.* Fort Worth: Harcourt Brace.

Rennison, Callie Marie, and Michael R. Rand. 2003. *Criminal Victimization, 2002.* Washington, DC: Bureau of Justice Statistics.

Richardson, Laurel, Verta Taylor, and Nancy Whittier, eds. 2004. *Feminist Frontiers.* 6th ed. New York: McGraw-Hill.

Richtel, Matt. 2000. "www.layoffs.com." *New York Times,* June 22, pp. C1, C12.

Rideout, Victoria J., Ulla G. Foehr, Donald E. Roberts, and Mollyann Brodie. 1999. *Kids & Media @ the New Millennium.* New York: Kaiser Family Foundation.

Ridgeway, Cecilia L., and Lynn Smith-Lovin. 1999. "The Gender System and Interaction." Pp. 191–216 in *The Annual Review of Sociology 1999,* edited by Karen Cook and John Hagan. Palo Alto, CA: Annual Review.

Riding, Alan. 1998. "Why 'Titanic' Conquered the World." *New York Times,* April 26, sec. 2, pp. 1, 28, 29.

Rifkin, Jeremy. 1995. "Afterwork." *Utne Reader* (May/June):52–62.

Riley, Matilda White, Robert L. Kahn, and Anne Foner. 1994a. *Age and Structural Lag.* New York: Wiley InterScience.

Riley, Matilda White, and Robert L. Kahn, in association with Karin A. Mock. 1994b. "Introduction: The Mismatch between People and Structures." Pp. 1–36 in *Age and Structural Lag,* edited by Matilda White Riley, Robert L. Kahn, and Ann Foner. New York: Wiley InterScience.

Ritzer, George. 2000. *The McDonaldization of Society.* New Century Edition. Thousand Oaks, CA: Pine Forge Press.

———. 2004a. *The McDonaldization of Society.* Revised New Century Edition. Thousand Oaks, CA: Pine Forge Press.

Roberts, Lynne D., and Malcolm R. Parks. 1999. "The Social Geography of Gender-Switching in Virtual Environments on the Internet." *Information, Communication and Society* 2 (Winter).

Robertson, Roland. 1988. "The Sociological Significance of Culture: Some General Considerations." *Theory, Culture, and Society* 5 (February):3–23.

Roethlisberger, Fritz J., and W. J. Dickson. 1939. *Management and the Worker.* Cambridge, MA: Harvard University Press.

Rose, Arnold. 1951. *The Roots of Prejudice.* Paris: UNESCO.

Rosenberg, Douglas H. 1991. "Capitalism." Pp. 33–34 in *Encyclopedic Dictionary of Sociology,* 4th ed., edited by Dushkin Publishing Group. Guilford, CT: Dushkin.

Rosenthal, Robert, and Lenore Jacobson. 1968. *Pygmalion in the Classroom.* New York: Holt.

Rossides, Daniel W. 1997. *Social Stratification: The Interplay of Class, Race, and Gender.* 2d ed. Upper Saddle River, NJ: Prentice Hall.

Roszak, Theodore. 1969. *The Making of a Counterculture.* Garden City, NY: Doubleday.

Rubin, Alissa J. 2003. "Pat-Down on the Way to Prayer." *Los Angeles Times,* November 25, pp. A1, A5.

Ryan, William. 1976. *Blaming the Victim.* Rev. ed. New York: Random House.

"Sabbathday Lake." 2004. Interview by author with Sabbathday, Lake Shaker Village. July 29.

Sadker, Myra Pollack, and David Miller Sadker. 2003. *Teachers, Schools and Society,* 6th ed. New York: McGraw-Hill.

Safire, William. 1996. "Downsized." *New York Times Magazine,* May 26, pp. 12, 14.

Sagarin, Edward, and Jose Sanchez. 1988. "Ideology and Deviance: The Case of the Debate over the Biological Factor." *Deviant Behavior* 9 (1):87–99.

Sale, Kirkpatrick. 1996. *Rebels against the Future: The Luddites and Their War on the Industrial Revolution* (with a new preface by the author). Reading, MA: Addison-Wesley.

Salkever, Alex. 1999. "Making Machines More Like Us." *Christian Science Monitor,* December 20, electronic edition.

Samuelson, Paul A., and William D. Nordhaus. 2005. *Economics.* 18th ed. New York: McGraw-Hill.

Samuelson, Robert J. 1996a. "Are Workers Disposable?" *Newsweek* 127 (February 12), p. 47.

————. 1996b. "Fashionable Statements." *Washington Post National Weekly Edition* 13 (March 18), p. 5.

Saukko, Paula. 1999. "Fat Boys and Goody Girls." In *Weighty Issues: Fatness and Thinness as Social Problems,* edited by Jeffrey Sobal and Donna Mauer. New York: Aldine de Gruyter.

Sax, Linda J., Alexander W. Astin, Jennifer A. Lindholm, William S. Korn, Victor B. Saenz, and Kathryn M. Mahoney. 2003. *The American Freshman: National Norms for Fall 2003.* Los Angeles: Higher Education Research Institute, University of California, Los Angeles.

Schaefer, Peter. 1995. "Destroy Your Future." *Daily Northwestern,* November 3, p. 8.

Schaefer, Richard T. 2005. *Racial and Ethnic Groups.* 10th ed. Upper Saddle River, NJ: Prentice Hall.

Schellenberg, Kathryn, ed. 1996. *Computers in Society.* 6th ed. Guilford, CT: Dushkin.

Schnaiberg, Allan. 1994. *Environment and Society: The Enduring Conflict.* New York: St. Martin's.

Schulman, Andrew. 2001. *The Extent of Systematic Monitoring of Employee E-mail and Internet Users.* Denver, CO: Workplace Surveillance Project, Privacy Foundation.

Schur, Edwin M. 1965. *Crimes without Victims: Deviant Behavior and Public Policy.* Englewood Cliffs, NJ: Prentice Hall.

————. 1968. *Law and Society: A Sociological View.* New York: Random House.

————. 1985. "'Crimes without Victims': A 20 Year Reassessment." Paper presented at the annual meeting of the Society for the Study of Social Problems.

Schwab, William A. 1993. "Recent Empirical and Theoretical Developments in Sociological Human Ecology." Pp. 29–57 in *Urban Sociology in Transition,* edited by Ray Hutchison. Greenwich, CT: JAI Press.

Schwartz, Howard D., ed. 1987. *Dominant Issues in Medical Sociology.* 2d ed. New York: Random House.

Scott, Alan. 1990. *Ideology and the New Social Movements.* London: Unwin Hyman.

Scott, Richard W. 2003. *Organizations: Rational, Natural, and Open Systems.* 5th ed. Upper Saddle River, NJ: Prentice Hall.

Seager, Joni. 2003. *The Penguin Atlas Women in the World.* Rev. ed. New York: Putnum.

Second Harvest. 2003. *America's Second Harvest: How We Work.* Accessed March 3 (www.secondharvest.org/aboutash/how_work/html).

Segall, Alexander. 1976. "The Sick Role Concept: Understanding Illness Behavior." *Journal of Health and Social Behavior* 17 (June):163–170.

Segerstråle, Ullica. 2000. *Defense of the Truth: The Battle for Science in the Sociobiology Debate and Beyond.* New York: Oxford University Press.

Seidman, Steven. 2002. *Beyond the Closet: The Transformation of Gay and Lesbian Life.* New York: Routledge.

Sernau, Scott. 2001. *Worlds Apart: Social Inequalities in a New Century.* Thousand Oaks, CA: Pine Forge Press.

Shcherbak, Yuri M. 1996. "Ten Years of the Chernobyl Era." *Scientific American* 274 (April):44–49.

Sheehy, Gail. 1999. *Understanding Men's Passages: Discovering the New Map of Men's Lives.* New York: Ballantine Books.

Sherman, Lawrence W., Patrick R. Gartin, and Michael D. Buerger. 1989. "Hot Spots of Predatory Crime: Routine Activities and the Criminology of Place." *Criminology* 27:27–56.

Shinkai, Hiroguki, and Ugljea Zvekic. 1999. "Punishment." Pp. 89–120 in *Global Report on Crime and Justice,* edited by Graeme Newman. New York: Oxford University Press.

Short, Kathleen, et al. 1999. "Experimental Poverty Measures: 1990 to 1997." *Current Population Reports,* ser. P. 60, no. 205. Washington, DC: U.S. Government Printing Office.

Sigelman, Lee, et al. 1996. "Making Contact? Black-White Social Interaction in an Urban Setting." *American Journal of Sociology* 5 (March):1306–1332.

Silicon Valley Cultures Project. 2002. The Silicon Valley Cultures Project Website. Accessed November 10, 2002 (www.sjsu.edu/depts/anthropology/svcp).

Simmons, Ann M. 1998. "Where Fat Is a Mark of Beauty." *Los Angeles Times,* September 30, pp. A1, A12.

Simpson, Sally. 1993. "Corporate Crime." Pp. 236–256 in *Introduction to Social Problems,* edited by Craig Calhoun and George Ritzer. New York: McGraw-Hill.

Sjoberg, Gideon. 1960. *The Preindustrial City: Past and Present.* Glencoe, IL: Free Press.

Smedley, Brian D., Adrienne Y. Stith and Alan R. Nelson, eds. 2002. *Unequal Treatment: Confronting Racial and Ethnic Disparities in Health Care.* Washington, DC: Institutional Medicine.

Smelser, Neil. 1963. *The Sociology of Economic Life.* Englewood Cliffs, NJ: Prentice Hall.

Smith, Buffy. 2004. "Leave No College Student Behind." *Multicultural Education* (Spring), pp. 48–49.

Smith, David A. 1995. "The New Urban Sociology Meets the Old: Rereading Some Classical Human Ecology." *Urban Affairs Review* 20 (January):432–457.

———, and Michael Timberlake. 1993. "World Cities: A Political Economy/Global Network Approach." Pp. 181–201 in *Urban Sociology in Transition,* edited by Ray Hutchison. Greenwich, CT: JAI Press.

Smith, Michael Peter. 1988. *City, State, and Market.* New York: Basil Blackwell.

Smith, Patricia K. 1994. "Downward Mobility: Is It a Growing Problem?" *American Journal of Economics and Sociology* 53 (January):57–72.

Snyder, Thomas D. 1996. *Digest of Education Statistics 1996.* Washington, DC: U.S. Government Printing Office.

Sohoni, Neera Kuckreja. 1994. "Where Are the Girls?" *Ms.* 5 (July/August):96.

Sorokin, Pitirim A. [1927] 1959. *Social and Cultural Mobility.* New York: Free Press.

Spar, Deborah L. 2001. *Ruling the Waves: Cycles of Discovery, Chaos and Wealth from the Compass to the Internet.* San Diego: Harcourt.

Spitzer, Steven. 1975. "Toward a Marxian Theory of Deviance." *Social Problems* 22 (June):641–651.

Stack, Megan K. 2001. "E-Mail Capability Changes Lives of Sailors Far Away." *Los Angeles Times,* October 23, p. A3.

Staggenborg, Suzanne. 1989a. "Stability and Innovation in the Women's Movement: A Comparison of Two Movement Organizations." *Social Problems* 36 (February):75–92.

———. 1989b. "Organizational and Environmental Influences on the Development of the Pro-Choice Movement." *Social Forces* 36 (September):204–240.

Starr, Paul. 1982. *The Social Transformation of American Medicine.* New York: Basic Books.

Steffensmeier, Darrell, and Stephen Demuth. 2000. "Ethnicity and Sentencing Outcomes in U.S. Federal Courts: Who Is Punished More Harshly?" *American Sociological Review* 65 (October):705–729.

Stoops, Nicole. 2004. "Educational Attainment in the United States: 2003." *Population Reports.* ser. P. 20. no. 550. Washington, DC: U.S. Government Printing Office.

Strauss, Gary. 2002. "'Good Old Boys' Network Still Rules Corporate Boards." *USA Today,* November 1, pp. B1, B2.

Sugimoto, Yoshio. 1997. *An Introduction to Japanese Society.* Cambridge: Cambridge University Press.

Sumner, William G. 1906. *Folkways.* New York: Ginn.

Sunstein, Cass R., Reid Hastie, John W. Payne, David A. Schkade, W. Kip Viscusi, and George L. Priest, eds. 2003. *Punitive Damages: How Juries Decide.* Chicago: University of Chicago Press.

Sutherland, Edwin H. 1937. *The Professional Thief.* Chicago: University of Chicago Press.

———. 1940. "White-Collar Criminality." *American Sociological Review* 5 (February):1–11.

———. 1949. *White Collar Crime.* New York: Dryden.

———. 1983. *White Collar Crime: The Uncut Version.* New Haven, CT: Yale University Press.

———, and Donald R. Cressey. 1978. *Principles of Criminology.* 10th ed. Philadelphia: Lippincott.

Szasz, Thomas S. 1971. "The Same Slave: An Historical Note on the Use of Medical Diagnosis as Justificatory Rhetoric." *American Journal of Psychotherapy* 25 (April):228–239.

Tafoya, Sonya M., Hans Johnson, and Laura E. Hill. 2004. *Who Chooses to Choose Two?* New York: Russell Sage Foundation and Population Reference Bureau.

Tannen, Deborah. 1990. *You Just Don't Understand: Women and Men in Conversation.* New York: Ballantine.

———. 1994a. *Talking from 9 to 5.* New York: William Morris.

———. 1994b. *Gender and Discourse.* New York: Oxford University Press.

Taylor, Verta. 1995. "Watching for Vibes: Bringing Emotions into the Study of Feminist Organizations." Pp. 223–233 in *Feminist Organizations: Harvest of the New Women's Movement,* edited by Myra Marx Ferree and Patricia Yancy Martin. Philadelphia: Temple University Press.

Therrien, Melissa, and Roberto R. Ramirez. 2001. "The Hispanic Population in the United States, March 2000." *Current Population Report,* ser. P. 20, no. 535. Washington, DC: U.S. Government Printing Office.

Thomas, Gordon, and Max Morgan Witts. 1974. *Voyage of the Damned.* Greenwich, CT: Fawcett Crest.

Thomas, William I. 1923. *The Unadjusted Girl.* Boston: Little, Brown.

Thompson, Ginger. 2003. "Money Sent Home by Mexicans Is Booming." *New York Times,* October 28, p. A12.

Thornton, Russell. 1987. *American Indians Holocaust and Survival: A Population History Since 1492.* Norman: University of Oklahoma Press.

Tierney, John. 1990. "Betting the Planet." *New York Times Magazine,* December 2, pp. 52–53, 71, 74, 76, 78, 80–81.

———. 2003. "Iraqi Family Ties Complicate American Efforts for Change." *New York Times,* September 28, pp. A1, A22.

Tilly, Charles. 1993. *Popular Contention in Great Britain 1758–1834.* Cambridge, MA: Harvard University Press.

Tönnies, Ferdinand. [1887] 1988. *Community and Society.* Rutgers, NJ: Transaction.

Toossi, Mitra. 2002. "A Century of Change: The U.S. Labor Force, 1950–2050." *Monthly Labor Review* (May):15–28.

Touraine, Alain. 1974. *The Academic System in American Society.* New York: McGraw-Hill.

Treiman, Donald J. 1977. *Occupational Prestige in Comparative Perspective.* New York: Academic Press.

Trotter III, Robert T., and Juan Antonio Chavira. 1997. *Curanderismo: Mexican American Folk Healing.* Athens, GA: University of Georgia Press.

Tuchman, Gaye. 1992. "Feminist Theory." Pp. 695–704 in *Encyclopedia of Sociology,* vol. 2, edited by Edgar F. Borgatta and Marie L. Borgatta. New York: Macmillan.

Tumin, Melvin M. 1953. "Some Principles of Stratification: A Critical Analysis." *American Sociological Review* 18 (August):387–394.

———. 1985. *Social Stratification.* 2d ed. Englewood Cliffs, NJ: Prentice Hall.

Turkle, Sherry. 1995. *Life on the Screen: Identity in the Age of the Internet.* New York: Simon and Schuster.

———. 1999. "Looking toward Cyberspace: Beyond Grounded Sociology." *Contemporary Sociology* 28 (November):643–654.

———. 2004. "How Computers Change the Way We Think." *Chronicle of Higher Education* 50 (January 30):B26–B28.

Turner, J. H. 1985. *Herbert Spencer: A Renewed Application.* Beverly Hills, CA: Sage.

Twaddle, Andrew. 1974. "The Concept of Health Status." *Social Science and Medicine* 8 (January):29–38.

Tyler, William D. 1985. "The Organizational Structure of the School." Pp. 49–73 in *Annual Review of Sociology, 1985,* edited by Ralph H. Turner. Palo Alto, CA: Annual Reviews.

Tyre, Peg and Daniel McGinn. 2003. "She Works, He Doesn't." *Newsweek* 141 (May 12), pp. 45–52.

United Jewish Communities. 2003. *The National Jewish Population Survey 2000–2001.* New York : UJC.

United Nations. 2000. *The World's Women 2000: Trends and Statistics.* New York: United Nations.

United Nations. 2003. *Water For People, Water for Life: Executive Summary.* New York: United Nations World Water Assessment Programme.

United Nations Development Programme. 2001. *Human Development Report 2001. Making New Technologies Work for Human Development.* New York: UNDP.

———. 2004. *Human Development Report 2004.* New York: UNDP.

United Nations Population Division. 2004a. *World Population Prospects Population Database.* Accessed October 4, 2004 (http://esa.un.org/unpp).

———. 2004b. *Population Division Homepage: World Percentage Urban."* Accessed October 4 (http://esa.un.org/unpp/ p2kOdata.asp).

United States Trade Representative. 2003. *2002 Annual Report.* Washington, DC: U.S. Government Printing Office.

Urbina, Ian. 2004. "Disco, Rice, and Other Trash Talk." *New York Times,* July 31, p. A11.

Veblen, Thorstein. 1919. *The Vested Interests and the State of the Industrial Arts.* New York: Huebsch.

Verhovek, Sam Howe. 1997. "Racial Tensions in Suit Slowing Drive for 'Environmental Justice,'" *New York Times,* September 7, pp. 1, 16.

Vidaver, R. M., et al. 2000. "Women Subjects in NIH-funded Clinical Research Literature: Lack of Progress in Both Representation and Analysis by Sex." *Journal of Women's Health Gender-Based Medicine* 9 (June):495–504.

Wagley, Charles, and Marvin Harris. 1958. *Minorities in the New World: Six Case Studies.* New York: Columbia University Press.

Waitzkin, Howard. 1986. *The Second Sickness: Contradictions of Capitalist Health Care.* Chicago: University of Chicago Press.

Wallace, Ruth A., and Alison Wolf. 1980. *Contemporary Sociological Theory.* Englewood Cliffs, NJ: Prentice Hall.

Wallerstein, Immanuel. 1974. *The Modern World System.* New York: Academic Press.

———. 1979a. *Capitalist World Economy.* Cambridge: Cambridge University Press.

———. 1979b. *The End of the World As We Know It: Social Science for the Twenty-First Century.* Minneapolis: University of Minnesota Press.

———. 2000. *The Essential Wallerstein.* New York: The New Press.

———. 2004. *World-Systems Analysis: An Introduction.* Durham, NC: Duke University Press.

Walzer, Susan. 1996. "Thinking about the Baby: Gender and Divisions of Infant Care." *Social Problems* 43 (May):219–234.

Watts, Jerry G. 1990. "Pluralism Reconsidered." *Urban Affairs Quarterly* 25 (June):697–704.

Weber, Max. [1913–1922] 1947. *The Theory of Social and Economic Organization.* Translated by A. Henderson and T. Parsons. New York: Free Press.

———. [1904] 1958. *The Protestant Ethic and the Spirit of Capitalism.* Translated by Talcott Parsons. New York: Scribner.

Wechsler, Henry, et al. 2002. "Trends in College Binge Drinking during a Period of Increased Prevention Efforts: Findings from Four Harvard School of Public Health College Alcohol Study Surveys: 1993–2001." *Journal of American College Health* 50 (5):203–217.

Weeks, John R. 2005; *Population: An Introduction to Concepts and Issues.* 9th ed. Belmont, CA: Wadsworth.

Weinberg, Daniel H. 2004. *Evidence from Census 2000 About Earnings by Detailed Occupation for Men and Women.* CENSR-15. Washington, DC: U.S. Government Printing Office.

Weinstein, Deena, and Michael A. Weinstein. 1999. "McDonaldization Enframed." Pp. 57–69 in *Resisting McDonaldization,* edited by Barry Smart. London: Sage.

West, Candace, and Don H. Zimmerman. 1983. "Small Insults: A Study of Interruptions in Cross Sex Conversations between Unacquainted Persons." Pp. 86–111 in *Language, Gender, and Society,* edited by Barrie Thorne, Cheris Kramarae, and Nancy Henley. Rowley, MA: Newbury House.

———, and ———. 1987. "Doing Gender." *Gender and Society* 1 (June): 125–151.

White, Jonathan R. 2002. *Terrorism: An Introduction.* Belmont, CA: Wadsworth.

Whyte, William Foote. 1981. *Street Corner Society: Social Structure of an Italian Slum.* 3d ed. Chicago: University of Chicago Press.

Wickman, Peter M. 1991. "Deviance." Pp. 85–87 in *Encyclopedic Dictionary of Sociology,* 4th ed., by Dushkin Publishing Group. Guilford, CT: Dushkin.

Wilford, John Noble. 1997. "New Clues Show Where People Made the Great Leap to Agriculture." *New York Times,* November 18, pp. B9, B12.

Williams, Wendy M. 1998. "Do Parents Matter? Scholars Need to Explain What Research Really Shows." *Chronicle of Higher Education* 45 (December 11):B6–B7.

Wilson, Barbara J., Stacy L. Smith, W. James Porter, Dale Kunkel, Daniel Linz, Carolyn M. Colvin, and Edward Donnerstein. 2002. "Violence in Children's Televisions Programming: Assessing the Risks." *Journal of Communication* 52 (March):5–35.

Wilson, Edward O. 1975. *Sociobiology: The New Synthesis.* Cambridge, MA: Harvard University Press.

———. 1978. *On Human Nature.* Cambridge, MA: Harvard University Press.

———. 2000. *Sociobiology: The New Synthesis.* Cambridge, MA: Belknap Press, Harvard University Press.

Wilson, John. 1973. *Introduction to Social Movements.* New York: Basic Books.

———. 1978. *Religion in American Society: The Effective Presence.* Englewood Cliffs, NJ: Prentice Hall.

Wilson, William Julius. 1996. *When Work Disappears: The World of the New Urban Poor.* New York: Knopf.

———. 1999. *The Bridge over the Racial Divide: Rising Inequality and Coalition Politics.* Berkeley: University of California Press.

Winter, J. Alan. 1977. *Continuities in the Sociology of Religion.* New York: Harper and Row.

Wirth, Louis. 1928. *The Ghetto.* Chicago: University of Chicago Press.

———. 1931. "Criminal Sociology." *American Journal of Sociology* 37 (July):49–60.

———. 1938. "Urbanism as a Way of Life." *American Journal of Sociology* 44 (July):1–24.

Wolf, Naomi. 1992. *The Beauty Myth: How Images of Beauty Are Used against Women.* New York: Anchor.

Wolff, Edward N. 1999. "Recent Trends in the Distribution of Household Wealth Ownership." In *Back to Shared Prosperity: The Growing Inequality of Wealth and Income in America,* edited by Ray Marshall. New York: M. E. Sharpe.

———. 2002. *Top Heavy.* New ed. New York: New Press.

Wolinsky, Fredric P. 1980. *The Sociology of Health.* Boston: Little, Brown.

Wolraich, Mark, et al. 1998. "Guidance for Effective Discipline." *Pediatrics* 101 (April):723–728.

Woodard, Colin. 1998. "When Rote Learning Fails against the Test of Global Economy." *Christian Science Monitor,* April 15, p. 7.

Wooden, Wayne. 1995. *Renegade Kids, Suburban Outlaws: From Youth Culture to Delinquency.* Belmont, CA: Wadsworth.

World Bank. 2000. *World Development Report 2000/2001.* New York: Oxford University Press.

———. 2003. *Development Indicators 2003.* Washington, DC: World Bank.

———. 2004. *World Development Indicators 2004.* Washington DC: World Bank.

World Resources Institute. 1998. *1998–1999 World Resources: A Guide to the Global Environment.* New York: Oxford University Press.

Wright, Erik Olin, David Hachen, Cynthia Costello, and Joy Sprague. 1982. "The American Class Structure." *American Sociological Review* 47 (December):709–726.

Wurman, Richard Saul. 1989. *Information Anxiety.* New York: Doubleday.

Yamagata, Hisashi, et al. 1997. "Sex Segregation and Glass Ceilings: A Comparative Statistics Model of Women's Career Opportunities in the Federal Government over a Quarter Century." *American Journal of Sociology* 103 (November):566–632.

Yinger, J. Milton. 1970. *The Scientific Study of Religion.* New York: Macmillan.

———. 1974. "Religion, Sociology of." Pp. 604–613 in *Encyclopaedia Britannica,* vol. 15. Chicago: Encyclopedia Britannica.

Young, Alford A., Jr., and Donald R. Deskins, Jr. 2001. "Early Traditions of African-American Sociological Thought." Pp. 445–477 in *Annual Review of Sociology, 2001,* edited by Karen S. Cook and John Hagan. Palo Alto, CA: Annual Reviews.

Zarembo, Alan. 2003. "Funding Studies to Suit Need." *Los Angeles Times,* December 7, pp. A1, A20.

————. "A Theater of Inquiry and Evil." *Los Angeles Times,* July 15, pp. A1, A24, A25.

Zellner, William M. 1995. *Counter Cultures: A Sociological Analysis.* New York: St. Martin's Press.

Zia, Helen. 1993. "Women of Color in Leadership." *Social Policy* 23 (Summer):51–55.

Zimbardo, Philip G., Ann L. Weber, and Robert Johnson. 2003. *Psychology: Core Concepts.* 4th ed. Boston: Allyn and Bacon.

————. 2004. "Power Turns Good Soldiers into 'Bad Apples.'" *Boston Globe,* May 9 (www.prisonexp.org).

Zola, Irving K. 1972. "Medicine as an Institution of Social Control." *Sociological Review* 20 (November):487–504.

————. 1983. *Socio-Medical Inquiries.* Philadelphia: Temple University Press.

Zook, Matthew A. 1996. "The Unorganized Militia Network: Conspiracies, Computers, and Community." *Berkeley Planning Journal* 11:1–15.

Zweigenhaft, Richard L., and G. William Domhoff. 1998. *Diversity in the Power Elite: Have Women and Minorities Reached the Top?* New Haven, CT: Yale University Press.

Acknowledgments

Chapter 2:
P. 46: Cartoon © 2006 by Sidney Harris. Used by permission.

P. 59: Figure 2-1 from "Growing up Wired: Survey on Youth and the Internet in the Silicon Valley." (#3340), The Henry J. Kaiser Family Foundation and the *San Jose Mercury News,* May 2003. This information was reprinted with permission from the Henry J. Kaiser Family Foundation. The Kaiser Family Foundation, based in Menlo Park, CA, is a nonprofit, independent national health care philanthropy and is not associated with Kaiser Permanente or Kaiser Industries.

Chapter 3:
P. 73: Cartoon TOLES © The Buffalo News 2000. Reprinted with permission of UNIVERSAL PRESS SYNDICATE. All rights reserved.

Chapter 4:
P. 95: Table 4-1 from Robert K. Merton. 1968. *Social Theory and Social Structure:* p. 194. Reprinted with permission of The Free Press, a Division of Simon & Schuster Adult Publishing Group. Copyright © 1967, 1968 by Robert K. Merton. All rights reserved.

P. 104: Cartoon © 2006 by Sidney Harris. Used by permission.

Chapter 5:
P. 122: Table 5-2 from James A. Davis, Tom W. Smith, and Peter V. Marsden. 2003. *General Social Surveys, 1972–2002.* Chicago: National Opinion Research Center. Used by permission of National Opinion Research Center.

P. 124: Figure 5-2 from Edward N. Wolff. 1999. "Recent Trends in the Distribution of Household Wealth Ownership." In *Back to Shared Prosperity: The Growing Inequality of Wealth and Income in America,* edited by Ray Marshall. NY: M.E. Sharpe. Reprinted by permission of the author.

Chapter 6:
P. 151: Cartoon by Michael Ramirez, Copley News Service. Used by permission.

Chapter 7:
P. 172: Cartoon © 2006 by Sidney Harris. Used by permission.

Chapter 8:
P. 190: Figure 8-1 in part from Joseph A. McFalls, Jr. 2003. "Population: A Lively Introduction." 4e, *Population Bulletin* 58 (December):23. Used by permission of the Population Reference Bureau.

Chapter 9:
P. 220: Figure 9-1 from G. William Domhoff. 2001. *Who Rules America,* 4th ed.:96. © 2001 by The McGraw-Hill Companies, Inc. Reproduced by permission of the publisher.

P. 228: Cartoon TOLES © The Buffalo News 2000. Reprinted with permission of UNIVERSAL PRESS SYNDICATE. All rights reserved.

Chapter 10:

P. 239: Table 10-1 based on Gideon Sjoberg. 1960. *The Preindustrial City: Past and Present:*323–328. Copyright © 1960 by The Free Press; copyright renewed 1968 by Gideon Sjoberg. Adapted with permission of The Free Press, a division of Simon & Schuster Adult Publishing Group. All rights reserved. And based on E. Barbara Phillips. 1996. *City Lights: Urban-Suburban Life in the Global Society,* 2/e:132–135. Copyright © 1981 by E. Barbara Phillips and Richard T. LeGates, 1996 by E. Barbara Phillips. Used by permission of Oxford University Press, Inc.

P. 241: Figure 10-1 from Chauncy D. Harris & Edward Ullman. 1945. "The Nature of Cities" in *Annals of the American Academy of Political and Social Science,* Volume 242, November 1945.

Chapter 11:

P. 273: Cartoon © 1985 Carol * Simpson. Reprinted by permission of Carol * Simpson Productions.

Photo Credits

Chapter 1: P. 1   A balloon artist entertains his young audience at a street fair in New York City. Sociologists study all kinds of social behavior, from impromptu street gatherings to formally organized meetings. Photo © Bryan Bedder/Getty Images.

Chapter 2: P. 33   In a classroom in Havana, members of the Young Cuban Pioneers learn to weave. Culture is transmitted from one generation to the next through formal schooling and informal experiences with family and friends. Photo © Paul Conklin/ PhotoEdit Inc.

Chapter 3: P. 64   These teenagers may look as if they are just having fun playing miniature golf, but they are also learning. People acquire their norms, values, and expectations by participating in groups. Photo © SW Productions/Getty Images.

Chapter 4: P. 87   Pro-cannabis demonstrators march through New York to promote the legalization of marijuana. The march was one of almost 200 events held around the world in May 2002 under the name "Million Marijuana March." Because deviance is a socially constructed concept, the behaviors a society considers deviant can change over time as society changes. Photo © Spencer Platt/Getty Images.

Chapter 5: P. 111   A prosperous-looking businessman passes a beggar on a city street in Australia. Social inequality exists worldwide, even in relatively well-to-do indus-trialized nations. Up to 20 percent of Australians live in poverty, despite government strategies meant to narrow the growing gap between rich and poor. Photo © Greg Wood/AFP/Getty Images.

Chapter 6: P. 142   College students share a quiet moment between classes. Though people tend to socialize with those who are similar to themselves, the nation's grow-ing diversity, mirrored in the student bodies at our colleges and universities, has increased the likelihood of inter-ethnic and interracial contact. Photo © Doug Menuez/Getty Images.

Chapter 7: P. 165   U.S. Army Privates Cherish Cooper and Atiyhia Goldbold prepare to leave on a mission in Ramadi, west of Baghdad. In the United States today, women are assuming new roles that were once said to be beyond their abilities. Photo ©Patrick Baz/AFP/Getty Images.

Chapter 8: P. 184   In the Republic of Georgia, a family relaxes after a cheese-and-bread dinner around the small wooden table in their two-room apartment. Despite cultural differences from one country to the next, worldwide, the family is probably the most central, vital social institution. Photo ©Jonathan Alpeyrie/Getty Images.

Chapter 9: P. 205   Students at New York University attend their graduation ceremony in Washington Square Park. Higher education has a significant impact on a person's income and career opportunities. Photo ©Mario Tama/Getty Images.

Chapter 10: P. 232   College students clown around on the beach at South Padre Island, Texas, during spring break. Some 125,000 revelers descend on the beach each year for a wild week of sun, sand, and partying. Such large concentrations of people raise serious public health issues, including binge drinking, sexually transmitted diseases, and date rape. Photo ©Joe Raedle/Newsmakers/Getty Images.

Chapter 11: P. 264 Visitors at the Mori Art Museum in Tokyo use the Apple "iPod," a portable digital music player, to listen to a guided tour of an exhibition. New technologies change the way people live, altering their culture in the process. Photo ©Toru Yamanaka/AFP/Getty Images.

Index

Abercrombie, Nicholas, 44, 119
Aberle, David E., 187
Abortion, 276
  and sex selection, 279
Absolute poverty, 125, 289
Abu Ghraib prison, 65
Achieved status, 67–68, 112, 289
  and social mobility, 130
Activism, social, 265–270
Adam, Barry D., 249
Addams, Jane, 11–12, 12, 171
Adler, Freda, 101, 102t
Adler, Patricia A., 25
Adler, Peter, 25
Adolescents
  African American, 53
  drug and alcohol use, 57
Affirmative action, 159, 208, 226, 289
Africa
  AIDS in, 297
  and "brain drain", 247
  life expectancy, 247
  poverty in, 132–133
African Americans
  in adolescence, 53
  and the criminal justice system,
    100
  and discrimination, 158–160
  and education, 208
  and environmental justice,
    259–260
  family support, 195
  and health and illness, 252
  and Internet access, 285f
  media stereotypes, 180–181
  and political power, 222
  in poverty, 127, 127t, 128
  and racial profiling, 99–100,
    142–143
  and slavery, 112, 249
  social mobility of, 131–132
  as sociologists, 12, 15
  U. S. population, 147t
    projected, 148f
  women, 180–181
  in the workforce, 226
African countries, as periphery
  nations, 134
Age, and health and illness, 254–255
Agrarian societies, 75, 77t, 289

AIDS (acquired immune deficiency
    syndrome), 250
  in Africa, 297
  persons with (PWAs), 68, 249
Air pollution, 256–257
Al-Qaeda, 80
Alain, Michel, 266
Alba, Richard, 150
Alcohol use, 57
Alfino, Mark, 37
Allen, Bern P., 90
Allport, Gordon W., 155
Alzheimer's Association, 254
Ameican Medical Association
    (AMA), 275
American Sociological Association
    (ASA), Code of Ethics, 27, 28
Americans With Disabilites Act, 83
Amish community, 56
Andersen, Margaret, 172
Anderson, Sarah, 114
Andrews, Edmund L., 255
Anomie, 94, 289
Anomie theory of deviance, 94–95,
    102t, 289
Anthrax, 72
Anticipatory socialization, 55–56
Appelbaum, Richard, 137
Apple corporation, 264
Applied sociology, 28–29, 289
Arab cultures, 4, 47, 52
Arabs, and racial profiling, 100,
    154–155
Argot, 44, 289
Aristotle, 6
Armer, J. Michael, 138
Ascribed status, 66–67, 112, 289
  and social mobility, 130
Ashe, Arthur, 68
Asian Americans, 147t, 148f, 226,
    285f
Asian countries, as periphery nations,
    134
Associated Press, 260
Astin, Alexander, 43, 214
Australia, crime rates, 107
Authority, 216–222
  definition, 289
  and power, 216–217
    political, 218–222

  types of, 217–218
Avarey, D'Aunn Wester, 98
Aviation and Transportation Security
    Act, 158
Avon corporation, 178
Azumi, Koya, 78

Babad, Elisha, 211
Bachu, Amara, 177
Baker, Wayne E., 138
Bales, Robert, 170
Barbie doll, 37
Barnett, Ida Wells, 12
Basic sociology, 29, 289
Bates, Colleen Dunn, 254
Bauerlein, Monika, 276
BBC (British Broadcasting
    Corporation), 34
Beagan, Brenda L., 248
Beauty myth, 92
Beck, Allen J., 91
Becker, Howard, 99, 249
Beeghley, Leonard, 115
Belgium, gross national income, per
    capita, 133
Bell, Daniel, 76, 276
Bell, Wendell, 138
Belsie, Laurent, 277
Benford, Robert D., 265
Berger, Peter, 189
Best, Amy, 92
Bhandari, Shailesh, 129
Bharadwaj, Lakshmik, 259
Bhutan, cultural change in, 33–34
Bianchi, Susan, 195
Bielby, Denise D., 194
Bielby, William T., 194
Bilateral descent, 289
Bin Laden, Osama, 80
Biological terrorism, 72, 250
Biology, impact on socialization, 50
  and gender differences, 169
Biotechnology, 278–281
Bioterrorism, 72, 250, 280–281
Birth control, 234
Birthrate, 235, 289
Black, Donald, 40, 91
Blau, Peter M., 131
Blauner, Robert, 154

Blumer, Herbert, 265
Body image, 92–93
Bond, James T., 179
Borman, Kathryn M., 213
Bornschier, Volker, 138
Bottomore, Tom, 272
Bourgeosie, 115, 289
Bowles, Samuel, 57, 208, 214
Bradford, Calvin P., 187
Brady, David, 126
Brain drain, 247, 289
Brainard, Jeffrey, 280
Brainard, Lael, 229
Brannigan, Augustine, 77
Brannon, Robert, 168
Bray, James H., 195
Brazil, popular culture, 37
Brettell, Caroline B., 168
Brimmer, Andrew, 161
Brittingham, Angela, 147t
Broad, William J., 281
Brown, D., 209
Brown v. Board of Education, 208
Browne, Irene, 181
Browner, Carol, 260
Buddhism, 197t
Budrys, Grace, 253
Buerger, Michael D., 98
Bulle, Wolfgang F., 40
Bullying, 58–59
Bunzel, John H., 156
Bureau of Justice Statistics, 106
Bureau of Labor Statistics, 83, 179
Bureau of Primary Health Care, 251
Bureaucracy
 characteristics of, 78–81, 79t
 definition, 78, 289
 educational, 211, 212–214
 and organizational culture, 82
 values of, and conflict with pro-
 fessionalism, 214
Burgess, Ernest, 241
Burns, John R., 175
Bush, George W., 154, 198, 218, 255
Butler, Daniel Allen, 111

Caesar, 253
Calvin, John, 199
Cambridge University, 233
Campaign for 100% Access and Zero
 Health Disparities, 251
Canada, popular culture, 37
Capitalism, 115–116, 222–223, 225,
 289
Caplan, Ronald L., 247
Carpenter, Susan, 87

Carter, Jimmy, 129
Carty, Win, 257
Cassidy, Rachel C., 147t
Castells, Manuel, 84
Castes, caste system, 113, 200
 definition, 289
Castro, Fidel, 265
Catalano, Shannan, 106, 107f, 129
Catton, William R., Jr., 258
Causal logic, 20, 289
Cavanagh, John, 114
CBS News, 70
Census, 235, 289
Center for American Women and
 Politics, 174
Centers for Disease Control and
 Prevention (CDC), 250
Cha, Ariena Eunjung, 283
Chambliss, William, 99
Charismatic authority, 218, 267, 290
Chase-Dunn, Christopher, 134, 135,
 138
Chavira, Juan Antonio, 253
Cherlin, Andrew, 195
Chernobyl nuclear accident, 256
Chesney-Lind, Meda, 101, 102t
Childcare, lack of, 179–180
Children
 internet use, 59t
 TV watching, 59, 60
China
 under communism, 224, 225
 as periphery nation, 134
Chinese immigrants, 154
Chinese, U. S. population, 147t
Christ, Jesus, 218
Christianity, 197t, 200
Christians, born again, 202
Chuck D, 264
CIA (Central Intelligence Agency), 80
Cities
 "edge", 242–243
 industrial, 238–239, 239, 239t
 postindustrial, 239t, 240
 preindustrial, 237–238, 239t
Civil Rights Act of 1964, 158
Clark, Burton, 215, 245
Clark, Candace, 249
Clarke, Adele E., 278
Class consciousness, 115–116, 290
Class, social, 113–115, 290
 and health and illness, 129,
 251–252
 and internet access, 278, 284–285
 measuring, 120–122
 multiple measures, 121, 122
 objective method, 121
 in preindustrial societies, 237

and stratification, 120–130
Class system, 113–114, 290
Classical theory, 82, 290
Clinard, Marshall B., 96
Clinical sociology, 29, 290
Clinton, Bill, 260, 280
Cloning, 280
Closed system, 130
Coca-Cola corporation, 138
Cockerham, William, 250
Code of ethics, 290
Code of Ethics (American
 Sociological Association), 27, 28
Cohen, A. K., 187
Cohen, Lawrence E., 98
Cole, Mike, 208
Collective decision making, 83, 290
College students
 binge drinking, 88
 religiosity of, 6
 subcultures, 215
Collins, Randall, 118, 119, 199, 274
Colonialism, 133–134, 290
Colvin, Carolyn M., 27
Commission on Civil Rights, 158,
 176
Commoner, Barry, 234, 257, 257–258
Communication
 nonverbal, 17, 39
 and symbols, 52
 and technology, 72, 281–282
Communism, 115–116, 224–225, 290
Communist governments, collapse of,
 273–274
Communist League, 10
Communist Manifesto (Marx and
 Engels), 10, 135
Communities, early, 236–237
Community, definition, 236, 290
Computer Security Institute, 104
Computers. *see* Internet; Technology
Comte, Auguste, 8, 270–271
Concentric-zone theory, 241–242, 290
Conflict perspective, 14–15, 18t, 290
 on culture, 48t
 on deviance, 100–101, 102t
 on educational institutions,
 208–211, 212t, 213–214
 on the environment, 258–259
 on the family, 193, 194, 196t
 on gender inequality, 173t
 on health and illness, 246–247
 on immigration, 152–153
 and Marxist theory, 118–119, 272
 on modernization, 138
 on multinational corporations,
 137–138
 on religion, 199–200, 202t

on schools, 58
on sex selection, 279
on social control, 88
on social inequality, 154–155,
    170–171
on sociobiology, 50
on stratification, 118–119, 120t
    and access to technology, 284
on study of social institutions,
    187–188
on subcultures, 45
on urbanization, 243–244
on white-collar crime, 105
Conformity, 89, 290
    in anomie theory of deviance, 95
Conrad, Peter, 245, 246, 247
Constitution, United States, 235
Contact hypothesis, 155, 290
Content analysis, 290
Contraception, 234
Control group, 26, 290
Control variable, 23, 290
Cooley, Charles Horton, 11, 51, 70
Cooper, Richard T., 60
Core nations, and periphery nations,
    134–135
Corporate crime, 104
Corporate downsizing, 227
Corporations, multinational, 136–137,
    294
Correlation, 21, 290
Correll, Joshua, 143
Coser, Lewis, 119
Cosmetic surgery, 93
Couch, Carl, 218
Council on Scientific Affairs, 253
Countercultures, 45–46, 290
Cox, Oliver, 154
Credentialism, 209, 290
Cressey, Donald R., 98
Crime, 102–108, 290
    corporate, 104
    definition, 101
    organized, 103
    and the poor, 129
    professional, 102–103
    statistics, 105–108
    technology-based, 103–105,
        283–284
    victimless, 105
    violent, 102, 107
    white-collar, 103–105
Crime rates
    international, 107
Criminal justice system, 100
    and DNA evidence, 284
    rates of incarceration, by nation,
        108

Cromwell, Paul F., 98
Crouse, Kelly, 111
Cuba, 224, 225
Cuff, E. C., 119
Cullen, Francis T., Jr., 100
Cullen, John B., 100
Cultural relativism, 48, 290
Cultural transmission theory, of
    deviance, 97–98, 102t, 290
Cultural universal, 36, 290
Culture, 34–47, 290
    development of, 35–36
    elements of, 38–43
    variation in, 44–47
Culture lag, 275–276, 290
Culture shock, 46–47, 290
Curanderismo, 253, 290
Currie, Elliot, 108
Curry, Timothy Jon, 246
Cushman, John H., Jr., 260
Cussins, Choris M., 192
Czechoslovakia, 225

Dahl, Robert, Who Governs?, 221
Dahrendorf, Ralf, 15, 119, 273
Dalaker, Joseph, 126
Darwin, Charles, On the Origin of
    Species, 9
Das Kapital (Marx), 272
Data collection and analysis, 21–22
Daugherty, Kevin, 212
Davies, J. A., 23t
Davis, A. K., 187
Davis, James, 131
Davis, James A., 122t
Davis, Kingsley, 14, 50, 118, 238
Davis, Nanette J., 100
De Andra, Roberto M., 181
De Bois, W. E. B., 15
De la Cruz, G. Patricia, 147t
Death penalty
    and DNA evidence, 284
Death Penalty Information Center,
    284
Death rate, 291
Declaration of Independence, 176
Decriminalization, of victimless
    crime, 105
Degradation ceremonies, 56, 291
Deindustrialization, 227–228, 229,
    291
Deinstitutionalization, of mentally ill,
    128
Demarest, Jack, 168
Demography, 233–237, 291
    elements of, 235–237

Demuth, Stephen, 100
DeNavas-Walt, Carmen, 114, 115,
    123t, 125, 129, 161t, 251f
DePalma, Anthony, 37, 229
Department of Justice, 102, 106
    Computer Crime and Intellectual
        Property section, 284
Department of Labor, 157, 179
Dependency theory, 291
Dependent variable, 20, 291
Descent, patterns of familial, 192
Deskins, Donald R., 16
Developing countries, 132–139
    access to modern technology, 278
    influence of colonialism, 133–134
    poverty in, 132–133
Deviance, 92, 92–108, 102t, 108, 291
    biological theories of, 93
    conflict perspective, 100–101,
        102t
    cultural transmission theory,
        97–98
    Durkheim's theory of, 94
    feminist perspective, 101, 102t
    functionalist perspective, 94–96
    interactionist perspective, 96–100
    and labeling theory, 99–100
    Merton's theory of, 94–96
    theories of, comparison, 102t
Dickson, W. J., 82
Differential association, 97–98, 291
Diffusion, 291
Digital divide, 284–285
DiMaggio, Paul, 84, 284
Disability, as master status, 68
Discovery, 36, 291
Discrimination, 156–158, 291
    gender, 210–211
        and sexism, 174
    institutional, 157–158
    measuring, 159–160
Diversity in the Power Elite
    (Zweigenhaft), 221
Division of labor, 79, 79t, 80
Divorce rates, 190
DNA evidence, criminal, 284
Domhoff, G. William, 220f, 221
Dominant group, privileges of,
    143–144
Dominant ideology, 43–44, 291
Donnerstein, Edward, 27
Downie, Andrew, 37
Downsizing, corporate, 227, 291
    global perspective, 227–229
Doyle, James, 168
Dramaturgical approach, 54, 291
Dreier, Peter, 137
Drezner, Daniel, 229, 306

Drown, Rachel, 214
Drug abuse, 57
Drug use, illegal, 105
Duncan, Otis Dudley, 131
Duneier, Mitchell, 188
Dunkin' Donuts, 138
Dunlap, Riley E., 258
Durkheim, Emile, 7–8, 9, 27, 94, 196, 196–197, 270–271
DWB (driving while black), 99

Eastern Europe, 224–225, 273–274
Economic system, 291
    definition, 222
Economic systems, 222–225
    capitalism, 222–223, 225
    communism, 224–225
    socialism, 224
Economist, The, 52
Edalitarian family, 291
Edge cities, 242–243
Edquilibrium model, 291
Education, 206, 291
Education Week, 214
Educational institutions. *See also* Schools
    conflict perspective, 208–211, 212t, 213
    functionalist perspective, 206–208, 212t
    and hidden curriculum, 209
    interactionist perspective, 212t
    sexism in, 210–211
Educational level
    and income, 23t, 160
        median, by race and sex, 161t
    and social mobility, 131
Educationan Act of 1972, 211
Efron, Sonni, 210
Egalitarian family, 192
Ehrlich, Paul R. and Anne H., 257
    The Population Bomb, 234
Einstein, Albert, 72
Ekman, Paul, 39
Elderly, and health and illness, 254–255
Electric shock expiments, of Milgram, 89–90
Elite model of authority, 218, 291
Ellison, Katherine, 257
Elmer-DeWitt, Philip, 282
Engelberg, Stephen, 281
Engels, Friedrich, 10–11, 17, 135, 193, 266
    The Origin of the Family, Private Property, and the State, 171

England. *See* Great Britain
Entine, Jon, 137
Environment, and socialization, 49–50
Environment, the, 255–260
    conflict perspective, 258–259
    pollution, 256–257
Environmental activists, 269
Environmental justice, 259–260, 291
Environmental Protection Agency (EPA), 260
Epidemiology, social, 250–251, 297
Epstein, Cynthia Fuchs, 180
Essays on the Principle of Population (Malthus), 233–234
Estate system, of stratification, 113, 291
Esteem, 121, 291
Ethnic group, definition, 291
Ethnic groups, 145–146
    U. S. population, 147t
        projected, 148f
    white, 149
Ethnicity, 148–149
Ethnocentrism, 47, 156, 291
Ethnography, 25, 291
Etzioni, Amitai, 78
European Union, economic system, 225
Evans, Peter, 138
Evolutionary theory, 291
    of social change, 270–271
Experiment, 26, 291
Experimental group, 26, 28t, 291
Exploitation, 291
Exploitation theory, 154
Expressiveness, 170, 291
Extended family, 189, 291
Exxon Valdez oil spill, 257

FAIR US, 152
Faith-based organizations, 198
False consciousness, 116, 267, 292
Faludi, Susan, 169
Family
    as agent of socialization, 56–57
    authority patterns, 192
    conflict perspective, 193, 194, 196t
    definition, 189, 292
    dual-income, 195
    egalitarian, 192
    extended, 189
    feminist perspective, 195–196, 196t
    functionalist perspective, 193–194, 196t

interactionist perspective, 194–195, 196t
    nuclear, 189
    single-parent, 195
    as social institution, 189–191
    structure, 189–192
Farr, Grant M., 192
FBI (Federal Bureau of Investigation), 80, 104
Feagin, Joe R., 216, 243, 244
Featherman, David L., 131
Feketekuty, Geza, 135
Felson, Marcus, 98
Female circumcision, 176
Feminist perspective, 16, 292
    on deviance, 101, 102t
    on the family, 195–196, 196t
    on gender inequality, 171–172, 173t
Feminization of poverty, 175, 292
Ferree, Myra Marx, 268
Fertility, 233, 292
Fertility rate, total (TFR), 236
Feuer, Lewis S., 135, 171
Fiala, Robert, 276
Fields, Jason, 190f
Filipinos, U. S. population, 147t
Finkel, Steven E., 266
Fishman, Jennifer R., 278
Fitton, Laura, 260
Fitzgerald, Kathleen J., 267
Flacks, Richard, 46
Folkways, 40, 292
Foner, Anne, 276
Force, 216, 292
Formal norms, 39, 292
Formal organizations, 78, 292
Formal social control, 91, 292
Fortune 1000, 178
Fortune magazine, 157
Foster, Jodie, 49
France, Muslim culture in, 52
Francis, D. W., 119
Free enterprise system, 223
Freidson, Eliot, 246
Fridlund, Alan J., 39
Friedland, Jonathon, 247
Friedrichs, David O., 103
Friends (TV show), 145
Frohne, Ursula, 283
Functionalist perspective, 13–14, 18t, 117–118, 292
    on culture, 48t
    on deviance, 94–96, 102t
    on educational institutions, 206–208, 213
    on ethnocentrism, 47
    on the family, 193–194

on gender inequality, 173t
on health and illness, 245–246
on immigration, 152
on modernization, 138
on multinational corporations, 136–137
on poverty, 128
on religion, 196–197, 197–198, 202t
on schools, 58
on sex selection, 279
on social change, 271–272
on social control, 88
on social inequality, 153–154, 169–170
on sociobiology, 50
on stratification, 120t
on study of social institutions, 185–187
on subcultures, 45
on urbanization, 241–242
Furstenberg, Frank, 195
Fusket, Jennifer Ruth, 278

Galinsky, Ellen, 179
Gamson, Joshua, 267
Gandhi, Mahatma, 218
Gans, Herbert, 128
Gap clothing, 137
Garfinkel, Harold, 56
Garner, Roberta, 268, 269
Garreau, Joel, 242
Gartin, Patrick R., 98
Gates, Henry Lewis, Jr., 284
Gauette, Nicole, 58
Gecas, Victor, 51, 55
Gelbspan, Ross, 255
Gemeinschaft, 74, 282, 292
Gender
    and health and illness, 253–254
    and income, median, 161t
    social construction of, 166–169
    and social mobility, 132
    and social movements, 268
    switching, internet, 282
Gender inequality, 165–183
    conflict perspective, 170–171, 173t
    and discrimination, 174, 210–211
    feminist perspective, 173t
    functionalist perspective, 169–170, 173t
    global perspective, 175–176
    interactionist perspective, 172–173, 173t
    and sex selection, 279

Gender roles, 57, 166, 167–168
    definition, 292
    nature vs. nurture, 169
General Accounting Office, 178
General Motors corporation, 227
General Social Survey (GSS), 22
Generalized other, 53, 292
Genetic engineering, 279–280
Genetically modified foods (GMO), 280
Genital mulilation, female, 176
Germany, 47
Gerth, H. H., 10, 116, 127, 128, 209
Gesellschaft, 74, 282, 292
Gezari, Vanessa, 279
Gibson, William, 282
Gintis, Herbert, 57, 208, 214
Giordano, Peggy C., 54
Glass ceiling, 157, 177, 292
Glass Ceiling Commission, 157
Global perspective
    on health care, 247
    on inequality, 132–139
    on Internet access, 278
    on job outsourcing, 227–229
    on social change, 273–274
    on social structure, 73–78
    on stratification, 117–118, 243–244
Global Reach, 277
Global warming, 255
Globalization, 36–37, 292
    cultural, 37–38
    and poverty, 135–136
Goal displacement, 81, 292
Goffman, Erving, 54, 55, 92, 93
Golden, Frederic, 280
Golden West Financial, 178
Goldman, Benjamin A., 260
Goode, Erica, 129
Gorbachev, Mikhail, 274
Gottdiener, Mark, 243, 244
Gouldner, Alvin, 272
Gramsci, Antonio, 43–44
Great Britain, 16, 107, 108
Greece, rate of incarceration, 108
Greeley, Andrew M., 199
Greenhouse, Linda, 175
Greenwald, Anthony G., 142–143
Grieco, Elizabeth M., 147t
Grimes, Peter, 134, 135, 138
Groups, 70–71
    definition, 70, 292
Growth rate, 236, 292
Guardian, The, 33, 34
Gun use, in U. S., 5
Guterman, Lila, 50

Hacker, Andrew, 219
Hacker, Helen Mayer, 171, 181
Hage, Jerald, 78
Haines, Valerie A., 271
Hajj, 201–202
Hall, Mimi, 279
Hall, Robert H., 252
Hallinan, Maureen, 210, 273, 274
Hammack, Floyd M., 212
Haney, Craig, 64
Harap, Louis, 200
Hargittai, Eszter, 84, 284
Harnan, Vera, 216
Harris, Chauncy D., 241f, 242
Harris, Judith Rich, 56
Harris, Marvin, 146
Hartman, Chris, 114
Hastie, Reid, 257
Haub, Carl, 247, 248, 250
Hauser, Robert M., 131
Havel, Vaclav, 265
Haviland, William A., 38, 184
Hawkins, Darnell F., 100
Hawthorne effect, 26, 27, 292
Hawthorne studies, 82
HBO (Home Box Office channel), 33
Head Start program, 208
Health and illness, 244–250
    and age, 254–255
    conflict perspective, 246–247
    functionalist perspective, 245–246
    and gender, 253–254
    interactionist perspective, 248
    and labeling theory, 248–249
    occupational illness, 252
    and poverty, 251
    and race and ethnicity, 252–253
    and social class, 129, 251–252
Health care
    folk medicine, 253
    global perspective, 247
    inequities of, 247–248
Health, definition, 244–245, 292
Health insurance, 251–252
Heckert, Druann, 92
Hedley, R. Allan, 138
Henry L. Stimson Center, 250
Heredity
    vs. environment, 48, 49
    and socialization, 50
Hewlett-Packard, 178
Hickman, Jonathan, 157
Hidden curriculum, 209, 292
Hierarchy of authority, 79t, 80
    minimal, 83
Hill, Laura E., 145
Hill, Stephen, 44, 119
Hindu cultures, 175

Hinduism, 197t
  and caste system, 200
Hispanics, 148–149
  and the criminal justice system, 100
  and discrimination, 159–160
  and education, 208
  and health and illness, 252, 253
  and Internet access, 285f
  and political power, 222
  in poverty, 127t, 128
  U. S. population, 147t
    projected, 148f
  women, 181
  in the workforce, 226
History, of sociology, 5
Hitler, Adolf, 218
HIV (human immunodeficiency
    virus), 249, 250
  persons with AIDS (PWAs), 249
Hochschild, Arlie, 179, 195
Hodge, Robert W., 121
Hoebel, E. Adamson, 153
Hoffman, Lois Wladis, 50
Hollingshead, August B., 215
Homans, George C., 49
Homophobia, 292
Horizontal mobility, 130, 292
Horowitz, Helen Lefkowitz, 215
Horticultural societies, 75, 237, 292
Household, U. S., by family types,
    190f
Hout, Michael, 132
Howard, Judith A., 172
Howard, Philip E., 283
Hughes, Everett, 68
Huie, Stephanie A. Bond, 129
Hull House, 12
Hull, Raymond, 81
Human ecology, 241, 257–258, 292
Human Genome Project, 280
Human relations approach, 82, 292
Hummer, Robert A., 129
Hunter, David, 198
Hunter, Herbert M., 154
Hunting-and-gathering societies, 75,
    77t, 236–237, 293
Hurn, Christopher J., 208, 209
Hussein, Saddam, 218
Hussey, Mark, 167
Hutchinson, Ray, 243, 244
Hypothesis, 20, 293
  fornumating, 20–21
  supporting, 22–23

Ideal type, 10, 293
Ijime, 58–59

Illness. *See* Health and illness
Immigration, 149–153
  conflict perspective, 152–153
  functionalist perspective, 152
  history of, 150–152
Impression management, 54, 293
In-groups, 71, 293
In vitro fertilization, 279
Incarceration, rate of, 108
Incest, 184
Incidence, 250, 293
Income, 111, 293
  distribution, United States,
    122–123, 123t
  and educational level, 23t, 160
  inequality, 113–114, 122–124
  median, by race and sex, 161t
  and wealth, 122–124
Independent variable, 20, 293
India, 200
Industrial city, 293
Industrial revolution, 238–239
Industrial societies, 76, 77t, 293
Infant mortality rate, 236, 293
  in Africa, 247
  and race, 252
  in United States, 248, 252
Influence, 216–217, 293
Informal norms, 40
Informal social control, 90, 293
Inglehart, Ronald, 138
Innovation, 36, 293
  in anomie theory of deviance, 95t,
    96
Inpersonality, bureaucratic, 79t, 81
Institute of International Education,
    208
Institutional discrimination, 157–158,
    293
Institutions, social. *See* Social institu-
    tions
Instrumentality, 170, 293
Interactionist perspective, 16–17, 18t,
    293
  on culture, 48t
  on deviance, 96–100, 102t
  on educational institutions, 211,
    212t
  on the family, 194–195, 196t
  on gender inequality, 172–173,
    173t
  on health and illness, 248
  on racism, 153
  on religion, 200–203, 202t
  on sociobiology, 50
  on study of social institutions,
    188–189

  on urbanization, 242–243
  on the workplace, 226
Intercom, 232
Intergenerational mobility, 130, 293
International Crime Victim Survey,
    107
International Monetary Fund, 134,
    135
Internet, 277–278
  access
    in developing countries, 278
    and social class, 278
  and crime, 103–104
  and gender-switching, 282
  music downloading, 264
  and social interaction, 282
  and social movements, 268
  use, by children, 59t
Interviews, 24, 28t, 293
Intragenerational mobility, 130, 293
Invention, 293
Iraq, 47, 218
  prisoner abuse scandal, 65
"Isabelle", 49–50
Islam. *See* Muslim rituals, 197t,
    201–202
Islamic fundamentalism, 274
Isolation, social, 49–50
Israel, as core nation, 134
Italy, crime rates, 107

Jackson, Elton F., 97, 98
Jackson, Philip, 209
Jacobson, Lenore, 211
Japan
  as core nation, 134
  culture, 47
  economic system, 225
  gross national income, per capita,
    133
  management style in, 83
  popular culture, 37
  school experience in, 58–59
Jasper, James M., 269, 275
Jenkins, Richard, 114
Jesus Christ, 218
Jiang Zemin, 225
Jobtrak.com, 60
Johnson, Benton, 272
Johnson, Hans, 145
Johnson, John M., 25
Jones, Del, 178
Jones, James T., IV, 175
Jones, Steve, 283
Judaism, 197t
Juhasz, Anne McCreary, 54

Kahn, Robert L., 276
Kalb, Claudia, 93
Katovich, Michael A., 90
Katsillis, John, 138
Kelly, John, 195
Kennedy, John F., 117, 218
Kerbo, Harold R., 118
King, Elliot, 278
King, Martin Luther, Jr., 218, 267
Kinship, 191, 293
    patterns of, 184, 191–192
Kitt, Alice S., 72
Kochhar, Rakesh, 160
Kolata, Gina, 279
Komarovsky, Mirra, 16
Koolhas, Rem, 240
Koreans, U. S. population, 147t
Korn, William S., 214
Kortenhaus, Carole M., 168
Kottak, Conrad, 184
Krueger, Patrick M., 129
Ku Klux Klan, 156
Kunkel, Dale, 27
Kyoto protocol, 255

Labeling theory, 99–100, 293
    and health and illness, 248–249
Labor force, composition, by race and
    ethnicity, 226f
Laden, Osama bin, 80
Laissez-faire, 223, 293
Landtman, Gunnar, 117
Lang, Eric, 26
Language, 38–39, 293
    and subcultures, 44–45
Larry King Live (TV show), 33
Lasswell, Harold, 216
Latent functions, 14, 293
Latin American countries, as periph-
    ery nations, 134
Latinas. *See* Hispanics, women
Latinos. *See* Hispanics
Lauer, Robert H., 272
Law, 91, 293
Leavell, Hugh R., 245
Legal-rational authority, 217–218,
    293
Leinwand, Donna, 57
Leng, M. J., Jr., 187
Lengermann, Patricia Madoo, 9, 12
Lenski, Gerhard, 37–38, 73, 74–75, 77,
    120, 237, 271
Leondar-Wright, Betsy, 114
Levin, Thomas Y., 283
Lieberman, David, 285
Life chances, 128–129, 293

Life course approach, 55, 293
Life expectancy, 236, 293
    developing countries, 247
    and race, 252
Lin, Nan, 72, 121
Lindbergh, Anne Morrow, 179
Lindsey, Linda L., 167
Linz, Daniel, 27
Lipset, Seymour Martin, 124
Lipson, Karen, 49
Litam, Robert E., 229
Literature review, 20
Livernash, Robert, 259
Lohr, Steve, 285
Looking-glass self, 294
Love Canal, 256, 257, 258
Lucent Technologies, 178
Luckmann, Thomas, 189
Luddites, 276, 294
Lukacs, Georg, 43–44
Lynn, Barry, 227
Lyotard, Jean Francois, 77

MacDorman, Marian F., 252
Mack, Raymond W., 187
Maguire, Meredith B., 105
Maharaj (author), 133
Malcolm X, 68, 202, 218
Malthus, Thomas, Essays on the
    Principle of Population, 233–234
Mandela, Nelson, 265
Mangum, Garth L., 128
Mangum, Stephen L., 128
Manifest functions, 14, 294
Margolis, Eric, 209
Mark, Karl, 10–11
Maro, Laura, 278
Marriage
    rape in, 101
    types of, 190–191
Marsden, Peter V., 122t
Martin, Philip, 150f
Martin, Susan E., 69
Martineau, Harriet, 8–9
Marx, Karl, 10–11, 112, 115, 118,
    135, 154, 171, 193, 199–200,
    219, 224–225, 234, 266, 267
    Das Kapital, 272
Marxist theory, 10–11, 15
    and class differentiation,
        115–116, 154
    and conflict perspective, 118–119,
        272
    and neo-Malthusians, 234
    and relative deprivation approach,
        266

and resource mobilization
    approach, 267
Massachusetts Department of
    Education, 215
Master status, 68, 294
Material culture, 275, 294
Mathews, T. J., 252
Matriarchy, 192, 294
Matrilineal descent, 192, 294
Matsushita, Yoshiko, 59
McBride, Bunny, 184
McCreary, D., 169
McDonald, Kim A., 254
McDonaldization, 37, 278
McFalls, Joseph A., Jr., 190f
McGinn, Daniel, 195
McIntosh, Peggy, 143–144
McKinlay, John B., 246
McKinlay, Sonja M., 246
McSpotlight, 283
Mead, George Herbert, 16–17, 51,
    51–52, 282
    theory of the self, 53–54
Mead, Margaret, 171
    Sex and Temperament, 169
Media, as agents of socialization,
    59–60
    and stereotypes, 167–168, 180–181
Medical establishment
    racism in, 249, 252–253
    resistance to change, 275
Medicalization of society, 246–247
Melia, Marilyn Kennedy, 226
Menacker, Fay, 252
Merrill, David A., 268
Merton, Robert, 12, 14, 72, 81,
    94–95, 102t
Mexico, rate of incarceration, 108
Michels, Robert, 267
Microsoft corporation, 223
Middle class, African American, 132
Middle Eastern cultures, 4, 47, 52,
    201–202
Midgley, Elizabeth, 150f
Milgram, Stanley, 89–90
Mill, John Stuart, *The Subjection of
    Women,* 171
Miller, David, 3, 4
Miller, G. Tyler, Jr., 259
Miller, Judith, 281
Miller, Robert F., 96
Mills, C. Wright, 3, 116, 128, 209,
    219–220
    The Power Elite, 219
Mills, Robert J., 129
Minimal hierarchy, 83
Minimum wage, 124–128, 125f

Minorities
    and political power, 222
    in the workforce, 225–226
Minority groups, 146, 294
Mirant, 178
Mississippi, 240
Modernization, 138–139, 294
Modernization theory, 138
Monogamy, 294
Monopoly, 223, 294
Monsanto corporation, 277
Monteiro, Lois A., 249
Moon, Youngme, 282
Moore, Wilbert E., 60, 118, 264
Morbidity rate, 250–251, 294
Morehouse Medical Treatment
    Effectiveness Center, 253
Mores, 40, 294
Morris, Aldon, 267
Morrison, Denton E., 266
Mortality, 233
Mortality rate, 250, 294
    infant, 236
Mosley, J., 195
Mulinowa, Adolphe, 132–133
Mullins, Marcy E., 281
Multilinear evolutionary theory, 271,
    294
Multinational corporations, 294
    conflict perspective, 137–138
    functionalist perspective, 136–137
    and global poverty, 136–137
Multiple-nuclei theory, 242, 294
Mumola, Christopher J., 57
Murdock, George, 36, 185, 191, 192
Murphy, D., 243
Murray, Velma McBride, 195
Muslim. See Islam cultures, 4, 47, 52
    racial profiling of Muslims, 100,
        154–155
    religious rituals, 197t, 201–202

NAACP (National Association for the
    Advancement of Colored People),
    15, 285
Nader, Laura, 176
Nash, Manning, 153
Nass, Clifford, 282
National Advisory Commission on
    Criminal Justice, 103
National Center for Education
    Statistics, 208
National Center for Health Statistics,
    252
National Center on Women and
    Family Law, 101

National Crime Victimization Survey,
    129
National Marriage Project, 190
National Opinion Research Center
    (NORC), 22
National Rifle Association (NRA), 5
Native Americans
    and health and illness, 252
    in poverty, 126
    U. S. population, 147t
        projected, 147t
Natural science, 4, 294
Nature vs. nurture, 48, 49
    and gender differences, 169
Nell (film), 49
Nelson, Alan R., 253
Nelson, F. Howard, 214
Neo-Malthusian view, 234
Neocolonialism, 134, 294
    and multinational corporations,
        136
Networking, 72
    women, 188–189
Neuborne, Ellen, 283
Neuman, W. Russell, 84, 284
New Guinea, 117
New Orleans Medical Journal, 249
New social movements, 269, 270t,
    294
New urban sociology, 243, 294
New Zealand, crime rates, 107
Newport, Frank, 202t
Nichols, Martha, 137
Nie, Norman H., 283
Niebrigge-Brantley, Jill, 9, 12
Nigeria, body image in, 92
Nike corporation, 137
Nikitah, Imani, 216
NIMBY (not in my backyard), 45,
    275
Nolan, Patrick, 37–38, 75, 120, 237
Nonmaterial culture, 275, 294
Nonverbal communication, 17, 39,
    294
Noonan, Rita K., 268
Nordhaus, William D., 122
Norms, 42t, 294
    acceptance of, 40–41
    formal vs. informal, 39–40
Norway, gross national income per
    capita, 133
Nuclear family, 189, 294
Nussbaum, Daniel, 257

Obedience, 89, 294
Oberlin College, 210

Oberschall, Anthony, 267
Objective method, 294
    and measurement of stratification,
        121
Observation, 28t, 295
Occupational mobility, 131
Occupations
    dangerous, 252
    gender-stereotyped, 177
    prestige rankings of, 121, 122t
O'Connell, Martin, 177
Office of Justice Programs, 103
Ogburn, William F., 38, 194, 275, 280
Okamoto, Dina G., 173
Okano, Kaori, 209
Oliver, Melvin L., 124
Olson, James N., 98
On the Origin of Species (Darwin), 9
Open system, 130, 295
Operational definition, 18, 295
Organizations, formal, 78
Organized crime, 103, 295
*Origin of the Family, Private
    Property, and the State* (Engels),
    171
Orum, Anthony M., 266
Ouchi, William, 83
Out-groups, 71, 295
Outsourcing, job, 227–229
Ozone layer, 257

Pager, Devah, 159
Pakistan, and "brain drain", 247
Papua, New Guinea, 117
Park, Bernadette, 142
Park, Robert, 241
Parks, Malcolm R., 282
Parrott, Sarah A., 214
Parsons, Talcott, 13–14, 170, 245, 271
Patriarchy, 192, 295
Patrilineal descent, 192, 295
Paul, Pamela, 255
Pearlstein, Steven, 135
Peer group, as agent of socialization,
    58–59
People's Republic of China, 224, 225
Periphery nations, and core nations,
    134–135
Perrow, Charles, 82
Personality, 34, 295
Peter, Laurence J., 81
Peter principle, 81, 295
Petersen, William, 234
Phillips, E. Barbara, 240
Piller, Charles, 283
Pinderhughes, Dianne, 222

Pinkerton, James P., 210
Plastic surgery, 93
Pluralist model, of power, 221, 295
Poland, Solidarity movement, 224–225
Political power, U. S., 218–222
  and minority groups, 222
Politics, 216, 295
Polletta, Francesca, 269
Pollution, 256–257
Polyandry, 191, 295
Polygamy, 191, 295
Polygyny, 295
Poor, urban, 240, 243, 244
Population
  growth, 232–233
  study of, 233–236
  modern, 235
Population Bomb, The (Ehrlich and Ehrlich), 234
Porter, James, 27
Postindustrial cities, 240, 295
Postindustrial societies, 76, 77t, 295
Postmodern societies, 77t, 295
Poverty, 124–133
  absolute, 125
  feminization of, 126–127, 132, 175
  functionalist perspective, 128
  global, 132–133
  and health and illness, 247–248, 251
  and Internet access, 284–285
  and life chances, 128–129
  and race, 127, 128, 131–132
  relative, 126
  studying, 125–126
Poverty line, 125
Power, 117, 295
  and authority, 216–217
Power elite, 295
  models, 219–221, 220f
Power Elite, The (Mills), 219
Preindustrial cities, 237–238, 295
Prejudice, 156, 295
Prestige, 121, 295
Prevalence, 250, 295
Priest, George L., 257
Primary group, 70, 295
Prins, Harald E. L., 184
Prison experiment, 64–65, 68
Prisoner abuse, in Iraq, 65
Proctor, Bernadette D., 126
Professional crime, 102
Professional criminal, 102, 295
Project Head Start, 208
Proletariat, 115, 295
Prostitution, 105

Protestant ethic, 199, 295
Protestant Ethic and the Spirit of Capitalism (Weber), 199
Psychology, 5
Pure sociology, 29
Pythagoras, 6

Qaeda, al-, 80
Qualitative research, 25, 295
Quantitative research, 25, 295
Questionnaires, 24, 28t, 295
Quinceanera ceremony, 54
Quinney, Richard, 100, 102t

Race
  and educaiton, 208
  and health and illness, 252–253
  and income, median, 161t
  and Internet access, 284–285
  social construction of, 144–145
  and social mobility, 131–132
Racial and ethnic inequality, 153–155
  conflict perspective, 154–155
  functionalist perspective, 153–154
  interactionist perspective, 153
Racial groups, 145, 295
  U. S. population, 147t
    projected, 148f
Racial profiling, 99–100, 142–143, 154, 295
  of Arabs and Muslims, 100, 154–155
Racism, 99–100, 142–144
  definition, 156, 296
  environmental, 259–260
  in the medical establishment, 249, 252–253
Rainie, Lee, 283
Ramet, Sabrina, 265
Random sample, 21, 296
Rantala, Ramona R., 104
Rape, 101
Raybon, Patricia, 180
Reagan, Ronald, 129, 218
Reality, defining, 65–66
Rebellion, in anomie theory of deviance, 95t, 96
Reddick, Randy, 278
Reebok corporation, 137
Reference groups, 71–72, 296
Relative deprivation approach, to social change, 266, 270t, 296
Relative poverty, 126, 296
Reliability, 22, 296
Religion, 296

conflict perspective, 199–200, 202t
  definition, 196
  functionalist perspective, 196–197, 197–198, 202t
  interactionist perspective, 200–203, 202t
  and social change, 198–199
Religions, major world, 197t
Religiosity, of college students, 6
Religious behavior, 200–203
Religious beliefs, 201, 296
Religious experience, 202, 296
Religious fundamentalism, 274
Religious rituals, 201–202, 296
Research design, definition, 296
Research designs, 24–27, 28t
Research, qualitative vs. quantitative, 25
Resocialization, 55, 296
Resource mobilization approach, to social change, 266–267, 270t, 296
Retreatism, in anomie theory of deviance, 95t, 96
Richardson, L., 195
Richtel, Matt, 227
Rideout, Victoria J., 60
Ridgeway, Cecilia L., 173
Riding, Alan, 111
Rifkin, Jeremy, 276
Riley, Matilda White, 276
Rites of passage, 54–55
Ritualism, in anomie theory of deviance, 95t, 96
Ritzer, George, 37, 278
Roberts, Lynne D., 282
Robertson, Roland, 44, 119
Robinson, John P., 84, 284
Rodenburg, Eric, 259
Rodgers, Diane M., 267
Roethlisberger, Fritz J., 82
Rogers, Richard G., 129
Role conflict, 69, 296
Role strain, 69–70, 296
Role taking, 52, 296
Roles, 68–70
Roosevelt, Franklin D., 218
Rose, Arnold, 153
Rosenberg, Douglas H., 115, 223
Rosenthal, Robert, 211
Rossi, Peter H., 121
Rossides, Daniel, 114–115
Roszak, Theodore, 46
Routine activities theory, 98, 296
Rubel, Maximilien, 272
Rubin, Alissa J., 41
Rule, James B., 266

Russia
    under communism, 224
    crime rates, 107–108
    rate of incarceration, 108
Ryan, William, 128

Sabbathday Lake, 185
Sadker, David Miller, 210
Sadker, Myra Pollack, 210
Safire, William, 227
Sale, Kirkpatrick, 276
Salkever, Alex, 281
Sample, 21, 296
Samuelson, Paul A., 122
Samuelson, Robert J., 227
Sanctions, 41–42, 42t, 88, 296
Sanger, Margaret, 265
Sargent, Carolyn F., 168
Saukko, Paula, 93
Sax, Linda J., 6, 43, 214
Schaefer, Peter, 283
Schaefer, Richard, 3, 4, 155, 157
Schellenberg, Kathryn, 283
Schkade, David A., 257
Schnaiberg, Allan, 259
Schneider, Joseph W., 246, 247
Schools. *See also* Educational institu-
    tions
    as agents of socialization, 57–58
    as formal organizations, 211,
        212–214
    funding for, 160
Schulman, Andrew, 283
Schur, Edwin M., 91, 105
Schwab, William A., 242
Schwartz, Howard D., 249
Science, definition, 4, 296
Scientific management approach, 82,
    296
Scientific method, 296
    definition, 18
    using, 18–24
Scott, W., 83, 269
Seager, Joni, 191
Second Harvest, 3–4
Second shift, 179, 296
Secondary analysis, 27, 28t, 296
Secondary group, 70, 71, 296
Segall, Alexander, 245
Segerstrale, Ullica, 50
Seidman, Steven, 167
Self, 51, 296
    concept of, 50–54
    Mead's stages of, 51–53
September 11, 2001, 4, 6, 46, 80, 135,
    158

and racial profiling, 100
    social reaction to, 186–187
Serial monogamy, 190, 296
Sernau, Scott, 132
Sex and Temperament (Mead), 169
Sex selection, 279
Sexism, 174, 296
    in education, 210–211
Sexual harassment, 174–175, 296
Shapiro, Thomas M., 124
Sharrock, W. W., 119
Shcherbak, Yuri M., 256
Sheehy, Gail, 169
Sherman, Lawrence W., 98
Shim, Janet K., 278
Shinkai, Hiroguki, 108
Shintech corporation, 260
Short, Kathleen, 126
Sick role, 296
Sigelman, Lee, 155
Significant others, 53–54, 296
Silicon Valley Cultures Project, 60
Simmons, Ann M., 92
Simpson, Sally, 104
Single mothers, 195
Sjoberg, Gideon, 238
Slavery, 112–113, 249, 296
Smedley, Brian D., 253
Smelser, Neïl, 223
Smith, Adam, 223
Smith, Buffy, 209
Smith, David A., 240, 244
Smith-Lovin, Lynn, 173
Smith, Michael Peter, 243
Smith, Patricia K., 132
Smith, Stacy L., 27
Smith, Tom W., 122t
Snyder, Thomas D., 276
Social change, 264, 297
    evolutionary theory of, 270–271
    functionalist perspective, 271–272
    global perspective, 273–274
    resistance to, 274–277
Social constructionist theory, of
    deviance, 99–100, 102t
Social control, 88, 297
    formal vs. informal, 90–91
    and technology, 283–284
Social epidemiology, 250–251, 297
Social inequality, 111, 297
Social institutions, 72–73, 184–204,
    297
    five major functions, 185–187,
        205
    studying, 185–189
        conflict perspective, 187–188
Social interaction, 64–65, 297
    electronic, 282

Social mobility, 129–132, 297
    occupational, 131
    in the United States, 130–132
Social movements, 265, 265–270
    and gender, 268
    new social movement theory, 269,
        270t
    relative deprivation theory, 270t
    resource mobilization theory,
        266–267, 270t
    and technology, 268
Social networks, 72, 297
Social roles, 68–69, 297
Social science, definition, 4–5, 297
Social structure, 64–78, 297
    elements of, 66–73
    global perspective, 73–78
    groups, 70–72
    networks, 72
    roles, 68–70
    statuses, 66–68
Socialism, 224, 297
Socialization, 34, 297
    agents of, 56–61
    anticipatory, 55–56
    and gender roles, 169
    and the life course, 54–55
    role of, 48, 49
    and the self, 50–54
    studying, 185–187
Societal-reaction approach, 99, 297
Society, 297
Society for the Psychological Study
    of Social Issues, 50
Society for the Study of Social
    Problems, 12
Sociobiology, 50, 297
Sociocultural evolution, 75, 297
    stages of, 77t
Sociological approach, 17–18
Sociological imagination, 3–4, 297
    definition, 3
Sociological theory, 6–7
Sociology
    applied, 28–29
    basic, 29
    clinical, 29
    and common sense, 5–6
    definition, 2, 297
    development of, 8–13
        modern, 11–13
    pure, 29
Sohoni, Neera Kuckreja, 279
South Korea, as periphery nation, 134
Soviet Union, 224
    collapse of, 273–274
Spar, Deborah L., 264
Spencer, Herbert, 9, 271

Spitzer, Stephen, 100
Spring, Joel H., 213
Stack, Megan K., 72
Staggenborg, Suzanne, 267
Stanford University, 64
Starbucks coffee, 137
Starr, Paul, 247, 275
State, the, as agent of socialization, 61
Status, 297
    achieved, 67, 67–68, 112, 130
    ascribed, 66, 67, 112, 130
Status groups, 116–117, 297
Steffensmeier, Darrell, 100
Stereotypes, 145, 297
    gender, 167–168
    racial, 156
    in the media, 180–181
Stigma, 92, 93, 297
Stith, Adrienne Y., 253
Stone, Lucy, 210
Stoops, Nicole, 205, 206
Stratification, 111, 29
    and access to technology,
        284–285
    conflict perspective, 118–119,
        120t
    functionalist perspective,
        117–118, 120t
    open vs. closed systems, 130
    by social class, 120–130
    systems of, 112–115
    universal nature of, 117–118
Strauss, Gary, 178
Street Corner Society (Whyte), 25–26
Students
    binge drinking, 88
    religiosity of, 6
    subcultures, 215
Subcultures, 44–45, 215, 297
Subjection of Women, The (Mill), 171
Sugimoto, Yoshio, 59
Suicide, 6–7, 27
Sum, Andrew M., 128
Sumner, William Graham, 47, 71, 146
Sunstein, Cass R., 257
Supreme Court, United States,
    158–159, 208
Surveys, 24–25, 28t, 297
Susi doll, 37
Sutherland, Edwin H., 97–98, 102t,
    103, 104
Sutton, F. N., 187
Swanberg, Jennifer E., 179
Switzerland
    gross national income, per capita,
        133
Symbolic ethnicity, 149, 150, 297

Symbols, 297
    and communication, 52
    of social stigma, 93
Szasz, Thomas, 249

Tafoya, Sonya M., 145
Taggers, 97
Tannen, Deborah, 173
Task forces, 83
Tattoos, 65–66
Taylor, P. J., 211
Taylor, Verta, 268
Teacher-expectancy effect, 211, 297
Teaching profession, 214
Technology, 37, 75
    advancement of, 277
        and culture, 281
    as agent of socialization, 59–60
    biological, 278–281
    and communication, 72, 281–282
    computer, 277–278
    and crime, 103–105, 283–284
    definition, 277, 297
    impact on the workplace, 83–84
    resistance to, 276–277
    and social control, 283–284
    and social movements, 268
Telecommuters, 83–84, 297
Television, as agent of socialization,
    59, 60
    and stereotypes, 167–168
Terrorism, 4, 6, 46, 80, 135, 158
    biological, 72, 250, 280–281
    social reaction to acts of, 186–187
Theoretical perspectives, major,
    13–18
    comparison, 18t
        and role of culture, 48t
Theory, definition, 7, 297
Third World countries. *See*
    Developing countries
Thomas, Gordon, 151, 152
Thomas, William I., 66, 145
Thomson, E., 195
Tibbits, Clark, 194
Tierney, John, 47, 234
Tilly, Charles, 269
Timberlake, Michael, 240
Titanic (ocean liner), 111
Tonnies, Ferdinand, 73, 74, 77, 282
Toossi, Mitra, 226
Total fertility rate (TFR), 236, 298
Total institutions, 55, 298
Tracking, in education, 210, 298
Traditional authority, 217, 298
Trained incapacity, 80, 298

Treiman, Donald J., 121
Trotter, Robert T., III, 253
Trow, Martin, 215
Tsuchiya, Motonori, 209
Tuchman, Gaye, 16, 171
Tumin, Melvin M., 118
Turkle, Sherry, 282
Turner, Bryan S., 44, 119
Turner, J. H., 271
Twaddle, Andrew, 245
Tyler, William D., 213
Tyre, Peg, 195

Ullman, Edward, 241f, 242
Unilinear evolutionary theory,
    270–271, 298
United Nations, 176, 257
    Development Programme, 133,
        247
    Population Division, 232, 240
United States
    Constitution, 235
    as core nation, 134
    divorce, 190
    economic system, 225
    gross national income, per capita,
        133
    households, by family type, 190f
    infant mortality, 248
    racial and ethnic groups in, 147t
    Supreme Court, 158–159
United States Committion on Civil
    Rights, 158
United States Trade Representative,
    136
University of Georgia, 195
University of Washington, 142–143
Up Against The Wal, 283
Ur (Mesopotamian city), 237
Urban ecology, 241
Urbanism, 240, 298
Urbanization, 240–244
    conflict perspective, 243–244
    early, 237–238
    functionalist perspective, 241–242
    interactionist perspective,
        242–243
Urbina, Ian, 45
USSR (United Soviet Socialist
    Republics), 224

Validity, 22, 298
Value, 298
Values, 42–43

Variables, 20, 298
  control, 23
  independent vs. dependent, 20, 23
Veblen, Thorstein, 274–275
Verhovek, Sam Howe, 260
Vermont, 240
Verstehen, 10, 298
Vertical mobility, 130, 298
Vested interests, 274–275, 298
Victimization surveys, 106, 298
Victimless crime, 105, 298
Vidaver, R. M., 254
Vietnam, 225
Vietnamese, U. S. population, 147t
Vindication of the Rights of Women
  (Wollstonecraft), 171
Violence, 87
Violent crime, 101, 102, 107
Viscusi, W. Kip, 257
Vital statistics, 235, 298

Wagley, Charles, 146
Waitzkin, Howard, 253
Wal-Mart, 137, 283
Walesa, Lech, 224, 265
Wallerstein, Immanuel, 134, 136,
  243–244, 278
Walrath, Dana, 184
Walzer, Susan, 180
Water pollution, 257
Watts, Jerry G., 222
Wealth, 298
  and income, 122–124
Weber, Max, 10, 79, 81, 116–117,
  128, 216, 217
  The Protestant Work Ethic and
    the Spirit of Capitalism,
    198–199
Wechsler, Henry, 88
Weeks, John R., 234
Weibel, Peter, 283
Weinberg, Daniel H., 161
Weinstein, Deena, 278
Weinstein, Michael A., 278
Wells-Barnett, Ida, 171
West, Candace, 167, 173
West Virginia, 240
Western Electric Company, 26
Western Europe, crime rates, 107

White-collar crime, 103–105, 298
White-collar jobs
  downsizing, 227
  outsourcing, 228–229
White ethnics, 149
White, Jonathan R., 281
Whites
  as dominant group, 143–144
  and Internet access, 285f
  U. S. population, 147t
    projected, 148f
Who Governs? (Dahl), 221
Whyte, William Foote, *Street Corner
  Society,* 25–26
Wickman, Peter M., 92
Widows, in India, 175
Wilford, John Noble, 75
Williams, Wendy M., 56, 253
Wilson, Barbara J., 27
Wilson, Edward O., 50
Wilson, J., 266
Wilson, John, 200
Wilson, William Julius, 132, 155, 198
Winter, J. Alan, 199
Wirth, Louis, 240
Witts, Max Morgan, 151, 152
Wolf, Naomi, 92
Wolff, Edward N., 124
Wolinski, Fredric P., 245
Wollstonecraft, Mary, *A Vindication
  of the Rights of Women,* 171
Wolraich, Mark, 90
Women
  and body image, 92, 93
  as criminals, 106
  in education, 210–211
  genital mutilation, 176
  income
    median, 161t
    as percentage of men's,
      178–179, 180
  media stereotypes, 167–168
  and networking, 188
  in politics, 173, 174
  in poverty, 126–127, 175
  as primary breadwinners, 195
  and social mobility, 132
  status of, worldwide, 175–176
  in the workforce, 157, 177–181,
    210–211
    minority, 180–181

  percentage by occupation,
    178
  percentage in paid labor
    force, 177t
  social consequences, 179–180
Wooden, Wayne, 97
Woods, Tiger, 145
Work teams, 83, 298
Workforce, changing, 225–226
Workplace
  as agent of socialization, 60–61
  bureaucratization of, 82
  changes in, 83
World Bank, 118, 234, 278
World Health Organization (WHO),
  244–245, 256–257
World systems analysis, 134,
  243–244, 278, 298
World Trade Center attacks, 4, 6, 46,
  80, 135, 158
  social reaction to, 186–187
World Trade Organization (WTO), 135
Wrestling, backyard, 87
Wright, Eric Olin, 119
Wurman, Richard Saul, 277

Xerox corporation, 178
Xie, Wen, 121

Yale University, 89–90
Yamagata, Hisashi, 157
Yelsin, Boris, 265
Yinger, J. Milton, 199
Young, Alford A., Jr., 16
Yugoslavia, 225

Zarembo, Alan, 65, 257
Zellner, William M., 46
Zia, Helen, 181
Zimbardo, Philip, 64–65, 68
Zimmerman, Don H., 167, 173
Zola, Irving K., 246
Zook, Matthew A., 268
Zvekic, Ugljea, 108
Zweigenhaft, Richard L., *Diversity in
  the Power Elite,* 221